Breakthrough
Strategic IT and
Process Planning

Breakthrough
Strategic IT and Process Planning

Bennet P Lientz

UCLA Anderson School of Management, USA

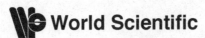 World Scientific

NEW JERSEY · LONDON · SINGAPORE · BEIJING · SHANGHAI · HONG KONG · TAIPEI · CHENNAI

Published by

World Scientific Publishing Co. Pte. Ltd.

5 Toh Tuck Link, Singapore 596224

USA office: 27 Warren Street, Suite 401-402, Hackensack, NJ 07601

UK office: 57 Shelton Street, Covent Garden, London WC2H 9HE

Library of Congress Cataloging-in-Publication Data
Lientz, Bennet P.
   Breakthrough strategic it and process planning / by Bennet P. Lientz.
      p. cm.
   ISBN-13 978-981-4280-08-2
   ISBN-10 981-4280-08-9
   1. Information technology--Planning. 2. Strategic planning. 3. Management information
systems. I. Title.
   HD30.2 .L535 2010
   658.4'012--dc22

                                                    2009034619

British Library Cataloguing-in-Publication Data
A catalogue record for this book is available from the British Library.

Typeset by Stallion Press
Email: enquiries@stallionpress.com

Printed in Singapore.

Preface

The Challenge

An obvious statement — all organizations use information systems and technology to support their key business processes. Value of IT and systems is reflected in the performance of the business through the processes. The business has a mission or vision and strategic business plan. Many have strategic IT plans. Even with all of these, there are problems and many instances of failure. Some of them include the following:

- The value of IT is questioned.
- Systems get implemented. Nothing changes in the work. Benefits are not achieved.
- Alignment of IT to the business is questioned.
- Failures in process change systems' implementation are frequent.

Of course, not everything is bleak. The situation, however, raises some questions.

- How can you develop a strategic IT plan with limited time and resources?
- How do you address planning for the business processes?

- What if you have not done IT planning before, or have had limited success in the past?
- Even if you develop the plan, how do you market it to management, business units, and IT?
- Even if you develop and market the plan successfully, how can you get resources to implement the action items of the plan?
- How do you implement and track the implementation of the action items of the strategic plan?
- After implementing, how do you measure whether it was worth the effort?
- How can you maintain the plan with limited time and resources?

It gets more complicated. You have the strategic systems plan in your right hand and the business plan in your left. Other questions like the following also arise:

- How do you know if the two plans mesh and are aligned?
- More generally, how do you assess the operational and intermediate term alignment along with strategic alignment?
- Business relies on processes. Systems and technology support processes. Where is the process plan? What is the direction of the work?

Planning Failures

We define success for strategic IT and process planning as the cumulative improvement to business value and competitive position through the measurable improvement of key business processes using information systems, technology, and project management. This is a very tall order.

Why? Because there are many instances and degrees of planning failure. Here are some of them:

- The plan is never completed.
- The plan is completed, but management and/or business departments ignore it.
- The plan is supported but, too bad, there are no resources to do anything.
- The plan action items are implemented, but there seems to be no change.
- The systems changed, but the organization and business processes remained the same.
- There appear to be no tangible benefits from the plan.
- Many of the planning actions are too long range and require a lot of resources — so they never even get started.
- The plan is there, but it seems too general and hard to map to day-to-day work.
- The plan just sits on the shelf and gathers dust.

The General Objectives

Here are the critical objectives for strategic IT and process planning and the plan.

- Get improvements in the business and IT through planning, strategic resource allocation, and implementation.
- Develop a real-world strategic plan so as to generate political support.
- Assess and exploit IT-business alignment on three levels: operations, intermediate term (projects and strategies), and strategic.
- Effect cumulative improvement and time and effort reduction in future planning.

- Address commonly encountered problems and roadblocks.
- Be capable of being in any country, any type, and size of organization.

The Detailed Goals

Key issues and questions were mentioned above. Answering these and more is the purpose and scope of this book. More specifically, our goal is to provide you the methods and tools so that you can:

- Understand the business, process, and systems environment.
- Develop the strategic IT and process plan that includes the direction of key processes (hence, the business process and strategic systems plan).
- Get involvement, support, and endorsement from management, business employees and IT staff.
- Put in place an organized approach for allocating resources between the planning action items, projects, maintenance and enhancement, and support.
- Implement the planning action items and measure the results.
- Employ an affordable method for updating the plan — fast.

Our Approach

The method presented has been distilled over a period of over 25 years. The method is a combination of:

- Strategic planning
- Change management
- Process improvement
- Project management

- Business process management
- IT architecture and systems

Change management acts as the umbrella over all. Project management governs how it is done in a strategic planning framework. Changes are affected through: process improvement, business process management, and IT architecture and systems.

We have collected a library of over 100 strategic IT plans. A planning database has been created with over 200 objectives, 500 strategies, and 800 action items. This information has been invaluable to the content and examples in the book.

The method in this book has been implemented in over 50 organizations in 20 countries including North America (United States, Canada, and Mexico), South America (Peru, Brazil, Chile, and Colombia), Europe (Great Britain, Ireland, France, Spain, Germany, Italy), Asia (China, Singapore, Thailand, Taiwan, Japan, Korea, India, Saudi Arabia, Dubai), Africa (South Africa, Egypt, Nigeria), and Australia and New Zealand.

Industries that have employed the plan include:

- Banking and insurance
- Manufacturing
- Distribution
- Transportation and shipping
- Utilities
- Government agencies
- Agricultural firms
- Natural resources and energy firms
- Aerospace and defense
- Technology and Internet firms
- Education
- Logistics
- Telecommunications

The method is scalable. It has been implemented in organizations ranging from a three-person IT group to several with hundreds of employees in multiple locations and countries.

Why has it worked? Here are the key ingredients.

- The approach is inclusive of processes as well as information systems and technology — ensuring that the technology and systems are relevant and useful to the actual work.
- We map the strategic business planning elements to those of the strategic systems and process plan through business processes — ensuring alignment and generating more support.
- We employ checklists for issues and opportunities, objectives, action items — all planning elements — getting you off the ground and running fast.
- Lessons learned and potential problems are provided to get you over hurdles you may encounter.
- Developing the plan is treated and organized as a project — giving more structure for the method.
- The method is step-wise with multiple steps in parallel — to reduce the elapsed time and get results faster.
- Focusing on not just project ideas but also policy changes, procedures, organization, workflow, etc. provides you with Quick Wins to gain more support for the plan, and to get these implemented before the plan is totally implemented.
- The method addresses resistance to change and the many political factors that can crush the planning effort.

The approach is based on the emerging integration of four areas:

- Information systems and technology
- Project management
- Process improvement and business process management
- Change management

These are all related. You do not want to implement a new system or technology with business impact and benefit — process improvement. You cannot get lasting process improvement through reengineering, Six Sigma or some other method unless there is automation to prevent regression and deterioration. Implementing last process change and systems requires a structured project management approach. The mention of change instills resistance in many — they see it as a threat to their jobs, positions, and power. Thus, we include change management to deal with the politics.

The method components are based on the following:

- Examine the business by examining the vision and mission, several key processes, and industry environment; measure the processes.
- Analyze and measure the current work in IT and systems to see where changes can be made, new technology employed, and resources obtained to support the planning action items.
- Develop the plan (issues and opportunities, objectives and constraints, and strategies and action items).
- Implement Quick Win changes consistent with the plan, generating more support for the plan.
- Perform a structured approach for allocating resources between the planning action items and other IT activities.
- Implement and measure the results of the plan action items.
- Update the plan using structured lists and tables.

To implement the method we employ:

- Extensive checklists and tables that effectively are the core of the plan.
- Collaboration with the business and IT during the entire process.
- Lessons learned from past planning efforts.
- Roadblocks, barriers, and problems that you may encounter and how to deal with them.

- A parallel approach for most of the work limited by available resources. If you followed a sequential approach, you might never finish.
- Don't strive for perfection the first time — you won't make it. Instead, work toward improvement of the processes through the strategic plan.

The book follows the method from the initial start through the update of the plan. Each chapter contain an introduction, lists and tables to help you get going, examples, a discussion of the political factors at work when doing the tasks in the chapter, lessons learned, and things to do next. At the end of the book is a complete example within the space allowed. This example, an Irish farming organization, contains many of the factors of other organizations — technology challenge, resistance to change and new ideas, limited IT resources, and very busy business employees — to name a few.

You will note that the word "breakthrough" appears in the title. The approach is quite different than others in that it employs change management as the umbrella for the planning and project management to get it done. Rather than being restricted to IT, it encompasses IT architecture and systems, process improvement, and business process management. This is shown in the diagram below. Here, change management is over the IT and strategic business process planning. Project management governs the planning work. The middle area is the subject of planning — IT and business processes.

How the Book is Organized

This book is divided into four logical parts. Part I presents the method and give guidelines for the various presentations and informal communications related to the planning effort. Part II involves collecting information for plan from both internal and

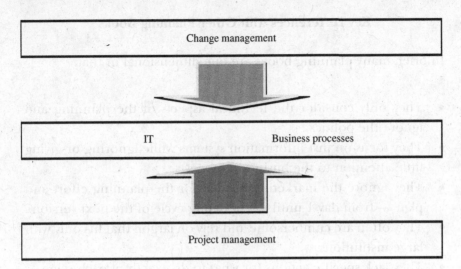

external sources. This part also includes a chapter on alignment of processes and IT to the business. Part III focuses on developing each part of the strategic plan. Also, there is an additional chapter on how to develop strategic plans for business units. This is often neglected in other planning books. Part IV addresses implementation and provides an in-depth example. Both short-term Quick Wins and longer term change are addressed. There is a chapter on measurement and updating the plan with the minimal effort as well.

Note that there is some intentional overlap. For instance, during the planning effort there are two instances of data gathering by interview. One is in the gathering of information related to past planning efforts (Chapter 4). The other is in the data collection for the new plan — in Chapter 6. A summary project plan for developing the strategic plan is given in Chapter 1, while a more detailed plan appears in Chapter 5. The purpose of the one in Chapter 1 is to explain the scope of the planning work. The business mission and vision are covered in Chapter 5 (data collection) and in Chapter 6 (analysis).

Key Differences with Other Planning Books

In brief, many planning books are one dimensional in that:

- They only consider the technical aspects of the planning and ignore the politics.
- They focus on just information systems while ignoring or giving little attention to the business processes.
- They ignore the marketing needed for the planning effort and plan — from day 1 until the updating cycle of the next version.
- They often are cumbersome and rely on jargon that fits only with large institutions.
- They lack specific actions for what to do exactly at each stage.
- They fail to consider the politics of planning and resistance to change. They do not realize the impact of the changes affected by the plan on the business and IT and their corresponding political power structures.

What You Will Get from the Book

This is a nuts and bolts approach to strategic systems and process planning developed and honed over the past 15 years. Firms and people that have used the method have received the following benefits:

- Integrated examples throughout the book
- Standardized lists of planning issues, objectives, action items, strategies, and constraints
- Integrates process and systems planning
- Jargon-free methods
- Easy to read format
- Extensive checklists and examples
- Specific tips on how to develop the plan

- Scalable to large and small organizations
- Proven in over 50 organizations in 20 countries
- Method allows you to measure progress as you go
- Realistic approach to developing the plan with limited resources
- How to deal with the real-world politics of planning

The Audience

In our management, consulting, and seminars, we have found that the audience for this material includes:

- Business managers and senior staff involved in overseeing business work
- Business planning and control staff
- IT managers and senior staff
- Consultants involved in IT, process improvement, planning, and change management

The materials have also been used in classes at the upper division and graduate level in IT, process improvement, change management, and project management.

Contents

PART I

THE PLANNING APPROACH

Chapter 1

Introduction

In a 2002 survey Cutter Consortium found that 39% of IT groups had no formal IT strategy at all. The survey also found that 1/3 of the survey respondents had no business strategic plan either. When everything is stable in the business and in technology, then you could make the argument that there is no need to expand the work to create a strategic plan for IT and processes. However, either due to business dynamics or technological change, this has seldom been the case. It is not just the benefit of the planning, but the harm and impact if business process and IT strategic planning is not done.

At the other extreme are the firms that generate strategic IT plans of over 100 pages. Is long length good? Probably not. Why? Because too much effort was consumed in the planning. Moreover, it is more difficult to use such an extensive plan. Often, these just end up sitting on the shelf. A related problem is that if the plan is too long, then it will take a major effort to update the plan. That is why our goal is to give the methods and tools to create a realistic plan in less time and one that is shorter, is more usable, and can be updated easily.

To show the growing importance of a strategic IT plan, consider the American federal government. The Paperwork Reduction Act of 1995 specifies that agencies shall "develop and maintain a strategic information resources management plan that shall describe how information resources management activities help accomplish agencies' missions."

10 Reasons Given for Not Planning

From consulting and doing over 75 strategic IT and process plans, we have heard a variety of reasons for not developing or doing a strategic IT plan. Why start this book this way — in a seemingly negative way? Because many of you will have to justify the planning effort.

Reason 1: We have never carried out an IT planning effort before

Lack of experience is a reason commonly given. However, there are too many benefits to taking on the planning effort as discussed in a later section. Moreover, using the approach in this book you can develop the plan quickly and logically and gain management, user, and IT support.

Reason 2: We are doing fine without the plan

Without a plan work requests from management and users come in without structure or coherence. The IT group tends to be reactive and not proactive.

Reason 3: Our business does not even have a strategic plan.
So why have a strategic IT plan?

In the example in Chapter 18, there was no business plan. Just because this does not exist is no reason not to do the strategic IT planning. After all, many organizations have standardized processes that have not changed in years. The strategic IT and process plan can enhance business performance through the processes.

Reason 4: We tried doing a strategic IT plan before and it failed

This has been encountered often. One of the early tasks in any planning effort is to gather information on past efforts and assess what worked and what didn't. Just because a past effort failed is not a reason not to try again. Here is a political tip. You often should market the plan as a way to head off problems similar to those that occurred in the past.

Reason 5: We are an organization with very limited IT resources so we cannot afford to do planning

A number of the strategic planning efforts we have helped with or carried out involved an IT group of less than 10 people. A small or stretched IT group needs a strategic IT and process plan as much or more than larger organizations to help structure and control the IT work, given limited resources.

Reason 6: We don't have the expertise to do the planning

If we were proposing a complex method, then this would be valid. However, the approach in the book is common sense, jargon free, and can be started as you read the book. One can argue that having a great deal of experience can inhibit the effort by giving too much structure.

Reason 7: We cannot afford a consultant to do the planning

Many people think that you need a consultant to develop the plan. While we have helped to develop many planning strategies, we have also initiated plans using the method in this book. We have even provided chapters of the book to individuals who then developed their own plans. Remember if you do it yourself, you own it and are more confident in it.

Reason 8: We have a very standard IT environment
and do not require a strategic IT plan

A number of IT groups support standardized computing and technology environments — so why do planning with such stability? The strategic IT and process plan goes beyond the systems and technology, and encompasses processes, user requests, and alignment to management and the business.

Reason 9: We are too busy to carry out the planning effort

Busy people tend to find the time to do additional work through time management. The planning approach here is NOT a full-time effort. Planning is most successful when there is a great deal of coordination. We have seen many project leaders develop the basic plan rather quickly in addition to their regular work.

Reason 10: We did a plan and it was approved. But then no one
paid any attention to the plan

This is a common problem. It happens in other areas as well. It is estimated that 10% of the books purchased are never read. So, how can you ensure that this planning approach will work when the last one failed to deliver results? One reason is collaboration. Another reason is the generation of quick, short-term ideas that can be implemented during the planning effort without management approval. This then generates support for the plan since they see results prior to approval.

Why Do Strategic IT and Process Planning Together?

There are many books on strategic IT planning. There are fewer books on strategic process planning. Why combine them? More fundamentally, what is the value of IT? The value or worth of IT is a subjective concept. Some think IT's value lies in competitive advantage, cost savings, efficiency of the business, business flexibility, and agility as measured through a mixture of performance measures or Return on Investment (ROI). What do all of these things have in common?

> The value of IT lies in its contribution to the business through business process performance and use of knowledge and information for cumulative improvement.

From this discussion it is clear that process and IT performance, management, and planning are closely related.

Who delivers the value of IT? IT alone? No. Experience reveals that IT can deliver systems, projects, and capabilities on-time and within budget. But to what end? If the business does not change to utilize these capabilities, then it is wasted. That is why much IT efforts have resulted in little tangible benefit. A corollary to this has been the theory that it takes time, maybe over a year before the benefits of an IT project are realized. One theory that has been advanced is a W-shaped graph (see Figure 1.1, Chatterjee, D. and A. Seagars, Presentation to SIM Advanced Practices Council, Chicago, 2002). In this chart the value of the work declines after initial implementation. Then simple, easy changes are made to the business (stage 2), leading to the capability of handling additional complexity (stage 3). The final stage that delivers value is to make the business simpler. Sound familiar? Accepting this leads to overall lower IT value due to the elapsed time required to realize the benefits of the IT investment.

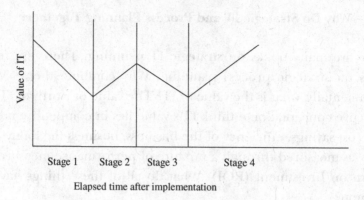

Figure 1.1 Delivery of IT Value after Project Completion.

To realize the value of IT faster without this delay, it is necessary to more closely link IT to process management. The area of focus of this book lies in joint IT and process planning. Not included here is the linkage of process change and IT project and work performance. This was addressed in Breakthrough IT Change Management (Lientz, 2003).

What are the Objectives of the Planning Effort?

One short-term goal is to complete the plan on time and within budget. This is much too narrow. It neither addresses implementation of the plan, nor does it include measuring results. Also, it does not include the on-going planning effort.

Here are some desirable and realistic objectives.

- The plan action items, strategies, and objectives should point to measurable, substantial business benefits through the processes.
- The plan must be understood and supported by management and employees.
- The plan should lead to more effective internal IT processes and infrastructure so as to increase IT's ability to support strategic business initiatives and operations.

- It should be easier to develop successive strategic IT and process plans in the future, based on experience and lessons learned.
- The plan should result in greater control of IT resources so that more effort is devoted to supporting strategic business goals.

Overall,

> The purpose of IT and process planning effort is to enhance business performance and agility through the improvement of business processes and IT systems, technology, and resources.

This is a very tall order. What does it mean? First, it means that the planning process must generate political support for both the plan and IT. Second, the plan must indicate both short- and long-term efforts that improve the business as well as IT. Now look at the last point. Experience has shown that in the absence of a plan, IT tends to be reactive to the business. With the plan, IT has the opportunity to be proactive. How is this achieved? Through the channeling of some IT resources toward projects and work of strategic importance as opposed to maintenance and operations support. In addition, this reveals that strategic IT and process planning must include resource management and allocation. After all, you can develop a great plan, but without resources it dies.

There is also a negative objective. What happens if the plan is not done? A common answer, from experience, is that there will be maintenance and enhancement work. IT will perform tactically fine. The systems "run on time." Projects are completed on time and within budget. However, it won't have much of an impact since some of the key strategic business needs were not addressed.

Benefits of Strategic IT and Process Planning

A key benefit of joint IT and process planning is to enable the delivery of more rapid benefits of IT to the business through process change. In other words, to shrink or eliminate the graph in Figure 1.1.

Process planning is carried out on a rare basis. Why? Essentially, for the same reasons given at the start of this chapter. However, processes and IT are very closely related. Thus, the IT plan is more credible and realistic if it contains changes to the business processes joint with future IT work. Linking them together ensures that process planning occurs. Moreover, including process planning helps to make IT objectives, strategies, and action items more realistic.

IT systems are multifunctional and complex — requiring planning. It logically follows that implementing new or modified processes to fit with the new systems requires planning. Another reason for linking.

But there is another basic benefit. When management reviews and approves a strategic IT-only plan, what do they expect? Obviously, they expect the benefits cited in the plan. How can the benefits come true if there is no strategy for process change? Thus, combining IT and processes in the strategic planning process gives more credibility to the plan and serves to explain HOW the benefits will be achieved.

The strategic IT and process plan can help address some of the common complaints about IT from the business. Here is a list of complaints cited in the literature.

- IT is not working on the right things. The plan reveals the alignment of IT to the business through the processes.
- The value of IT is questionable. By including the processes, you more clearly show the benefit of IT to the business.
- IT takes too long to implement projects. Since process change is included in the plan, it is clear that the implementation time extends due to the process work.

- IT is too rigid. By showing the current business issues and objectives, and then mapping IT objectives, strategies, and action items to these, you can demonstrate that IT is current and flexible with respect to business needs.

What is Success?

One answer is that you complete the plan on time and within the budget. A successful project, right? Wrong. This does not ensure that the plan is even read or used. Our definition of success is broader.

> As a result of the plan, action items are completed that generate tangible benefits to both the business and IT and improve the alignment of IT to key processes and the business.

This is very ambitious, but necessary. In order to achieve this success, the following have to be achieved.

- Understanding and support of the plan and planning method.
- Allocation of resources to the planning action items.
- Successful implementation of both the short- and long-term action items of the plan.
- Measurement of the results of the action item implementation.

But here is the dilemma. No person involved in planning has the power or authority to ensure that success is attained. This means that the planning method and planners have to be political and work to gather support and enthusiasm for the plan, and especially the action items. This is proven in their support or lack of support for resources to be allocated to the implementation of the action items.

What is Realistic IT and Process Planning?

Many IT and non-IT planning methods assume some or all of the following:

- There is plenty of time to do the plan.
- There are dedicated people to do the plan.
- Consulting help is available.
- You have time to study a planning method in-depth or take seminars and classes in planning.
- Management supports the planning effort.
- It is easy to gain participation in the planning effort.
- You need to follow a number of formal steps in a sequential order.

Get real! In the real world we have found that:

- The planning effort is under great time pressure due to other work and the timing with respect to the business plan.
- Any and everyone involved in the planning effort has other work that is often pressing and viewed as more important than the planning work.
- There is often no consulting budget for the planning.
- There is also often no resources or time for in-depth learning.
- In reality, many business managers do not really understand IT. They see it as just another department. So, why have the plan when the average department does not have the plan? We have found that most managers tolerate the planning effort as long as the other work gets done.
- People in the business departments and IT are busy. This is one reason for them not wanting to participate. Another reason is that they do not see the benefit or self-interest to participate.
- In many business and IT activities, it is necessary that steps be undertaken in sequential order. This can be a killer in strategic IT and process planning. You want to do as much of the work in parallel.

The Timing of the Strategic IT and Process Planning Effort

As they say, "Timing is everything." Can you just do the planning anytime? Not if you want to maximize the impact and benefit of the planning effort. Let's take a common example. Suppose the business fiscal year starts on January 1. Backing into this date means that the strategic business plan must be completed to allow time for budgeting and more detailed operational planning. So let's say that the business plan is approved on October 1 of the preceding year. Now, you need to consider how much time will be needed to review and approve the strategic IT and process plan. Let's assume three months. This would mean that the plan should be completed by July 1. Thus, there is a six-month time period from the start of the fiscal year. This gives sufficient time to get project ideas into the budget.

How do you know about the projects and other work six months in advance of getting started? That is part of the reason for the plan. The plan is strategic so the project ideas generated are also strategic. They and changes to the related processes will be implemented through the plan.

In fact, we have found that the strategic IT and process plan is just one of four key IT documents and presentations that IT should provide management. The other three are:

- *Report on the results of the IT work and performance*. This could politically best be done by October 1. Why this date? So as to influence the budget process.
- *Technology and process assessment*. This is an evaluation of the internal systems, technology, and processes as well as new technologies and systems available and relevant to the business. This could be done by April 1. This serves to stir up interest in IT work and in the plan.
- *Resource allocation of IT resources*. This is the prioritization of resources across all IT activities — development, maintenance, enhancement, operations support, and so forth. This could be given by January 1 just as new year begins.

As you can see, timing is very political. It is like being a director of a movie. You control timing but not the cast or the budget.

The Relationship between IT, Process Improvement, and Change Management

People often see these three things as separate. Companies have wasted a great deal of treasure and time in doing these separately. Look at the failures of Six Sigma, Re-engineering, and Total Quality Management. While there have been some successes, their failure has often stemmed from a lack of linkage to IT and change management.

Here is the logical connection and reasoning behind joining the three.

- To get IT results and benefits, you have to most often change the process as well. This relates process improvement to IT.
- You can improve a process with systems, but there is still a problem. Many people resist change. Moreover, after the new process and system are installed, the actual work sometimes reverts back to the old form. This is due to many factors including resistance to change, the need for senior business users to regain power, and habit. "Old habits die hard." This ties in with change management.

Change management serves as an umbrella for IT and business process strategic planning. Project management provides the guidance to achieving the change. IT, process improvement, and business process management (BPM) are all factors involved in the change effort.

The Risks of IT and Process Planning and What Can Go Wrong

Let's recap what we have so far. There is both benefit and need for linking IT and processes in strategic planning. There should also be a highly organized approach. Why? Because from experience there are many risks in planning. Here are some of the ones surfaced in prior planning efforts.

- Management expectations are raised. The objectives and action items in the plan should be good. The benefits are great. However, it will take many more steps to realize these including fighting for resources and doing the work.
- The planning effort seems to drag out. There are waiting periods for reviews and feedback. There is the need to gather information from people who are busy.
- There are such limited resources that even with a winning plan, there is only so much that can be done.

Developing the strategic plan is a major piece of work — even if you have done it many times. This is due to the risks mentioned.

Treating the Planning Effort as a Program and Project

Given the above risks, it makes common sense to treat the planning effort on a single time as a project. Over years the planning effort then becomes a program. Yes, yes, so what? Turn now to the structure of project management. In a project, you have to define your goals. Basically, there are four dimensions to consider:

- *Technical goals* — carry out the planning effort in an efficient and cost-effective manner.
- *Business goals* — ensure IT aligns with the business that through the achievement of the plan strategies and action items improve business performance.
- *Political goals* — get the plan approved and the implementation of the plan completed.

- *Social goals* — use the planning effort to build collaboration and communications with management and the business.

Now turn to scope. We have already included the key processes with IT. From the previous section on planning objectives, we can also include resource management and allocation. Another part of scope is measurement. If we don't measure where we are now, then even if the plan is wildly successful, we won't know how much it is so unless we measure.

Another area of project planning or the project concept is that of roles and responsibilities. The role of the head of the planning effort or project leader is to coordinate the development of the plan. The key operative work is "coordinate." This means that the project leader should not develop the plan alone, but should involve many members of management, IT, and the business. The more the better — up to a reasonable limit. Why? When people participate, they expend effort. They get involved. They begin to have a stake in and own the plan.

Next, we need to identify potential issues in doing the planning. Figure 1.2 contains a list of numbered potential issues. We hope that you will not encounter all of these. But if you list them ahead of time, before they appear, you will be more prepared.

The benefits of the planning effort have already been addressed. The costs are labor hours and the opportunity cost of not being able to deploy the time absorbed in planning other activities.

---

1. Deal with high management business expectations.
2. Cope with the limited available resources for planning.
3. Get all of the planning issues and opportunities.
4. Get people involved in the planning process.
5. Measure the improvement due to the plan.
6. Control resources consumed in support, maintenance, and related activities so as to pursue the action items of the plan.
7. Gather process information with limited resources and time.

Figure 1.2 Potential IT and Process Planning Issues.

A task template is given in Figure 1.3. A template is a set of high-level tasks and milestones. Later, we will examine all of the tasks in this template. The purpose of putting it here is to give you a starting point for your planning effort. Get you off the ground running, so to speak. Note that a more detailed plan is given in Chapter 5.

1000		Preparation for the planning effort
	1100	Review past planning efforts
	1200	Create an initial list of business processes
	1300	Define initial lists for business issues, mission, vision, objectives, and strategies
	1400	Create the planning project plan
	1500	Develop lists of IT objectives, systems, architecture components, constraints, strategies, and action items
	1600	Identify potential managers and employees for involvement in the planning effort
	1700	Identify web and other planning resources
	1999	M: Planning preparation completed
2000		Gather information on business objectives and issues
	2100	Analyze the mission and/or vision of the organization
	2200	Get initial feedback on the business objectives, strategies, and issues
	2300	Prepare initial business planning tables
3000		Gather information on business processes and on the competition
	3100	Identify problems with the current key processes
	3200	Assess the competition
4000		Assess the current IT architecture, technology, and infrastructure
5000		Analyze business processes
6000		Assess the alignment of IT and processes to the business
7000		Define the issues and opportunities for the plan
8000		Determine the objectives and constraints
9000		Identify the strategies and actions
10000		Construct planning tables and relate IT to the business
11000		Create and deliver the plan
12000		Implement short-term action items of the plan
13000		Perform resource allocation to gain resources for the plan action items
14000		Implement the long-term action items
15000		Measure plan results
16000		Gather lessons learned and prepare for updating the plan

Figure 1.3 Template Tasks for the IT and Process Planning Effort.

This is just the first version. We will expand on this later.

Here, the architecture refers to the ensemble of the hardware, software, and network components in use along with supporting technologies. The infrastructure includes the architecture as well as the support resources for maintenance, enhancement, and projects. Note that all tasks are numbered. This is for several reasons. If you number tasks and milestones, it is easier to refer to them and is clearer in meaning during meetings. Second, by having zeros in the numbering you can add more subordinate tasks. Third, the project management approach and template give you credibility by showing that you are organized.

For the planning effort to be an on-going program, there has to be a regular, standardized process for not only developing, but updating the plan.

The Need for a Realistic, Scalable Planning Method

What are the requirements for a planning method? Here is a list.

- The method should be scalable. That is, it can be employed by small and large organizations.
- The method should be neutral in terms of cultures and countries. This means that it can be applied anywhere.
- The planning method should be easily understood without jargon.
- You must be able to get up to speed in employing the method quickly. A few days, not weeks or months.
- You should be able to use the method without outside assistance.
- The method should be cumulative in construction. This means that the plan grows incrementally. This allows you to easily track status of the work and provide this to management and others.
- The method should result in a completed plan in a few months in elapsed time.

- The method should not require full-time effort or on-going substantial effort.
- The method should support updating the plan without a major effort.
- The method should result in a plan that includes short-term action items unrelated to project ideas.
- The method should be collaborative in nature to gain support and commitment from both management and the employees who will be involved and affected by the plan.

Our Approach in a Nutshell

The approach includes the following activities:

- Assess past planning efforts and gather lessons learned.
- Identify key business processes, systems, projects, and infrastructure.
- Collect information and build the project plan.
- Assess the business and competitive environment.
- Understand business strategies, objectives, vision, mission, and issues.
- Evaluate the technology, systems, and architecture.
- Analyze the processes and determine their alignment to the business.
- Define issues and opportunities for the plan.
- Determine objectives and constraints for the plan.
- Identify strategies and action items.
- Create lists and tables to map business and IT factors.
- Develop a vision for business processes and IT assuming the successful implementation of the plan.
- Produce the plan and market it and the method.
- Fight successfully for resources for the longer-term action items.
- Implement short-term action items.
- Implement longer-term action items.

- Measure the results.
- Update the plan.

Note that we purposely did not list these numerically since we want these to be in parallel to the extent possible.

A number of points must be explained more to have this make sense.

- *Lessons learned* are both positive and negative points that can be used not only in planning, but in operations as well. These are drawn from the business, the processes, the planning effort, and IT.
- *Vision* is the long-term view of where the business is headed. *Mission* is the directional approach to achieve the vision.
- *Business objectives* are general goals for carrying out the mission to achieve the vision.
- *Business strategies* is the intermediate term to achieve the business objectives.
- *Business issues* are potential and actual problems and opportunities that the business and its processes face.
- Because the plan includes both processes and IT, the issues and opportunities relate to both. The *issues* are potential or actual problems that need to be addressed. **Opportunities** are things that can be done to improve process and/or IT performance.
- *Objectives* (labeled IT objectives in the book to distinguish them from business objectives) are directional goals that cannot be achieved except through years of effort and many projects and other changes.
- *Constraints* are roadblocks to objectives. They are issues that cannot be changed, but must be dealt with or gotten around. Going beyond limited staffing and money, they include existing technology, the nature of the business, the competition, the locations of the firm's operations, culture, and politics.

- **Strategies** are major initiatives to take to work toward the objectives around the constraints.
- **Action items** are specific steps that can be taken in support of the strategies to address the issues and opportunities and work toward the objectives. They include much more than project ideas. Often, they encompass changes in policies, procedures, facilities, staffing, processes, and so forth.
- The **vision for business processes and IT** is what you see as the combined result of successfully completing all objectives, strategies, and action items.

Figure 1.4 gives a graphical representation of these definitions. Here, the thicker solid line represents the strategies while the thinner lines represent action items. As you can see, the objectives cannot get at or reach the issues and opportunities directly due to the constraints. Strategies are needed. However, strategies are too general to be actionable so we require the specific steps in the action items.

What are lists and tables? Lists include both business and IT factors. Here are the ones that we will use in later chapters.

- Mission or vision elements
- Business objectives
- Business processes

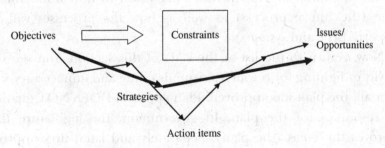

Figure 1.4 Graphical View of the Planning Elements.

- Business strategies
- Business issues
- Business departments
- Issues and opportunities
- IT objectives
- Constraints
- IT strategies
- Action items
- New IT and process vision
- Systems
- Projects
- Architecture elements
- Current work (e.g., maintenance, enhancement, and operations support)

A table relates one factor to another. There are three categories of tables. Business tables relate one business factor to another (e.g., business issues versus action items). The guts of the plan consists of the lists and tables. This is what you develop and what you update.

Another item in the list pertains to the vision of the business processes and IT. Often, in many plans there are detailed action items, and so forth. These sound good and make sense. However, management, employees, and IT staff naturally would like to know what this all summarizes up to after implementation. This is where the vision comes in. This includes the vision of how work will be done (the future process) as well as how the processes will be supported (IT and systems).

Now, return to the list at the start of this section. You see the activity of fighting for resources. Sounds crude and unnecessary, eh? After all, the plan was approved. Plan approval DOES NOT guarantee resources for the plan. In government, the legislature first approves the ideas (the plan). Separately and later, they approve funding (resources). It is often the same in business. Unfortunately, most planning methods, articles, and books stop with the approval of the strategic plan. Too bad. In the real world this is when the fun is just beginning. Resources have probably been completely or over committed to other work and priorities. The result is often that no action is taken. That is why we devote an entire chapter to the resource allocation.

The next items in the list at the start of the section refer to implementation. There are two parts: short term and long term. Long-term actions include facility changes, major process changes, and projects. Short-term actions encompass items that can be accomplished without major resources, costs, or management approval as a separate item. Examples are changes in procedures, policies, staff assignment, project priorities, and the like.

The next bullet in the list pertains to measurement. You need to measure both IT and process performance before and after the plan. Otherwise, how could you tell if and whether the plan made a difference?

The last item is that of updating the plan. How often should you update the plan? In most organizations this is an annual exercise. Bad idea. There is too much change and dynamism in the business and IT to enjoy this luxury. If the plan is not updated more often, then it can become obsolete and lose credibility. A better approach is to do the update several times per year. You ask, "What about the effort to do this?" That is one of the benefits of the method. You first review with others the lists. With these updated, you construct updated tables.

Next question. How are these activities undertaken? The following are some of the main techniques.

- *Project focus*. The strategic IT and process plan is created, implemented, and updated using project management methods giving structure, consistency, and coherence to the effort.
- *Collaboration*. The person in charge of the planning effort is really a coordinator and facilitator — NOT A DEVELOPER.

While this role can include generating lists and initial tables, the key to planning success is to gain involvement of managers, business employees, and IT staff members — the more the better. You want grassroots support for the plan.

- *Constant marketing.* You have to not only see the plan and planning method you also have to market the individual elements of the plan, the struggle for resources and priorities, and the actual implementation. These things, even if common sense and obvious to you, are not at all accepted by people. Remember, any organization contains both inertia and resistance to change.

- *Parallelism.* The technique is to perform the steps in the list in parallel. For example, there is no reason why you cannot create the initial planning lists all at the same time.

- *Communications.* You should constantly communicate with management and key employees on the plan. They should have multiple opportunities for review. The sign of success here is that the actual presentation of the plan contains hardly anything new that they have not been exposed to.

- *Problem-solving focus.* Key to acceptance of the plan is getting results. Results mean changes. Changes target solving problems and exploiting opportunities.

Alignment — A Magic Word

Years ago, the word "alignment" pertained mainly to automobile tires. The new application of the term occurred to perceptions that IT, while providing systems and support, was not doing enough to support key business activities and initiatives. In short, IT was often accused of not being aligned to the business. That is, IT activities did not adequately address business issues or support business vision/mission, objectives, and strategies.

What is alignment of IT and the business? Alignment of IT to the business can be seen in three dimensions.

- Current work (today).
- IT projects (intermediate term).
- The strategic IT and process plan (long term).

To be successful, alignment must occur in all three time frames. Here is an example. In a major retailer, the IT manager had directed IT efficiently and effectively. Support was excellent. Projects were completed on time and within budget. The IT manager was named "manager of the year" by a professional IT organization. Sounds great, right? Alignment was superb in both current work and projects. Too bad for him and the organization. The company declared bankruptcy three months after the award was given. Why? Because the company had not kept up with competition in new e-technologies.

In many firms, people create wonderful strategic IT plans — strategic alignment. However, the same projects and support continue on. Strategic but neither operational nor intermediate-term alignment.

How do you analyze alignment? For automobile tires, you look at the wear of the tread after the vehicle has been driven some distance. It is similar with IT and business alignment. IT supports key business processes. This is where "the rubber meets the road." Business performance is largely governed by the performance of key processes. Thus, you can assess IT alignment by considering performance *vis-a-vis* business processes. Here are three critical planning tables for alignment:

- Current work versus business processes. What is the distribution of support work across the processes? ***Tactical alignment.***
- Projects versus business processes. What is the expected benefit and impact of each IT project on business process performance? ***Intermediate-term alignment.***

- Strategic IT and process plan objectives versus business processes. What is the anticipated benefit of objective achievement on the processes? *Strategic or long-term alignment.*
- Strategic IT and process plan objectives versus business issues. What is the effect of achieving the objectives in terms of mitigating the business issues? *Negative alignment.*

Of course, for the plan, you could also consider strategies and action items in the same way. Negative alignment is often more important than positive alignment since business is often driven by problems today, rather than the long-term future.

Applications and Benefits of this Planning Method

The planning approach has been employed in over 100 organizations in 25 countries. It has been taught in seminars, classes, and through consulting. Applications have occurred in many areas, including:

- Government
- Manufacturing
- Banking and insurance
- Aerospace
- Telecommunications
- High technology
- Medical care and biotechnology
- Distribution
- Retailing
- Utilities
- Transportation
- Education
- Advertising
- Agriculture

- Shipping and logistics
- Cosmetics

There are a number of benefits of the planning approach. Here are some of the critical success factors of the method.

- The method works in many diverse settings.
- It delivers both short- and long-term tangible, measurable results.
- The method focus on both processes and IT to ensure that there will be benefits and relevance from the plan.
- The method is straightforward to use.
- The plan includes marketing and sales to ensure support for the plan and approach.
- The book contains many examples as well as guidelines and tips for doing work.
- The method and the book recognize the importance of political factors in planning.
- The approach is based on project management principles.
- The method is collaborative and provides for involving many different people and roles to generate support for change.
- The approach is not sequential so the plan can be completed faster.
- The method recognizes and deals with political factors such as resistance to change.
- The approach includes strategic resource management so that the plan can actually be implemented.
- The method provides for an easy way to update the plan.
- You know the status of the planning effort from the lists, tables, and involvement.
- The approach provides for measurement of both IT and processes.
- The method has been proven to uncover new opportunities during the planning process. Examples are given in Chapter 18 and other chapters.
- The approach does not require a long learning curve. Nor does it require a huge full-time effort. It is scalable.

How this Book is Organized

The approach for strategic planning is presented in detail in Chapter 2. The following 17 chapters proceed through the planning activities (no, not steps since this would be sequential). The first part of the book lays out the method and gives guidelines for communications during all activities. The second part focuses on information collection and assessment with the following chapters.

- Improve both formal and informal communications (Chapter 3).
- Analyze your past planning efforts (Chapter 4). This chapter discusses how to gather lessons learned from previous work.
- Collect information for the plan (Chapter 5). This includes both information gathering and organization as well as developing the plan for the planning effort.
- Assess the business and systems environment (Chapter 6). This is not an in-depth assessment since neither time nor resources are available. Rather, it focuses on the key processes, systems, and technology.
- Analyze processes and IT to determine their alignment to business goals (Chapter 7). This is important because it determines the relative importance of the processes in terms of positive alignment (business goals) and negative alignment (business issues).

The third part of the book covers the development of the plan:

- Develop issues and opportunities for the plan (Chapter 8). This includes IT and process-related issues and problems as well as new opportunities.
- Define objectives and constraints (Chapter 9). Objectives and constraints are best defined together. The constraints serve to indicate real world limitations faced by IT and the business processes.

- Create strategies and action items (Chapter 10). Not only are methods given for the development of strategies and action items, but many examples are provided.
- Develop IT and process strategic plans for key business units (Chapter 11). This is of importance to ensure that the overall plan maps into the business units — ensuring benefits from the planning work.
- Build and market the plan and method (Chapter 12). Here the plan is finalized and marketed.

The fourth part of the book turns to implementation:

- Perform strategic resource allocation (Chapter 13). This key chapter considers the process for allocating resources between projects, current work, and action items of the strategic IT and process plan.
- Implement the plan — short term (Chapter 14). This chapter deals with implementing Quick Wins during and after the planning effort. Examples are given here to suggest what to look for during planning.
- Implement the plan — long term (Chapter 15). This includes the project ideas generated by the plan as well as substantial policy and other changes.
- Measure planning results and update the plan (Chapter 16). Here we measure how we did. We also provide guidance on how to update the plan.
- Conclusions and actions to take (Chapter 17). This chapter sums things up and it provides a long list of specific actions you take to get going.

The last chapter (Chapter 18) presents a strategic IT and process plan that was developed by an Irish farming cooperative. This example is interesting in that it includes political factors, small IT organization, and limited time and resources.

At the end of the book are three appendices. These include:

- Useful web sites (Appendix A) which are drawn from experience.
- References (Appendix B) which includes both journals and books.
- Checklists and Tables (Appendix C) which is a summary of the key lists and tables in the book.

Each chapter includes topic specific material as well as the following:

- *Introduction.* This section relates the chapter material to the overall method and the other chapters. The purpose and scope are laid out.
- *Examples.* These are real-world examples and are in addition to the Chapter 18 example.
- *Lessons learned.* These are guidelines from past planning efforts to provide more on the "how" of the methods.
- *Politics.* Politics, resistance to change, and related topics must be addressed formally due to their importance and influence on the success or failure of your planning effort.
- *What to do Next.* These are specific things you can do after reading the chapter.
- *Summary*

Planning — Self-Interest

What is in all of this for you? It seems like a lot of work. Also, there is potential exposure if you screw up or fail. True, but there are benefits and the method here can reduce the risk of failure or problems. Here are some points to remember.

- Coordinating a planning effort means that you will have contact with a wide range of managers and departments. These can assist you in your career advancement.

- Doing a strategic joint process and IT plan gives you the opportunity to observe, assess, and understand key business processes. It is always valuable to know things work.
- The business and technology assessments provide you with a better understanding what is going on in the real world.
- Because you are using the incremental, collaborative approach, your chances of having problems or failing are minimized. In each area we provide examples (objectives, strategies, issues and opportunities, action items, and so forth).

Our advice is that if you are offered the chance to coordinate the planning effort, take it. Don't give up all of your regular work as you probably do not want to become a full-time planner. However, this staff role in larger IT groups has many benefits and can lead to the role of the IT manager.

Examples

Here is an example of an application of the method. A finance manager was given responsibility for IT in a large firm in Southeast Asia. He had no previous IT, project, or planning experience. Using the approach he developed the strategic IT and process plan and implemented 10 major projects so as to improve business profitability, reduce business costs, and improve overall business performance. He is now the CEO of the organization.

The example in Chapter 18 examines an Irish farming cooperative that was delivering marginal IT services and support. By doing the plan, the manager turned around not only IT, but also made a major improvement in the business to ensure its viability and growth.

Lessons Learned

This section is included in each chapter to give you more guidelines and tips for successful planning and implementation. Let's give a major guideline that will be emphasized in 'the book. The word here is "fear." Sounds negative, eh? Actually, it is positive in that using the fear of not doing the plan can gather more support. Similarly, for fear of not getting resources. When you implement change in processes and systems, you often encounter major resistance to this change. To cope with this, you should highlight the problems with the way things are and how they will get worse if the changes are not made.

This is not a new idea. Here is how it works in everyday life.

- For people who have a substance abuse, a key first step is to admit that they have a problem and that if it does not get addressed, life will be worse.
- A doctor uses fear to get patients to agree to an operation. After all, why would anyone want the pain, loss of income, potential infection, and so forth? These are all countered by the doctor explaining the impact of not having the operation.
- Parents want their kids to eat healthy food, like vegetables. Many learn that saying "These are good for you," leads nowhere. Instead, they give the impact of not eating properly — weakness and poor health.
- Anti-smoking campaigns. The most effective ads are those that give graphic detail of the impact of long-term smoking.
- Car salespersons. While you can give lists and show the wonderful features of the new car, the key is to have the customer no longer want their current car. That is why most salespeople want to look over and appraise your current car. They want you to desire the new car by not wanting your current car.

The examples are endless.

Politics

IT and business processes are closely intertwined. Thus, it is important to examine the business departments. The common department is composed of managers, senior employees, and other employees. The managers and supervisors rely heavily on these senior employees. They know the ropes. They have been there forever. They wield a great deal of informal power in the organization. You come along with a plan, a project, or some action that will improve a process in that department. Then you run into a wall of resistance. Management wants the change. The junior employees may support the change. The problem is with the senior business employees. We will call these people "king bees" and "queen bees." They will lose their informal power through change. They will not be seen as important. They could be replaced. They see no reason for change since what they have done and do has remained unchanged and working for a long time. From surveys we have done and experienced, the percentage of these people who resist change can be as high as 80%. The lesson learned here is that each activity in the planning effort must be sensitive to this potential resistance.

What to Do Next

Sit back and see if you start to build some items for the planning lists. It might seem too early since we have not covered these in detail, but it will help you get thinking in the planning framework given above.

Another action is to get copies of the mission, vision, and business plan. Ask yourself if the mission and/or vision has been used. Are they referred to often? Or do they just sit as words on walls and bulletin boards gathering dust?

Summary

We have laid out the roadmap for creating, marketing, implementing, and updating the strategic IT and process plan. The importance of business processes as a part of the plan was emphasized for a number of reasons. First, you need them to ensure the IT objectives, strategies, and action items are realistic. Second, often you have to have process change to realize the benefit of the IT investment.

The key themes of the planning method are:

- Organization through project management.
- Inclusion of processes, resource allocation, and implementation.
- Development of key lists and tables for business and IT factors.
- Collaboration during all parts of the planning effort.
- Parallelism of the planning activities.
- Communications during the plan not only to gather information, but also to gain support for the plan and the actions.

The plan is one of three dimensions in the alignment of IT to the business. If the plan is successful, you will be working on the right projects (strategic alignment). These two can influence the current work (tactical alignment).

The use of project management is valuable in doing strategic planning since it provides structure and a framework for all parts of the planning work. The project plan, tracking issues, and gathering lessons learned all assist in having more effective planning.

Chapter 2

Planning

Introduction

Let's first list the activities in the strategic IT and process planning work. As we go, we will note the changes from traditional strategic IT planning.

- *Analyze your past planning efforts.* This often does not receive much attention. However, here you will be able to employ the method with no risks and gain political support for the plan. There is a lot of good information here to help you technically and to assist you politically.
- *Define the purpose and scope of the planning work.* This seems obvious from the title, but it is not. This is because you will be doing process planning as well as IT planning. Here, you will also select your planning method.
- *Collect information for the plan.* Normally, this is very dry. It is very important because you are not only collecting information, but also identifying potential Quick Wins and generating more political support for implementation. Your political goal is to gain support for resources and implementation — not just plan for approval.
- *Assess the business and competitive environment.* This is easily a full-time activity. However, there is no time. Instead of learning about the industry, concentrate on key processes.

- *Evaluate the technology and architecture.* Since there is too much technology to consider and time is limited, you will be concentrating on what can be done with systems and technology in a three–five-year time horizon that is relevant to the business processes and supporting IT components.

- *Analyze processes and determine alignment to business goals.* This is a key part of the plan since it includes processes. You will want to indicate the key processes and problems — resulting in more support for IT action items that address these.

- *Assess the alignment of IT and systems to the business.* Techniques are given for analyzing alignment, both now and after the plan, is done. Alignment to general business goals will be carried out by relating them to the key processes.

- *Develop issues and opportunities for planning.* These include not only IT, but also process opportunities. You also may uncover some Quick Wins.

- *Define objectives and constraints.* Both process and IT objectives are defined. Constraints are immovable barriers or issues that prevent the immediate attainment of the objectives.

- *Create strategies and action items.* Strategies are intermediate term goals that support the objectives. Action items fall under the umbrella of the strategies in a many-to-many relationship. Many, if not most, of the action items should not be project ideas.

- *Build the plan and relate it to the business.* You will build the plan as you go through lists and tables. Here, a substantial effort is made in closely relating the plan to the strategic business plan and business units.

- *Get the strategic IT and process plan approved.* While this is important, it does not really matter if the plan does not get the resources or is implemented.

- *Obtain resources for the plan recommendations.* Most planning books ignore this part. Yet, if you do not have an approach for strategic resource allocation, many of the wonderful action items may never see the light of the day.

- *Implement the short-term plan action items.* Many action items should be Quick Wins that change procedures, improve processes, and make minor improvements in IT.
- *Implement the long-term plan action items.* These include project ideas as well as longer term organizational, process, policy, and other changes.
- *Measure planning results.* There are not only IT measurements, but also process measurements as well as measurements for alignment.
- *Update and maintain the plan.* We want to show how to do quickly and effectively, and continue to gain political support.

As you can see from the list, you are going to be implementing some action items before the plan is completed. This is not traditional. Normally, you develop the plan and gain approval. Then you work on implementation. That approach often fails since you will lose momentum. Instead, by implementing as you go, you create more enthusiasm for the plan. You also facilitate the review and approval process as managers are already seeing results.

Note that these tasks were not listed in a sequential step order. Why? Because you want to do as much of this in parallel as possible. From the first chapter remember that one goal is to get this done as fast as possible. Figure 2.1 indicates the activities that can be performed in parallel.

Analyze Your Past Planning Efforts

Sounds quite passive, doesn't it? Don't underestimate the significance of this step. Here you will be not only reviewing the planning documents, but also making contacts to see what happened in the past and what ideas people have for improvement. In this step you will be creating their first and lasting impression of the new planning work. Political? Very much so. Through your understanding of

First group — Definition

- Review past planning work
- Define purpose and scope of the planning effort

Second group — Assessment

- Collect data for the plan
- Assess the business and competitive environment
- Evaluate the technology and architecture
- Assess processes and determine alignment to the business
- Evaluate the alignment of IT to the business

Third group — Development

- Define issues and opportunities
- Develop objectives and constraints
- Identify strategies and action items
- Build the plan and relate it to the business

Fourth group — Implementation

- Perform resource allocation
- Implement the short-term action items
- Implement longer term action items
- Measure planning results
- Update and refine the plan

Figure 2.1 Parallel Approach to Strategic IT and Process Planning.

past work, you should not gather information that will help ensure future success, but also shorten the time required to develop the plan. Hence, you will create lists and tables that you will build upon later.

Another political aspect of this work is that you can see who is supportive and who is either doubtful or suspicious of the planning work. Useful to know as you perform later tasks.

At the end of this task you should have the following:

- Information from the past plan that can be used in the new effort.
- Data on who is friendly to the work and who is either questionable or opposed.
- The actual tangible benefits and results from the plan.
- How resources were allocated to planning action items.

- The effectiveness of the past planning effort.
- Lessons learned from the past effort — what worked and what to avoid.

Define the Purpose and Scope of the Planning Work

There is no specific chapter for this step. It is appropriate to work on it here. For any project, there are four purposes. There is the *technical purpose* — which is to create a high-quality plan that will be used. The second purpose is the business purpose. Here, the *business purpose* to get the plan completed on-time and within budget. Achieving both of these is insufficient to achieve the success discussed in the first chapter.

Most planning methods stop there — a bad idea. The third objective is the *political purpose*. This one is more complex. Let's see, after the plan is completed, you need to get resources. Then, the action items have to be implemented. So, it seems that a logical political purpose is to get management and employees behind and committed to the plan to the extent that both resource allocation and the planning action items are carried out successfully.

Isn't this enough? No, you could still achieve these, but you would not have involved other people to any degree. That is the reason for the fourth objective — the social purpose. The *social purpose* of the planning effort is to generate understanding in a collaborative way that the plan is important and that changes are needed as identified in the plan.

Another part of defining a project is to define the roles. Typically in the past, strategic IT planning has assumed or stated that the planner(s) will develop the plan. There is a problem here. If you or I do it and do not involve many people, there will be less buy-in and support since there was little or no involvement. Thus, the role of the "planners" is to coordinate the development of the plan and planning effort. Here is a basic point.

> The ownership of the plan is with management, line managers, employees, and IT — not the planners.

The challenge then is not only to get the plan done, but to generate substantial interest and involvement in the planning work so they will assume a greater degree of ownership.

Now we can turn to scope. The scope has already been broadened from just IT planning to strategic IT and process planning. But there are many processes. To do process plans for all major processes is impossible due to size and extent. Moreover, processes tend to be more interdependent. We will be selecting groups of processes that are aligned to the business in both a positive and negative way.

- *Processes are positively aligned* if their performance plays a key role in achieving business goals, the mission, and the vision.
- *Processes are negatively aligned* if their performance is so bad that they create or are major contributors to business issues and problems.

Experience shows that urgency compels most of the attention on processes in the second group.

Succeed in Communications

Planning cannot be done in a vacuum. If your planning effort is to be successful, your communications must be organized — both formally and informally. We consider the following formal communications and give tips for each as well as templates for all presentations.

- The planning approach — sell whatever you are using;
- The project plan for the strategic IT and process plan;

- Status of the planning work;
- Quick Wins from the planning effort;
- Present the plan and get it approved;
- Resource allocation;
- Plan results;
- Update the plan.

Informal communications are keys to success. Guidelines are given so that you don't fall into common pitfalls of overpromising results, and so forth. More importantly, the informal communications need to build political support for the plan action items.

Collect Information for the Plan

You already have captured information from past planning efforts — thereby reducing the effort in this step. Here we begin with an assessment of the mission, vision, and objectives of the business. Then, we turn to the business strategic plan. Our goal here is to relate the plan and work to the business all of the way. While this would be important if the plan included only IT, it is critical since processes are included. This will pave the way for aligning the processes to the business so that you can gain support for improvements to the key processes.

In the field you will be collecting information on these key processes. This does not mean an in-depth analysis of a process. Rather, it is an examination of common transactions and how the process has changed or deteriorated. Deterioration is important to show why actions are necessary.

Concurrently, you will be examining IT activities including:

- Current projects;
- Operations work and support;
- Maintenance and enhancement;

- Emergency work to fix problems;
- Resource allocation;
- The backlog of work.

In this chapter we include guidelines for developing the detailed project plan for the planning effort. To this end, the following are provided:

- Template for tasks and milestones;
- List of potential problems you might encounter;
- Guidelines for setting up the plan in Microsoft Project or some other project management system;
- Suggestions on how to create the project plan;
- Guidelines for updating and tracking the plan for planning effort.

Assess the Business and Competitive Environment

This part begins with getting business involvement so as to gather information on your industry, competition, and so forth. You are after trends in your industry segment. You will be identifying business issues that are due in part or whole to the processes and supporting systems and technology.

Having identified key processes, you will consider trends and issues in these processes. Guidance will be given on finding information on the future configuration of the processes. This includes both insourced and outsourced work.

Evaluate the Technology and Architecture

Many methods have been proposed for developing detailed IT architectures and structures. However, with greater standardization of hardware and software, the work required has been reduced. Important here is to pin down issues and problems in the systems and technology and relate these to the components of the architectural components. You will want to determine trends in both growth and deterioration.

Guidelines are provided for finding technology trends and applying these to the architecture. We are mainly interested in intermediate 3–5-year trends in hardware, communications and network, support, software, and Web-based tools and packages. The scope of the technology is that relevant to either the business processes and/or IT.

During this work, you have the opportunity to get IT staff and managers involved. What do you hope to achieve? A better understanding of the limitations of the current technology and systems and its impact on the business.

Analyze Processes and Determine Alignment to the Business Goals

Suggestions are provided for examining a business process. This is done at both a general and detailed level. By detail you want to look at a sample common transaction. Having the information on how the process works, its deterioration, and its problems, a vision for the future transactions will be developed. This can be expanded to a vision for the process.

Next, you can assess the alignment of the process to the business. As stated in Chapter 1, *Positive alignment* is the relation of the process to the business goals, mission, and vision. *Negative alignment* is the relation of the process to the business issues.

With the present and future of a process laid out, you can define a process plan. What is a process plan? Simply put, a *process plan* is a strategic plan for a single or group of related processes. The ingredients of a process plan include:

- Summary of the current process;
- Relation of the process to the business in both positive and negative terms;

- Problems, trends, and deterioration of the process;
- Vision of the future process;
- Benefits of the vision to the business;
- IT requirements generated by the process vision;
- Impact if the process is not improved — estimated future deterioration;
- Strategy for achieving the process vision.

Due to the work involved and limited time, you will only be able to do a few of these. Hopefully, you will generate interest to do more and to update these process plans.

Why do a process plan? Several reasons. First, if you have no process plan, it is difficult to see how strategic plans for IT and the business are realistic. Second, both business and IT depend upon the success of processes. Third, almost all process improvement methods do not address this critical step so that they can define many improvements, but do not tell people where it is all going. Fourth, it can provide both motivation and understanding of business employees involved in the processes.

Assess the Alignment of IT and Systems to the Business

This work involves determining the fit between IT and systems to the business — before, during, and after the planning effort. There are three kinds of alignment to be concerned with. These are:

- ***IT and systems internal alignment.*** Analysis here reveals the fit between the support, development, and operations parts of IT. It also includes the fit between the hardware, network, and software components for both operations and support.
- ***IT and systems alignment to processes.*** Having carried out the first step, each IT component can be related to business processes.

Here you are trying to determine the extent to which the IT components adequately support the business processes.

- *IT and systems factors alignment to business factors.* This is critical and is constructed from tables and lists of the previous two. Remember that alignment is a double edged sword. The positive side of alignment supports the operational, intermediate, and long-term goals of the business. The negative side of alignment deals with helping to resolve business issues through improvements in IT and processes.

Overall, there are three levels of alignment: current work, near term (strategies, projects), and long-term (the strategic IT and process plan).

In the next series of chapters (explained below in the following sections), a number of lists and possible tables will be created. This approach of lists and tables is a proven incremental method of doing the plan that makes planning easier, faster, and more understood. A cautionary note — while many tables are given, time and resources limit the actual number of planning tables you can generate. In each related chapter, we will indicate which ones are critical and give reasons for this selection.

The general technique is the same. After doing the lists, you relate the planning factor (issues and opportunities, objectives, etc.) to the business processes. Using these tables, you can then map the planning factor to the mission, vision, business objectives, and business issues.

Develop Issues and Opportunities for Planning

The next three steps take the information and create the essence of the plan components. The first is to identify issues and opportunities for both IT and processes. An *issue* is a problem while an *opportunity* is something that will improve something in IT or in a process. However, politically, it is sometimes good to point to these as opportunities — the chance to fix an issue.

To help you get going on these things quickly, we provide in each chapter a sample list of each of the planning factors: issues and opportunities, objectives, constraints, strategies, and action items.

Many think that these pertain to systems, technology, or new processes. But this is just a part of the story. These also encompass the following:

- Procedure changes;
- Policy changes;
- Facility changes;
- Organization change;
- Work assignment changes;
- Work rule changes;
- Training reinforcement and changes.

These changes can occur both within business units and IT. It is often either to fix some of these things than to embark on new projects. A bottom line that has served us well in the past is:

> You should seek to do new projects as a last resort for change.

Why? Because projects consume multiple resources and incur risk. Moreover, many problems faced by processes and IT cannot be fixed by some new projects. The political reason is that too many projects makes the strategic plan appear to self-serving — just more marketing for projects.

Once you have lists of issues and opportunities, you can map these to the business processes. This can be accomplished through tables in which the rows are specific issues and opportunities and the columns are processes. The table indicates the impact and importance of the issue or opportunity to the individual business process.

Now you can link the issues and opportunities to the business factors such as mission, vision, business objectives, and business issues through the processes. Three tables are created:

- *Issues and opportunities versus mission or vision.* This table shows the importance of a specific issue or opportunity to a mission or vision element.
- *Issues and opportunities versus business objectives.* Similar to the previous.
- *Issues and opportunities versus business issues.* The table reveals how an individual issue or opportunity contributes to an individual business issue.

A more detailed explanation of how to combine the tables is given in the next section. The usefulness of these tables lies in the fact that they show the impact of technical problems on business goals and operations. This is valuable because it is often hard to imagine in a business person's mind how some seemingly arcane technical network or software problem affects a general business objective or issue. Politically, this shows the relevance of the plan and the need to address the issues. It helps to sell the plan.

Define Objectives and Constraints

Objectives are directional goals for both processes and IT. Ideally, an objective should be timeless. That is, while you can make progress toward it, the resources, money, state of the technology, and other factors prevent you from achieving the objective in less than five years. Here are some areas of objectives.

- General IT objectives;
- General business process objectives;

- Application systems objectives;
- Architecture and infrastructure objectives;
- Project objectives;
- Methods and tools objectives.

What prevents the achievement of objectives? Constraints. You can think of *constraints* as immovable issues which you cannot overcome. Categories of constraints include:

- Financial constraints;
- Time constraints due to business pressures;
- Resource constraints;
- Technology constraints.

But this is just a start. There are more from the business side.

- Competitive constraints;
- Nature of the business and industry constraints;
- Geographical constraints;
- Regulatory and legal constraints;
- Cultural and social constraints;
- Customer constraints;
- Product and service constraints.

Why are constraints important? After all, they sound so negative. Constraints in the plan are a means of showing both IT and the business the factors that have to be accepted and restrict what is possible in terms of actions, strategies, and objectives.

Now you can proceed to relate these to each other and to the processes. The first table is that of objectives versus constraints. The entries here reveal how constraints restrict the objectives. Next, you can relate the objectives to the processes in a second table. The entry in this table shows the impact on a specific process if the objective is achieved. For example, if you achieve a major network objective you would enhance the performance of a number of processes.

You can next map the objectives to the business factors through the processes. Here are the tables to prepare:

- *Objectives versus business mission and/or vision.* This table shows the overall alignment of IT to the business. The rows are the objectives while the columns are elements of the vision or mission. The entry is how an objective supports a particular vision or mission element.
- *Objectives versus business objectives.* This table demonstrates how the plan objectives help achieve specific business objectives. The entries are similar to that for mission and/or vision.
- *Objectives versus business issues.* This table reveals how achieving the objectives will help resolve specific business issues. The rows are the objectives while the columns are the individual business issues.

How do you develop these tables? Many strategic plans are less than successful at doing this because of the generality of the objectives, mission, vision, business objectives, and issues. You proceed by linking the table of objectives versus processes to that of the business factor to the processes — combining tables or matrices. For example, suppose objective A supports and improves process Q. Mission element C relates closely to the performance of process Q. Combining the tables, you find that objective A supports mission element C.

There are added benefits to this approach beyond making the relationship between the plan objectives and business factors easier to develop. By using this approach you clearly demonstrate to management and employees the relationships. If someone questions the validity or need for an objective, you can move to the processes. In order to attack a plan objective, they have to attack the importance of their own business process. This method has been proven again and again. It works!

Another benefit is that you can build the tables incrementally as you go. This means that you can get reviews and involvement of some managers and staff. They get a chance to participate and buy into the work. Moreover, it is easier to show the status and progress of the planning effort through the lists and tables.

Yet another benefit lies in the updating of the plan. Updating the plan starts with the existing lists. Then after these are defined, you can update the planning tables — making the updating effort easier and less time consuming. In addition, you are building on what you have done so that you reduce the risk and potential problems.

Create Strategies and Action Items

A *strategy* is a method or approach to work toward one or more objectives while not violating any constraint. One strategy can support more than one objective so that the relationship between objectives and strategies is many-to-many. Here are categories of strategies for the strategic IT and process plan.

- General IT strategies;
- General business process strategies;
- Application systems strategies;
- Architecture and infrastructure strategies;
- Project strategies;
- Methods and tools strategies;
- Policy strategies.

Once the strategies for the plan have been developed, they can be related to the business processes through the table of strategies versus business processes. The rows are the strategies of the plan while the columns are the processes. The entry is how an individual strategy can improve the performance of a specific business process.

As with objectives and issues and opportunities, you can now relate the plan strategies to the business factors. The following tables can be produced using the same approach as described in the previous two sections.

- ***Strategies versus business mission and/or vision.*** This table shows the positive alignment of the intermediate level of the plan (strategies) to the mission and/or vision. Each entry explains how a strategy supports a mission or vision element.
- ***Strategies versus business objectives.*** Similar to the above.
- ***Strategies versus business issues.*** This table shows the negative alignment of strategies to the business. The entry is how an individual strategy helps to mitigate a specific business issue.

An ***action item*** is some specific, measurable activity or decision that is generated by the strategic plan. Many think of action items as project ideas. Yet, they include many other items that do not require projects and money, but instead are management actions. In the many strategic plans we have developed, over half of the action items are not project related. Here are the areas of action items.

- Technical and technology potential action items;
- Application system potential action items;
- Policy and procedure potential action items;
- Business process-related action items;
- Methods and tools potential action items.

A brief write-up of each action item is needed. This includes:

- Description of the action item;
- Steps needed to implement the action item;
- How to measure the success of the action item after implementation;

- Impact if the action item is not carried out;
- Tangible benefits of the action item.

The impact of not doing the action item is very important in that it shows the urgency of the action item. You have to overcome the feeling that:

We haven't done this action before so why now?

and

Our other work is much more important than the plan action items.

These write-ups sound like a lot of work. However, you will mainly write this up for the project ideas. Why? Because after approval of the strategic plan, the project related action items have to fight for available resources.

As with strategies and the other planning factors, you can relate the action items to the business processes. The rows in this table are the action items. The columns are the processes. The entry is the benefit or impact of carrying out an action item on the process.

Well, you know what comes next. We relate the action items to the business factors and generate the following tables.

- ***Action items versus mission and/or vision.*** This table shows the positive alignment of the action items to the business — hence, their importance. One action can map to several mission or vision elements. The entry is the contribution of the action item through the processes to the mission or vision elements.

- *Action items versus business objectives.* Similar to the previous.
- *Action items versus business issues.* This table reveals the negative alignment of the action items to the business. The entry is the benefit of the action item to resolving or mitigating the business issues.

Using these tables you can demonstrate how a technical or seemingly small action item is relevant to the business.

In the chapter covering strategies and action items, a substantial number of possible strategies and action items are presented. This will help you get started faster.

Pay attention to the categories as you should have action items and strategies in each of the areas. Politically, it is useful to have non-project action items since they can be implemented more easily — showing results from the planning. Here is another tip. Get some of the action approved and put into effect before the plan is finished. This will give the plan more momentum and credibility.

Build the Plan and Relate It to the Business

Up to this point you have created lists of the following:

- Issues and opportunities;
- Objectives;
- Constraints;
- Strategies;
- Action items.

You have also related all but the constraints to the business processes and produced the following tables.

- Issues and opportunities versus processes;
- Objectives versus processes;

- Strategies versus processes;
- Action items versus processes.

With these you have related each of the four planning factors to the business mission, vision, objectives, and issues.

Think of this as the parts. You now want to define the whole impact of the strategic plan if it is approved and implemented. There are several steps to carry out. First, you want to show how achieving the objectives will overall improve the performance of the business processes. You can develop a vision of several key processes.

The second step is to take the results of the first step and show how improvement of the processes helps to achieve the mission, vision, and business objectives. You can also show how process improvement contributes to resolving business issues.

Market the Plan and Planning Method

Even before the plan is started, you have to market the plan and the method. Chapter 13 gives some practical advice on how to undertake this. However, once sold you have to continually do selling and marketing. Why? After all, the planning work was approved. The continual justification is to stir more interest and involvement. It also helps to protect the resources assigned to the planning work. Now, you can spend all day extolling the wonderful benefits of planning. Managers with a short-term focus may not really listen to this or see it as of importance. Thus, much of the marketing is to stress negative importance. If you had a workable strategic IT and process plan, the problems X, Y, and Z could have been avoided. If you have a plan, then the deterioration of process Q, R, and S will stop and their performance will be enhanced in an organized manner. Marketing here is based upon self-interest.

You have to undertake negative marketing, emphasizing the impact of not doing something. This is as important as the positive marketing stressing the benefits.

Get Resources for the Larger Planning Action Items

This is an area seldom considered in the literature around IT planning. Instead, they focus on building the plan. Nice, but not complete. You can develop a wonderful plan, but if you can't get any resources for the action items, it is dead in the water. Chapter 13 addresses the import area of strategic resource allocation. This is highly related to strategic planning.

The planning action items have to be complete with the following activities that are already consuming resources:

- Existing projects;
- Operations support;
- Maintenance and enhancement work;
- Targets of opportunity;
- Emergency repairs and work;
- Backlog of approved work;
- Other project ideas not from the plan.

Some comments are useful here. Targets of opportunity should, where possible, be incorporated into the plan. Other project ideas should also be part of the planning effort. The backlog of projects should have been considered in the planning work.

However, these have something in common. They are either not consuming real, active resources or they consume a lesser amount of resources as compared to the other categories.

> The real target of strategic resource allocation is to control the resources devoted to maintenance, enhancement, and operations.

This struggle is made easier because this work is often only generally justified. Few answer the question: "What if some of this was not done? What would be the impact?" By controlling resources devoted to everyday work, you free up resources to work toward more strategic goals and resolve long-standing problems.

Here we come to a basic and major reason for doing a strategic IT and process plan.

> The strategic IT and process plan can be a management and political tool to control resources consumed in tactical work.

For an individual person this is effective time management. Without the plan, management has few tools to control resources. After all, what is the alternative to doing more tactical work? Answer — they would have to invent new project ideas on their own or reduce the resources in IT and elsewhere.

There is also inertia to overcome since many view the current work as the most important. Since there are often no spare resources, the key to getting resources for the project-related action items is to reduce the effort in these other activities.

You should not expect a major shift in resources toward the plan action items. This is because of the extent of resources required for operational support. Your goal should be a more modest goal — say 10% of the resources.

While the plan is updated either annually or twice a year, strategic resource allocation should be done at least four times a year. This will make IT more responsive to new business needs and requirements. In addition, it forces existing projects to show progress or otherwise lose support.

In the resource allocation you should not expect to get all project action items approved. Concentrate on the project action items that have either or both of a clear urgency or direct and tangible benefits.

Implement the Plan — Short Term

The implementation of the plan, once approved, can be divided into two parts: short-term Quick Wins and longer term work and projects. The first are the short-term changes that can be implemented with little or no resources. This is the subject of Chapter 14. We can partition the short-term actions or Quick Wins into the following types:

- Business process Quick Wins. These are modifications to processes in terms of work assignments, policies, procedures, and the like in both IT and the business operations.
- Infrastructure Quick Wins. These are enhancements to network, hardware, system software, and application software.
- Resource management Quick Wins. This consists of reassigning resources to meet more pressing needs. This follows from the strategic resource allocation.
- Methods and tools Quick Wins. Often, the planning effort reveals areas where the use of methods and tools can be improved. This includes gathering and sharing lessons learned.
- Staffing and skills Quick Wins. These are steps to improve the skills and knowledge of both IT workers and business employees.
- Project management Quick Wins. Included here are steps to either redirect or change internals of existing projects so as to increase their value and performance.

Implement the Plan — Long Term

The longer term action items consist mainly of projects. These can be divided into four categories:

- Projects related to processes and work;
- Projects related to application systems;
- Projects related to infrastructure and architecture;
- Projects related to new technology and systems.

Each of these has unique attributes that are explored in Chapter 15.

Measure Planning Results

Measurement of the planning work is not performed only at the end of the planning cycle, it is also undertaken during the work. Here are some of the key measurement areas.

- Business processes. You want to measure processes early in the work. Additional measurements occur after Quick Wins. This can generate more interest and support in the planning effort. There is also process measurement after the projects are completed.
- IT. Guidelines and measurements are provided for each area and major activity of IT.
- Projects. This applies to active projects as well as to those generated by the plan.
- Architecture. How to assess the effectiveness of the technology and systems architecture is examined.
- Planning process and method. Measurements here concentrate on how to analyze the effectiveness and efficiency of the planning approach.
- Planning. Measurements here deal with the actual planning work.

- Work and support. This area includes measuring the existing work in IT and the key business processes.

Note that the measurements extend well beyond the planning process and process. They include the business processes and IT. This is the control part of "planning and control."

Measurement results should be presented separate from the plan. This gives more visibility and supports concentration on the plan. It also provides a separate forum to present progress and results of the planning work.

Now let's suppose the worse. The plan is approved, but no new projects are started. What do you do? Keep up the measurement to show deterioration in the condition of processes and IT systems and technology. We have used this several times to later obtain resources for the planning projects.

Measurements deliver several benefits. First and foremost, people get an overall picture of what is going on. Second, measurements support the benefit and help to justify the planning work. Third, measurements provide a way to increase morale and gain political traction with business management.

This chapter also addresses updating the plan. Detailed tasks are defined and explained in detail. The goal of the plan update is not to just complete an updated plan. In addition, you have the opportunity to gain more support for change. Another objective in the update is to do this as quickly and effectively as possible. This is accomplished through the use of the planning lists and tables. Using the lists and tables method, you will find that the update can be accomplished with limited effort.

Examples

The method was applied for a number of years in a major energy firm with a large IT group. They already had an IT plan. But it was not really used. There was no formal strategic resource allocation. Resources were tactically applied. There was little enthusiasm for the planning work initially. Expectations were low. This was actually an advantage since it allowed us the opportunity to collect information easily because no one thought anything would come of it. The first Quick Wins changed this attitude and generated enthusiasm. While the planning work was done, a review of resource allocation was initiated. This led to several projects being canceled as well as reductions and reviews of enhancement and maintenance. A process was implemented for justifying maintenance and enhancement. These actions freed up resources for the plan action items.

In addition to the example in Chapter 18 for a small IT group in Ireland, the method was applied to a manufacturing firm in Indonesia. This firm had a limited IT staff. They had had no experience in either IT or process planning. They managed IT on a day-to-day basis. The first step was to sell the need for a planning effort at all. The methodology had to be simple and straightforward. The justification of the planning effort was successful because it was based upon the problems and lack of strategic progress in IT. A dismal scenario was developed for the impacts on the business if there was no change.

Even after the planning method was approved and resources allocated, there was resistance in both IT and the business. "Why do this when things are fine as they are?" To answer this and overcome the inertia, a two pronged-approach was adopted. The first or positive thrust was to demonstrate how their skills and marketability individually would be enhanced if the action items were completed. The negative marketing was to emphasize the effects on them individually and on the company if there was no change.

Let's consider another energy firm which we will call Omega Energy. Due to space constraints, this will be summarized and is not complete. We begin with issues and opportunities. Here are some of the ones developed. Only a few are given out of the over 60.

- Much of the technology used for exploration support is out-of-date.
- The systems at the retail level do not support business goals for growth and business expansion.
- Too much of IT resources are devoted to support of existing systems.

Before the planning effort, the IT objectives were:

- Be responsive to business needs.
- Implement new technology based on tangible benefits.
- Provide efficient support to meet user requirements.

What is the problem with these? They are too general and do not apply to the business. No wonder that some managers questioned whether IT was working on the right projects.

During the planning effort, these objectives were refined to match up to the business better, resulting in:

- Employ systems and technology to position the firm more effectively to support exploration.
- Support the streamlining of the refining and distribution processes.
- . Implement new technology that would provide a competitive edge in retailing, marketing, and operations management.

Note that these better position IT to the business — improved alignment.

Now turn to constraints. Here is a sample of the ones that were formulated.

- Individual profit centers mean that systems efforts are dedicated in each area — limiting resource flexibility.

- Management focus on short-term profit goals limits investment in long-term architectural improvement.
- Dispersed locations increase the support requirements.
- Existing and legacy technology consumes IT personnel's time.
- Distributed authority among business units restricts the IT role in getting improvements.

Next are the strategies. Let's take an example. One was to implement a new retail network to support retail operations. This seems OK, but in fact it is too general. A better strategy is:

> Design and implement a full function, flexible retail system, and network that will accommodate future operations as well as web-based technology.

This is preferable since it is more specific and complete.

Consider the exploration objective above. This relates to both hardware and network capabilities on the one hand, and data management and modeling software on the other. This led to two strategies:

- Establish a high capacity, reliable, and flexible network and hardware capability to address exploration requirements.
- Provide data management and analysis software necessary to support exploration data analysis.

Finally, we can list some of the action items.

- Improve IT staff training in new technology.
- Identify, evaluate, and select the appropriate software tools to support exploration.
- Define a new network architecture.
- Hire new petroleum engineers and geologists who are familiar with the latest software.
- Develop a business plan for streamlining refinery operations.

About 70% of the action items were not project related.

Lessons Learned

One lesson learned is not to oversell the method. The best approach is to emphasize the negative aspects of not having the plan. The reason for this is that people have heard many times about the wonders and benefits of some planning method. You want to avoid over-promising results.

We cannot underemphasize the importance of doing the planning work in parallel steps. You not only reduce the elapsed time for planning, but also generate results faster. This leads to the next lesson learned. You want to implement some Quick Wins during the planning work to show results. We have said this earlier, but it deserves repeating. Quick Wins often do not require the approval or even completion of the entire plan. In fact, the plan can indicate which Quick Wins were implemented and their respective benefits.

Politics

Why is planning political? Isn't it just another project? The answer is no. The plan and its action items threaten the status quo of both IT staff and management, and that of the business units. That is why you must continually work to sell the planning work. After you start using the method, do not try to sell the planning work based on the method. Instead, focus on the impact of doing nothing and having no change. Get the attention focused on the work not the planning method.

What to Do Next

One step is to review your past planning efforts. We explore this in-depth in Chapter 4. Another action is to review the method and start filling in some of the lists. You can also discover what information you can readily get your hands on.

Another action is to find problems that have occurred because the plan was not created or not followed. The same applies to resource allocation. You can see how resources are currently deployed. If operations consumes a great deal of resources, it could be that the IT staff are working hard, but the overall situation is standing still.

Summary

The planning method has been presented along with strategic resource allocation and measurement. These three things go hand-in-hand in achieving success in strategic IT and process planning.

Chapter 3

Undertake Effective Communications

Introduction

In this chapter we cover both formal and informal communications from the presentation of the planning approach to the results of implementation — the entire planning cycle. In any strategic planning effort there are a handful of key presentations:

- The planning approach. Here you present the overall method and what you hope to achieve with their involvement.
- The project plan for the planning work. This is sometimes combined with the first one, but we treat here separately to give you greater flexibility.
- Status of the planning work.
- Quick Wins.
- Presentation of the completed plan.
- The plan for a project action item.
- Results from the strategic resource allocation.
- Results stemming from the implementation of action items of the plan.
- Update the plan.

For each of these we provide templates, guidelines, and questions that you maybe asked along with a framework of responses. Other communications can relate to technology assessments and measurements. Tips for these are given in Chapters 6 and 16, respectively.

Here is our ranking of communications media.

1. Face-to-face. This is best and there is less chance of misunderstanding.
2. Voice mail. This is better than paper or e-mail since you can convey tone of voice.
3. E-mail. This is the preferred method for written communications since it is so common.
4. Paper. Mail often goes through intermediaries. Moreover, there is the usual delay of sending mail through the company.
5. Fax. This ranks the lowest of the five since there is no record of what happened to it. Faxes may arrive in a common area and people may not get to them for a while. Moreover, someone could inadvertently take your fax along with their own.

You can pursue a group of these. Suppose that you want to send someone a substantial draft of part of the strategic plan. You first contact them in person or by phone to alert them of what is coming and what response and time to review are requested. Then you can send an e-mail with a copy of the document attached. In the text of the e-mail you can give a summary. Since the document is substantial in length, separately you deliver or send a hard copy. Delivery in person is best since it gives you another opportunity for contact. This seems obvious, but people run into trouble because they do plan regarding the medium.

Steering Committees

In larger organizations, it is typical to establish a steering committee to review the planning materials. This group of managers represents the major stakeholders and business unit managers as well as representatives of upper management. This sounds fine in theory. In practice, the challenge is to ensure that managers really attend these meetings and not send lower-level staff members. Doing this can result in all managers sending lower-level people. One approach we have employed is to have two levels of steering committees. The operational steering committee deals with the details while the management steering committee conducts milestone reviews. This gets around the problem of time limitations of management. Experience shows that it does impose an undue burden.

To build interest, experience has shown that it is useful to start with issues and opportunities. Issues and opportunities can be linked to the business processes. These tend to be precise, detailed, and so more interested. Having gotten their interest, you might think that you would present IT objectives. In many firms this is the case. However, these can be very general. Some managers may have a hard time connecting the issues to the objectives.

Since this is both a business process and strategic IT plan, we suggest that you get them involved in reviewing the process plans (see Chapter 7). This should really get their interest since the business depends on the processes for success. Here they can see the vision for the work.

A good next step is to present potential action items and strategies. Why? These are more detailed than objectives. You can demonstrate how the strategies and action items deal with the issues and opportunities, and support the process plans. After all of this, you can present the objectives.

This approach has been proven to keep managers' interest and not bog them down in fuzzy concepts like objectives. Moreover, the approach clearly shows that IT is being aligned to the processes and, hence, to the business.

If You Don't Communicate...

Often, if management has assigned you to do something, you just go ahead and do it. People often assume that the only communications are the formal ones. Not so. You should make the following assumptions.

- If you fail to regularly communicate, they may lose interest.
- If you fail to regularly communicate, you will have to present much more information to get them up to speed. If you communicate fairly often, then the update of information is incremental.
- You want to keep their interest because you will require their support and involvement to get the strategic plan approved, to get approval for Quick Wins, to get resources for project action items, and to approve the update.

In short, communications must be planned to the same extent as the planning effort itself.

There are other benefits to communications. First, you get the people involved and interested — therefore, more supportive. A second reason is that you want them to own the plan. It is your plan — it is theirs. Third, you receive valuable feedback and opinions that can help shape tasks in the planning work. Fourth, they can aid you politically in gaining support for changes generated by the planning effort.

Informal versus Formal Communications

Prior to, during, and after the strategic planning work there are a limited number of formal presentations to prepare and deliver. For formal presentations in general, here are some guidelines.

- Try to get to some of important members of the audience before the presentation and give them a one-on-one view of the presentation. This will head off questions and problems later.

- Your goal in each formal presentation is to achieve an objective — get something approved, and so forth — not to just do the presentation.
- Try to get the message across quickly — hopefully, in less than 15 minutes.
- Make sure that the slides have complete thoughts. It is frustrating to read the presentation later and not see what was meant. Moreover, there will be people missing from the presentation and you want them to understand the material.
- Try to have good eye contact around the room.

The next section provides guidelines and tips for informal communications. As you will see, this requires an organized approach. Here are some general tips for communicating informally.

- Seek out managers on one-on-one basis. The best time is early in the morning or at the end of the day, or during breaks.
- Try to avoid scheduling a formal meeting. They may get the wrong impression that there is a major problem even when there is none. They may defensively gather a number of staff members. So much for the one-on-one.
- If you are on good terms with the secretary or assistant to the manager, don't hesitate to stop by and give them a "casual" update. Indicate that you know the manager is busy so that you just wanted to stop by and provide some information.
- Keep a log of the manager informal contacts. This sounds like a lot of additional work, but it is not. You want to record the date and time of contact, the subject, and any comments they made. This is important for a number of reasons. First, we have found that problems often arise with the managers with whom you had.

Informal Communications

Informal communications occurs when you do not make a formal presentation. So, it covers everything else outside of this. Many think that "informal" means unplanned or casual. Far from it! You have to be organized about this communication form as well. Otherwise, you will repeatedly curse yourself for not bringing up something when you had the opportunity.

First up is communicating about the planning approach and planning in general. Get some war stories and examples from the web and your organization's to show the need for planning. In explaining any planning method, stress the following:

- The method is common sense.
- It has been used many times by a wide range of organizations.
- With the method it can be done rapidly and with limited interference and effort so as not to disturb regular work.

This last point is one of the most important. Note what is missing from the list — you are not explaining the method in detail. If you should do this, people may think that you are either unsure of the method and need reinforcement. Alternatively, they may think that you want them to get more involved than they are willing to be.

The planning effort has been authorized. Now, you create a project plan and are preparing to communicate about it. Here are some tips.

- Cover only some of the initial major activities and first milestones. Informally, you don't want to cover the whole plan.
- Mention, almost as an aside, some potential problems that might be encountered. This gets them ready if they materialize.
- Emphasize again that you have scheduled meetings, and so forth that will minimize people's time.

Now you have started doing strategic planning. Assume that you will meet some managers in the hallway and that they ask how things are going. Be ready with the following:

- Have information on status ready at all times. This includes current tasks as well as the overall schedule and costs. Also, be ready to identify short-term future tasks.
- Have a story or interesting finding from the planning effort so far. This should be non-political and hopefully related to favorable work in departments you are working with.
- Identify a few potential Quick Wins. This often gets manager interested and even excited. It also helps you justify the planning cost, time, and effort.
- Have two or three issues ready to mention and discuss if they show interest. Never have just one issue. It makes the discussion too focused. If these are brought up, your goal is just to provide information and status on the problems. Not to get resolution.

You have something that is ready for review. Using our method this might consist of lists and/or some tables. Indicate that you will be sending this to them. Point something interesting from the information — maybe, something that was a surprise or that was unexpected. Also, indicate the number of items in the lists or tables. Also, point out the status so that they can sense that work is on schedule. In addition, mention some Quick Wins.

Later, you have a draft of the plan. You will be giving them a copy. This is not the final version leading to the strategic plan presentation. Indicate what the draft covers. What is probably most interesting to them is to highlight how the plan addresses key issues and opportunities and objectives from a business point of view. If interest is shown, then you can mention a few non-project action items. Why not mention project ideas? They require resources and money. But if you can mention some Quick Wins, they will feel more comfortable.

Because of the planning effort, several Quick Wins have been identified. You want to get their support before you formally present them. Indicate what they are and the benefit to their department and the organization as a whole. Point out that little effort is needed. You might give an example of before and after the Quick Win. They may ask you "Why wasn't this done before?" A suitable and often accurate answer is that "People get tied up in their daily work and miss things like this." Many cannot see the forest through the trees — but you don't say this.

The plan is completed. You will be scheduling the presentation. However, you also informally want to get them prepared for the strategic planning document. What should you do? Here are some tips.

- Give them an example of an issue or opportunity that affects them and the corresponding action items. This makes the plan relevant to them.
- Indicate the level of cooperation and involvement that you have received. Here you want to reinforce the idea that it is their plan and not yours. Give them all of the credit. Take none for yourself.

After the plan has been presented, you may want meet informally to see the action items. Instead of mentioning the great benefits of the action items, focus on the impact if nothing is done — further deterioration. Also, reinforce the fact that many of the things do not require funding or resources — the Quick Wins.

You are developing a project plan for one of the project action items out of the strategic plan. You want to convince managers that it is worthy of getting resources and funding. As before with other items, point out the downside if the project is not done. Also, you want to indicate that the schedule, costs, and resource demands are in line with what was mentioned in the plan.

You are working to convince managers that a new resource allocation method is needed. Instead of referring to the projects you want to start, turn attention to the shortcomings of the present resource allocation method. Emphasize the need for a more proactive approach.

Later, it is time to communicate the need to do a strategic planning update. Here you want to indicate some of the things that have changed since the strategic plan was developed. Also, demonstrate that since the plan relies on tables and lists, it will be easy and cost-efficient to update.

How can you test yourself for these types of informal communications? At home or the office, sit down and assume you meet a manager right now. What do you say? This helps to test your readiness.

Here is another tip for informal communications, try to have these one-on-one. In that way, you can interpret the information in a way that applies to their department and work. You are in essence presenting a relational view of the information.

Here are some additional observations on informal communications.

- When using the telephone speak clearly and distinctly into the phone. This seems obvious but we have all gotten calls that were difficult to understand.
- When speaking on the telephone, smile. Yes, you heard right. When you smile, your voice changes and becomes more positive. You sound more upbeat.
- Make a decision before calling. Do you really need to talk to the real person? Or will voice mail or a secretary or assistant suffice?
- Make a note on a piece of paper of the purpose of the call and any other critical information. This will get you organized before the call.

Comments on Written Communications

For any written communication, it is wise to avoid mentioning any problems that you are having. Try to have discussions on these verbally. Why? Because they may fall into the wrong hands. They could be misinterpreted.

When you write either for paper or e-mail, make an outline first. Write the note and then store it as a draft. Wait at least a few hours. Then go back and review it before you send it out.

To aid you in writing, here is a checklist of things to consider:

- Why can't this message be conveyed verbally?
- Who is your audience? How technical are they?
- What is the message that you are trying to convey?
- Is the note clear and unambiguous?
- What is the tone of the words used?
- Will the title of the e-mail or note attract attention?
- Is the note short and direct?
- Is there a connection between this note and previous correspondence?
- Put yourself in the position of the recipient. Is your desired action spelled out clearly?

Be careful who you copy on a note or e-mail. Sometimes, if a high-level manager sees lower-level people on the distribution list, he or she may ignore the note. For e-mail messages, make sure that the message is in the first few lines since that is what people will read first to determine if they should open the message.

Many people write sentences and paragraphs that are too long and not to the point. They ramble on and on. How can you break old habits? Through a radical change. Try these three tips for informal notes.

- Make all paragraphs three sentences or less in length.
- Make all sentences 10 words long or less.
- Ensure that each word has no more than three syllables.

These rules will have to be violated due to the nature of the planning. However, you should try to do this. Remember that the simpler the writing, the clearer the message will be. And the greater the likelihood that the message will get across to the receiver. After all, that is the goal, right?

One suggestion is to keep politics out of all written material.

> You should assume that all written material will be read by many people.

Another lesson learned from communications is the following:

> If there is a failure in communication, it is always the fault of the sender, not the receiver.

This is because the sender makes the decisions about the messages. Now let's consider some of the formal presentations that you will be making.

Present the Planning Approach

Ten specific formal presentations are discussed in this and following sections. These cover almost all of the potential presentations that relate to strategic IT and process planning. For each we provide an outline or template for the presentation along with guidelines on what to cover and points to emphasize. While you can use any outline you want it is useful to employ standardized templates. This makes the structure of the presentation very clear from the start so that the audience can concentrate on the content and not on the format.

First up is the presentation of the planning method or approach. If you are using a method employed in the past, this is, of course, not needed. The purpose of the presentation is to gain commitment and involvement in the planning effort. It is not to have the audience understand the details of the planning method. If you present too much detail on the method, managers may think that you are unsure and need their involvement in managing the strategic planning project.

The first part of the presentation focuses on the need for strategic planning. Even if everyone is behind this, you still want to emphasize the need and benefit. It is useful here to highlight some of the areas that need planning. Then, during the presentation verbally you can point to the impact if these areas are not addressed.

Second, you should provide a sample general outline of the resulting plan and what they should expect to see. This can be followed up with some examples of action items. Why not objectives and issues, and so forth? Well, issues are negative. Objectives are too general. Action items are more tangible and positive. Make sure that a majority of the action items are not projects. If they are all projects, then management will just put more demands for resources and funding. Here you want to show that changes in policies, procedures, work assignments, and other modifications can lead to Quick Wins and tangible results.

At this point you have talked about the need and the end products of the planning work. This is the "What." Go to the "how." Give a summary set of tasks and milestones for the plan. This includes the projected schedule. Make sure that these are worded in business terms. This is where a summary explanation of the method can be delivered.

This naturally leads to the question of resources. Provide a slide on what business units will be asked to provide in terms of information and involvement. Verbally, indicate how much time and the type of people you want to contact. Make sure that you leave the impression that this is a limited effort.

You are almost done. The final step is to present a list of next steps and actions in the planning process.

To kick off the planning effort after this presentation, many would seek a memo or e-mail from management endorsing the planning effort and its importance. Our experience has shown that this can be mixed. It could raise expectations of fast results. Alternatively, if people have been getting a lot of management messages, they may ignore it.

A better approach is to have the managers of the individual business units introduce you and the planning to their employees. This is more direct and will often lead to greater support and participation.

Present the Project Plan for the Planning Effort

Sometimes this is combined with the first presentation. However, to cover the widest range of possibilities, we will consider this as a separate presentation following that of the approach. The purpose of this presentation is to ensure that the audience understands what is ahead and reinforces their limited involvement. Here, you also want to make sure that the managers see clearly the scope of the effort. There should be no immediate actions from this presentation except the initial planning activities.

The project plan presentation should give the elements in Figure 3.1.

Looks fairly complete, doesn't it? But where are the costs and benefits? These were covered earlier. If you give benefits, you will often be drawn into those of the action items. However, you cannot promise this since these are not known and approval of project ideas and other action items is separate from the planning work itself.

- *Purpose of the planning effort.* There are actually four purposes. The business purpose is to initiate change that will improve the performance of IT and the processes. The technical purpose is to do this with minimal time and effort and still cover the key IT and process areas completely. The political purpose is to gain support for getting resources and implementing Quick Wins. The social purpose is to involve a substantial number of people to a limited extent so that they feel that they are participating and even owning the contents of the plan.
- *Scope of the plan.* Here, you want to emphasize that the plan includes not only IT, but also critical processes. In terms of range, you want to show that Quick Wins are included. You can give a list of areas of Quick Wins to indicate what you mean.
- *Tasks, milestones, and schedule.* Rather than bulleted lists, present a GANTT chart. This will reinforce the idea that the planning effort is a project, not just more work. In the list of tasks ensure that implementation of some Quick Wins occurs before the completion of the plan.
- *Potential issues and opportunities to be addressed.* Here, you want to reveal some of the things that the plan will address. This is another aspect of showing what the scope is. You are not promising to resolve the issues or implement all opportunities.
- *Roles and activities.* This includes what you will need from the business units in terms of types of people and information to be gathered. Indicate here that it is in their own self-interest to involve more than one or two people.
- *Potential problems.* Here, you can give a list of potential problems. Examples are lack of available time due to other commitments, the difficulty of getting external information, and so forth.
- *Detailed next steps.* These are activities that will be undertaken in the first month.

Figure 3.1 Elements of the Project Plan Presentation.

Present Status on the Plan

The purpose of providing status is to make the managers comfortable about the progress of the work. Yet, there is also another goal. Presenting status gives you the opportunity to get them more interested in the work, to get their involvement in problem resolution, and to gain support for action items. How often should you present status? This obviously depends on the size and scope of the planning effort. Informally, you should provide status updates on a weekly basis. Formal status could be given either every two weeks or once a month.

The key ingredients of the status presentation whether in slides or a document include the list in Figure 3.2.

What is missing? There is no budget or cost information. This is because it is basically labor hours of a small number of people.

- GANTT chart that shows summary tasks for all work, the corresponding milestones, and detailed tasks for a date range of the past month and next one and two months.
- Milestones completed since the last status report was given.
- Findings. This consists of information that you found in the work in this period. This is beneficial since it makes the presentation more interesting.
- Involvement and activities by the business unit managers and staff. Here, you can give them credit for participating.
- Outstanding problems and their status. If there are no significant problems, then this can be omitted. However, sometimes it is politically useful to give a few. One that we employed frequently is "some feel that the plan will not lead to any change." If you mention this one, then you can indicate your response referring to the impacts if there is no plan. This has the political benefit of indirectly indicating that management support for change will be needed.

Figure 3.2 Elements of the Project Status Presentations.

Notice too that you are not giving findings. This is separate and, if presented, would cloud the status. You want each presentation to have a single point of focus.

Present Quick Wins

Remember that a *Quick Win* is an idea generated by the planning work that can be done quickly, with very few resource demands, and show results in a short time. Since some of these changes are minor, it is often useful to present Quick Wins in related groups. One group might be some that relate to one area of IT. Another is a set of changes to a business process.

The purpose of this presentation is to gain approval for implementing the group of Quick Wins. The audience might be IT or business unit managers. This is a short presentation.

- Activities addressed by the Quick Wins.
- Impact of the problems if the Quick Wins are not carried out.
- Estimated benefits from the Quick Wins.

- An example of before and after for one or two Quick Wins. This makes the changes more tangible and benefits more obvious.
- Actions and schedule for the changes.

This presentation is often best made by either an IT or business unit manager since it will indicate commitment.

Another related presentation is to present the results of Quick Wins. This is similar to the one above, but you also would include some lessons learned from the Quick Win implementation. For credibility this is often best presented by someone involved in the work affected by the Quick Wins.

Get the Strategic Plan Approved

The purpose is not only to get approval of the plan, but also to gain support for obtaining resources and implementing changes. Presenting the entire plan is often impossible due to the length and time available.

A template for the plan presentation appears in Figure 3.3.

- Introduction. Give the number of people involved and contacted, the range of information resources used, and a summary of the key milestone dates.
- List of key issues and opportunities. Keep this to 10 or less.
- IT and process objectives.
- Mapping of the objectives to key business processes.
- Mapping of these objectives to business goals, vision, and mission. This will show positive alignment.
- Mapping of these objectives to business issues — revealing negative alignment.
- IT and process strategies.
- Tables and mapping of strategies to issues and opportunities to show coverage.
- Action items.
- Table or mapping of action items to issues and opportunities. This indicates that the plan is addressing the problems.
- Table or mapping of action items to business processes. This shows more detailed benefits and alignment.
- Quick Wins implemented so far along with their respective benefits.
- Lessons learned from the planning effort.
- Immediate next steps for action items.

Figure 3.3 Elements of the Strategic Plan Presentation.

You could put a lot more into this — provide more lists and tables, and so forth. However, usually this is not possible. Time is too short. Moreover, adding to this will detract from the attention needed for the key items listed above.

Present a Strategic Plan for a Business Process

A *process plan* is the strategic direction for a major business process. As such, it shows the long-term state of the process given process and IT improvements. Process plans are seldom developed — for many reasons. One is that processes are often taken for granted. Another is that it is assumed to be part of the IT only work.

But there are many benefits to having a process plan. The employees will have a vision for future work and their place in it. IT gets clearer direction and requirements for what is needed in the future — reducing requirement changes, providing more focus, and cutting back on scope creep. Another benefit is that user requests can be structured within the process plan, thereby making such request more planned and predictable.

The goals of the process plan presentation are:

- Increase the understanding of the process and its importance. This includes a vision of how work would be performed in three–five years.
- Enhance the desire for actions to fix and improve the processes.
- Gain support for IT efforts to increase and restructure processes so as to improve performance of the work.

The template for the presentation of the process plan is given in Figure 3.4.

- Summary of key activities in the process.
- Problems and their impacts in the current work.
- Example transaction highlighting the problems and impacts.
- Vision of the long-term process.
- Benefits resulting from the realization of the vision.
- Same example transaction in the future process.
- Barriers to changing the process. This includes not just IT work, but also politics, resistance to change, competition, and other factors.
- Phased approach for getting to the vision. The first phase usually consists of Quick Wins followed by change generated by IT projects. Even so, it is often not possible to achieve the vision quickly due to limited resources, existing work, and so forth.
- Action items for the process in terms of Quick Wins.

Figure 3.4 Elements of the Process Plan Presentation.

Present a Plan for a Project Action Item

After the plan has been approved, you have to get plans ready for the approved project ideas. These in turn will be employed in the struggle for resources during strategic resource allocation. The goal of the presentation of a project plan is to get support for the resources required.

Elements of the presentation for a project action item are given in Figure 3.5.

Present the Resource Allocation

To gain resources for the plan project action items, there must be a reallocation of resources. This is addressed in detail in Chapter 13. The goal of the presentation for the results of the resource allocation is to gain acceptance of this allocation. The thing you are trying to avoid is to have the allocation undone later by some manager's decision. Hence, you want to make sure they understand the downside if the resources are taken away from the project action items.

- Purposes of the project. Here you give the business, technical, and social goals. The political goal can be mentioned verbally.
- Impact if the project is not done. This "cuts to the chase" by showing a sense of urgency.
- Benefits of the project and how these benefits will be measured.
- Examples of business transactions or work before the project, and after, the project results are implemented.
- Summary tasks and milestones presented in a GANTT chart.
- Budgeting and costs for the work.
- Resources required as well as roles and responsibilities.
- Potential issues and problems that may arise. This is very useful since it helps to dampen expectations and make them more realistic. Also, it shows that you are aware of what can happen from your experience — adding to your credibility. A third benefit is to reduce future expansion of the scope of the project.
- Immediate actions to take after project approval.

Figure 3.5 Elements of the Presentation of a Project Action Item.

- Existing resource allocation. This includes division of labor among projects as well as that between projects and non-project work.
- Impacts of the current resource allocation. Problems and issues are given showing the negative effect if the status quo is maintained.
- New resource allocation.
- Comparison of the old and new allocation.
- How the new allocation supports process plans as well as the business goals. This reveals alignment of the resource allocation to the business.
- Impacts on the areas for which resources will be extracted. This shows that you are aware of the negative effects. However, resources are limited.
- Steps to take in implementing the new resource allocation.

Figure 3.6 Elements of the Resource Allocation Presentation.

We have employed the following outline or template for this presentation (see Figure 3.6).

Present Plan Results and Lessons Learned

The plan Quick Wins have been implemented. Some project work is done. More is in progress. The goal of presenting the plan results is

NOT to show how wonderful the planning effort way. That is self-serving. Rather, the objective is to gain support for further change and improvement. Or, put another way you want to continue momentum for change. You achieve this here in several ways. First, you demonstrate tangible results from the work. Second, you provide lessons learned from the entire effort that will increase future performance. In a later chapter examples of lessons learned will be covered along with how to gather these. Notice how this approach differs from a traditional one in which results are presented in a dry form.

IT has often presented benefits achieved before. Often, there is a lack of credibility. Why? Because the benefits, although due to IT work, really resulted from business change. That is why the logical person to present the benefits is from the business, not IT. You can create the presentation and coach some managers, but they should give it. This gives them credit and instills a sense of ownership in change. Both of you can present the lessons learned.

Here is what to cover for plan results and lessons learned (Figure 3.7).

What seems to be missing? The benefits of the planning. However, this is covered indirectly by real results. Now look at these bullets again. Notice the one on deterioration. This is important. Many assume that if the changes had not been done, things would have remained the

---

- Recap of the action items from the plan.
- Quick Wins implemented and their benefits.
- Example of benefits from Quick Wins.
- Summary of project ideas status — which projects were approved, which were completed, and what is in progress.
- Benefits of completed projects.
- Deterioration that would have occurred if neither the Quick Wins nor the projects had been undertaken.
- Lessons learned. This can be a morale booster by showing that people are enthusiastic about the changes.
- Recommended actions in terms of additional actions and changes to resource allocation.

Figure 3.7 Elements of the Presentation on Results and Lessons Learned.

same including the problems. However, this is most often not the case. Things get worse in the same way that our bodies, clothes, cars, houses, and so forth decay. By pointing out deterioration you again demonstrate the positive benefits of strategic IT and process planning.

Present the Plan Update

The update to the plan follows that of the presentation of original strategic IT and process plan. However, you want to also include the following list in Figure 3.8.

Examples

Many times people approach the formal presentations in an *ad hoc* way. Just get started a few days before the presentation with a blank piece of paper. Time and time again we have seen the failure of this in companies. Without a structured approach to communications, the following problems may arise:

- The audience has trouble understanding the format, leaving less time to understand and absorb the content of the presentation.
- You seem to get approval for actions, but nothing happens.

- Summary of the benefits achieved since the last planning effort.
- New issues and opportunities that have arisen or that were not addressed in the last plan. This includes the projects that were not done due to lack of resources.
- Updated strategies and a recap of the objectives which should not have changed.
- Table or mapping of strategies to business processes.
- Table or mapping of strategies to business goals, vision, and mission.
- Table or mapping of strategies to business issues.
- New action items.
- Action items versus issues and opportunities.

Figure 3.8 Elements of the Presentation on the Plan Update.

- You fail to pre-sell the presentations to key managers so that too many questions and disputes arise during the presentation — leading to failure.
- You fail to have regular contact with managers so that when there is contact, it is like you are starting all over again.

In contrast, the entire communications approach was implemented in a Chinese manufacturing firm in which management had a limited understanding of IT and IT planning. Processes were treated informally. After the approach was implemented, the results were not only improved processes and IT systems and technology, but also improved management. Upper management insisted that all business presentations follow standardized templates and outlines. Presentations were shortened. There were more favorable results. This helped when the company was rapidly expanding, but gave even greater benefit when cutbacks were made.

Lessons Learned

You want to start preparing the presentations as soon as you have sufficient information to begin. The longer elapsed time that you have for the presentation, the better will be the presentation.

Another lesson learned for formal presentations is to review them with key managers one-on-one prior to the presentation. There are a number of benefits of this. First, you can give an interpretation of the plan to them — a relational view. Second, they can ask questions that they might not pose in the presentation meeting. Third, you can sense any resistance or problems and deal with them prior to the presentation. If you are, say, presenting to five managers, then you should attempt to meet with at least two or three of them ahead of time. Is there a downside to this? Yes, the presentation might seem very boring to them. However, this also has a benefit in that they may just cut you off and approve what you have done. Nothing wrong with that.

When preparing a presentation, consider having business employees and managers involved in doing the presentation. This was discussed under each presentation, but deserves to be emphasized. As the "planner," you have a vested interest in the presentation. Hence, your credibility is less. Better to have business managers and staff involved.

Politics

Let's turn our attention to your attitude. It would seem natural that you should be enthusiastic and supportive of the plan ingredients — action items, and so forth. True, but this shows people you have too much of a vested interest. Answer this basic question, "What do you lose if the plan is approved, but that no actions are taken?" Or, "What if the plan is not approved?" You go on to other work. Who suffers if either of these events happens? The business and secondarily IT. What does this discussion point toward?

When communicating on the strategic plan, you should be positive neutral.

What? The words positive and neutral seem to contradict each other. Not at all. You should be positive about the plan and the benefits. However, you should be neutral because (1) you cannot make the action items come true and happen and (2) most of the benefits of the plan help the business, but not you directly.

If you adopt this attitude, then you will be seen as more unbiased. People will listen to you more. In meetings, you can say that things will deteriorate or never change, unless actions are taken from the plan.

Communicating regarding the strategic plan is always political. Part of this is based on three different views. One is that the planning process is viewed as a waste of time. In communicating you should frequently stress that the planning effort is very limited and of relatively short duration.

The second is that some may expect results from the plan. This can be partially avoided by never overpromising. Indicate that even if the plan is completed and approved, the action items must still be approved, funded, and given resources. However, if you downplay the potential benefits too much, then people question the planning effort itself. So, you must also emphasize what will happen if there is no plan.

A third view is that some may fear the impacts on their work and projects if the plan is enacted. Let's face it — the implementation of the plan entails change. Change maybe threatening. To counter this, point to the reasonableness of the action items as well as the seriousness of the issues.

What to Do Next

Here are some tips that you can pursue now.

- Review the frequency of your communications with managers. Make a list of five or so names. For each one, write down the last time you met with the person.
- Start making a log of your communications. This seems tedious but if you get in to the habit, it takes little time. Here are the columns for the log:

  o Date, time
  o Contact

    o   Medium (in person, phone, and so forth)
    o   Purpose
    o   Comments
    o   Rating

All but the last are obvious. What is the rating? It is your rating of how successful you were in two dimensions. Did you get your message across? Did you see the desired action or result? How do you know if the message got across? By the receiver's reaction.

- Review the last 10 or so e-mails and ask the questions that were posed earlier about your written messages.

Summary

Let's summarize some of the key points of this chapter.

- There should be structure to both informal and formal communications.
- You need to measure proactively your communications so as to improve your communication skills and results.
- In strategic IT and process planning there are only a limited number of formal presentations. These have been presented and discussed. There is no need to use these templates and outlines as is. Adapt them to suit your needs.
- If you follow standardized methods, you achieve real results. First, the time to prepare presentations will drop. Second, the audience will spend more time on understanding the content of the presentation or communication, rather than the format.
- A major point of emphasis has been that of politics. You deal with political situations and issues through communications. The more you are aware of this, the better you will communicate.
- Success for formal communications is to get decisions. Success for informal communications is to get understanding and support.

- Remember a key lesson learned — the sender of the message is responsible if the message does not get through correctly.
- The structured approach applies also to casual conversations and e-mail. This takes more thought when you first do this, but it gets much easier as you get into the habit of planning your messages.

PART II

INFORMATION GATHERING
AND ASSESSMENT

Chapter 4

Analyze Your Past Planning Efforts; Market the New Planning

Introduction

When people start something new, they often just plunge in and get started. They neglect the lessons of the past. As the old saying goes, they then sometimes repeat the same mistakes over and over. That is why part of this chapter is devoted to past planning. You want to collect and analyze information on both the planning process or method and the plan itself — regardless of its degree of success or failure.

What is the goal of this work? Your technical objective is to understand what happened, what worked, what failed, and why. Your business goal is to ensure a better chance of success for your new planning work. The social goal is to get people interested in the planning effort and gain support. The political goal is to demonstrate two things:

- There is a need and benefit for a new effort, regardless of the past.
- Drawing upon the experience of the past, people see that this effort has a greater likelihood of success.

Note that the emphasis is on the political. When you collect information, you have the opportunity to influence how people think about planning and the plan itself. Do this right and you have more motivation and support. Do it wrong, or not do it all, and you may later encounter many problems and resistance. Probably, the same things that were encountered in the last planning effort. In the next section, we will refine these goals in terms of political factors.

This part of the planning effort is like a small project with the above goals. The scope of the attention to the past includes:

- Business and IT planning documents;
- Individuals involved in creating the past plan;
- IT managers and staff who were involved in implementing the plan;
- Business managers who oversee IT and key processes;
- Employees who were involved in projects generated by the plan.

The scope expands if the organization used Six Sigma, Total Quality Management (TQM), or re-engineering. Then you would include:

- Individuals involved in the application of the method;
- Managers and staff of business units involved with the method.

We begin with how to position the data collection — old, new, or not planning at all. Why discuss this? Politics. The chapter then turns to a discussion of how and what to collect in terms of the past. Then, we move to checklists for both the planning method and plan itself. These are separate because you could have a wonderful planning method, but the plan results are not implemented. Alternatively, you might have a decent plan, but the process needs work.

Then, we turn to the analysis of the information as well as its application to the new effort. We close the discussion with coverage of how best to present what you have learned to management, IT staff, and employees.

The remainder of the chapter is concerned with marketing. Just because everything endorses the planning does not turn it into reality. Just like learning from the past planning effort, you have to plan the marketing work. Marketing will have to be performed all of the way — from inception to implementation. The more effort and thought you put in, the better the results. Marketing not only helps to sell some activity of strategic planning, but it also gives you more opportunities to deal with resistance to change.

The Label — A New Effort, Implementation of the Old, or Not Planning at All

In the academic sense, you could just announce that there is a new planning effort. This can be very politically damaging. Because it is new, people naturally blame someone for the failure of the last one. Unpleasant memories are raised again. There is a reluctance to participate due to the problems in the last effort. These ideas should give you sufficient grounds to pause and ask "How do you want to position the new planning effort?" You have to do it now — even before the new effort starts. This is because you are gathering information about the past planning effort — raising questions in many minds.

Now suppose that instead of outright failure, the picture is mixed. Management approved the plan. Some action items were implemented. But there is not much enthusiasm for planning. Perhaps, few people participated in the effort. Overall, it may seem that there has not been much change despite the plan. Some people may feel that the same things would have occurred without the planning effort and plan. This is more common than you think.

So, do you position the data collection as old or new? Actually, neither. Here is the political strategy:

Position the data collection as information gathering on processes and systems.

This avoids a "planning" label. Moreover, it illuminates the emphasis on improving the work. This will put some ground between you and the plan. During the data collection, your political goal is to:

> Gather information on issues, problems, and opportunities that show the need for a planning effort and for change through implementation of the plan.

Remember that this may be in spite of management's endorsement of the planning work. You have to gain more grassroot support that will lead to more change later. Experience shows that this will be more successful than announcing the measurement as the start of yet another planning effort.

After this discussion, we can return to the purpose of the data collection.

- Collect information on problems and opportunities in the processes and systems that can be addressed in the plan. Fixing small things (called Quick Wins) can sometimes be undertaken during the planning work. However, most of the action items will require resources and implementation planning and support.
- Through the above identification, generate support for dealing with the problems and opportunities. Remember that to be cured of a disease, you first have to admit that you have a problem.

These represent a political refinement of the earlier, more general goals. Thus, if you are successful, people will see the need to get something going, regardless of what it is called.

We have used this approach many times — even where there was widespread support for the planning work from both management and employees. Why the stealth approach? It turns the attention toward the issues and opportunities, rather than the plan — which is where the attention should go.

How to Gather Information from the Plan?

It is time to analyze the previous strategic IT plan. To do this, you will create a series of lists and tables. These are not only useful in determining the impact of the planning effort, but also can give you a head start on the new plan.

Extract both the issues and opportunities, and the action items. Depending on the planning approach that was employed, this may be easier said than done. From these make a list of the processes that should have been affected, the systems that should have been changed or implemented, and the departments that should have been affected.

Before collecting detailed information for the plan, make a list of critical business processes. A checklist is given in Figure 4.1.

Go to the last strategic IT plan and create a list of issues and opportunities that the plan was designed to address. Based on your

---

- Payroll
- Accounts payable
- Accounts receivable
- General ledger
- Cash management
- Sales
- Distribution
- Manufacturing planning
- Customer service; customer relationship management (CRM)
- Web-based sales
- Web-based fulfilment
- Web-based customer service
- Human resources — benefits, hiring, promotion, and performance reviews
- Supply chain management
- Processes in IT

Figure 4.1 Examples of Key Processes.

knowledge write down what has happened to these since the plan was done. Status could be: eliminated through the action items, eliminated through other work, active (unresolved), and inactive-no longer significant. You can also subjectively determine if the impact of the issue worsened for those issues that were not addressed.

Also, make a list of the action items from the plan. For each one, document the status of the action item today. You could use: never approved, approved but not acted upon, carried out and completed, and started but never completed.

In what follows a number of tables are identified that can be derived from the strategic IT plan. We provide more than you can do so that you can select the best ones. "Best" tables are those that contribute to the new strategic IT and process plan.

You can map the processes to the issues and opportunities, and action items by creating two tables.

- *Issues and opportunities versus processes.* Here, you can place an "X" if the issue or opportunity pertains to the process. Otherwise, the entry is blank.
- *Action items versus processes.* Similar to the previous table.

These tables indicate which processes should have been improved through the plan actions. You want to do both issues and opportunities, and action items since there is a many-to-many relationship between the action items on the one hand, and the issues and opportunities on the other. Also, it could be that some processes with issues were not addressed by the action items.

Now, you want to relate the processes to the application systems. That is, to pin down the systems that support the key processes — either directly or indirectly. For example, the ERP system supports a range of processes as does the network, while the general ledger enables the accounting area. You can do this via a table of systems versus processes. Again, an "X" is placed in a table cell if an individual system supports that process. With Supply Chain Management

(SCM), Customer Relationship Management (CRM), and Enterprise Resource Planning (ERP) systems covering multiple processes, this will be a many-to-many relationship.

It is also time to relate the planning elements to the systems. You can now create two additional tables.

- *Issues and opportunities versus systems.* Here, you place an "X" if the issue or opportunity applies to the particular system. Otherwise, it is blank.
- *Action items versus systems.* Similar to the preceding table.

Now you have mapped the beginning and ending elements of the strategic IT plan to the processes and systems.

What about the objectives and strategies? Here, you can examine the internal consistency of the past plan. Identify both the IT objectives and IT strategies in the plan. Since both of these are general and directional, it is difficult to see if they have been totally achieved. Nevertheless, you can relate these to both issues and opportunities and action items. Here are some useful tables.

- *IT objectives versus IT strategies.* The entry is an "X" if the strategy supports the objective. This table will validate consistency in that the objectives should be totally covered by the strategies.
- *IT strategies versus issues and opportunities.* The issues and opportunities should be covered by the strategies.
- *IT strategies versus action items.* All strategies should be supported by at least one action item.

From these you can establish the following derived tables. These are interesting because they complete the cycle in understanding the plan.

- IT objectives versus issues and opportunities.
- IT objectives versus action items.

Let's turn to the currently active IT projects. You can construct some useful tables to reveal the alignment of the projects to the plan and IT. The place to start is the table: projects versus processes. Here, the entry is an "X" if the project supports the specific process. You are almost done because now you can put some of the above tables with this one to develop.

- *Projects versus action items.* Which projects were generated from the action items? What projects were targets of opportunity after the plan was approved?
- *Projects versus IT strategies.* To what extent do the current projects support the strategies?
- *Projects versus IT objectives.* To what extent do the projects align to the IT objectives?
- *Projects versus issues and opportunities.* To what degree do the projects address the issues and opportunities of the plan?

If you find that many projects were created outside of the plan, then you might question the value and credibility of the plan. If you think that the plan is correct and find that the projects do not strongly support either the strategies or objectives, then the projects are not aligned well to the plan.

Doing this work is straightforward if the plan was structured around these elements. However, if the plan is long in text and short in tables and lists, then you have more work. A warning here. Don't assume that consistency analysis was carried out to ensure everything hangs together. It may not. If you encounter this situation, learn from it that you have now found a problem with the plan that may provide insight into any problems faced in implementation.

One benefit of doing this analysis is that it is likely that the strategies and objectives were not achieved in one year. Thus, these can be useful as a starting point for the new plan. You can enter them as candidates in the new plan. If you fail to do this, someone may see them and raise questions.

In building these lists, start thinking about the following important and impact factors:

- Support for sales
- Support for customer relations
- Number of employees involved or supported
- General condition of the process
- General condition of the application system and infrastructure

If you collect data in a sequential mode, it will take too long. You will lose both credibility and momentum. So, you should initiate several parallel efforts. Detailed checklists are given in the next two sections. Here, we concentrate on the process of the data gathering.

Let's summarize what we have so far. These actions have been based on your assessment of the strategic IT plan. You have not gone out yet to gather information from people who were either involved or impacted by the planning work.

These steps seem like you have really started the planning. Well, you have and you haven't. This chapter relates to the past planning efforts. But to understand how these went, you should begin to assess the processes and systems. This is so that you can determine if the previous strategic IT planning effort made a difference. Note here that we said "IT planning" and not "IT and process planning." Most organizations have in the past restricted the strategic IT plan to IT factors only with some mention of processes. A political goal here is that you want to show the advantages of combining IT and process planning. Thus, you might show that while the plan resulted in some new systems and capabilities, the processes were not changed to take maximum advantage of these. The result — lost benefits while the plan was approved.

Techniques in Interviewing and Politics

Now, you can proceed to make contacts in the organization regarding the past effort. Let's start with the individual who did the planning. If you did it yourself, you can ask these things yourself. A list of questions to cover is given in Figure 4.2.

From this information, you can proceed to contact some of the managers involved. Start in IT where the audience might be more friendly. Figure 4.3 contains some questions to pose to the IT manager. Notice that there is overlap here with the questions in Figure 4.2. This is because you want to get different perspectives on both the plan and planning process.

For both the strategic IT plan and process improvement methods, you can undertake to collect information from business managers. Questions are included in Figure 4.4.

When you collect the information, you will obviously write up notes. But do yourself a favor. Take it a step farther. Document guidelines for the future planning effort below the notes. Here, you are starting to gather planning lessons learned — useful to avoid making the same mistakes.

Checklist for the Planning Process

A checklist for the past planning process is given in Figure 4.5. Note that many of these items are subjective. Remember that you want learn — not gather quantitative data for statistical analysis.

How should you collect information? Of course, you can pose some of the questions directly. However, this could make some people defensive. Why not ask questions along the following lines?

- What has changed over the past year (since the last plan was created)?
- On what tasks do they spend time?
- How would like to spend time differently?
- If they could fix something, what would it be?
- What is their understanding of how the business plan affects them?

- What was the position of the person before the planning? What is their position now? Were they rewarded for the planning work? If there was a positive change, this could indicate success. However, often the person goes back to the previous role such as project leader or analyst.
- How they apply the knowledge of IT and the business gained during the planning? The same question applies to contacts.
- How long did the planning take? Did they have to do other work as well — that slowed the planning down? If the elapsed time is too long, momentum is lost. The business or IT situation may have changed.
- What training and prior experience did they have before the planning work? What books, articles, and sources did they use?
- Did they follow a formal planning methodology? If so, does the plan reflect the method? What do they think of the method? Did they have to perform additional work to follow the method step-by-step?
- How did they spend their time during planning? How much, for example, was data collection versus analysis versus communications? How much time was spent in planning versus their other work?
- Who was contacted in the creation of the plan? Do they have any notes, memos, or documents that they are willing to share? Which managers were supportive and participated?
- If they could do it over, how would they spend their time differently? This is less political than asking what they would have done differently, but it can yield the same results.
- Were they able to get easy access to people to collect information or get plan reviews? What changed in the planning drafts due to the reviews?
- How did they organize their notes, documents, and presentations? Obviously, you want to get copies of these, if possible.
- How did they develop plan elements such as objectives, action items, and so forth? In meetings, alone, or through reviews?
- What resistance did they run into during the planning? From whom?
- Looking back, what things did they miss that surfaced after the plan was approved and implementation began? In hindsight, what could have been done differently?
- How was the plan communicated to management, IT managers and staff, and employees? Was it mostly through formal presentations?
- What changes to the plan did management make, if any? This might reveal the political realities surrounding IT.
- If they had more time, resources, or money, what would they have done differently? If they had less time, what would they have cut out?
- What happened after the plan was approved? How were resources allocated to the plan action items?
- After the plan was produced, did the IT organization refer to the plan? If so, how often? Or, did they just go on as business as usual?
- Based on their experience, what changes would they make in any future planning work?

Figure 4.2 Interviewing the Planners.

- What were the goals of the planning work? Were these achieved? How?
- How were they involved in the planning effort?
- What lessons learned were gained from the plan and planning process?
- What was their view of how the planning effort was started? What did they learn?
- What was their opinion of the planning effort itself? And the planning method?
- Were sufficient people at the right levels involved in the effort?
- What were some of the problems that were encountered?
- How effectively was the plan communicated within IT?
- How was the plan communicated to management?
- What was the communications of the plan to business departments?
- How was the plan employed to set priorities for work and resources?
- If the plan had not been done, what would have been done in terms of work and projects?
- What surprises surfaced during the planning work or as a result of the plan?
- Did management view IT any differently after the plan than before?
- How were resources allocated after the plan was completed?
- Is their work any different after the planning? If so, how?
- What factors, events, and so forth got in the way of implementing the plan?
- Based on their experience, what changes would they make in any future planning work?

Figure 4.3 Questions for the IT Manager.

- What was their involvement in the IT planning effort?
- Have they been involved in previous planning efforts?
- What was the communications process during the effort?
- How was the plan communicated to them?
- Did they understand the plan? Was it too technical?
- What was their understanding of IT before the plan? Did this change through the planning work?
- What changes occurred as a result of the plan in their department? In their work?
- Did the plan cover the areas that were important to them?
- What did they learn from the plan and planning process?
- Based on their experience, what changes would they make in any future planning work?
- What were the benefits of the IT plan for them?
- What was their involvement in the process improvement effort?
- What resources were required to support the process improvement work?
- What were the short-term benefits of the process improvement effort? What were the long-term benefits?
- What lessons did they learn from the process improvement effort?

Figure 4.4 Questions for Business Managers and Employees.

- Was the planning process clearly understood and communicated?
- Did the planning process deliver interim results as well as the plan itself?
- If outside help was required for the planning development, was there a transfer of knowledge from the consultants or contractors on the process and information found during the process?
- Involvement by management in the planning process. This goes beyond just kick off and approval. What role did they play, if any, during the work?
- Involvement by IT staff in the planning process. What active role and contribution did they make?
- Involvement by users in the planning process.
- Percentage of action items in the plan that were implemented.
- Extent to which support and maintenance have been controlled. This speaks to whether this work was reduced due to the action items. You hope that it is so that IT can deliver new value to the business.
- Number and type of projects killed off by the strategic IT plan. There is nothing wrong with using the strategic plan as a weapon to kill off marginal work. Again, another political value of planning.
- Number and type of technologies considered and discarded due to the plan. Most of the time this will be minimal.
- Effort required to develop the plan. This includes both full-time and part-time.
- Elapsed time to generate the plan.
- Is there a formal process for implementing resource management?
- Effort that was required to support and update the plan.
- Were lessons learned gathered during the planning process?
- Were there any Quick Wins generated? If so, what were the tangible benefits?

Figure 4.5 Checklist for the Past Planning Approach.

These questions (and we give more later) are focused on people's work and self-interest. Answers can lead you to the list in Figure 4.5.

Checklist for the Plan

Figure 4.6 provides a checklist for the strategic IT plan itself.

Answering or even thinking about these questions will help you later and enhance the likelihood that you will develop a successful plan. Underlying these questions is a basic one:

How serious do both business and IT management take the planning effort and the plan?

- Is the plan written in business or in technical terms? You write for the intended audience — more the business than IT. The strategic plan is NOT an education tool on systems and technology for management.
- After the plan was adopted, how often has it been used or referred to by either managers in IT or business?
- Do the objectives cover the issues and opportunities?
- Is the tone of the objectives positive or negative in that they refer to or imply current problems?
- Can you clearly ascertain the difference between strategies and objectives?
- Do the strategies cover the action items?
- What percentage of the action items are project ideas versus changes in policies, procedures, and so forth?
- How do the action items map to the issues and opportunities?
- Is there a mapping from the IT objectives to the business mission and vision?
- Were business issues defined in the plan? Were these related to the plan objectives, strategies, and so forth?
- Did the plan indicate the impact if the action items were not undertaken?

Figure 4.6 Checklist for the Strategic IT Plan.

How to Assess Your Past Efforts

With the tables and checklists started, you can begin to analyze the past planning work in terms of the planning process and the plan itself. After this we will turn to the resource allocation and project selection work that occurs after the plan is approved. Our first suggestion is to organize lists and tables for your future effort. To recap, observe the lists include those in Figure 4.7.

Tables are given in Figure 4.8.

In addition, you have lessons learned from the planning process, the review of the plan, and the resource allocation that followed the plan adoption.

You also may want to assess what happened to the project ideas that were not carried out — essentially rejected. Here is a list of questions to get you going.

- What processes would have been affected by these projects?
- Can you estimate the potential benefits that would have accrued?

- Business related

  - o Business processes
  - o Business goals
  - o Business vision and/or mission
  - o Business issues

- IT related

  - o Issues and opportunities
  - o Objectives
  - o Strategies
  - o Action items
  - o Systems
  - o Projects

Figure 4.7 Planning Lists.

- Issues and opportunities versus processes
- Action items versus processes
- IT objectives versus IT strategies
- IT strategies versus issues and opportunities
- IT strategies versus action items
- IT objectives versus issues and opportunities
- IT objectives versus action items
- Projects versus action items
- Projects versus IT strategies
- Projects versus IT objectives
- Projects versus issues and opportunities

Figure 4.8 Planning Tables.

- Why were the projects rejected and not adopted?
- Are the project ideas still valid — are they still alive?

How was the allocation of resources to the projects done? Was it effective? You might not think that this involves the plan, but this would be wrong since the overall planning effort includes both generating the plan and getting resources to undertake the action items. Figure 4.9 contains a list of items to consider. You will not be

- Number of total project ideas that were considered. This should be substantial and affect many of the key processes.
- Number of project ideas that were proactively generated within IT.
- Number of project ideas that were reactively generated through requests.
- Percentage of project ideas approved. This depends on resource availability and urgency. Usually, it would be about 50%. Why not more? In a robust planning effort you want to generate many good ideas.
- Percentage of project ideas that result in true tangible benefits. Ah, this is good because it addresses the question of whether completed projects are measured.
- Percentage of project ideas that are:

    o Generated by management
    o Generated by process improvement
    o Generated by business requests
    o Generated by infrastructure need
    o Generated by competitive pressure

- Percentage of project ideas rejected

Figure 4.9 Resource Allocation Statistics.

- The planning effort was halted. What were the reasons given? What happened to the information gathered during the effort?
- New project ideas came along to uproot the planning action items. How were these ideas missed during the planning process?
- Resources were taken away from the planning action items, causing there to be no implementation. Did anyone raise a concern about this?
- The plan was approved, but no actions were taken. Did management later inquire what happened to the plan? Or, was it never brought up again?

Figure 4.10 Examples of Planning Surprises.

able to gather information on all of these, but the information will give you insight into both the planning process and the resource allocation.

Going beyond pleasant home experiences, surprises are often neither welcome nor wanted. A surprise is some event, fact, or piece of information that you were not expecting. In business and IT planning surprises are mostly unfavorable. Let's first list some possible *planning surprises* generated from the last planning effort and discuss how to deal with them (Figure 4.10).

Next, let's consider what you learn from surprises. Since such surprises were not predicted, it is valuable to answer the following questions:

- To what extent was there communications during the plan?
- Why weren't the new project ideas predicted and included in the plan?

The underlying result of the surprises is the same. Taking the worst political scenario, you could infer some or all of the following:

- IT management was not serious about the plan in the first place.
- The plan was viewed as window dressing so that IT appears as "well run."
- The plan focused on tactical and operational issues and did not address strategic business needs.

Sounds harsh, right? Well, you want to ensure that your planning effort will be more successful. The key thing to learn from this is that you must motivate management toward positive change. That is one of the key lessons learned from the past — the attitude of business and IT management toward the plan.

Present the Analysis Results

Some formal suggestions for presentations and communications are presented in Chapter 14. Here, we concentrate on some of the political aspects. A case can be made about not presenting any of it. Why? Because it brings up the past and you have not yet had time to develop parts of the new plan.

However, you may be under considerable pressure to show something from the time you have taken of the managers and staff. If you feel that you must present something, here are some tips.

- Don't be negative about the past efforts. Instead, emphasize the need for a plan to address key issues.
- Even if the planning effort has widespread support, focus on the improved use of resources and work on more strategic goals.
- If you want to go negative on the past, emphasize how little things have changed since the last planning effort.

The key in your presentations and communications is to be *positive neutral*. That is, you are positive about planning and the need for the plan. However, you are neutral as to the information itself. You want to show that you have no vested interest in the plan or the process. This is critical in enhancing your credibility.

What if This is the First Planning Effort?

This section applies to situations where there was no previous plan or where a number of years have passed since the last plan was created. Don't be depressed. This has some tangible benefits. First, there are few expectations since this is the first time. Second, you can point to the problems that occurred because of the lack of a plan.

Using the list of systems and that of processes, you can develop a table of systems versus processes. The table entry could be a comment on the extent to which the system supports the process. This table helps to reveal the extent to which the processes are supported by IT.

How was IT work selected and prioritized? Without a plan, much of the IT work and projects are reactive to short-term business needs. Therefore, it should be the case that IT is very busy, but over the past few years, there may have been few, if any, strategic initiatives. Remember that:

> Strategic IT and process planning is closely tied to strategic resource allocation.

What is strategic resource allocation? *Strategic resource allocation* is the directional assignment of resources to areas of work. Short-term resource assignments should be consistent with the strategic allocation. Strategic resource allocation indicates how much of the work will go into projects, maintenance, operations support, enhancements, and so forth.

Potential Problems

Figure 4.11 contains a list of problems encountered in the past that you should be prepared for.

Why do people say these things? One reason is that they have an honest concern. Another reason is political. Some IT managers and staff may resent the plan in that it gets in the way of working on things that they like. For the business managers the plan may seem to limit what they can do. They may see that their processes do not have a high priority. Overall, if the plan is successfully implemented, then what work is done, how it is performed, and how it is managed can all change.

Examples

The Irish farming cooperative

The Irish farming cooperative discussed in the last chapter had never developed a strategic IT plan. They had a very limited business plan.

- There appear to have been little benefits from the last planning effort. Maybe, the plan was never used. To answer this concern, indicate the downside if there is no plan. More projects and work are performed in a reactive mode. Some critical business needs may not be met.
- "I do not want to do it because I am too busy or have no experience or ...." They may see it as overhead and that they will gain nothing from doing the plan. That is not true. Doing the plan gives you several benefits.
  - o You will gain a better understanding of the business.
  - o You will have more knowledge of the systems and processes.
  - o You will be able to establish useful political contacts with business managers.
- "There are too many pressing short-term needs so that people are not available to participate in the planning." Our approach in this book limits people's involvement and aims to produce the plan through lists and tables — quickly.
- "I have never done it before." Everyone encounters new situations all of the time. By following the common sense approach here you do not have to have had a great deal of experience in either planning or IT.
- "We never needed a strategic plan before. Why now?" Point to the reactive work going on. Point to marginal projects. Consider the time consumed in marginal maintenance and enhancement.
- "Why include the processes? We did not do this before." By including the processes the plan is more closely aligned to the business. The business managers will be more likely to understand and support the plan.

Figure 4.11 Potential Resistance to the Strategic Planning.

While this example is discussed in-depth in the last chapter, some lessons learned can be gained here. Politically, we decided not to call it a planning effort at first. Instead, the work was positioned as a method to "find ways to have IT be more supportive of the business." This gained substantially more goodwill and support outside of IT.

There was resistance to the planning work within IT. Some of the reasons staff gave are given in the potential problems section below. To address this we did not question either their work or its quality. Instead, we drew attention to what was worked on and what time was wasted. So, the goal and benefit of the planning effort for the IT was that:

- They would be working on more strategic tasks than previously was the case.

- User requests would be evaluated in part on their relevance to the plan.
- There would be fewer interruptions to do small maintenance and enhancement work.

A major energy and natural resources firm

A major energy firm had a large IT group and had tried out several planning methodologies over the years. They had also developed it internally and with consultants. Nothing seemed to work well. Many viewed the planning work and plan as a necessary evil — something that a large IT group should do and have. What happened in real life was that the planning action items seemed to take a backseat to operational crises and work. Hence, the plan usually sat on the shelf and then was dusted off each year. There was no formal update process. Nor, was there a formal process for getting planning action items into the resource allocation process and budget process. The plan was over 120 pages long and was a monster to understand, present, update, and even use.

The planning approach in the book was used and positioned as a way to more quickly get the planning done. There was no mention of the planning methodology itself. Instead, the methodology was unveiled as the work was done — much easier to justify and explain. Hence, there was no need to sell a planning method.

Lessons Learned

The first lesson learned was that this is an area overlooked in the literature and in practice. There is a tendency to get going and finish it due to other pressing priorities.

Another guideline is to try and avoid spending a lot of time explaining the method (whatever method you are using). There are a number of reasons for this. First, it draws too much attention to the method. People's expectations may get raised too high. Second, if you feel you must explain it, some may see this as defensive and/or that you are unsure of what you are doing.

In doing the tasks we discussed, you should avoid raising any expectations. People will ask you "What will we get out of this plan?" Don't overpromise. All that will be done is to create the plan. This does mean automatic actions and quick fixes. How do you answer this question? By pointing to the downside. Discuss what will happen if there is no plan.

In doing the planning, a department manager may provide access to a specific person. Start there but also work to get closer to the processes and the actual work. Try to avoid lengthy interviews with business managers as this will raise expectations or engender ill will. Realize that almost everyone is busy and is short-term focused.

Politics

We have made some suggestions regarding political factors above. This first step is important in positioning the planning effort politically. You will be establishing the first, and often lasting, impression of the entire effort. When people question the effort, you could respond with "Management wants it done." However, this just shows you to be a lackey. Better to say, "Look at what could happen if the plan is not done." How do doctors get patients to undergo life-risking, expensive, and painful surgery? Fear. Use the same approach. Try to find examples in the past and present of projects and work that would not have been done, or done with less effort if the plan had been in place.

What to Do Next

The next step in the planning process is the analysis of the business plan — vision, mission, objectives, and issues. There are also some action items that you can take after reading this.

- Get a copy of the previous plan and try to quickly find the planning elements — issues and opportunities, objectives, and so forth.
- Obtain a list of the projects that are currently underway.
- Make a list of key processes. Go to the web and search for processes in your industry segment as well.
- Go to business process management web sites and research this area as it might prove useful.

Summary

Often, the review of the past planning effort is cursory and the focus is on the new plan. However, as we have seen, there can be many lessons learned from a more structured review of what happened in the past. This is one benefit.

Another benefit is that you can start to build the lists and tables for the new strategic IT and process plan. This is accompanied by gaining experience in creating the lists. You will be much better positioned when you create the new plan.

Chapter 5

Collect Information for the Plan

Introduction

This chapter covers a wide range of what can be gathered internally in preparation for your IT and process planning effort. External data collection on technology and business trends is included in the next chapter. We include many more items than you have time to address. This is to give you a large menu of choice.

Data collection is addressed in this and in Chapter 6. This chapter deals with internal collection up to the point of interviewing. Chapter 6 starts with external data collection and then moves successively to interview data collection, analysis, and the creation of initial planning lists and tables. So, why not include the interviews in this chapter? Because you want to have collected external information first — improving your preparation for the interviews.

Chapter 7 and later chapters deal with analysis. Any book is written sequentially. However, you do start doing the analysis detailed in Chapters 7–11 as you gather the information. While you want to produce a quality strategic plan that gets results and change, you also have to make efforts to cut the elapsed time. If the elapsed time is too long, then there is a risk that parts of the plan could become obsolete. More importantly, interest in the plan may diminish. Political support for action may wane. The areas of data collection in this chapter are given in Figure 5.1.

- The business mission and vision — long term
- The business strategic plan — long term
- Current business initiatives — intermediate term
- Current and projected work in the business — now
- IT overall
- Information on the previous planning work
- The planning method used
- Assessment of the current strategic IT plan — long term
- Current work in IT — intermediate term
- Projects in IT — intermediate term
- The existing IT architecture and infrastructure

Figure 5.1 Categories of Planning Data Collection.

The questions raised in this chapter are not only valuable for get-ting started, but they can also be employed to ensure that your planning remains on track. Also, you can more likely avoid the problems committed in the past during planning.

The last part of this chapter is concerned with developing a detailed project plan for the planning effort. Why do you have to do this? Isn't the time better spent on planning? No. Having a project plan for the strategic planning is politically useful. It shows that you are well organized. Politically, the project plan can also dampen resistance to the work. Moreover, it reveals the scope of the work.

The Business Mission and Vision

Most organizations now have defined either or both of a mission and vision. Collect these for analysis in the next chapter. Questions to answer related to the mission and/or vision appear in Figure 5.2. The answers here can give you insight into the value and use of the mission and/or vision.

Answers here can reveal the use and credibility of the mission and vision. Regardless of the degree of use, the strategic IT and process plan should map and align to the mission and vision.

- How was the mission or vision defined?

  o How many managers at what levels were involved?
  o What did any consultants contribute?
  o Was there a methodology used to define the mission and/or vision?

- How was the mission or vision announced?

  o What expectations were stated?
  o Was anything said about how it was to be used?
  o What is the level of awareness of the mission and/or vision in the organization?
  o Was there any follow up?

- Was the mission or vision updated?

  o When did the update occur?
  o What are the differences between the new and old versions?

- How has the mission or vision been employed?

  o Is it used to review new work?
  o Are elements of the business plan related to it?

- What is the level of awareness of the mission or vision in IT?
- What is the level of awareness of the mission or vision in the business units?

Figure 5.2 Questions Related to the Mission and/or Vision.

The Business Strategic Plan

In Figure 5.3 there are some questions pertaining to the strategic plan. Most of these are triggers for you to extract information from the business plan for the strategic IT and process plan. The answer on the role of IT in the business strategic plan can reveal a lot about management's perception of the importance and roles of IT.

Current Business Initiatives

Business initiatives are projects and programs that the business has initiated. These could pertain to geographical expansion, new products, cutbacks, and so forth. Potential questions to ask are given in Figure 5.4. The purpose and use of the answers is to be able to

- What are the key business objectives?
- What are the business strategies?
- Are the most important processes identified?
- Are objectives related to the mission/vision?
- Are strategies linked to the mission/vision?
- What are the key business initiatives?
- How is IT portrayed in the plan in terms of its role and importance?
- Are business issues identified? You may have to dig for these. Often, they are stated as opportunities.
- How do the objectives, strategies, and so forth differ from those in the previous business plan?

Figure 5.3 Questions Regarding the Business Strategic Plan.

For each business project or initiative you should consider the following questions:

- To what business units/departments does the initiative apply?
- Which processes are affected by the initiative?
- If the initiative is successfully completed, what is the impact on the business work and IT?
- What is the goal of the initiative *vis-a-vis* the processes?
- What are related initiatives?
- To what extent is IT involved in the implementation of the initiative?
- What elements of the IT architecture and infrastructure are required to implement the initiative?

Figure 5.4 Questions Regarding Business Initiatives.

later map and relate the planning elements to the business initiatives. This will demonstrate part of the intermediate-term alignment of IT to the business.

Current and Projected Work in the Business

In addition to the business initiatives, it is useful to consider both the current and projected work that is going on or planned. Sample questions appear in Figure 5.5. Projected work is either new or changed work that does not result from a business project or initiative.

For a single or a set of business processes, you can consider the following questions:

- How do these processes relate to the business objectives in the strategic plan?
- What is the extent of IT support for the process?
- To what extent is the process automated?
- To what degree does the process contribute to revenue or constitute a major part of the costs?
- To what degree does the process contribute to or cause business issues?
- What are related processes?
- What are the known problems and opportunities associated with the process?
- Has there been deterioration in the process? You can get information on this by comparing what is said about a process now and previously.

Figure 5.5 Questions Regarding Current and Projected Business Work.

- Has an IT mission and/or vision been created? What happened to it? How has it been used?
- Is IT work related to objectives?
- What is the method for justification method for new work?
- How are resources assigned to work?
- What is the focus of IT — on operations or projects? A greater project focus is favorable since it shows that IT is attempting to address strategic needs.
- What is the overall relationship between IT and the business — formal, informal, and so forth? Is IT more reactive than proactive?
- To what degree is IT management involved in business decisions? Or, is IT brought in after the decisions have been made?
- How stable are work assignments? Are they subject to frequent change? If so, this would indicate that IT is more reactive than proactive.
- To what extent is there teamwork among IT staff?
- Do the same mistakes seem to recur?
- What efforts are made to utilize experience in planning and executing new work?
- What are known IT issues? How have these been addressed?

Figure 5.6 Questions about IT in General.

Examine IT Overall

The above questions were business-centered. Now we turn to IT, followed by the existing strategic IT plan and the associated planning process as well as areas within IT. Questions appear in Figure 5.6.

A Review of the Past Planning

You should conduct a review of the strategic IT plan and the planning process that was employed. There·are several benefits in doing this. These appear in Figure 5.7. While these may seem obvious, they have proven useful in guiding the data collection.

Collect Information on the Previous Planning Work

Beyond the analysis of the strategic plan document, you should also consider some or all of these techniques of data collection in Figures 5.8–5.15. Under each are listed questions to address. Note that there are MANY more questions than you have time to answer. These lists are intended to serve as a starting point. Note that some of the questions here refer to the past planning effort too. This is an intentional overlap with those raised in the previous chapter to make them easier to use.

- You can gather and use lessons learned from the planning method implementation. These will help you improve your next effort.
- You can examine the detailed contents of the plan to assess quality, completeness, and business relevance. By doing this you can determine what ideas can be moved into the new plan. There is a political reason for doing this also. You can demonstrate that the new plan improves on the past plan.
- Examine what happened to the action items. Which were dropped? Why? Of those that were approved, were they implemented? What were the results from those that were completed?
- Knowing IT and the business you can assess the alignment of the strategic plan to the business mission and vision.
- Between the time of the creation of the plan and today, there have been changes in both the business and IT. Could the last planning effort have anticipated some of these changes? More to the point, were there any surprises that the plan did not uncover? A good strategic plan will result in few, if any, surprises.
- Since the last plan was approved, were actions taken or decisions made that contradicted the plan? This is very valuable in that it reveals the value that management placed in the strategic plan.

Figure 5.7 Benefits of the Review of Past Planning.

Interview the person(s) who developed the plan.

- How was this person(s) selected?

  o What previous planning experience did they have?
  o What training in planning did they receive?
  o What other work duties did they have during the planning? This can reveal the actual effort.

- What was the motivation for creating the plan?

  o Was it based on a specific IT or business need?
  o Was it based on problems or issues?
  o Or, was it based on the fact that organizations develop such plans?

- How was the timing and planning for the creation of the strategic plan done?

  o How was the IT plan synchronized to the business planning and business cycle?
  o Was a project plan prepared for the work?
  o What were the milestones in the plan?
  o How were these milestones evaluated?
  o What events caused slippage in the schedule?
  o What changes were made to the plan after work began?
  o How was progress measured?

- How did they select the planning method?

  o Did they survey available methods? If so, which ones? How did they identify them?
  o How did they evaluate the methods?
  o What were the criteria used in selection?
  o What firms use the method that was adopted?
  o Who made the final selection of the method?

- Was outside help used in the planning?

  o If so, what was their role?
  o Was knowledge transferred from the consultants?
  o What methods and tools were used by the consultants?

- If they had to do it again, what would be different?

  o What were the lessons learned?
  o Would they have involved business units more?

- What information was collected from the business?

  o What business units and departments were contacted?
  o How were these identified and selected? Based on importance? Based on relationship to IT?
  o What was the extent and nature of the contact?
  o When was the initial contact made in the planning cycle?

Figure 5.8 Data Collection from the Planners.

- How was the strategic business plan used?

  - What efforts were made to determine alignment?
  - Were business issues identified?
  - How were the mission and vision analyzed?
  - What contact was made with the individuals doing the business planning?

- How were IT managers and staff involved in the planning effort?

  - Was resistance to change encountered?
  - What was the level of participation?

- How was upper management involved?

  - How was the planning effort announced?
  - What reasons did management provide as justification?
  - What expectations were given as to what was to be accomplished?
  - How was management involved in doing reviews?
  - How was the completed plan announced?
  - What was the approval process?
  - What happened after the plan was approved?

- What were the biggest challenges in doing the planning?

  - What level of cooperation and participation was achieved?
  - How was contradictory information treated?
  - To what were managers available when needed?
  - How timely and thorough were the reviews of the work?

- Did business unit managers get involved in the planning?

  - If so, which ones? How?
  - What role did they have in reviewing the plan?
  - Did the business unit implement action items?

- How were drafts of the plan presented?

  - Were parts of the plan presented? If so, how?
  - What directions and suggestions were provided for the review?
  - Was there a formal presentation of drafts, or only the document?
  - How was feedback obtained?

- What methods of data collection were used for the plan?

  - What outside information was collected? From what sources?
  - What was the data collection for the business?
  - What was the data collection for IT?

- Were there any surprises during the planning work?

  - Surprises in IT work.
  - Surprises related to objectives and strategies.
  - Surprises related to the business.

Figure 5.8 (*Continued*)

- Did they run into any resistance regarding the action items? Action items can take resources from other work.

  o How was the resistance detected?
  o How was the resistance addressed?
  o What was the impact of the resistance?

- What was the general attitude toward the planning?

  o Were expectations raised in regard to change and improvement?
  o What was the attitude in general?

    - At the start of the planning
    - During the planning work
    - After the plan was completed
    - After action items from the plan were implemented

- What was the extent of changes that were made after the plan was reviewed? The absence of change does not necessarily mean that the draft was perfect. It is more likely that they did not take the planning work seriously.

  o Were any action items implemented before the completion of the plan? If so, it would indicate a degree of planning success.
  o Were there any surprises from the review?

Figure 5.8 (*Continued*)

Interview the IT manager and some of the supervisors.

- How did they participate in the past planning effort?
  o To what extent does the plan reflect the feelings of the IT manager?
  o Were IT employees allowed to participate, or was it just IT management?
  o Did their participation in a few meetings, or was it active across the duration of the planning?

- What opinions did they have of the planning?

  o How effective did they think it was?
  o If they could make changes, what would they do?
  o Do they have knowledge or experience with other planning efforts?

- Do they have any suggestion regarding the new planning work?

  o Ideas for collecting data
  o Suggestions on which areas to concentrate on
  o Hints on how to deal with business units

- What action items pertained to them from the last plan?

  o How were these action items generated?
  o Did the action as approved meet their needs?

Figure 5.9 Data Collection from the IT Manager and Supervisors.

o How were resources given to action items? What activities received fewer resources? Why?

- What were the results of the implementation of the action items?

  o Did the actual results meet expectations?
  o What was learned from the implementation?
  o Were there any surprises during the implementation? If so, how did these affect the implementation?

- What issues and problems do they have in their work?
- If they could spend more time doing something, what would it be?
- If they could spend less time doing something, what would it be?
- What is their most interesting work? Least interesting?
- What to them would be considered success in terms of the IT plan?
- What is the minimum that they would expect from the IT plan?

  o Ingredients of the plan
  o Results from the plan

- How successful do they think that the planning was?
- What improvements could be made to allocation of resources?
- What improvements could be made regarding implementation?

Figure 5.9 (*Continued*)

Contact business managers and staff involved in strategic business planning.

- Have they used the strategic IT plan as input into their business plan?

  o If they did, how was this accomplished?
  o Did the strategic IT plan provide sufficient information?
  o What would they have done if there had been no strategic IT plan?

- Did the timing of the IT planning effort fit with that of the business?
- Were they participants in the IT planning? If so, how?
- Are they familiar with the planning method that was used? If so, what are their opinions?
- What role would they like to have in the new planning effort?
- What communications and interfaces would they like during the planning?
- What to them would be considered success in terms of the IT plan?
- What is the minimum that they would expect from the IT plan?
- How successful do they think that the planning was? What could be improved?

Figure 5.10 Data Collection from the Business Planners.

You should contact upper management regarding the strategic IT planning. One reason is that this is beneficial before the onset of work. A second, more political, reason is to get them more informed and involved so that they will be supportive later. Examples of questions here are:

- How did they see their role in IT planning?
- How was the IT planning initiated before?
- What questions arose from line managers after the planning was announced?
- What involvement did they have during the planning?

  o To what extent was this proactive or reactive on their part?
  o Was involvement concentrated at the start and the end?

- What problems did they detect during the planning?

  o How did these problems surface?
  o How were the problems addressed?

- What to them would be considered success in terms of the IT plan?

  o For management and the organization
  o For employees
  o For the work and processes
  o For IT

- What is the minimum that they would expect from the IT plan?

  o Content
  o Action items
  o Results

- How successful do they think that the planning was?
- What was their role in the allocation of resources?
- How did they assign priorities to action items? What was the method for determining the source of the resources?
- Were they presented with results from the completion of the action items?
- How would they improve the new planning effort?
- Did the planning result in a change in relationship between IT and management?

Figure 5.11 Data Collection from Upper Management.

Analyze the Current Strategic IT Plan

Now we can turn our attention to the strategic plan itself. You can examine alignment of the plan to the business first. Here are some things to consider.

- How did the plan relate to the business processes?

Communicate with business unit managers that received benefits from the
implementation of the action items.

- How did they participate in the planning effort?

  o How were they invited to participate?
  o What activities did they take part in?
  o What information did they provide?

- What problems did they detect during the planning?
- What to them would be considered success in terms of the IT plan?
- What is the minimum that they would expect from the IT plan?
- Were there any difficulties in getting resources for the action items?

  o How were resources obtained?
  o Did they have to give up some work to do the action items?

- How did the implementation of the action items go?

  o Were there any surprises?
  o What was their role in implementation?
  o What was the IT role?

- What were the results of the action items?

  o Was this different from what was expected?
  o What did they learn from the implementation?

Figure 5.12 Data Collection from the Business Units.

Try to review any notes, e-mails, memos, and supporting documents written during
the development of the plan. Rather than questions, here are some tips.

- Try to arrange the documents in sequential date order.
- Make a note of any problems and issues that were mentioned.
- Review the documents for political nuances.
- What was the quality of communications? Did some things need to be explained
  several times?
- How long did it take to resolve issues?
- What was the tone of communications between business managers and IT, and
  within IT?

Figure 5.13 Data Collection from Documentation.

- Was there an effort to show alignment to the business for the IT
  objectives?
- What alignment was demonstrated for IT strategies and projects?
- Were IT operations aligned to business operations?

Here are some questions to start with regarding the assignment of resources to the implementation of the plan action items.

- What is the standard method for resource allocation?
- What information is collected prior to the allocation?
- Are alternative rankings of work carried out?
- How was the selection process undertaken?
- Were there any changes after the selection?
- What was the role of upper management in resource allocation?
- What was the role of IT during the selection process?
- What information on the action items was presented prior to and during the resource allocation?
- Who delivered and described the benefits of the action items?
- Scanning the items that were given lower priority, can you detect any common characteristics?
- Were the action items provided with resources selected because of:
  - o Urgency, impact if not done
  - o Benefit
  - o Alignment to the business objectives, mission, and vision
  - o Low risk
  - o Political power of departments benefiting from the action items

Figure 5.14 Data Collection from Resource Allocation.

This area is often neglected — especially if the planning cycle ends with the completion of the plan. It is useful to consider since it will likely provide you with guidance on how to be more successful in the new planning effort.

- How were action items organized to prepare for implementation?
- Were project plans developed for implementation?
- What surprises arose during the implementation?
- How were benefits measured after implementation?
- Were related action items implemented in groups?
- Were lessons learned gathered during implementation?
- Did the implementation of action items change due to the situation?
- Were any implementation halted during implementation? If so, what were the reasons?
- Was experience gained from earlier implementations applied to later installations of other action items?

Figure 5.15 Data Collection from Action Item Implementation.

- How was the alignment analysis undertaken?
- Does the analysis seem credible?

Turn now to the planning factors in the existing strategic IT plan. Figure 5.16 gives a list of questions.

Issues and opportunities

- How many business process and business-related items are there?
- Is there a wide range of issues and opportunities, or are they narrowly focused?
- Was the impact of the issue explained?
- Was the benefit of the opportunity explained?

IT objectives

- Is the objective clear?
- Does the objective have business meaning to a non-IT manager?
- Is there a clear statement of benefit and impact if the objective is achieved?
- Does the objective contain too many buzzwords or jargon?
- Does the objective implicitly give the feeling that there are problems today?

Constraints

- Are constraints explicitly stated?
- How are the constraints related to the IT objectives?
- Is the impact of the constraint clear?

IT strategies

- Are the strategies at a level more detailed than the IT objectives?
- Are the business benefits of completing strategies defined?
- Are the strategies related to the IT objectives?
- Are the strategies related to the issues and opportunities?
- Are the strategies related to each other?
- Are the strategies related to the business processes and business initiatives?

Action items

- What is the mix of project and non-project action items?
- Are implementation steps and resources needed defined for action items?
- Are the benefits to the business delineated for each action item?
- Are the action items related to IT strategies?
- Are the action items related to the issues and opportunities?
- Are the action items related to current IT work, projects, and infrastructure?
- Are the action items linked to each other?
- Are the action items connected to the business processes?

Figure 5.16 Analysis Questions Related to the Current Strategic IT Plan.

Examine Current Work in IT

Since the current work in IT depends on both the time and the organization, a list of questions cannot be developed. The purposes of the examination of current work are:

- Understand the current work so as to define issues and opportunities.

- Market the planning effort during the collection of the information.
- Identify areas and activities (e.g., maintenance, enhancement, and projects) from which resources could be drawn to implement the action items.

The last two make the data collection political. But, in reality, since the plan can result in change and modification of resource use, the entire planning effort from the start to the end is political.

In collecting the information in IT, focus your attention on the following:

- The age and condition of the methods, tools, and systems
- How new technology, methods, and tools are absorbed into IT
- The extent information is shared and teamwork exists
- How the work is measured (e.g., what constitutes a successful day or week?)
- The awareness of the current strategic IT plan
- The connections between IT and the business units
- How work is assigned to IT staff
- The knowledge and expertise in methods and tools

Review Projects in IT

This topic is almost a whole book in itself. In Figure 5.17 we present some questions that are most useful from experience.

Assess the Existing IT Architecture and Infrastructure

As with some of the other areas, this is specific to the organization. Your goals in data collection here include:

- Identify potential issues and opportunities.
- Define potential action items for the strategic IT and process plan.

- How are IT project selected — in terms of reactive or proactive criterion?
- What happens to rejected project ideas? Are these reviewed later?
- What is the effectiveness of the project management method on projects of all sizes?
- Under what conditions is IT work called a project?
- What are the ingredients of the project plan? Do these include potential issues and lessons learned?
- How is multiple project analysis performed?
- How are successful projects measured?
- Is the rate of success of projects increased?
- What determines project failure? Is there an organized approach to evaluate existing projects for potential termination?
- How are resources shared among projects?
- How is work allocated between project and non-project work?
- Are there standardized project templates in use?
- What steps are taken to improve the skills of project leaders?
- How are lessons learned gathered?
- How are lessons learned organized?
- How are the lessons learned used and refined?
- Who owns the IT projects that relate to business units and processes? What is the proof of ownership?
- What role does the business unit have in IT projects? How is this role defined?

Figure 5.17 Questions Regarding IT Projects.

- Build support for change through the implementation of the strategic plan.
- Determine how resources and knowledge are shared in support, upgrades, and implementation.
- Find out how lessons learned and problems are addressed.
- Ascertain what constitutes success in these activities.

Develop the Project Plan for the Planning Effort

To provide structure in developing the plan, consider using the template in Figure 5.18. Notice that the scope of the template includes resource allocation as well as measuring the results of the implementation of the action items. It does not encompass implementation since this would be specific to the type and nature of each action

1000 Setup the planning effort (plan the planning)

    1100 Identify the planning method and tools to be used
    1200 Determine the staff who will do the planning
    1300 Develop a communications approach
    1400 Review potential planning issues
    1500 Determine how the planning work will be accomplished along with regular work
    1600 Develop strawman lists and tables to simulate the plan
    1700 Review the resource allocation method used
    1800 Coordinate with management relative to the kick off of the planning work
    1999 Milestone: start of planning effort

2000 Collect internal information for the plan

    2100 Gather documents on previous plan
    2200 Collect the business information

        2210 Business strategic plan
        2220 Mission and vision
        2230 Business initiatives
        2240 Business processes
        2299 Milestone: basic business information organized

    2300 Collect strategic planning information

        2310 Strategic IT plan and drafts
        2320 Planning memos, e-mail, and notes
        2330 Analyze information
        2399 Milestone: planning information extracted

    2400 Extract information to support the planning lists and tables

        2410 Business objectives, mission, and vision
        2420 Business processes
        2430 Business initiatives
        2440 Current and projected business work
        2450 Business issues
        2499 Milestone: analysis of business plan finished

3000 Gather external information relevant to the strategic plan

    3100 Identify relevant technologies to the business and IT
    3200 Conduct a limited technology and systems assessment
    3300 Identify key industries and processes
    3400 Conduct a limited business assessment
    3500 Take the information and add it to the lists in the plan
    3999 Milestone: external information collected

4000 Analyze the past planning process

    4100 Determine evaluation criteria
    4200 Conduct review of planning process
    4300 Identify lessons learned
    4400 Develop guidelines for the new planning effort
    4999 Milestone: assessment of the planning process completed

Figure 5.18 Example of Project Template for Strategic Planning.

5000 Analyze the current strategic IT plan

    5100 Assess IT issues and opportunities
    5200 Evaluate IT objectives
    5300 Define IT constraints
    5400 Analyze IT strategies
    5500 Review the action items
    5600 Assess the strategic resource allocation
    5700 Evaluate the implementation of the action items
    5800 Determine items for inclusion in the new plan
    5900 Collect lessons learned
    5999 Milestone: review of the current IT plan completed

5000 Conduct plan analysis and produce lists and tables for review

    5100 Refine business lists

        5110 Mission/vision
        5120 Business objectives
        5130 Business strategies
        5140 Key business processes
        5150 Business issues
        5199 Milestone: submit business lists for review and update

    5200 Create IT lists

        5210 Issues and opportunities
        5220 IT objectives
        5230 Constraints
        5240 IT strategies
        5250 Action items
        5299 Milestone: submit IT lists for review and update

    5300 Develop planning tables

        5310 Business factor tables
        5320 IT factor tables
        5330 Business-IT factor tables
        5399 Milestone: submit tables for review and update

6000 Develop department IT and process plans

    6100 Identify key processes and departments
    6200 Collect information from the processes and departments
    6300 Assemble planning lists
    6400 Create planning tables
    6500 Map the department/business unit lists and tables to those in the strategic IT plan
    6600 Create a draft department business unit IT plan
    6700 Develop a draft process plan
    6999 Milestone: submit process and business unit IT plans for review and update

7000 Secure plan reviews and approvals
8000 Obtain resources for the action items
9000 Implement Quick Win action items
10000 Initiate project action items

Figure 5.18 (*Continued*)

item. Since the specific work under a number of these tasks has been discussed already, they are not included in the figure. Note that this is a refinement of the earlier general sets of tasks given earlier in Chapter 1.

Figure 5.19 give some of the potential problems that the strategic planning may run into. Why present this? It could make people depressed. Not so. By identifying potential issues you are more aware of what can go wrong so that: (1) you can take steps to prevent the problem from becoming an open, actual issue; (2) you show management that you are better prepared to do the planning; and (3) you can use this list to tip off people that you are tracking this and trying to prevent this. This last point may be a deterrent to people who might raise the issue or problems.

Note that the planning process covers more than planning. It encompasses resource allocation. In addition, implementation of the action items is included in Figure 5.19. As a sidenote, we have run into these many times and have compiled a database of planning problems. You will find that each of this is discussed in the appropriate section along with prevention and actions. The issues were common ones selected from a database of over 300 potential problems. We have purposely not included many political issues, due to their sensitivity. For example, for resistance to change during implementation, we have developed a checklist of excuses that people give to avoid change.

Examples

In several planning projects we collected data more than halfway through the duration of the planning. That proved useful for several reasons.

- You stay in touch with business units and IT.
- You can use the reason of data collection to get some draft lists and tables reviewed.

- Set-up for the planning

    o Some information from business units is not available.
    o People doubt or are unclear about what the plan can deliver.
    o The concept of alignment seems too fuzzy.
    o The benefits of the last planning effort are not clear.
    o Many actions were not implemented in the last effort.
    o There was turnover in the staff assigned to do the planning.
    o The staff that are assigned to participate in the planning lack experience.
    o The planning methodology was not easy to understand.

- During the development of the plan

    o It is difficult to get management attention.
    o The data collected seems contradictory.
    o People are reticent to share information.
    o It is difficult to relate business factors to the IT planning elements.
    o There are too many issues and opportunities.
    o Business units do not see how the plan can benefit them.
    o Senior management changes the direction of the planning work.
    o The scope of the planning increases due to the number of issues, action items, and so forth, but the schedule is unchanged.
    o The staff doing the planning have other work that takes priority.
    o The planning method used is taking too much time to understand and gain proficiency.
    o The consultants that are used are trying to dominate the planning work.
    o The consultants insist on using their own methods.
    o The consultants do not share information to the planners.
    o There is miscommunication between the business unit managers and consultants, leading to problems between IT and the business units.
    o Business units are reluctant to develop process plans.
    o What business employees tell you is at variance with the information provided by their managers and supervisors.
    o The IT staff say they are too busy to participate in the planning.

- Plan review and approval

    o It is taking too long to get feedback to the plan drafts.
    o Some managers think that plan approval means automatic implementation of action items.
    o Many managers give only a cursory review of the plan drafts.
    o There is no followup after plan approval.
    o As a result of the reviews, much of the plan must be redone.

- Strategic resource allocation

    o There is no formal process to prioritize work, including the action items of the plan.
    o The action items received resources on a case-by-case basis.
    o Resources are allocated, but then are pulled back due to urgent daily work.
    o The wrong people are assigned to the action item implementation.

Figure 5.19 Examples of Potential Problems during the Planning Process.

- Implementation of action items
  - The action items are interdependent.
  - It is difficult to track the implementation status of some of the action items.
  - It is difficult to determine the benefits and differences in the business process work before and after.
  - The scope of the implementation work expands as more potential work surfaces during action item implementation.
  - Some action items could not be implemented due to the pressures of daily work.
  - The employees affected by the action item resist the changes giving a variety of excuses.

Figure 5.19 (*Continued*)

Consider developing a department or business unit IT plan at the same time you are doing the overall strategic IT and process planning. This has benefits that justify the incremental effort.

- You validate the strategic IT and process plan elements at the business unit level.
- You gain direct political support from the business unit affected.
- You demonstrate flexibility and added value for the planning work.

Lessons Learned

Given the limited time, you should collect data in different areas concurrently. Start organizing these into the following lists:

- Business factors
  - List of mission and/or vision elements
  - Business objectives
  - Business strategies
  - Business initiatives
  - Business processes
  - Business issues

- IT factors

  - o IT issues and opportunities
  - o IT objectives
  - o IT strategies
  - o IT constraints
  - o IT action items
  - o IT projects
  - o IT infrastructure and architecture

These will be employed from Chapter 7 onwards.

Politics

Assume that as you gather data that the path is littered with political mines and time bombs. You have to be very careful about what and how you say things. You should adopt the tone of "positive neutral." Recall here that you are positive about the planning. However, you are neutral because you do not benefit directly from the strategic plan action items.

You do indirectly benefit by gaining exposure to managers, staff, and processes that you otherwise would not have touched. Use this carefully to your advance. In graduate school a key purpose is not just to gain knowledge and get good grades, it is also to establish a network of contacts. It is the same here.

What to Do Next

Given all of the areas of data collection, it is a challenge to determine where to start. Experience shows that the documentation maybe a good point. It is readily available. This includes not only documentation related to the planning effort, but also the mission/vision and strategic business plan.

There is another reason to start here. You are building up your knowledge and awareness. For example, it is valuable to see what people did and where they stood before you contact them.

In terms of contacts, start in IT since that is the easiest group to work with. Then, go to the individuals involved in business planning. Move next to business department and unit managers. This will increase your knowledge before you contact members of upper management. Make sure in the contacts that you do not raise expectations.

Remember that you cannot promise any benefits since you control neither resource allocation, nor implementation.

Summary

The chapter contained list after list of questions and areas in which to collect information. In failed planning efforts, we have found that a key factor in failure was the lack of planning and thought in the early work. Remember through these contacts you create lasting impressions of both the planning process and the plan. Do it right and things do not get harder. Do it wrong without planning and you may set yourself up for failure later. And, you have only just begun.

Chapter 6

Assess the Business and IT Environment

Introduction

This chapter focuses on two major activities that follow from your initial data collection. The first activity is that of external data collection pertaining to both IT and the business. Two areas that are very relevant to this are Business Process Management (BPM) and Service-Oriented Architecture (SOA). These are discussed in the next two sections. Another area that is emerging is Business Process Architecture. After this, we cover the external data collection.

Now note that in Chapter 5 you did not conduct interviews extensively with business and IT managers and staff. Again, the reasons are:

- You want to run some of the external and internal information by them.
- You want to be more knowledgeable about processes and IT so that your interviews and contacts are more effective.
- You are better to suggest potential action items, and so forth.
- Politically, you will be much more credible.

So, we provide tips for interviews. Then, we discuss how to organize the information. By the time the chapter ends, the analysis that leads to the creation of the strategic IT and process plan starts.

However, recall that we recommended that you do not approach this in a sequential mode. Do the analysis as you collect data.

Business Process Management (BPM)

A *business process* is basically an end-to-end related set of work to produce a specific result using both systems — people and other resources. The management and coordination of processes have been a struggle for centuries. Some of the challenges have been:

- How do you measure a process?
- How do you manage the interconnection among processes?
- How do you improve the work in the process?
- How do you automate a process effectively?
- How do you coordinate the IT and non-IT changes?
- How do you address the resistance to change?
- How do you detect and prevent deterioration?

For years, these things were given little attention. The focus was on the organization and department management. They owned the processes and so were supposed to answer these questions.

Then, a trend in many industries began and surged. This was to move from an organization focus to being process-centered. Processes began to span departments. No one department owned the process. Systems provided many more capabilities so that process integration through new systems (e.g., ERP, SCM and CRM) became not only possible, but essential to stay competitive.

These trends gave rise to BPM. *Business Process Management* is an organized function that employs business practices, methods, tools, and techniques to measure, create, and improve business processes. The alignment of IT to the business as well as both strategic IT and process plans fall into the areas of BPM. Other things that interrelate to BPM include:

- Creating standardized, modular systems, and architecture focused on processes. This falls under the area of SOA discussed in the next section
- Re-engineering
- Total Quality Management (TQM)
- Six Sigma
- Lean manufacturing
- Outsourcing
- Industrial engineering
- Voice of customer

The advantage of considering BPM is that it acts as an umbrella for all of these as well as new methods or techniques that may emerge in the future. Anything that can improve the work and its performance falls within BPM.

The reason we are bringing this up now and not earlier is that an area of external data collection is that of BPM, process software, and BPM software suites. There is great interest in this area since a relatively small improvement in process performance can translate into substantial, tangible business benefit.

Organizations have struggled with process improvement forever. Many of the efforts failed because of the following:

- They were not comprehensive.
- They worked in isolation from IT.
- The methods were piecemeal.

Failure here is defined as the lack of long-term process performance improvements. To support an overall BPM implementation, software designed specifically for process management and operations have been developed by a number of firms. All of the major software firms including Microsoft, Oracle, SAP, and so forth have software solutions. Then there are over 60 smaller firms that specialize in this area. Examples of functions of BPM software include the following:

- Process measurement
- Process analysis
- Process design
- Workflow automation
- Process management
- Implementation of standardized protocols in different industries
- Support for Six Sigma and other methods
- Processes created through mergers and acquisitions

A related area to BPM is Business Activity Monitoring (BAM). *Business Activity Monitoring* tools can provide real time, intervention-centered approaches for measuring, and managing business processes. Companies employ BAM to:

- Monitor the processes
- Identify failures in the process
- Determine exceptions and address them

BAM software tracks the executions of processes and so creates histories of behavior and actions that can assist in process improvement. Other benefits include:

- Manage compliance
- Reduce risk
- Support aspects of cumulative improvement

BAM tracks business events and so is more general than IT software monitoring. Examples of events include the following:

- Number of transactions
- Number of changes in a record

- Number of process events such as items consumed
- Transaction revenue
- Number and type of calls
- Process revenue
- Number of tickets closed
- Process costs
- Line of business revenue
- Margins
- Number of compliance events to support auditing

With all of this, you might expect us to suggest that you include the software of BPM as an action item. Not the case. You should track this area since the strategic planning includes business processes. However, you would have to consider the following:

- The learning and proficiency effort required.
- The substantial cost of implementation and continued use.
- The current maturity and flexibility of BPM software.
- The human resources to take advantage of the BPM methods and tools.

Service-Oriented Architecture (SOA)

SOA is a design methodology in which application functions or components are bundled and packaged into reusable services. SOA provides guidelines and principles for determining a systems solution based on the services. As such, SOA is a thinking process rather than some tool.

SOA can be contrasted with other approaches to software solutions.

- Traditional software applications address the needs of one process.
- Enterprise software addresses multiple processes.

Here, in SOA, you are attempting to fulfill the requirements of many processes through the use of reusable components. SOA goes beyond re-use and instead centers on multiple use.

The potential benefits of SOA include:

- Improved systems and process performance
- Greater flexibility and agility through modularity and components
- Simpler modifiability and extendability
- Lower cost

To adopt SOA, the organization has to deal with:

- Being extremely process oriented
- Being adaptable to changes
- Capable of dealing with a variety of technologies
- Handling a multi system deployment

SOA changes the thinking of multiple application systems to one of being shared and service-based.

In IT there has been some progress toward an SOA environment. From modules much software advanced to objects and then to components. The next step is to services.

We have used the term "service" a lot. Here are some characteristics of a **service**.

- Services are building blocks to organize capabilities.
- A service combines information and behavior while concealing its internal workings from the outside (so as to protect stability).
- A service provides a simpler, more straightforward interface.

For example, web services are the set of protocols by which services can be published, discovered, and used in a neutral, standard form.

SOA, since it deals with services, links IT more closely to the business. Ideally, the goal is to merge both business and IT processes. This is yet another reason why you want to include business processes with IT in strategic planning.

This sounds really good, but there are some real-world issues. Some of these are:

- The level of maturity of current SOA solutions.
- The problem of migrating to SOA from traditional software.
- The extensive cross business process analysis required.
- The challenge to get the IT staff aligned to SOA as well as creating SOA proficiencies and capabilities.

Collect External Information

Appendix A provides you with a number of web sites on:

- IT architecture
- IT management
- Business process management
- Re-engineering
- Change management
- Six Sigma
- Project management

At these web sites, you can sign up and enroll without cost. They have articles and white papers pertaining to:

- Guidelines for using methods
- Evaluations of relevant software products
- Implementation tips and guidelines
- Case studies and examples
- Discussion of trends in both IT and business processes

You should start without an agenda. Just do some general scanning of materials. Do this early in the planning work — the earlier the better. Before you begin concentrating on building the strategic plan.

Keep in mind that some of the articles and stories are presented by software vendors, consultants, and other firms who have a vested interest in what they are saying. From these firms, the web sites provide a marketing channel. However, that said, many articles provide useful and current information.

Some additional guidelines are given in Figure 6.1.

For business processes and IT in general, consider researching the topics in Figure 6.2.

Now let's turn our attention to systems and technology. Many think that the technology rapidly changes. This is really not true. Here are some valid statements.

- Most new systems and technology are incremental. Why? Because the new is forced to be backward compatible with the old — to attract a wider marketing audience.
- Watch out for the maturity of the product or service. The test here is twofold. First, there should be case examples. Make sure that these refer to complete implementations and not just work in progress. Second, there should be available guidelines on how

---

- Organize the information, articles, and so forth into subfolders around specific topics.
- When you save the document (either as a HTML, PDF, or document file), try to indicate what key point or value is in the title. Otherwise, you could later waste time trying to find something.
- Extract information and collect it in either a database, spreadsheet, or document.
- As you are doing this, do not hesitate to return to the same web site multiple times. You may find new information.
- Go into the archives of articles and white papers. Stuff written 10 years ago is probably still useful today.
- Except for background, books tend to be limited in value since the materials in a book are typically at least a year older than the date of publication.

Figure 6.1 Guidelines for Organizing Information.

- Business process management
- Service-oriented architecture
- Business activity monitoring
- Business process architecture
- Change management
- Six Sigma
- Process improvement
- Process design
- Project management
- Outsourcing
- BPM software suites
- Re-engineering
- Business and IT alignment
- Strategic planning
- Strategic IT planning
- Information Technology Information Library (ITIL) — a methodology for creating and delivering more structured services

Figure 6.2 Research Topics for IT and Business Processes.

best to install, test, use, and manage the product or service. There should also be consultants who support it. Remember that if you adopt something new, you are a "pioneer." From American western movies, pioneers are the people who got arrows in their backs. Not good.

Make a list of IT-related areas, products, and services. This corresponding to that for business processes.

What questions should you ask about some new technology, service, or product? A list is given in Figure 6.3.

This list can be daunting. That is what is intended. Here are some basic lessons learned from what we have employed in managing IT groups and in doing consulting.

- *Consider the support costs of all systems and technology when you consider new products.*
- *Only adopt something new if it adds clear business value either directly in the business or indirectly through IT.*

- Is the product from an established firm?
- What is the track record of the firm's performance?
- Is the product available where we are? This is geographical availability.
- Is support available for us? This is support availability.
- Does the product apply to our industry? This is industry availability.
- Does the product replace anything we have today?
- What guidelines exist for installation?
- What guidance is there for operations and management?
- What are the life cycle costs of the product?
- What is likely life of the product until it is replaced?
- What is the opportunity cost if we don't get it?
- How would it integrate and interface with what we have?
- What would be the benefits and impacts to the business work?
- How would the business realize the benefits?
- What potential changes would be needed in the business?
- To what processes and business units is the product applicable?
- What are the proven benefits of the product?
- How would the product be measured and managed after installation?
- What are skill requirements to support operations, maintenance, and enhancements?
- What time and effort are required to gain proficiency?
- If we get this product, how would we verify the benefits?
- If we don't acquire the product, what do we lose?
- If we delay getting the product, what do we lose?
- How did we survive without this product up to now?

Figure 6.3 Questions Related to New Systems and Technology.

- *When you are considering new products, evaluate what you have to see, what can be eliminated or combined.*

This pain and suffering of new systems and technology mandates that you at least consider the above items carefully.

Considering something new entails many costs. These are listed in Figure 6.4.

Many organizations and people don't think of these things. They just plunge in and get them. Here are some examples.

- Early PDA (personal digital assistant) devices. Cumbersome, limited, and difficult to interface with.
- Standalone PCs in business departments in the 1980s. No connectivity, wide use of minesweeper and solitaire, and lost productivity.

- Evaluation and selection cost
- Acquisition cost
- Installation preparation cost
- Training cost
- Cost of the effort to become proficient in the use of the product
- The cost of a pilot project
- Conversion cost to effectively use the product
- Cost of changes to other parts of IT due to the product
- Cost of business change due to the product
- Consulting costs for installation
- Operations costs
- Consulting and product costs for operations and upgrades
- Maintenance costs
- Enhancement and upgrade cost
- Replacement costs

Figure 6.4 Potential Cost Elements for New Systems and Technology.

- Early versions of "neat" products such as the iPhone. Limited features, capabilities, and capacity; high expense. Later versions were much improved.

The guideline overall is that there should be compelling needs and urgency arising from the business and/or IT to justify the expense.

Analyze the Business Mission and Vision

So, you have the mission and/or vision statement. It also sounds good. But is it complete and consistent? Many people trust these things and accept them at face value. However, often, they were not really carefully reviewed. One typical approach used to generate a mission or vision statement is to follow these steps:

- Hire a facilitator or consultant to assist in the definition.
- Conduct a meeting of one or more days. These are often held off-site so that the managers will not be distracted by work.

But, the cell phones still ring. And, there are distractions at the country club or other venue.

- The managers might be divided in groups to consider areas of IT.
- Brainstorming occurs to define objectives.
- The group gets back together and tries to gain consensus.
- The last part of the meeting is a feverish effort to finalize the mission or vision.

Sound familiar? As the infamous governor of Alaska often said, "You betcha." This is not a book on how to define a mission or vision. However, you can use the evaluation method presented here to actually generate it. Figure 6.5 gives a step-by-step approach for analyzing a mission or vision.

The purpose of the last step is to align the mission or vision to the business processes. Surprise! In doing this you may find that there are a number of processes that are not really affected by the mission or vision. This indicates that more needs to be said in the mission or vision statement in relation to one or more of the

---

1. Define the perspectives or views relevant to the mission or vision. These could include the following:

   o Stakeholders
   o Employees
   o The work or processes
   o Customers
   o Management
   o IT

2. Parse or segment the mission or vision into the above categories. You can use as a means of testing whether each of the perspectives is addressed.
3. List the key processes that were identified earlier.
4. Prepare a table of the mission or vision elements as rows and the processes as columns. You can place an "X" in the table if the mission or vision element relates to the business process.

Figure 6.5 Approach for Assessing the Business Mission or Vision.

perspectives. A bigger surprise is to find one or more of the per-spectives are left out.

Don't stop here. You can undertake one more task. Instead of placing an "X" in the table, write down how the process can help achieve the vision or carry out the mission. You can see that this is the business long-term goal of the process. Very useful. Process visions are seldom developed since the processes are not people and organiza-tions and since people assume what they are — when they really do not know. The process vision or mission is the aggregation of the text in the column of the process of all non-blank entries. This is a good thing to do as part of the strategic IT and process planning effort.

Push it further. A business unit oversees a number of processes and shares other processes with different business units. Now, if you accumulate all of the mission or vision statements for the processes in which they are heavily involved, you could get a mission or vision statement for a business unit.

These comments seem fuzzy. To help you see how this can be done, we examine as an example a mission statement and perform the analysis in a later section.

Assess Business Issues

This is the negative side of the business factors. Because people don't like to talk or write about negative things, especially in busi-ness, it is sometimes more difficult to do this analysis. Some guidelines for analyzing the business issues are given in Figure 6.6.

Develop and Organize Lists and Tables

Lists and tables appear through the chapters. However, you will find in Appendix C an overall list. Start with lists of business factors first. Since this can become tedious, only devote an hour or two here.

- What are the nature and type of the issue?
- When did this business issues first appear?
- To what processes does it apply?
- To what business units does it pertain?
- Are firms in the same or related industry saddled with the same issue?
- What has been the impact of the issue so far?
- Is the issue getting more severe in its impact?
- Do any business initiatives address this issue?
- How does the issue bear on IT?

Figure 6.6 Guidelines for Analyzing Business Issues.

Next, move to the IT factors. Experience shows that you can divide the work into groups.

- The somewhat negative factors — issues and opportunities and constraints.
- The general positive factors — IT objectives and IT strategies.
- The detailed positive factors — action items.

Put these on paper in front of you and move often between the lists. As you think of something new in issues and opportunities, it may trigger an idea for a new action items.

After you have made progress on the lists, don't try to be complete or comprehensive. Start constructing some of the tables. Here, concentrate on those that include either all business or all IT factors. You will relate the business and IT factors later.

Collect Data from Managers and Staff

There are three audiences that you should address in data collection through informal contacts or interviews: IT, business units, and upper management. Specific suggestions for each appear in Figures 6.7–6.9, respectively. Note that there is some overlap.

We favor informal contacts. If you have formal interviews, you incur several risks that impact the success of the strategic

The items in this list are all indirect. The danger of asking things like "What would you change?" might just provoke a canned response. The IT staff probably sees the planners as a tool of management so that whatever is said will be assumed to flow back to the IT managers.

- Start by getting an understanding of where they spend their time.
- Explore how their work has changed.
- Ask how they get work assignments.
- Ask how to learn about new things in IT.
- Probe which are easiest and most challenging tasks.
- Inquire as to what they think of specific departments, processes, and systems and technology.
- Ask about who they work with.
- Ask what they consider to be a good and bad day.

Figure 6.7 Guidelines for Data Collection in IT.

If you were doing just a strategic IT plan, these contacts would be more strained. However, you are including processes.

- Put them at ease. The reason why processes are included is that the IT plan by itself lacks meaning unless the interaction with the business work is included.
- Indicate that you want a brief review of some of the processes for the plan — no in-depth, not requirements.
- Put expectations in the context that some process improvements can be in the plan as action items.
- Now, you can relate the planning process by giving them some sample tables. Also, point out that the critical decision points are the resource allocation and the implementation. Results count. Raise the specter of fear — if they don't support it, it won't get done.
- Next, have them describe their own involvement in reviews. Because the plan involves the processes, indicate you would like to have very brief meetings with some of the supervisors and employees. Tell them that these can be informal contacts.

Figure 6.8 Guidelines for Data Collection in the Business Units.

planning work. First, a formal request for an interview means the manager will likely prepare canned answers — not good. Second, the manager may feel threatened and assemble a number of people in the meeting. What you thought was going to be one-on-one turns out to be one-on-many. This will shade the information that you provide.

Here, assume you have at most 10 minutes. You cannot cover much. Your purpose is to explain what you are doing, that you are competent to do the planning work, and get some guidance from them relative to the business processes and business units.

- Indicate that you are using the mission and vision as well as the strategic business plan. This should help politically.
- Start with reviewing the long-term positive things like objectives. Get them to comment on what strategies and business issues these apply to.
- Ask if they would like to interim drafts of lists and tables. This gives you the opportunity to indirectly explain the planning method. Give them a sample of the lists and tables.
- Inquire as to what business activities would benefit most from new IT work.
- Related to that you can ask what additional contribution IT could make to the business.

Figure 6.9 Guidelines for Data Collection from Upper Management.

Another guideline is to avoid acting too smart. As a planner you are looking for information. You are coming with answers. Related to this is their likely fear that the plan is being used as an IT tool to jam a project down their throat. Don't come with solutions.

During a formal interview, take notes in summary form. Don't write too much as this will detract from eye contact. Be aware of the manager's body language and tone of voice. For informal contacts, sit down right afterwards and make some notes. Use the log that is presented later in the chapter.

After each formal contact, you should write up a summary and send it to them for feedback. This means that there is extra work with formal contacts. Informal contacts have no such problem. You can catch a manager spontaneously. Experience shows that early in the morning is sometimes the best time to make contact.

Examples

Let's take one item from the chapter and give an example. Figure 6.10 gives an example of a mission statement. Please note that we did not develop this. We later modified it as part of the strategic IT and process planning effort.

XXX is an electronic commerce company committed to providing a high quality, one-to-one customer experience that exceeds expectations and exceeds expectations in long-term relationships. We provide excellent customer service and a vast selection of products and services through unique channels and partnerships. We foster high morale among our team members by providing them with an energizing work environment and clear direction, and by valuing all team member contributions. Long-term profitability, creating value for our shareholders and partners, and enhancing the communities we share are essential to our success.

Figure 6.10 Example of a Mission Statement.

Following our method in the chapter, we first identify the areas of the mission. Recall that these include the following:

- Stakeholders
- Employees
- The work or processes
- Customers
- Management
- IT

Next, you can parse the mission statement into these categories. Notice that this is a multirelationship.

- Stakeholders

  o Long-term profitability
  o Create value

- Employees

  o High morale
  o Energizing work environment
  o Clear direction
  o Value of their contributions

- The work or processes

  o Excellent customer service
  o Wide range of products/services

- Customers
  - High quality
  - One-to-one experience
  - Excellent customer service
  - Wide range of products and services
- Management
  - Long-term profitability
  - Create value
  - Clear direction
  - High morale
- IT
  - Energizing work environment
  - Wide range of products/services
  - Excellent customer service
  - Long-term profitability

The next thing to do is to create a table of the mission perspectives (as organized above) versus processes. Space limitations do not permit an entire list of processes. However, by focusing on one area, you can get the idea. The example in Tables 6.1 and 6.2 pertain to human resources. The processes in human resources include:

- Hiring
- Assimilation or familiarization

Table 6.1 Sample Table of Mission Elements versus Human Resources Processes.

Mission area	Hiring	Assimilation	Retention	Training	Sharing
Stakeholders			X	X	X
Employees	X	X	X	X	X
The work				X	X
Customers		X	X	X	X
Management	X		X	X	
IT				X	X

Table 6.2 Example of Mission Elements for Human Resources.

Area	Mission element
Hiring	Ensure that the most qualified people are hired
Familiarization	Ensure that new and current employees are familiar with the organization, mission, and business processes
Retention	Provide for retention and career paths for dedicated employees, including lessons learned from terminations
Training	Provide training in processes, methods, and tools to support higher productivity
Information sharing	Support the sharing of information and lessons learned among

- Retention
- Training
- Information sharing

We could have place more "Xs", but only the ones with at least moderate association were selected. Note also, that we could make the table more detailed by including as the second column the specific mission elements. Keep in mind that these are subjective. What you would do here is to create a sample or draft table and then have it reviewed and updated by the managers in human resources.

Table 6.2 provides information on the mission for each of the processes in human resources listed above.

What happened as a result of doing this work? Here were some of the benefits.

- The business department managers became enthusiastic about the planning work.
- Some of the managers circulated their process mission statements.
- The mission statements became part of the training.
- The missions were a useful aid in mapping planning factors to the business processes.

Lessons Learned

From experience some of the guidelines that will help you do the work described in this chapter include the following:

- Do not be too open with the analysis of the mission or vision. Upper management has probably set this in stone. So, what you should emphasize is the application of mission or vision to the business processes.
- If you find gaps in the mission or vision relative to processes, try to fill these in. You can use the web to search for samples.
- As a trial rule, go on the web and find a mission or vision statement and parse it.
- When you are collecting information from managers and staff, keep a log of contacts. For each include the following:

  o Contact
  o Date of contact
  o Subject
  o Results
  o Body language, tone of voice, and impressions
  o Any insight into politics and their opinions

Politics

A downbeat mood was purposely employed with respect to new technology. This was by intent. You do not want to use the strategic IT and process plan to push new technology. It will not likely work. IT may just raise expectations that cannot be fulfilled. Your purpose is to show how the business and IT will be harmed or affected negatively if you fail to adopt new systems and technology. In past consulting projects, we employed this approach to demonstrate the need for enterprise software. This was in spite of: (1) the fact that the old application systems were adequate and (2) resources were limited. Competitors implemented such systems and were on the brink of realizing the benefits of integrated information. To have started later would have reduced market share of products.

Another example where the same politics played a role was in e-business. In one case, the threat of not being cost-competitive encouraged an organization to pursue electronic transactions with suppliers. In another instance, it was employed to get a company to implement e-business to reach new customers. This was in a very traditional machine tool business. E-business was used to reach potential with less than 50 employees. In the end over 40% of their sales originated from these smaller firms.

What to Do Next

The beauty of this chapter is that you can get started with this data collection right away. You can start the external data collection as well as the analysis of the mission and/or vision. This will help you build momentum.

Since you can do this alone, you can treat it as a background task in between meetings and as a break in doing planning analysis. If you start early, you will accumulate a substantial amount of knowledge that you can then use in meetings, interviews, and contacts along with use in the strategic plan itself.

Summary

In this chapter, guidelines were provided for external data collection. More were provided for systems and technology since they are more common than business factors across organizations.

A step-wise approach was described for assessment of the mission and/or vision. Doing this analysis will help you really understand what the mission or vision means and how it applies to the business.

On the reverse side of the coin of mission and vision are business issues. Since these can be general as well as not self-evident or stated, it is critical to assess these with reference to the business processes. Don't try at this time to relate them to IT planning factors since it is too much of a leap.

In this chapter you began to assemble some of the basic planning tables. Keep in mind that this is the beginning. As you construct more tables, it will become easier to create these as well as update them.

Another area addressed data collection through interviews and contacts with different audiences: IT, business departments, and upper management. While some of the suggestions were similar, the nature of the audiences and their self-interest is distinct.

Chapter 7

Determine Alignment of IT and Processes to the Business

Introduction

The work covered in this chapter paves the way for the creation of the lists and tables of the strategic IT and process plan. At the start, we consider the alignment of the IT and business processes to business objectives, mission, vision, and issues. The following sections center their attention on business processes: (1) how to analyze processes; (2) how to develop a vision for a business process; and (3) how to develop a process plan. A *process plan* defines both the issues and opportunities in the process as well as defining its future direction and strategies for advancing the process.

With the process assessment in place, we turn to relating this and business factors to IT in terms of alignment. Alignment is viewed in terms of three time periods — now, intermediate term, and long term.

The importance and benefits of these methods cannot be underestimated. They address:

- How to select processes for attention in the strategic IT and business process plan.
- How to assess process performance — now and later on with improvements.

- How to determine both negative and positive alignment of processes to the business.
- How to discover the alignment of IT to both business processes and business factors such as mission and issues.

Dimensions of IT and Process Alignment

Alignment can be thought of in three parts. The first is to define how processes align to the business in both negative and positive ways. This is valuable for several reasons.

- It provides a basis for selecting processes to include in the strategic plan.
- It helps IT determine the importance and relevance of their work and support to the business.

Many people think of alignment in terms of factor A helps achieve B. For example, IT objectives could be aligned to the business mission or vision in that if the IT objectives are achieved, there is substantial progress toward achieving elements of the mission or vision. This is an example of *positive alignment*. It is the one found in many IT management books. Alignment will be covered in several chapters as we construct the strategic plan.

The situation is different in the real world. When you are at home, you could pick up a language book to learn French. That would be work toward a goal of getting more out of travel. However, the reality is much different. There is meal preparation. You have to do some cleaning and laundry. The kids need attention. Then it is time to go to bed — and start all over again. The lesson learned here is most of us do work that aligns with issues and problems. This example reveals another type of positive alignment. We are doing work to deal with problems or issues.

Thus, there are two types of alignment:

- The factor helps to achieve positive goals (i.e., positive alignment).
- The factor works to mitigate, ease, or eliminate problems (i.e., negative alignment).

You can also have the situation where a business process or IT factor has negative impacts on the business. The example here would be some marginal project that consumes resources, but does not contribute either to solving a problem or achieving a goal. Some regard watching television or playing a video game as fitting into this area.

This section examines many of the planning tables that will be used in this book. So, consider this in detail and bookmark the pages since you will likely want to refer back to them often. The number of tables you can create depends on the number of entries in the lists and the available time. You are also restricted by the number that managers are willing to review. Also, you will likely create more tables than you will use. You will use the tables that meet some or all of the following tests.

- The table reinforces the benefits of the strategic planning.
- The table can be employed later for before and after comparisons.

In this and later chapter we consider both positive and negative alignment. Let's consider some examples. An IT project is being carried to support the sales and marketing processes. These are critical processes for business success. In this case, we would say that the project is positively aligned to the business. Now, let's suppose that there is another project that addresses changes to the payroll system to incorporate new tax rates. This would be negative alignment in that a substantial problem will occur if the changes are not made in time.

From Chapter 5 we have a list of major processes. In the preceding chapter (Chapter 6), the analysis of the business mission and

vision was undertaken. Each was parsed into areas related to shareholders, employees, management, customers, processes, IT, and
suppliers. The chapter also outlined steps to identify significant
business problems and issues. It is now time to put these together to
assess alignment. There are seven tables in Figure 7.1. Note that
since business objectives, mission, and vision use similar analysis, we
discuss only one of these three.

- *Mission versus business processes.* The first column contains the mission elements
  (employee, management, and so forth). The second column contains the specific
  items in the mission statement that pertain to the mission element. For example,
  within the customer area, we might improve customer service, increase repeat
  business, and reach a broader range of customers. The remaining columns
  contain the processes — one to a column. The entry in the table is the degree to
  which a process is related or important to the achievement of that mission
  element. In our example, the customer service process relates to the first two of
  the customer mission while the sales process applies to all three. The entry could
  be a number from 1 to 5 (1 is low, 5 is high), or high, medium, or low.
- *Vision versus business processes.*
- *Business objectives versus business processes.*
- *Business strategies versus business processes.* The business strategies are the
  directions taken to achieve the long-term goals. For example, a business strategy
  relating to e-business would impact supply chain processes as well as internal
  processes.
- *Business units versus business processes.* Depending on the size and type of the
  organization, you could use departments instead of business units. The table
  would indicate the degree of involvement of a particular business unit in a
  business unit. In the past this could have been ownership. However, since many
  key processes span departments and business units, involvement is probably more
  relevant.
- *Business initiatives versus business processes.* An example of a business initiative is to
  expand geographically or to a new range of products or services. The entry
  indicates the extent to which the process is important to the success of the
  individual business initiative.
- *Business issues versus business processes.* The first column of this table contains the
  business issues while the others are for individual processes. The entry is the
  extent to which the performance of the process contributes to the specific
  business issue. This is equivalent to using the importance or degree of relevance
  of the process to the issue. For example, suppose that sales are down. There is
  high turnover of staff in the telemarketing department — contributing to the
  falling sales. This is an example of negative alignment.

Figure 7.1 Alignment of Business Factors to Business Processes.

Some comments are useful. Each table is a many-to-many relationship table. That is, several processes may be applicable to one mission, vision, and so forth element, and vice versa. The first three tables assess the positive alignment of the processes to the mission, vision, and business objectives. These tables are not likely to change overtime, unless there is a radical change in the business. In the past, the move into e-business was such as example. The fourth one is more likely to vary overtime. A process could be improved leading to the business issue to diminish. Or, changes in the business reduced the importance of the issue. For example, in a robust economy, there is a drop-off in military recruitment due to many jobs being available. When the economy sours, jobs disappear in the private sector and recruitment quotas are full. The issue disappears. There was no change in a business process.

What is an effective approach for creating tables such as these and others? Well, you could hand out the table in blank form and have people fill it in by themselves. Then you could gather these up and average the results. This can take too much time and is not often necessary. Another method is to employ the results of your data collection from Chapter 5. Following this, you would prepare sample or "strawman" tables for people to review. The feedback can be used for an update. More important, it will likely trigger useful discussions about the content of the tables.

How are these things employed in the creation of the strategic IT and process plan? It is very difficult to try to relate an IT objective, project, and so forth directly to the mission, vision, business objectives, or business issues. The former is specific while the latter is general. What you can do is to relate the IT factor to the business processes (the next part of this section). Then, you can combine the tables from this and the next part to relate IT and business factors.

In the remaining parts, you are assessing the current situation before the creation of the strategic IT and process plan. Later chapters will provide more guidance and suggestions for these tables when you create the corresponding tables for the new strategic plan.

The second part is to assess the alignment of IT to the business processes. Earlier, you examined the existing strategic IT plan as well as the current work in IT, IT projects, and other areas. This can serve as the basis for doing this part of the work. Figure 7.2 gives the potential tables that can be created along with comments.

- *IT objectives versus business processes.* IT objectives are often worded in IT terms. This is often the case in the current strategic IT plan. It will not be the case when we develop the objectives for the new strategic plan. You can start by placing an "X" if an objective when achieved would help a specific process. A guideline is to develop a second version in which the entry is text that explains how the objective would aid the process. Suppose, for example, that you had an objective to provide a much more robust IT computing and communications environment. This would help all processes, but you would want to put text in some of the entries.
- *IT strategies versus business processes.* An IT strategy might be to implement several CRM modules or systems. This would impact a number of business processes. The entry in the table might be the new capabilities that are provided by these systems. Alternatively, they could be the benefits. Since other tables such as those related to projects and operations give benefits and support, you might want to emphasize capabilities here.
- *IT operations versus business processes.* Here, you do not have time to list all of the detailed operations carried out in IT. You might limit this to user support, software maintenance, enhancements, and operations. The entry would indicate an estimate of the percentage of resources devoted to that resource. There may be a need to average these based on the size of the user base related to the processes. This table is useful for several reasons. First, you can employ it to examine "fairness" in the deployment of resources. Second, you can discover business processes that are neglected or given less resources.
- *IT projects versus business processes.* Some projects focus on one process. Some relate to application systems such as ERP, CRM, and SCM apply to multiple processes. Network and infrastructure projects impact most processes. This table is very useful in showing the relevance of the projects to the actual business work. The table entry could be an "X" if a project, when completed, helps the performance and capabilities of a process. Start with this. Later, you can add specific benefits to replace the "X". This is a great way to show the importance of the projects. Moreover, it reinforces the justification for the projects — especially those involving infrastructure.
- *IT infrastructure and architecture versus business processes.* An exhaustive list of technical components is infeasible. Instead, group these. The entry could be the importance of that component to the performance of the process. This would indicate dependence of the processes on the architecture. This is politically useful in that it may help justify improvements in the architecture components.

Figure 7.2 Potential Tables Relating IT Factors to Business Processes.

The third part deals with the alignment of IT to business factors. These tables are created by combining the corresponding tables from the first two parts. This is done by mapping the two matrices or tables together. For example, if IT objective A relates to business process B, and process B relates to mission element C, the objective A aligns to mission element C. The table element can either be an "X", or, better, a comment on how achieving the objective supports the attainment of the mission element.

The potential tables are listed in Figures 7.3–7.7 for positive alignment and Figure 7.8 for alignment to business issues. Note that there is usually insufficient time to develop many of these. For example, for those involving business objectives, mission, and vision, you would often just pick one of these. The reason that the list is exhaustive of possibilities is to provide you with tips to help you select which to use. In each case we discuss why it might be useful and how it might be used.

There are both positive and negative reasons for developing some of these tables before you start the construction of the new strategic IT and process plan. On the positive side these are valuable later in showing a comparison between the old and new after the creation of the strategic plan. On the negative side, they can help in marketing the planning effort by indicating issues that should be addressed and potential opportunities that might be pursued later.

Strategic Alignment of IT to the Business

In the previous sections we examined many of the potential tables that can be created to examine and assess the alignment of IT to the business. This and the following two sections pull this together on three levels: strategic (long term), intermediate (mid term), and

- **IT objectives versus business objectives.** This and the next two tables are keys to showing the strategic, long-term alignment of IT to the business. You could put an "X" in the entry if a specific IT objective supports or applies to a specific business objective. However, it is better if you can provide text in bullet form to show how the IT objective applies to the business objective. One advantage of this and next two tables are that they are unlikely to change from one year to the end.

  In one management position we used this table to show the importance of infrastructure to streamlining government operations to better serve customers. Previously, it had been a challenge to get this funded. These three tables are valuable because management built their own objectives. Thus, the only debate is the extent to which an IT objective really does give benefits in achieving a business goal.

- **IT objectives versus mission.** Recall that the mission is the general direction for achieving the vision. Therefore, the comments in the above table apply here.

- **IT objectives versus vision.** The vision is the state that the organization seeks to reach over the long term. It might seem more natural to create a table of IT vision to the business vision. However, this is too presumptuous. Instead, you use this table to reveal how the achievement of the IT objectives work to achieve the vision. Given the generality of both things we have found that the use of the "X" is sufficient. That typically will generate some interesting discussion.

  There is a political point here. This and the previous table are useful because after the mission and/or vision is created, they are often seldom used. Now, you come along and use these to show alignment. This helps management justify in their minds the cost and effort of developing these in the first place.

- **IT objectives versus business units.** This table can really help market the strategic IT and process plan since it shows how the IT objectives are relevant to the individual business units. The table entry is how the department key processes are improved with the attainment of the objective. In one case a business unit manager was very negative to IT and to the strategic planning. He thought that IT was needed, but not key to his business operations. We first showed the table of IT objectives versus processes. No reaction. Then we showed this table. He suddenly showed a great deal of interest. He then later became an IT advocate.

- **IT objectives versus business strategies.** If you have the table for business objectives, then this one might be dropped. The main use of this table is to show how IT is supporting the top three and four strategies. The entry is text on how they are supported.

- **IT objectives versus business initiatives.** A business initiative can be a specific project within a business strategy. Suppose, for example, that a retailer has as its strategy the expansion into a geographical region. The business initiative could be the expansion into specific cities or a country. The entry would show the relevance of the IT objective. Of course, there is also a difference in levels — the IT objective is general and the business initiative is specific.

Figure 7.3 Potential Positive Alignment Tables Relating IT Objectives to Business Factors.

This group of tables along with those in Figure 7.5 addresses the intermediate level of alignment — between the long term of IT objectives and the details of operations today. The strategies show the IT approach for supporting the business overall. The IT projects, however, are very specific.

- *IT strategies versus business objectives.* This table along with the next two tables shows how more specific IT elements, namely strategies, can help achieve the objectives, mission, and vision. These three tables provide the detail to flesh out the IT objectives. We recommend that you use only one of these three. The entry should be text that shows the benefits of achieving the strategy related to the business.
- *IT strategies versus mission.* See the table above.
- *IT strategies versus vision.* See the table on IT strategies versus business objectives.
- *IT strategies versus business units.* Like the corresponding one for IT objectives, this can really show how IT is working to support individual business units. The entry can be the capabilities that the strategy delivers to the business unit through the business process.
- *IT strategies versus business strategies.* We list this for completeness. However, we seldom use it. Time and effort limitations restrict the number of tables. If you do want to use this one, it can reveal the fit of the intermediate-term activities of IT to those of the business.
- *IT strategies versus business initiatives.* This table can serve as an umbrella for IT projects and work to indicate how the total IT effort over the intermediate term is supportive of specific business initiatives. The entry should focus on the overall benefit of the IT strategy and go beyond a specific project.

There have been several applications of this table. In the most common case, you would gain support for the IT strategies because they want the business initiatives to be successful. In a few cases, it was shown that the IT strategies that were required were so expensive, extensive, and time consuming, that the business initiative was impossible to achieve. In one case it was dropped. In another instance, the initiative was scaled back.

Figure 7.4 Potential Positive Alignment Tables Relating IT Strategies to Business Factors.

operations (today). You need to have alignment on all three levels to be successful as was discussed earlier.

The key tables for strategic alignment of IT to the business include both negative and positive alignment. These are:

- **IT objectives versus business processes.** This show relevance to the work.

This group of tables can provide much needed management support for the projects since the tables show the importance of completing the projects to the business. When these have been employed, the result often has been a greater management commitment to the projects.

- *IT projects versus business objectives.* A project delivers benefits either directly to business processes, or indirectly through improvements in the IT infrastructure and architecture. The benefits of the projects to the processes have been developed in the table of IT projects versus business processes. This can be combined with the table on processes versus business objectives. The entry in this new table can summarize the benefits in terms of how the processes are changed and improved.
- *IT projects versus mission.* Similar to the one above.
- *IT projects versus vision.* Similar to the table of IT projects to business objectives.
- *IT projects versus business units.* Mapping via the processes versus business units table and IT projects versus processes, you can show how departments and business units benefits directly from the projects. This can not only generate more support for the projects from the business managers, but also overall support for IT work. The entry is the impact of the project completion on a specific business unit.
- *IT projects versus business strategies.* This table can provide information on how a group of projects can support an individual strategy. By looking down a column, you can see which projects deliver benefit and value to the business strategy. This can help in marketing a group of projects — so that key projects can support lesser, but essential projects.
- *IT projects versus business initiatives.* Similar to the previous table.

Figure 7.5 Potential Positive Alignment Tables Relating IT Projects to Business Factors.

- *IT objectives versus mission/vision/business objectives.* This is the overall strategic alignment of IT to the business.
- *IT objectives versus business issues.* This is the negative alignment.

Intermediate Alignment of IT to the Business

Intermediate alignment is in reference to IT strategies and projects. The key tables are listed here in Figure 7.9.

Potential tables relating to business objectives, vision, and mission are not included since it is often not necessary to justify current operations in terms of these long-term business goals. Recall that IT operations includes production systems, maintenance, enhancements, and other daily IT work.

- *IT operations versus business units.* This table is valuable in showing how IT operations work is spread across business units. The entry could be an estimate of the percentage of labor effort applied to the processes that involve an individual business unit. Network, hardware, and related activities could be assessed in terms of volume of work or number of users.

  This table has been employed to show that IT resources are spread in a fair manner across the business units. That is the positive use. The other application is to show that a disproportionate share of resources is devoted to some key departments. In one case, this analysis revealed that too much support was going to the accounting area. This table enabled management to reset IT priorities.
- *IT operations versus business strategies.* The achievement of a business strategy requires that there not only be IT projects, but also improvements to existing systems and technology. This table can show what changes are needed and their impacts. The table entry could either be the benefit of the work, or the additional capabilities required by the business strategy.
- *IT operations versus business initiatives.* Similar to the table above.

Figure 7.6 Potential Positive Alignment Tables Relating IT Operations to Business Factors.

The main tables of interest here relate to business units, strategies, and initiatives. They are constructed in a manner analogous to those of IT operations. The tables are of use in that they can reveal the extent to which the business unit, strategy, and initiative depend on the particular element of the IT infrastructure and architecture.

- *IT infrastructure versus business units.* The table entry can be the degree of importance of a particular part of the infrastructure to the business unit through its processes.
- *IT infrastructure versus business strategies.* Business strategies can be rather grand in scope. Reaching these can require substantial infrastructure and architecture change. Thus, the table entry should reveal the importance of work with the specific element of the infrastructure to the individual business strategy.
- *IT infrastructure versus business initiatives.* Similar to the above table.

Figure 7.7 Potential Positive Alignment Tables Relating IT Infrastructure to Business Factors.

Most books and articles that are concerned with alignment focus on the positive side as we have done in the preceding figures and tables. However, as we have said people and organizations do things because if they are not done, there will be pain and suffering. Seems exaggerated, but it is not. Negative alignment as revealed in the following tables can serve as very powerful motivation to support IT work, projects, and direction. This reflects the fact that IT is necessary, but not sufficient for process change since you still have to modify the process to take use of the systems and technology. In the context of what has been said, it is unlikely that IT alone can solve a business issue. Thus, these tables should demonstrate how they are necessary to resolving the business issues.

- *IT objectives versus business issues.* The table entry is impact of achieving the objective on the business issue. For example, let's suppose that a major IT objective relates to exploiting web 2.0 technology. This could be applied to the issue that there is a lack of communications among business units and employees.
- *IT strategies versus business issues.* This is similar to the previous table. However, since strategies are more specific, it is of interest to show why the individual IT strategies are good for helping resolve the business issue. It is useful to view this table by considering a column. In one column are all of the impacts on one issue across all strategies. This can show management the importance of these IT strategies taken together.
- *IT projects versus business issues.* Like the one above this applies to the intermediate term. The table entry should indicate the direct benefit of the project. Now you created this table by combining those of IT projects and business processes, and business processes versus business issues. The combined table can show the cumulative benefits across multiple processes. By considering a column you can see the overall benefits of multiple projects to helping resolve a business issue.
- *IT operations versus business issues.* There can be a wide range of business issues. Some of these issues relate to daily work. This table helps for these local issues. So, you may want to restrict the issues to those that are concerned with daily work. The entry would be the benefits of the enhancements, maintenance, and so forth to the business for the specific issue.
- *IT infrastructure and architecture versus business issues.* Some business issues apply to organization structure, policies, and business direction. Others relate to limitations that the business faces. IT infrastructure and architecture improvements can assist in dealing with these issues. The table entry could describe the additional capabilities that the architecture work would deliver.

Figure 7.8　Potential Negative Alignment Tables Relating IT to Business Factors.

- IT strategies versus business processes.
- IT projects versus business processes.
- IT strategies versus business units.
- IT projects versus business units.
- IT strategies versus business strategies.
- IT projects versus business strategies.
- IT strategies versus business initiatives.
- IT projects versus business initiatives.
- IT strategies versus business issues.
- IT projects versus business issues.

Figure 7.9　Tables Relating to Intermediate Alignment.

Operations Alignment of IT to the Business

The third level of alignment is that of tactical or operations alignment to the business. This can involve IT operations and IT infrastructure and architecture. If you envisioned major IT infrastructure work, then this could be included in the intermediate alignment. The tables of interest are listed here. The first four pertain to positive alignment to business work. The last two deal with negative alignment.

- IT operations versus business processes.
- IT infrastructure and architecture versus business processes.
- IT operations versus business units.
- IT infrastructure and architecture versus business units.
- IT operations versus business issues.
- IT infrastructure and architecture versus business issues.

Analyze Business Processes

The key business processes were identified in the previous chapter. That is our starting point. Now is the time to analyze a process. Why should this be part of a book on strategic planning? There are several reasons. First, the strategic plan includes processes as well as IT. Second, this planning requires that you understand the current work as well as defining the direction of the process. The next section addresses defining a vision for a business process. The following section covers the creation of a process plan. This is a strategic plan for a business process.

Why does this material appear with alignment? Because the more you know about the processes, the easier it will be to do the alignment analysis. In practice, you would proceed with both of these, alignment and process planning, in parallel.

In traditional IT systems analysis, you would proceed to analyze all of the transactions in the process. Then you would develop with the business users the requirements for the systems work. This approach has led to many failures. First, it does not take into account the fact that even though management wants a new system, the employees involved in the work may see no need for change. This is particularly true with many senior business staff (called here King and Queen Bees). These King and Queen Bees often resist changes. They are happy with things as they are. They possess tremendous informal power. New employees are often handed over to them to get trained. This training is often very selective to preserve their power.

Wait! The situation is worse. A process often is composed of standard transactions and work that many do. In addition, there are exceptions that require the knowledge and skills of the King and Queen Bees. There are also informal additional workarounds and systems, methods, and procedures that only the employees are aware of. These will be called *shadow systems*. Physically, they can be spreadsheets, checklists, and so forth. The department really depends on these shadow systems. However, the department management may not even be aware that they exist. Shadow systems represent both major risk and an opportunity. The risk lies in the fact that only one or a few people know how to use them. If a key person leaves, the work performance is at risk. They are not documented. They have not been formally tested. This means that they could be wrong and give bad results. This happened with a major American airline that had to dispose of routes to cut costs. They sold the route from the western United States to Australia to a competitor for a cheap price. But the flights had always been full. There was little competition on the route. Why did this happen? The analyst who performed the examination of routes had his own spreadsheet. But it was insensitive to currency. He did not know the difference between the US dollar ($) and the Australian dollar (A$)!

After reading all of this, you can see why a modification of the old approach is needed. Here are the analysis steps and guidelines that we have used for over 18 years.

- Concentrate on the common, frequent transactions. This is where the volume is. If you start gathering data on some exceptions, it will be hard not to do them all. Then you will never finish. This is politically useful as a tradeoff with the King and Queen Bees who oversee the exceptions. You give these to them in return for them helping you on the common work.
- Start with identifying the problems and the impacts of these problems on the work performance. This comes before requirements since you have to get the employees to recognize the need for change. It is just like drug and alcohol abuse — a person has to recognize they have a problem to be willing to modify their behavior. You can create the following table. The first three columns are basically playscript. This is simple for the employees to create and review. Since you are focusing on only a few common transactions, this is not too much work.

Transaction: _____

Step	Who	What	Problem	Impact

Next, you can roll these tables up to create the following one.

Transaction	Problems	Impacts

These tables serve as the basis for the process planning.

- Try to uncover the shadow systems. These are important in terms of defining requirements. Their elimination, automation, or organization will directly reduce the risk to the department.
- Gather information by observation of the work. This is often more effective than interviews. You might also have the employees provide you with some training in the process. That way you will learn their terminology.

Define a Vision for a Business Process

You might think that the next step is to define the requirements. However, this is difficult if you do not know where you are going. Requirements gathered in the traditional manner without a vision of the work are often either incomplete or inconsistent. Moreover, they are subject to change later — ah, the dreaded scope creep.

If you attempt to define a vision for the process in general, you might slaving on this for weeks. From experience a better approach is to start with the transactions that you analyzed before. It is much easier to explore how a specific piece of work might be performed more effectively and efficiently.

For a transaction you would define the following table. The first three columns are, respectively the new steps, who, and what. The next column is the difference at the step level with the old transaction. The fifth column gives information on how the issues were resolved. Column six gives the benefits of the new step. The last column can give requirements.

Transaction: _____

Step	Who	What	Difference	How issue is handled	Benefit	Requirements

You can then create a summary table that rolls up the analysis.

Transaction	Issues	Impacts	Difference	Benefits	Requirements

This analysis can then to defining the overall new process. Shadow systems would be included here. Exceptions would fit into the framework on the new process.

Create a Real-World Process Plan

If you have no overall analysis of a critical business process, you find that you are always responding to problems and opportunities. It is difficult to be proactive if you don't know where the process is going. Before seeing what the details are, let's consider how it will be used. Here is a list from experience.

- The process plan can help structure business unit requests.
- IT can become more proactive in supporting the business process.
- The process plan can reveal to the business unit management the non-IT shortcomings in the work.
- The process plan can be employed by IT to get new IT staff familiar with the business.
- The process can be used by IT to evaluate both upper management and department requests.

With all of these benefits, it is difficult to understand why anyone would want to have a major process without a process plan. We wondered the same thing. Here is what we discovered.

- The process is not an organization so it cannot speak for itself.
- Some think that the process plan is contained in a department plan. Not so. Many processes cross multiple departments. Also,

the department plan usually deals with staffing and budgets — rather than the work itself.

- There is the attitude that "We have gotten along OK with a process plan so far. Why do one now?"

With this motivation let's list the contents of the process plan. This appears in Figure 7.10. The first part is an overview that provides background. Here, history is useful to give perspective. The performance measures are valuable since process improvement efforts initiated through the strategic IT and process plan would affect these.

Given that we want to develop a process plan, how can we do it with limited time? First, if you depend on the employees of a department to do it, they will have problems due to lack of experience and direction. You start with the process analysis discussed in the earlier chapter. Then you move to define the future process. This information can serve as the basis for the process plan.

- Overview of the business process

  o Description
  o Purpose
  o Business units involved
  o Performance measures (cost, number of employees, and volume of work)
  o History of the process

- Current performance and issues

  o List of common transactions
  o Transaction analysis (as shown before)
  o Summary transaction analysis table (shown above)
  o List of sample exceptions
  o List of shadow systems and potential actions

- Future vision of the process

  o Transaction analysis for future (shown above)
  o Summary future transaction analysis table (shown above)
  o Major differences between the old and new
  o Benefits of the new over the old

- General requirements for process improvement

Figure 7.10 Contents of a Process Plan.

While you can start the process planning yourself, you really want employee involvement in both the process analysis and the definition of the future vision of the work. Since the process plan draws heavily on this analysis, you can create the first draft of the process plan. Since it is mainly composed of lists and tables, it is relatively easy to review. Our ideal review approach is to have simultaneous reviews at the management, supervisory, and employee levels. If you proceed top down, then politics might enter the scene (surprised?).

Examples

In one organization management was concerned with the direction of and work in IT. Yes, IT kept systems running. But the systems were old. There was a lack of new ideas and new technology. Before creating the strategic IT and process plan, we first wanted to show management some of the problems. We created a number of alignment tables for management. These revealed a good tactical alignment with operations work. There was less alignment with business initiatives and strategies. The alignment of the projects was quite poor. A number of the projects appeared to deliver no strategic benefit. Instead, they were linked to operations. At the strategic level — forget it. There was no alignment.

We wanted to beef up this analysis with an example. So, we took one key operational process and developed a process along the lines presented in this chapter. This revealed directly the problems and limitations of the IT work and support. Only one issue in the process was being addressed by IT out of six that could have been handled by systems and technology.

The alignment work and process plan were presented to management. The IT manager who had an opportunity to review it ahead of time raised few questions. When questioned by management, he went back to the excuses that "There are not enough people," "The users really do not know what they want," and

"We never had to do process plans or show alignment before." This triggered the creation of the strategic IT and process plan. The example has a nice ending. The manager got behind the plan and carried it out. The plan could never have been done without both the alignment analysis and the process plan example.

Lessons Learned

One thing from experience is that you want to assess the alignment at the start of the planning effort. This accomplishes several purposes. First, it serves as the basis for the planning work. Second, it is politically useful in revealing the problems and limitations in the current relationship between IT and the business. Most IT staff and managers would probably not see any problems since they are deeply involved in the everyday work. They are working on daily alignment. But as you read above, alignment needs to be on three levels.

Another lesson learned involves the process plan. You will sometimes run into resistance when you present the idea. To get around this and prevent it, consider not using the term. Here is what you might do. Look at the common transactions and identify issues. Then work at the transaction level to identify both the long-term view of the transaction as well as the requirements. This bottom-up approach is more tangible and real to both the employees involved in the work and the management. After you generate interest and support, you can move up to the process in general.

Politics

At first glance, the subjects of alignment and process planning would seem to be politically neutral. Not at all. As soon as the alignment tables are revealed, politics can get hot and heavy. Departments who feel they have been shortchanged in terms of IT resources may now have justification. Others may see that their processes are not that critical.

Thus, you need to plan for the politics ahead of time. In one case, we knew that the key areas for IT were operations and financial services. Supporting services such as facilities management were significant, but not key. An important political goal was to help the managers of various supporting services understand why their areas could not be addressed immediately. The alignment analysis was critical here.

There is also the politics of process planning. If one or several business units have worked to create process plans, they receive many political benefits. To management they appear more organized. The same applies to IT. The process plan is a political tool for managers over the process to exert more direction and control. Politically, this can be good or bad. However, improved business knowledge is beneficial either way.

What to Do Next

Several action items flow from the materials in this chapter. In the area of alignment, you can start right now to create some of the lists and tables developed here. You should initially focus on those involving the business processes. Take one process with which you are familiar and develop the tables for this one. This has several benefits. First, it helps you by providing experience in creating the tables. Second, this work can serve as a model to involve others in the creation of the tables (since the example represents an individual row or column of a table).

The other part of the chapter dealt with process planning. Why should IT be involved in this? As we said, one answer is self-interest. The action item here is to select a process for which you have substantial experience and knowledge. Then, you can build the lists of items within the process plan. Be careful on getting the related business unit too involved. It may really raise expectations for IT work that cannot be delivered!

Summary

This chapter has addressed several key topics. The first is that of alignment. While we included the standard elements of positive alignment, we also gave attention to the negative alignment to business issues. After all, IT is important not only because it delivers value and capabilities, but also because IT work can help resolve business problems. Alignment is often treated as a fuzzy term so that it is difficult for people to determine their degree of IT alignment — either positive or negative. Here a method based on tables and combining tables drawn from earlier lists was presented. This is a very useful step-by-step approach that can be rapidly improved and updated with incremental effort. Moreover, these tables are much easier to understand than pages and pages of text.

When most people think of alignment, they think of IT overall, and more specifically of the alignment of IT objectives. However, as we have seen, you can be perfectly aligned long term, but fail in terms of daily work (operations) or intermediate direction and effort (projects and strategies). That is why we defined three levels of alignment. A successful IT organization will be able to demonstrate alignment in all three time horizons.

The chapter also focused on specific business processes and gave techniques for analyzing them. This not only gives IT more valuable information about a process, but also provides for the strategic direction of a business process. That is why we stressed the importance of creating the business process plan. The process plan gives the problems, impacts, direction, and summary requirements for the process. Experience shows that the process plans lead to both immediate and long terms to both IT and the business.

PART III

DEVELOP THE PLAN

Chapter 8

Develop Issues and Opportunities for the Plan

Introduction

Let's recap some definitions. An *issue* is a problem or situation that can be addressed. By way of contrast, a *constraint* is an issue you have to accept and live with. An *opportunity* is a potential change, addition, or enhancement that provides additional capabilities, capacity, new functions, and other improvements. In doing many strategic plans, we have found that difficulties arise from the start if you do not have an organized, structured approach.

When is an issue for the strategic plan? The same question applies to opportunities. To be included, a potential issue or opportunity should meet at least one of the following tests:

- The performance of a business process will be measurably improved. Notice that we did not say in a major way since we want to allow for Quick Wins.
- The relationship between IT and business units will be positively affected.
- Vendor coordination and management will increase in effectiveness.
- The cost and performance of IT will improve.

187

These tests tend to eliminate minor improvements. However, if you uncover an issue that can be addressed during the planning, you shouldn't ignore it. Instead, get it fixed and give the credit to the people for the repair and to the planning effort for uncovering the issue.

Another observation is that an issue is just the flipped version of an opportunity. For example, let's suppose that in a department there is no sharing of knowledge about how to perform the work more effectively. This is the issue. The opportunity would be that work improvements can result from gathering and using experience and lessons learned. That is why we group these together in this chapter.

In this chapter we first provide a framework for issues and opportunities. This is in two parts. One is the list of areas that can be examined for issues and opportunities. The second is to identify what to look for in each area. This is followed by lists of potential issues in each area that you can use a starting point. Obviously, the more you have to start with, the less time it will take to develop the list of issues and opportunities.

Structure of Issues and Opportunities

Let's begin with the areas of issues and opportunities. Figure 8.1 gives a list of these. It is not comprehensive, just a starting point. You will add that are specific to your organization, industry, country of operation, and other factors.

Note that you should employ this as a starting point. However, we have found that this list is often complete.

Now, if you take an area or topic from the list, you can search for issues and opportunities. However, it is useful to have additional structure here too. Figure 8.2 provides a short list of what to look for.

Obviously, not all questions are relevant. However, this is a complete list of what can be done with something.

- *Process issues and opportunities.* These pertain to the work and normally would not be in a strategic plan restricted to IT.
- *Multiprocess issues and opportunities.* Many of the challenges faced by IT and upper management relate to cross department processes — which are becoming more of the rule than the exception.
- *Application system issues and opportunities.* There are examples of problems with both in-house developed software and software packages.
- *IT vendor issues and opportunities.* This category reflects the fact that in many organizations there is substantial outsourcing of IT work.
- *Architecture and infrastructure issues and opportunities.* This category covers the hardware, system software, and network as well as supporting components.
- *IT methods and tools issues and opportunities.* These pertain to systems analysis, design, development, operations, maintenance, enhancement, end user support, and other activities across IT.
- *IT staffing and organization issues and opportunities.* This includes both the staff and their skills as well as the organization and structure of IT.
- *IT-business department issues and opportunities.* This area applies to the many interfaces between IT and business units.
- *IT-management issues and opportunities.* This area includes both internal IT management and relations with upper management.
- *Project and project management issues and opportunities.* This encompasses both the work in projects and the project management process.

Figure 8.1 Areas of Potential Issues and Opportunities.

- Option 1: *Repair.* What repairs are needed to make it run as originally planned?
- Option 2: *Prevention.* What actions are needed to prevent future problems?
- Option 3: *Management.* What can be done to manage it better?
- Option 4: *Measurement.* What can be done to measure it?
- Option 5: *Enhancements.* What additional capabilities could be added?
- Option 6: *Replacement.* Should the item be replaced?
- Option 7: *New.* Should new technology, facilities, and so forth be added?
- Option 8: *Elimination.* Should it be eliminated?

Figure 8.2 Questions to Ask in Search of Issues and Opportunities.

Let's take two different examples to see how the above list can be employed. A large brokerage firm requires access to quotations for securities and other instruments. For years the company relied on an internal system. However, it was slow and downtimes were long. Brokers and other employees were forced to use the Internet. In fact, some switched entirely to the Internet. The IT group had proposed a major rewrite of the software that would require a lot of money and time. Moreover, it would divert resources from other work. Drop the first, fifth, and sixth option. To prevent future problems would require a stable, steady access to the markets (the second option). Management was having a difficult time directing the brokers in terms of what access to use (the third option). Measurement of the problem was subjective — just a lot of complaining and excuses from brokers to managers and clients (the fourth option). Elimination was the winner and a Quick Win.

This example reveals several things. First, while it is true that Quick Wins and other actions could be uncovered without the strategic planning effort, there is substantial inertia and a resistance to move from the status quo. The planning effort can serve as a trigger to take advantage of opportunities. Second, the example shows that you can implement Quick Wins during the planning effort for which implementation can be done long before the completion of the plan.

The second example is to deal with network problems in capacity and response time. Let's consider each option:

- Option 1. Network repair had been going on for years. More repairs would not seem to have much appeal. A more drastic option is needed.
- Option 2. Some problems that have recurred could have work done to prevent their reoccurrence — a short-term action.
- Option 3. The management of the network needs more attention — a Quick Win.
- Option 4. The measurement of the extent of the problem had not been done systematically. Measurements could be a Quick Win action item.
- Option 5. Substantial enhancements constitute a project action item for the plan.
- Option 6. Components can be replaced following option 5, but wholesale replacement is infeasible.

- Option 7. Total replacement with a new network is probably infeasible in terms of business impact and cost.
- Option 8. While the network cannot be eliminated, the support and maintenance could be outsourced.

From this example you can see that one area can generate a number of potential action items. These would probably not have been considered without the planning effort. Instead, the firm would likely have just continued maintenance and repair.

Tips on Defining Issues and Opportunities with Collaboration

In the following sections, specific issues and opportunities are provided as examples to get you started. Space does not permit a more complete collection. To be consistent the wording is that for issues. However, as we have seen, you can easily turn these into opportunities. For each issue the following items are discussed:

- Cause — how the issue arises.
- Impact — the effects of the issue on IT and the work.
- Detection — tips on how to detect the issue.
- Actions/prevention — these include potential Quick Wins to address the issue.

Note that you should employ this as a starting point. However, we have found that this list is often complete.

In developing the issues and opportunities, experience has shown that it is more time consuming if you just ask for these. It is sometimes better to provide a checklist. For this you can begin with the 60 issues in the following sections.

Attention needs to be given to the wording of issues and opportunities. Below you have the wording of the issue. Let's take an example.

> The employees in the business unit seem to work in isolation and do not share information.

That seems fine. However, it does not explain the impact. Thus, we would add this to the end to get:

> The employees in the business unit seem to work in isolation and do not share information so that business work is inconsistent and inefficient.

Now let's turn the issue into an opportunity. The result is:

> There are opportunities for business staff to share their knowledge and experience.

But, wait. You want to add the benefit of this opportunity. Doing this, you obtain:

> There are opportunities for business staff to share their knowledge and experience so that work performance is improved.

In general,

- For issues — issue followed by impact.
- For opportunities — opportunity followed by benefit.

A key benefit in developing these with collaboration is that you raise awareness of the issue or opportunity and raise desires to have them addressed. For issues you also can get a sense of importance and urgency.

Process Issues and Opportunities

These issues are important not only because of the fact that the strategic plan includes processes, but also because you have to get process change to realize the benefits of the IT work and investment. Figure 8.3 gives some examples of process issues and opportunities. Note that the one sentence attributes under each represents tips and not intended to be a complete discussion.

Multiprocess Issues and Opportunities

Increasingly, processes integrate and heavily depend on each other. This gives importance to identifying issues and opportunities that involve multiple processes. Figure 8.4 provides some examples.

Application System Issues and Opportunities

Included here are both systems and information issues and opportunities. Figure 8.5 gives some examples.

IT Vendor Issues and Opportunities

Outsourcing and the use of consultants has greatly expanded over the past years. This has yielded benefits, but also raised issues. Some of these are given in Figure 8.6.

- The employees in the business unit seem to work in isolation and do not share information.

  Cause — This may be due to the nature of the work, but often it is just habit.

  Impact — Productivity suffers and the potential benefit of IT solutions is less.

  Detection — Observe the work.

  Actions/Prevention — Involve many users in the project work. Keep in closer touch with department processes.

- The performance of the business process is deteriorating.

  Cause — This can be due to the fact that the basic process has not been changed due to new systems or changes in the mix of work.

  Impact — Productivity declines. Morale in departments may, as well.

  Detection — Consider measurements of the process as well as contacts with users to find out what has changed over the past year.

  Actions/Prevention — Conduct an assessment of the process and work. Try to identify some Quick Wins to eliminate exceptions.

- There is a resistance of some department staff to making changes in their work.

  Cause — The supervisors may not want to confront the employees and do not interfere since they are still completing some work.

  Impact — The capabilities of the system are not being exploited. The benefits are not achieved since there was less than adequate change.

  Detection — Suggest possible small changes during the planning work and test their reactions.

  Actions/Prevention — Plan ahead for resistance and even explain to them that this is normal. This will indicate that you are prepared to deal with it, should it arise.

- The process involves too many exceptions. There is an over dependence on King and Queen Bees.

  Cause — The process was not changed sufficiently after the system was installed.

  Impact — The process is not efficient. IT could get blamed for the lack of benefits.

  Detection — Same as some of other issues. Observe the work. Try to get trained in doing some of the work.

  Actions/Prevention — Conduct a review of the business process and highlight the problems and their impacts. Isolate the exceptions from standard, frequent work.

- There is substantial turnover in some business units.

  Cause — This could be due to the work environment, wages, and other factors.

  Impact — New employees are often not adequately trained in the process and system. They fall under the influence of the King and Queen Bees.

Figure 8.3 Examples of Process Issues and Opportunities.

Detection — Visit the department now and then informally.

Actions/Prevention — You want to talk to the employees regarding the process and their work — not about the system. Then, you can determine what can be done. In one planning effort, we initiated more process training and motivation improved. Turnover dropped. This is more than paid for the planning effort.

- The business employees do not seem to have a good understanding of the systems they use.

Cause — This can be due to employee turnover, lack of training in the process, and lax line management.

Impact — The benefits of the system are not fully realized. Unnecessary shadow systems maybe created.

Detection — Observe how employees use the system to do their work.

Actions/Prevention — One of the best actions is to gather tips through group meetings with employees on how to use the system. Then, you can initiate training in the business process that includes both the system and the guidelines on the process.

Figure 8.3 (*Continued*)

- There is a lack of coordination across departments for a process.

Cause — One cause is lack of management direction. Another reason may be politics among departments.

Impact — Redundant effort results in loss of effectiveness.

Detection — Observe how the work moves between departments by following some transactions through the process.

Actions/Prevention — Treat the interface between departments as a separate project — giving it more attention. Get down to the details of the work to avoid the politics. The truth is in the details.

- The transfer of information from one department to another is awkward, time-consuming, and ineffective.

Cause — No formal analysis or procedures were put in place. The handoff is ad hoc.

Impact — Loss of productivity and decline in performance.

Detection — Same as that for the previous issues.

Actions/Prevention — Same as that for the previous issue.

- There are political issues between different department managers.

Cause — This is probably deeply rooted and cannot easily be changed.

Impact — The problems carry over to their employees and their work.

Figure 8.4 Examples of Multiprocess Issues and Opportunities.

Detection — Observe how the managers interact with each other.

Actions/Prevention — Appeal to their self-interest and focus attention on detailed work. This may result in them putting aside their politics for awhile.

- Customer service and overall performance suffer because the work has to be handled by several departments.

  Cause — You probably have experienced this when you contact a firm. The organization was not set up for efficiency. There are only single department performance measures.

  Impact — Less customer satisfaction; higher cost of providing service.

  Detection — Follow some exception transactions through the process.

  Actions/Prevention — Focus on these transactions and take a customer-centric view.

- There are incompatible and/or redundant shadow systems across departments.

  Cause — This naturally occurs since departments improvised on their own at different times.

  Impact — Loss of effectiveness and efficiency.

  Detection — This takes a more detailed look at how work is done in each department.

  Actions/Prevention — Don't question the reason for the shadow systems. Try to understand to see if they can be standardized or replaced.

- It is difficult to coordinate process change across departments.

  Cause — Process change often fails if it progresses separately in different departments.

  Impact — The overall benefits of an integrated system and process are weakened.

  Detection — Look at how the process change was carried out.

  Actions/Prevention — Concentrate on cross department work.

Figure 8.4 (*Continued*)

- Several of the systems are very old, legacy systems that require a lot of handholding and support.

  Cause — Insufficient resources for modernization. Lack of priority from management.

  Impact — Morale of both IT and business staff can suffer. Users create more workarounds and shadow systems.

  Detection — Examine the work requests for the older systems. If there is little activity, this could mean that the business unit has given up.

  Actions/Prevention — Wholesale replacement is usually not practical. Instead, reduce the risk by having the IT staff share more knowledge. Consider what can be done outside of, but interfacing to the system.

Figure 8.5 Examples of Application Systems Issues and Opportunities.

- The application system does not support enough of the work in the business unit.

  Cause — The requirement gathering failed to handle a substantial part of the processes. Or, the application that was selected never was intended to cover all of the process.

  Impact — Business units must improvise to handle the missing pieces — through shadow systems.

  Detection — Observe the work in the process.

  Actions/Prevention — Start a project with the goal of potentially expanding the system as well as modifying the business process.

- The application systems do not interface or integrate well with each other.

  Cause — Each application was implemented separately.

  Impact — The suite of applications requires more support.

  Detection — Look at how systems interface with each other.

  Actions/Prevention — Focus on the interfaces as a separate effort instead of each system separately.

- Too much effort is expended on maintenance and minor enhancements.

  Cause — There is often more individual freedom and less pressure doing this work versus project work.

  Impact — Resources are frittered away on work of marginal value.

  Detection — Track what the IT staff spend their time on.

  Actions/Prevention — Construct a gateway to more carefully review this work. Treat the work as projects to increase accountability.

- Some new software packages were not fully installed.

  Cause — Resources could have run out as could have energy.

  Impact — The benefits originally estimated from the package are not realized.

  Detection — Determine how the system is being used.

  Actions/Prevention — Update the requirements based on what is used and then use this to see whether process change and/or additional installation is the course of action to take.

- The application system has very limited flexibility in meeting diverse business needs.

  Cause — The system was designed for one set of needs. The needs change.

  Impact — The business units improvise solutions to get around the limitations.

  Detection — Determine how the business is using the application.

  Actions/Prevention — Concentrate on the common work and not exceptions. Determine what can be done to deal with this part of the process.

Figure 8.5 (*Continued*)

- Vendor staff do not share information with IT employees.

  Cause — Unless there is a mandate that information be shared, it often will not occur.

  Impact — The organization has a continued dependence on the vendor.

  Detection — Look at how work is turned over to internal staff. What was conveyed on how the work was performed?

  Actions/Prevention — Encourage communications with the vendor staff doing the work. Consider using joint tasking.

- Vendors are not very responsive in resolving problems.

  Cause — This probably started with too much trust on the part of the company.

  Impact — The vendor feels that they are more in control. Problems remain unaddressed affecting the schedule and cost.

  Detection — Give the vendor a few issues and really track them in detail.

  Actions/Prevention — Make a list of issues and go over the status of these with the vendor. Then implement meetings wherein the only subject is that of issues — not progress or status.

- There is miscommunication between vendor management and their staff.

  Cause — This is often due to the intermediaries in the vendor organization between the company and the vendor staff doing the work.

  Impact — The vendor staff are doing the work wrong. Experience shows that this issue is a major cause of failure of outsourced work.

  Detection — Try providing some information to the intermediary and see what happens.

  Actions/Prevention — Assume that vendor intermediaries will screw up. Insist that there be direct communications with vendor employees doing the actual work.

- There is substantial vendor staff turnover.

  Cause — Internal vendor issues.

  Impact — Turnover slows the work down. Inadequate and incomplete turnover creates errors.

  Detection — Establish contact between your staff and those of the vendor. These can be informal and can provide a lot of early information about changes in the vendor organization.

  Actions/Prevention — Insist on regular contact with the technical staff of the vendor.

- It is difficult to obtain the true status of vendor work.

  Cause — The vendor manager does not want to be the carrier of bad news. So, it is delayed.

  Impact — Problems remain hidden.

Figure 8.6 Examples of Vendor Issues and Opportunities.

Detection — Don't ask about status. Focus instead on issues and questions. This will reveal more about the work.

Actions/Prevention — Active issue tracking along with regular, reviewable milestones will help.

• The vendor has competing priorities related to work for their staff.

Cause — They want to get more work out of the same people and so over commit.

Impact — Your work suffers.

Detection — See how the vendor performs in dealing with issues and deliverable items.

Actions/Prevention — Implement more informal contacts with the vendor. Have meetings on issues. The more contact there is, the more they will listen to you. Quick clients are often given a lower priority. "The squeaky wheel gets the attention."

Figure 8.6 (*Continued*)

Architecture and Infrastructure Issues and Opportunities

There are, almost, unlimited number of issues and opportunities here. So, in Figure 8.7 we direct attention to some of the common ones we have seen.

IT Methods and Tools Issues and Opportunities

IT methods and tools include those in all areas: operations, development, project management, and so forth. Some examples are provided in Figure 8.8.

IT Staffing and Organization Issues and Opportunities

Listed in Figure 8.9 are some of the commonly encountered issues and opportunities that pertain to IT staffing and organization.

- IT lacks expertise with new technologies such as those for collaboration and web 2.0.

  Cause — New technologies emerge. People are so busy with the current work that they cannot spend time on the new.

  Impact — It takes time to gain expertise. As a result, more outside help is sought. Morale internally drops.

  Detection — Look at the degree of awareness and knowledge of new technologies among IT management.

  Actions/Prevention — Proactively gather information on new technologies with the criterion being business application.

- There are performance and stability problems with the hardware/network vendor.

  Cause — Multiple reasons.

  Impact — The business suffers along with IT credibility.

  Detection — Contact almost daily performance reviews.

  Actions/Prevention — Service-level agreements are useful as long as they are accompanied by active issues management.

- There is a shortage of staff to address the problems and upgrades to the technology.

  Cause — The IT staff are spread too thin.

  Impact — Lack of upgrades causes decline in service.

  Detection — Create and track the outstanding issues.

  Actions/Prevention — This type of work should be prioritized with other work.

- There is a lack of integration of the hardware and network components.

  Cause — Products and services came from a range of different vendors.

  Impact — More staff is devoted to building and maintaining interfaces.

  Detection — Track the open issues related to these components.

  Actions/Prevention — Similar to that for the previous issues,

- We are too busy to assess, select, or install new technology.

  Cause — Everyday work is consuming resources.

  Impact — Missed opportunities. IT is put in a reactive mode as business units discover the technology first.

  Detection — There are surprises presented by business units.

  Actions/Prevention — Assign technology assessment as a background task to several staff members.

- We lack in-depth knowledge of the technology and have to rely on vendors.

  Cause — Shortage of IT staff.

  Impact — Increased dependence on the vendor.

  Detection — Determine the nature and frequency of vendor contacts.

  Actions/Prevention — Identify the most important areas and assign internal staff to work more closely with the vendor.

Figure 8.7 Examples of Architecture/Infrastructure Issues and Opportunities.

- There is an over dependence on consultants for some tools.

  Cause — Internal training and takeover were not given a priority.

  Impact — Higher costs.

  Detection — Consider the amount of work that the vendor is doing along with the costs.

  Actions/Prevention — Review the value of the tools and build a plan to establish internal expertise.

- There are gaps in either methods or tools.

  Cause — This is almost always the case given the wide range of IT activities.

  Impact — IT staff have to create workarounds that may not be consistent.

  Detection — Have IT staff share lessons learned in how they do their work.

  Actions/Prevention — Create a table that gives the methods, tools, guidelines, expert, and management expectations for each area of methods and tools.

- There is a lack of standard methods in use.

  Cause — Methods were adopted on a case-by-case basis.

  Impact — Lack of consistency in work.

  Detection — Take several projects and see how the methods are used.

  Actions/Prevention — Have the IT staff share experiences in using methods to identify good standard procedures.

- Some methods do not have the right tools and vice versa.

  Cause — This is often the case because of the attention to either the method or tool, but not both.

  Impact — The gaps will be filled on an ad hoc basis.

  Detection — Determine what guidelines exist for these.

  Actions/Prevention — Create a table that gives the methods, tools, guidelines, expert, and management expectations for each area of methods and tools.

- There is an overreliance on a few key staff for tool expertise.

  Cause — This is often the case due to time pressures and staff limitations.

  Impact — These individuals can experience a large backlog of work.

  Detection — Determine how these key staff members spend their time.

  Actions/Prevention — Have these staff members share more of their knowledge in lessons learned meetings.

- There is mixture of old and new tools and methods in use.

  Cause — Individual methods and tools were acquired from different sources at different times.

  Impact — Loss of efficiency and effectiveness.

  Detection — Determine what guidelines exist for these.

  Actions/Prevention — Create a table that gives the methods, tools, guidelines, expert, and management expectations for each area of methods and tools.

Figure 8.8 Examples of IT Methods and Tools Issues and Opportunities.

- The IT staff tend to work alone. There is a lack of teamwork.

  Cause — This is due to the nature of the work, the layout of facilities that isolate people in cubicles, and pressure to do the work.

  Impact — Information and knowledge is in silos.

  Detection — Observe the interaction of the employees.

  Actions/Prevention — Implement meetings on lessons learned to share knowledge. Implement joint tasks on projects.

- The workload cannot be spread evenly around since much of the work requires specialized knowledge.

  Cause — There is an emphasis on efficiency rather than on cumulative improvement.

  Impact — Some people have way too much to do. Others have much less.

  Detection — Look at the work levels assigned to staff.

  Actions/Prevention — Implement meetings on lessons learned to share knowledge. Implement joint tasks on projects.

- There is a lack of awareness of best practices.

  Cause — Management does not give importance to best practices.

  Impact — Lack of ability to measure the techniques in the work.

  Detection — See what methods and techniques the staff uses.

  Actions/Prevention — Gather information on best practices.

- New IT staff are not well assimilated into the organization.

  Cause — There is no organized approach for handling new employees.

  Impact — New employees may feel isolated. It will take them longer to get up to speed.

  Detection — Observe how the last two employees were handled.

  Actions/Prevention — Implement shared tasks for new employees. Have them participate in lessons-learned meetings.

- The established practices and procedures are not followed.

  Cause — The procedures may be too bureaucratic. There is no enforcement.

  Impact — The procedures and practices are largely ignored.

  Detection — See how a sample of work is performed.

  Actions/Prevention — Review the practices and procedures, and develop guidelines and measurements for effective use.

- There is a lack of work reviews.

  Cause — There is too much to do and people feel that there is no time for reviews.

  Impact — Work may have to redone.

  Detection — See how the last few milestones were addressed.

  Actions/Prevention — Focus reviews on the work with issues and risk.

Figure 8.9 Examples of IT Staffing/Organization Issues and Opportunities.

IT-Business Department Issues and Opportunities

Since you are creating a strategic plan that includes processes, it is important to identify those issues and opportunities for the relationship and interface between IT and the business units and departments. Some examples to get you started appear in Figure 8.10.

IT-Management Issues and Opportunities

This is a category that is often ignored in planning. Maybe, this is because of how it reflects on IT management. Nevertheless, if you are ever going to fix a problem, you have to recognize it first. Examples appear in Figure 8.11.

Project and Project Management Issues and Opportunities

In previous books we cited over 150 issues and opportunities related to IT projects (see for example, Lientz and Larssen, 2006 and Lientz and Rea, 2003).[1] Some examples are provided here in Figure 8.12.

Examples

In one planning effort, we became overwhelmed with too many issues that required attention and that had a major business impact. Using the planning method, here, we were able to place the planning work on hold for three months. During this time the entire focus was on Quick Wins. However, we related the Quick Wins to data collection for the planning — thereby giving political assistance to the planning work.

---

[1] Lientz, B.P. and L. Larssen, *Risk Management for IT Projects: How to Deal with over 150 Issues and Risks*, Elsevier, 2006; Lientz, B.P. and K.P. Rea, *Breakthrough IT Change Management: How to Get Enduring Change Results*, Elsevier, 2003.

- Business units provide neither sufficient nor accurate information in systems requests.

  Cause — They do not assume ownership of the work.

  Impact — It takes longer for IT to respond to the requests.

  Detection — Determine the differences between the request and actual analysis for the last few requests.

  Actions/Prevention — Implement a request approach that has the business unit specify their role, how benefits will be determined, and what will happen if the work is either deferred or not done.

- There is a lack of communications with departments during projects.

  Cause — Once the technical work begins, the contact with users drops off. It resumes as the project reaches completion.

  Impact — New requirements can surface leading to scope creep. Resistance to change may intensify.

  Detection — What degree of contact occurred in the last two projects?

  Actions/Prevention — Adopt an approach in which users continue to participate in the work through Quick Wins, procedures, testing, and training.

- User requests are handled in mostly political ways.

  Cause — This could have been developed as a pattern over time.

  Impact — Business unit employees and IT staff see everything as political and get turned off.

  Detection — Look at the distribution of labor among requests and business units.

  Actions/Prevention — Implement a more formal review process of requests that focuses on true, demonstrable business need.

- A number of valuable user requests have remained untouched for too long.

  Cause — Too much work to do in too little time.

  Impact — Business units turn to solutions from others or other solutions.

  Detection — Visit the departments to see what was done.

  Actions/Prevention — Review these to kill them off. Try to eliminate this backlog as new higher priority work will keep these requests in the backlog.

- There is no assessment of the value of IT to business units.

  Cause — IT may assume that the value is well understood.

  Impact — Distrust builds between business managers and IT.

  Detection — Review recent communications with management.

  Actions/Prevention — Implement a regular assessment of IT alignment as presented in Chapter 7.

- Work with some business departments seems very tactical and ad hoc.

  Cause — IT tends to be in a reactive mode.

  Impact — The business process does not advance strategically.

  Detection — Review the most recent work.

  Actions/Prevention — Implement the process planning approach in Chapter 7.

Figure 8.10 Examples of IT-Business Department Issues and Opportunities.

- It appears that the same mistakes are made again and again.

  Cause — Each project and piece of work is treated as new and separately.

  Impact — These is no improvement in skills. The same mistakes are committed repeatedly.

  Detection — Look at the most recent errors and surprises. Shouldn't these have been predicted?

  Actions/Prevention — Focus on gathering and organizing lessons learned on a regular basis. Insist that all work planning reflect past experience.

- Projects and work do not receive consistent management attention.

  Cause — Management often focuses on the larger projects and work.

  Impact — The work and projects with issues and risk do not receive the necessary attention.

  Detection — See how issues management is performed.

  Actions/Prevention — Focus management attention on the work with issues, regardless of size.

- There are often surprises in requests from upper management.

  Cause — This often reflects a lack of communications with management.

  Impact — Surprises tend to disrupt work — reducing productivity.

  Detection — What are the nature and extent of management communications?

  Actions/Prevention — Set up more informal contacts with multiple managers.

- IT managers spend too much time with upper management.

  Cause — This is the opposite of the previous issue. The IT manager want to promote his or her self too much.

  Impact — The management of IT activities receives less attention or delegated. Issues then pile up unresolved.

  Detection — Same as that of the preceding issue.

  Actions/Prevention — Present the IT manager with more issues so that they become more involved.

- IT supervisors tend to work directly with business users without informing IT management.

  Cause — Over time it is natural for contacts to become firmer.

  Impact — The supervisors may have marginal work performed because they want to please their business unit friends.

  Detection — Examine at a given time what work is being performed in detail.

  Actions/Prevention — Establish a review and justification process that goes beyond the supervisor.

- IT supervisors are too involved in doing programing and other work.

  Cause — Many supervisors used to perform technical work. People tend to gravitate to work that they are familiar with.

  Impact — Supervisory activities such as oversight and business unit contact suffer.

  Detection — Determine what the supervisor is working on and where they spend their time.

  Actions/Prevention — Get them to be out with business departments more.

Figure 8.11 Examples of IT Management Issues and Opportunities.

- It is difficult to share resources among projects.

  Cause — Project leaders tend to hold on to resources. There is a lack of management priority for sharing.
  Impact — Opportunities for productivity gains are lost.
  Detection — Look at the teams of the projects to see how much they have in common.
  Actions/Prevention — Insist on resource sharing and joint tasks.

- There is too much expansion of project scope or scope creep.

  Cause — Changes to requirements are accepted without adequate review. IT maybe politically weak.
  Impact — The project is delayed.
  Detection — Look for new and unplanned work in the project.
  Actions/Prevention — Get users involved in the project more and implement Quick Wins. This will help keep requirements stable.

- Projects are completed, but there is no real measurement of results.

  Cause — The project ends with the turnover of a system. Process change is not within the project scope so it does not occur.
  Impact — IT loses credibility and resources have been wasted.
  Detection — What does the project scope include in terms of end user participation and tasks?
  Actions/Prevention — Beyond including process change in the scope, initiate process change before the system is implemented.

- There is no method for dealing with small projects.

  Cause — This is the curse of many formal project management methodologies. They maybe great for big projects, but small projects are not included so that they are managed less effectively.
  Impact — Small projects can yield big problems and issues.
  Detection — See how small projects are tracked.
  Actions/Prevention — Adopt methods that are scalable down to smaller projects. Give more management attention to small projects.

- Projects take too long to complete.

  Cause — Many classic reasons here.
  Impact — Loss of benefits; decline in morale.
  Detection — Track open issues and deal with them. These are predecessors to slippage in cost or scheduled.
  Actions/Prevention — Manage the issues in the project. The handling of the issues represents an early warning of project failure and problems.

- There is a lack of user ownership of project results.

  Cause — Users often want IT to own the project so that they are not accountable for the benefits.
  Impact — There are often no benefits. IT and the business unit exchange accusations.
  Detection — Look at the extent of user participation.
  Actions/Prevention — Get users involved in the project at the start and keep them involved in Quick Hits, data conversion, testing, training, and procedures. Participation and involvement lead to commitment.

Figure 8.12 Examples of Project/Project Management Issues and Opportunities.

You might see this as negative since it appeared to delay the planning effort. Such was not the case. The Quick Wins were more than paid for the planning work. Also, the number of issues and opportunities in the plan were reduced so that the scope of the plan was reduced. The results were: (1) greater support for the plan and the required resources for implementation and (2) a reduced time horizon given the reduced range of issues and opportunities.

One thing to learn from this example is when you are doing strategic planning that involves business processes, you are likely to uncover some really juicy opportunities. Why? Because no one looked at it this way — from a different perspective. IT staff often just want the requirements and don't examine the whole process. The business employees are tied up in everyday work.

Lessons Learned

One approach is to develop a candidate list of issues and opportunities. Don't divide this into categories. That will look too contrived. Have managers and employees rank these on two criteria: urgency and impact. The urgency is the need to solve the problem. The impact is the effect if the issue is not solved or the opportunity is missed.

Concentrate now on the issues and opportunities that have medium to high urgency, regardless of importance. To this add the issues and opportunities that have high importance. Organize these into categories.

Write them up and include the impacts and urgency. Submit these for review. As you are getting these reviewed, start to build the following tables.

- *Issues and opportunities versus business processes*. This table can help flesh out which issues and opportunities are important relative to the importance of the business process to the business.

Include in each entry a rating of the urgency and importance relative to the corresponding process.

- *Issues and opportunities versus IT operations.* This table reveals the effect on IT work. As with the preceding table, include both the urgency and impact.
- *Issues and opportunities versus IT projects.* Here, the effect of issues on projects is given along with potential project improvements through the opportunities.
- *Issues and opportunities versus architecture and infrastructure.* The impact of the issue or the benefit of the opportunity on elements of the infrastructure is the subject of this table.

Guess what? You are starting to build the strategic plan.

You can use the table related to the business processes to create the following:

- *Business issues versus issues and opportunities.* This table shows how an issue or opportunity contributes to a business issue.
- *Business units/department versus issues and opportunities.* This useful table reveals the relevance of the issues and opportunities to specific business departments through the processes in which they are involved.
- *Business initiatives versus issues and opportunities.* Issues and opportunities can impact either the attainment of a business initiative or reduce results.

Politics

When you are gathering data on a business process, you want to uncover problems so that people will see the need for change as well as the value of the strategic planning. Tips were provided for this in Chapter 5. After this initial data collection, it is often best politically to emphasize the positive. Thus, you would center attention on the opportunity that addresses the issue. When you get to the point of presenting the strategic plan, you will return to issues to show the problems that require attention. The opportunities then are realized in the action items of the strategic plan.

What to Do Next

Make a list of the issues and opportunities that were identified in the last strategic IT plan. Answer the following questions.

- Is there any effort to determine either urgency or impact?
- Could any of these been addressed by Quick Wins and not included in the plan?
- Were the issues and opportunities restricted to IT activities?
- How many of the issues and opportunities were addressed by Quick Wins?
- How many were not addressed at all? What were the reasons?
- Were the issues and opportunities rated in terms of the importance of the business processes to which they apply?

Summary

In many IT planning efforts, there is much attention early on in gathering up issues and opportunities. One problem that occurs is that they are rated in terms of urgency and impact. They appear to all have the same rating. However, as we have seen, urgency and impact are in the eyes of the beholder. That is, there is a difference in perspective with each of the following views:

- The people doing the work
- IT managers and staff
- The overall business

What is important or urgent to one person may not be to another. Through a collaborative effort you can gain support and consensus on the critical issues and opportunities.

There is another agenda. Because this is a strategic plan that includes business processes, you can consider some of the issues and opportunities as candidates for Quick Wins. If you can fix something and deliver benefit without disrupting the planning, experience shows that you really gain support for the planning. See Chapter 14 for tips on implementing Quick Wins.

Chapter 9

Define Objectives and Constraints

Introduction

IT *objectives* are directional goals that are: (1) broad in scope; (2) directional to provide focus; and (3) relatively timeless. *Constraints* are factors that: (1) cannot be changed and (2) prevent the immediate attainment of the objectives. By understanding the constraints, managers can better understand the challenges of attaining the objectives. The objectives would support progress toward achieving an IT vision, should that be define. The action items and strategies in the next chapter support the achievement of the objectives. As such, they are the first steps in transforming a vision of IT into action. A mission or vision statement for IT can be generated from the IT objectives, if needed.

Our approach in this and the next chapter is to define how to build these planning factors. In both chapters the middle of the chapter gives examples of the planning factors along with comments. From experience we have found that it is easier to start with some of these and then adapt them to your organization.

There are several possible approaches to developing these. One is a group approach. Here several facilitated sessions are held with IT managers, staff, business managers, and employees. This typically is best suited for larger organizations. Here, it is useful to recall the discussion of steering committees in Chapter 3.

The other approach is to circulate potential lists of objectives, etc. and have people react and respond individually. Then you collect their comments and make the appropriate changes. After the changes have been completed, you can then hold a meeting to get any final input. This is lower profile and, we have found, suitable for organizations of any size. You can still have a meeting to finalize the items.

Structure of Objectives and Constraints

Many people just start writing down objectives and constraints. The problem with this is that they are not likely to be complete. Also, they may not be consistent with each other. That is why, in this chapter, we have organized both objectives and constraints into categories. The categories for objectives are presented in Figure 9.1.

- General IT objectives
- IT staffing objectives — pertains to both staffing and organization.
- General business process objectives — needs to be included since this is both an IT and strategic process plan.
- Application systems and information objectives — some separate information from systems, but to business employees they are linked.
- Architecture and infrastructure objectives — this is most frequently cited type of objective. These need to be in common English.
- Project objectives — the goals of projects and the project management process.

Figure 9.1 Categories of Objectives.

For constraints, we grouped these into fewer categories. Here are the four.

- Constraints on resources.
- Constraints due to the business and organization.
- Constraints due to culture and politics.
- Constraints due to systems and technology.

Of course, you are not restricted to these. The purpose of all this is to help you get started as well as to assess your current strategic IT plan.

Guidelines for Developing Objectives and Constraints

Let's start with the importance of wording of objectives and other planning factors. If they are too technical, the business managers will ignore them. They will see this as verification of a lack of alignment. If they are too fuzzy, they will be discarded. It is like Goldilocks — you want these to be just right. Wording is key.

As with issues and opportunities there are good, proven tips for defining these. Let's begin with objectives. This should be a complete sentence. Consider the following examples in Figure 9.2. These are not very useful for the following reasons: (1) they do not relate to the business; (2) as such, they are puzzling outside of IT and (3) as the comments show, they are actually negative about the current situation. In short, they fail. Look at the specific comments. We tried to make these sarcastic to show the problems and give a sense of humor.

A better approach is to state some of these in a positive way that points to improvement, rather than referencing today's problems.

> You really didn't want to use the wording of an objective to reveal that you have a problem.

This is the first part of the objective. The second part of the sentence describes the benefit to the business. If we take this approach, let's see if we can fix the above list (see Figure 9.3). Don't these sound better? Yes, they have to be general, but they should be understandable and directly apply to the business.

- Effective and efficient customer-based operations and services.

  o This implies that the current level of service is lacking.
  o No benefit is specified, nor is the direction of how to get there.

- Performance, accountability, and value.

  o Sounds good at first glance, but what is going on now? To what does it apply?
  o What is value?
  o Who is accountable?
  o This is really fuzzy.

- Privacy, security, and integrity.

  o Sounds, but what does this mean about today's systems?
  o These are very general terms.
  o Nothing is said about affordability.

- Productive employees.

  o Does this means that they are not very productive now?
  o Remember this is a goal or objective. Nothing is said about improvement.

- Agile management and infrastructure.

  o Ah, agility — a recent buzzword.
  o If something is too agile, it can change too often and nothing gets done.
  o Infrastructure can be scalable and to a degree flexible, but agile — we do not think so.

- Shared solutions, standards and flexible, open boundaries.

  o It must be that today there are limited standards, boundaries are firm, and nothing is shared.
  o What do these words mean to a business manager? Nothing, unless they are really into IT.
  o Flexible boundaries imply something of a rubber band approach to systems.

- Maturation and modernization of solutions.

  o This must mean that what is in IT now is less mature and outdated, eh?
  o Mature solutions tend not to be flexible due to maturity.

- Innovation and Transformation.

  o Everyone is for innovation. However, having it as a long-term objective implies that there will be less innovation until then.
  o These two things should either be action items or strategies. You should already be innovation and aiding in transforming the business.

Figure 9.2 Examples of Fuzzy Objectives.

- Effective and efficient customer-based operations and services.
  Support the delivery of full functioned, effective, and efficient services that improve customer service levels and satisfaction.
- Performance, accountability, and value.
  Continue to improve IT performance so as to add value of IT to business processes.
- Privacy, security, and integrity.
  Ensure, within constraints of funding and resources, the privacy and security of all information and systems.
- Productive employees.
  IT will continue to measure and work to improve productivity of both IT and business employees so as to affect continuous improvement through capitalizing on lessons learned and experience.
- Agile management and infrastructure.   -
  All parts of IT and its management will strive to respond to new, emerging, and existing business needs in a cost-effective way.
- Shared solutions, standards and flexible, open boundaries.
  IT will continue and expand efforts to reuse, share, and implement systems and solutions that respond to current and emerging business requirements.
- Maturation and modernization of solutions.
  IT will continue to improve its systems and technology solutions to increase business value by employing established, proven, and modern methods, tools, and systems.
- Innovation and Transformation.
  IT will continue to pursue innovative solutions that improve or transform business processes to add tangible business value.

Figure 9.3 Repaired Objectives.

Note that many objectives in strategic plans are not totally complete since they lack a phrase that links them to the business or IT. However, you can see that this is not that hard to do. Moreover, it really adds value and effect of the objectives. Moreover, you again demonstrate alignment to the business.

Let's now turn to constraints. Figure 9.4 gives a list of commonly stated constraints in strategic IT plans. As with objectives, we add some comments.

As with objectives, let's see if we can fix these in Figure 9.5.

- Limited funding.
  - o This is a permanent problem.
  - o This does not give the impact of the lack of money.
- Available resources.
  - o There will never be enough.
  - o What will suffer if there are no more resources?
- Legacy, old systems.
  - o Nothing is said about the impact.
  - o Almost everyone has these. The issue is whether some of these are business critical.
  - o Sometimes, old is better than new.

Figure 9.4 Some Commonly Encountered Constraints.

- Limited funding.
    As with the business, limited funding will restrict the number of new IT initiatives projects that can be started.
- Available resources.
    Restrictions on available resources will cause IT to focus on business critical functions and support.
- Legacy, old systems.
    Maintaining and supporting legacy systems restricts the resources and attention that can be devoted to new work as well as preventing business improvements to work.

Figure 9.5 Repaired Constraints.

General IT Objectives

There are some basic guidelines for objectives that cover all of IT. These include:

- The objectives should be worded in business terms.
- The number should be restricted to three or four.
- The objectives listed in the categories in the following sections can either be one of these or represent a subobjective.
- Each objective should start with an action verb for the first phase; the second part of the wording would give the business benefit.

Consider objectives in the areas of Figure 9.6.

- Customer.
  - o Emphasis on customer service.
  - o Support a range of services.
  - o Track and analyze customer activity.
  - o Enhance the customer experience.
- Processes.
  - o This is the place to emphasize the alignment of IT to the business.
  - o Improve and measure process performance in terms of effectiveness and efficiency.
  - o Provide flexibility for new types of work in new locations.
  - o Support cumulative improvement of processes.
- Employees.
  - o Improve worker productivity.
  - o Reduce clerical and routine work.
  - o Help to reduce turnover.
  - o Support collaboration among employees to improve work quality.
- IT itself.
  - o Reliable, secure computing environment (infrastructure).
  - o Provide applications and capabilities that meet current and future needs (applications).
  - o Effect cumulative improvement in productivity, knowledge sharing, and teamwork (staffing).
  - o Ensure that projects are focused on critical business needs and provide tangible benefits adhering to cost and schedule conditions (projects).

Figure 9.6 Areas of IT Objectives.

In the remaining part of this section, we examine a number of IT objectives and make comments on their use or how they could be changed (Figure 9.7). The intention here and with other planning elements is to provide you with a large menu of options. This will get you started earlier since you can select some of these to begin.

IT Staffing Objectives

IT staffing objectives should aim at cumulative improvement in the use and capabilities of the IT staff. As such, IT staffing objectives should include:

- Sharing of information and knowledge so as to improve skills.
- Collaborative work.

- Drive a business-intelligent IT organization and an IT-intelligent business operation.

  This is a good objective in that it points to alignment of business and IT. It also shows that IT is business-driven.

- Provide technology solutions and support services to the processes and programs of the company.

  This also shows alignment of IT to the business. However, it is restricted to technology solutions. To be flexible, you should include non-technical solutions related to change management and process improvement.

- Improve the cost and delivery of IT services.

  This is commonly seen in strategic IT plans. The problem is that it implies that the current cost and delivery of IT services falls short. Additionally, it should also include some measurement of delivery.

- Make IT a business-driven line activity, not a technology-driven activity.

  Sounds good, eh? However, it implies that IT has been technology-driven in the past and is so currently. This one has problems. Another issue is the word "line." In this objective IT could be seen as asserting itself to be a line organization. This puts it on a par with other line organizations — not good. IT should span the organization.

- Strive to maximize the productivity of customers.

  The problems here are several fold. How do you measure customer productivity? Does it matter? Also, there is no real goal here in terms of what the productivity will buy. Productivity should be replaced by capabilities that increase business from the customers.

- Provide quality service.

  This might mean that quality today is subpar. Moreover, quality should be linked to affordability and improved performance. Quality has to be traded off with value and cost.

- Minimize costs and complexity.

  This one is a common goal. However, there is no disagreement that IT is complex. If it were simple, business units could do it for themselves. In addition, complexity is not bad. If you minimize complexity, you could make the systems solutions too simple and deliver less than needed functions. As long as complexity stays in IT and is dealt with by IT, that is sufficient. With respect to minimizing costs, this sounds nice. But if you really minimize costs, then service levels are bound to be impacted. Costs should be proportionate to the value of the services provided.

- Ensure delivery of new and enhanced capabilities on time, on budget with high business satisfaction.

  This is acceptable since it associates delivery with added value constrained by time and money. The inclusion of business satisfaction validates that value has been delivered.

- Identify the forces affecting the business and those that are significant primarily to IT.

  We have problems with this one. The first is the word "identify." This is not action oriented. An objective should always reach beyond identification. The next problem is the last half of the objective. What is significant to IT? This is very fuzzy and with the integration of IT and systems into the business, very little is off limits to IT. Another problem is who would determine this. Reading this part in a negative manner, it might mean that IT wants to restrict its scope of work.

Figure 9.7 Examples of General IT Objectives.

- Identify technical challenges and develop specific solutions.

    Well, this one and the one that follows include solutions. However, management challenges cannot be easily separated by technical challenges. There is also confusion here because the technical challenge comes through the solution while the management challenge is the cause.
- Identify management challenges and develop solutions.

    Humorously, management challenges could be interpreted to mean management that is too challenging. This and the previous one should be combined to indicate that the goal is to "meet business challenges with innovative, cost-effective solutions."
- Place customer service as the highest priority.

    This goal must imply that customer service is not now the highest priority. It could also be misinterpreted to mean that good customer service should be attained without regard to costs and resources. In fact, for many organizations, good customer service is a constraint since you fail if you violate it.
- Use feedback to determine strategic direction for new services and improvement to existing services.

    The problem starts here with feedback. This must mean that there is not much today. Feedback makes IT reactive instead of being proactive. Feedback is in response to an action.
- Implement new services that increase customer value and are competitive.

    This should probably include existing services. Value includes capabilities at an affordable cost.
- Implement measurements for assessing performance and effectiveness of IT resources.

    The problem with this one is that measurement is too passive. This goal should include either or both of adding value to the business, or taking actions for improvement. It also is implicit that measurements are not currently in place.
- Provide innovative, timely, reliable, and secure IT services.

    This is a mouthful. It looks like everything is here except affordability. The wording suggests that there are some problems with the current IT services. Also, nothing is said about value to the business. The focus is too much on IT performance and not enough on business performance. In addition, there is nothing on where the services go in the business.
- Provide business value through understanding, knowledge, communication, agility, and a strong customer focus.

    Sounds good, eh? The problem is that there is nothing about the solution — just the process of doing the work. This should be internal to IT since doing all of these well will not deliver business value without a solution.
- Partner with key business units and contribute to the strategies and goals of the organization by leveraging technology to achieve clear business results.

    This implies that we are not doing "partnering" now. Why, all of a sudden, is partnering a good idea? This goal focuses on technology solutions. In an IT and strategic process plan you want to widen the range of solutions include process improvement as well as technical ones.
- Set priorities based upon business drivers and adapt to changing business needs.

    The problem here is that just setting priorities does not translate into action. The objective should be centered on results not just priorities.

Figure 9.7 (*Continued*)

- Demonstrate how IT contributes to business value and is cost-effective and efficient.

  This is too negative. The word "demonstrate" could mean marketing, or that some managers question IT's value and effectiveness. Neither of these is positive.

- Encourage risk taking for strategic alignment to the business.

  With recent events in the world, risk taking should be downplayed. It seems that there is enough about risk already. It implies that only through risk is strategic alignment possible. If you risk averse, you don't want to go for strategic alignment. This also implies that risk is required to align to the business. If so, this may say something about the business.

- Leverage technology to solve business problems.

  This, like some of the others, depends too much on technology. In addition, you want to go beyond business problems to improve capabilities. New capabilities may add value, but do not address any current problem.

- Make IT a key element of business strategy.

  This may be seen as too intrusive of IT. IT should become part of business strategy through actions and projects.

- Make IT driven by business and not technology so as to add value.

  This implies that IT is now technology-driven — not good. IT should be driven by business using available, established, and value proven technology and process improvement solutions.

- Use IT to address business requirements and achieve cost reduction through more efficient and effective use of IT resources.

  This implies that IT resources and systems are sufficient to address business requirements. This should include business involvement and ownership of change. The objective could be modified to be "address business needs through an effective combination of IT resources and business participation and support for improvement."

- Balance leadership of IT direction between benefits of scale through organization-wide activity and specific business requirements of individual business departments.

  IT work is not a "balancing act." This also implies that IT assumes it is in a leadership role — not good. Rather, it is work to improve business processes to aid both department and enterprise performance aligned to the goals of the business.

- Drive continuous productivity improvements through monitoring best-in-class benchmarks.

  Measurement is good. Benchmarking could be both expensive and subjective. However, you could be best in class in efficiency and not be working on key projects for the business. Productivity improvements should be a strategy, not an objective, since it relates to how the work is done.

- Establish an environment that spans organizational boundaries and promotes the sharing of information and technical resources.

  This one is too general to have much meaning. In addition, there is nothing said about the result of doing this.

Figure 9.7 (*Continued*)

- Recruit, retain, and invest in a highly skilled workforce that responds quickly to the ever-changing technology world.

  This is a good start. However, it should also include the applicability of the skills to the business work. The phrase "technology world" is too presumptuous. Instead, it should be replaced by business environment.
- Invest in staff to sustain and enhance a quality workforce.

  This should also be specific to the business. Another version might be "invest in staff to increase work quality and capabilities to improve business process performance."
- Recognize and reward exceptional employee performance.

  This is OK as far as it goes. However, it could relate to performance that contributes significant business value. Also, does this mean that individuals who perform critical, but only good, work are neither recognized nor rewarded? In addition, nothing is said about the importance of the work. It might be better to say "Recognize and reward team members who perform excellent work in critical activities."

Figure 9.8 Examples of IT Staffing Objectives.

- Improved communications with business units.
- Staff hiring, advancement, and retention.
- Promotion of training and skill improvement.

Some examples of IT staffing objectives are given in Figure 9.8.

General Business Process Objectives

This would be new to an strategic IT plan. The business process objectives should relate to the following:

- Cumulative improvement of business process performance.
- Process improvement through IT work, change management, and process change.
- Increase the reliability, stability, and flexibility of business processes.

Figure 9.9 gives some examples of process objectives.

- Streamline business operations by adopting integrated, consistent processes.
    This presumes that IT has the ability alone to do this. This really steps on the toes of the business units and implies that IT owns the processes. Not likely. Probably never. How about "Facilitate increasing business operation performance through improved business processes?"
- Improve workforce productivity through the use of technology.
    At first glance this sounds good. However, technology in itself is not sufficient for change. Why not use "Improve employee productivity and job satisfaction through improved use of systems and processes?"
- Support lasting and sustainable improvements in business processes through both IT work and business unit commitment.
    This is one of ours. It addresses the need for business ownership. Also, it points to the need to have improvements that last. Many process improvements later fail because the business unit staff revert back to their old ways.

Figure 9.9 Examples of General Business Process Objectives.

Application Systems and Information Objectives

In many strategic IT plans, information management and application are treated as separate objectives. To the business they are linked. Application systems and information objectives should include:

- Ensure that the applications and information continue to meet business needs (*value*).
- Promote process improvement to take advantage of the IT capabilities (*business alignment*).
- Take advantage of methods and tools to reduce maintenance and support requirements so as to address more business needs (*productivity*).

Some examples are provided in Figure 9.10.

Architecture and Infrastructure Objectives

The IT architecture provides the link between the company's mission and the technology that helps to support the mission.

- Maximize interoperability, the use of components and reuse.
  Sounds good, but to what does it apply? This should probably be a strategy not an objective. Also, the business benefit should be included.
- Promote a data architecture based upon relational database technology that is implemented to support access across multiple business units.
  Again, this is a strategy. More clear business benefits should be included.
- The company will move from an environment where there is little or no data standardization and sharing to one in which data is commonly collected once and utilized many times. This will reduce duplication, inconsistencies, and errors.
  Issues should be included in issues. This goal also is extremely difficult to achieve without a complete rework of the applications.
- Deliver and maintain a robust, flexible, secure, and efficient technology portfolio.
  This is closest to the best strategy. However, it should define what the benefits to the business are.
- Enhance the overall management of information technology and service delivery.
  The focus should not be on management, but on the actual delivery of service.

Figure 9.10 Examples of Application Systems and Information Objectives.

The infrastructure includes all hardware, system software, and network components. Objectives here should address the following:

- Support a high level of availability, performance, reliability, and security (*performance*).
- Support changing and evolving business needs within the limits of the technology (*flexibility and scalability*).
- Be cost-effective in terms of life cycle costs (*affordability*).

Figure 9.11 gives some examples of objectives pertaining to architecture and infrastructure.

Project Objectives

Project objectives include both the projects themselves as well as the project management methods. Project objectives should include:

- Ensure that projects are managed consistently regardless of size and that project performance increases over time through the application of experience (*structure, scalability, and cumulative improvement*).

- Continuously improve the delivery of services to our customers through strategic enterprise technology investments.

  This sounds good. However, continuous improvement is not possible. Technology improvement occurs in discrete chunks.
- Strengthen our technology architecture to take advantage of emerging trends.

  Why do you want to do this? Don't you want to wait until the emerging trends are realized in proven products and services? There is nothing to give the benefits except to strength an apparently weak architecture. Overall, it appears as being too self-serving.
- Limit the range of available technology options.

  This is really a strategy and should indicate the options are limited to those that provide direct business value. What if some option could yield real business value, but is outside the range? How about "Limit the range of technology options to optimize both business value and IT cost-effectiveness?"
- The key technologies will be built on a common architecture and standards to ensure interoperability among systems and applications.

  This is good. The thing to add is the benefit to the business in terms of expanded support and increased capabilities.

Figure 9.11 Examples of Architecture/Infrastructure Objectives.

- Identify and select projects that either deliver direct, tangible business benefits, or that improve the capabilities and efficiency of IT (*benefit and alignment*).
- Ensure that business projects include business ownership and involvement as well as process improvement and change (*business unit role*).

Note that accurate estimation of costs and schedules and other more detailed areas of project management are not included since these would be strategies.

Discussion of Constraints

Constraints are issues that cannot be changed. Most constraints mentioned in strategic IT plans relate to costs, but there are many categories of constraints. These include:

- Resources
- Line of business and processes

- Business organization
- Technology
- IT staffing
- Facilities
- Methods and tools

Culture and politics are usually not mentioned, but they are factors to consider. In the next group of sections we center attention on three areas. Cultural and political factors are included in the business.

Constraints on Resources

Some examples of constraints are:

- Resources are limited in both size and range of skills and knowledge so that it is challenging to accomplish all of the work (*IT staff resources*).
- There are limited financial resources available so that work must be carefully selected based on true business benefit (*cost constraints*).
- Business unit employee resources are limited due to work commitments so that use of business unit time and resources must be carefully planned to deliver the greatest value to the work (*business involvement*).
- Establish technology products and services limit the flexibility of capabilities that can be provided to the business *(systems and technology)*.

Constraints Due to the Business and Organization

These constraints relate to business units and processes.

- Business processes have limited flexibility which represents a challenge to effect lasting change (change management).

- Processes tend to become less efficient over time so that IT effort must be directed last improvements (long-term benefit).
- Operations in different countries have different cultures and practices which challenges the implementation of regional technical solutions (cultural and geographical diversification).

Constraints Due to Systems and Technology

Several types of constraints apply here. First, there is that of the available technology. Second, there is the constraint of the application systems and portfolio. Third, there are constraints in methods and tools. Some do not like to mention these in the strategic plan, but they are useful in explaining why the immediate achievement of objectives is not possible. They are in the plan, but politically you don't want to draw too much attention to them. This avoids the perception that IT is making excuses.

- The potential technology that is available is limited by the benefit to the business, the life cycle cost of the technology, and the effort to integrate the new into the existing architecture (new and emerging technology).
- The application systems were developed or acquired at different times from a variety of sources limiting the flexibility of the application systems to respond to business needs (application system performance).
- IT generally uses a variety of methods and tools which change overtime so that it is a challenge to select a set of methods and tools as a standard (methods and tools).

Examples

We have given a number of examples of objectives from various plans. Some of the common problems have been:

- Being overly technical;
- Not relating to the business;
- Objectives being given when they are really strategies.

You cannot easily train people to develop objectives perfectly. Instead, we have found that the best and quickest approach is to use examples.

Lessons Learned

One lesson learned from experience is that when developing the objectives, you should follow these steps:

- Settle on the areas of the objectives.
- Develop a tentative short bullet list of objectives for each category. Don't be concerned about the wording at this point.
- Circulate the list of objectives for review and rankings.
- Create an updated list of objectives.
- Now, add the business impact and benefit of the objectives as if they were achieved.
- Check the wording of the objectives to ensure they are in business language and that they do not refer to any current problems.
- Distribute the final list of objectives.

It is similar with constraints. Here are the steps:

- Identify the areas of the constraints.
- Create a strawman list of constraints.

- Have this list reviewed and ranked.
- Create an updated list.
- For each constraint add the business benefit.
- Check the wording of each constraint to see that it is not self-serving, but appears neutral and matter-of-fact.
- Conduct a final review.

You can develop both the objectives and constraints in parallel. Once you have the lists of objectives and constraints and in review, you can prepare the following tables.

- ***IT objectives versus constraints.*** This shows that every objective is affected by one or more constraints. Doing this validates both the objectives and constraints within IT.
- ***IT objectives versus business processes.*** This assists in validating that the objectives benefit the business processes, if achieved. Moreover, it can reveal which processes are not touched by an objective. This may cause you to add an objective.

With the second table you can use this to relate the IT objectives to business planning factors to develop the following:

- ***Business mission/vision/objectives versus IT objectives.*** This table represents strategic alignment. The entry indicates how the objective helps in achieving the business planning element.
- ***Business issues versus IT objectives.*** This is a table of strategic negative alignment. How achieving an IT objective helps relieve a business issue is the entry.
- ***Business initiatives versus IT objectives.*** This table shows how achieving an objective in IT contributes to the success of business initiatives.
- ***Business units/departments versus IT objectives.*** Here, the impact and benefits of the objectives to business units are defined.

These tables will be employed in Chapter 12 wherein you will build the plan. You want to distribute these tables as well so that you again validate both the objectives and constraints.

Politics

We spend considerable time on the wording of the objectives and constraints. You might think that this is not worth the effort. In reviewing many strategic IT plans, we have that the wording is considered as an afterthought. The words seem to be thrown together from an IT view. The wording is important because it is what leaves an impression on upper level managers who do not want to get into the details of the plan. They see if the objectives as they are worded are understandable and support the business. We have seen strategic plans fail because management got turned off.

What to Do Next

Here are some actions you can take:

- Analyze your current strategic IT plan and pull out lists of objectives and constraints.
- Carefully review these and ask the following questions:

  o Are the objectives stated in business terms?
  o Are the objectives too detailed and include too much of "how" instead of "what"?
  o Do the objectives cover the areas cited in this chapter?
  o Do the objectives include the business unit role in change and process improvement?
  o Are the benefits of achieving the objectives defined?
  o Are constraints given?
  o Are the constraints linked to the objectives?
  o Are the impacts of the constraints given?

Summary

Together with Chapters 8 and 10, the three constitute the creation of the key lists for the strategic IT and process plan. Throughout we have emphasized that great care and attention needs to be taken in defining the objectives. Most people naturally migrate to and give more attention to the strategies and action items since they are more detailed. Don't make this mistake.

Chapter 10

Create Strategies and Action Items

Introduction

A *strategy* defines what is to be accomplished in a 1–2 year time frame in an area relating to business processes and IT in support of one or more IT objectives. One strategy can support several objectives. One objective can require several strategies. Let's consider a simple example. Suppose that you have an objective to lose weight and keep it off. You also have a goal to have more fun and travel. Several strategies that are possible include: (1) adopt an organized program which provides food at reasonable prices; and (2) establish a travel program for the next five years.

Strategies provide for:

- A logical division of planned work to establish schedules and accountability targets. Objectives are too general for this.
- Identification of outcomes whose success leads to the achievement of the objectives.
- Measurement and tracking by management.

Examples of strategies could include:

- *New*. Provide new services to business units so as to improve process performance.

231

- *Improve and enhance*. Improve IT operations to reduce costs and improve reliability of service.
- *Eliminate*. Eliminate obsolete and ineffective technologies and systems that are consuming resources so that resources are freed up to be applied to major business needs.
- *Manage*. Implement a project management framework that applies to all IT work so as to deliver improved services to the business units.

An *action item* is a specific act that can be taken to support IT and the business processes. Most people think of action items as project ideas. This has problems. It makes the strategic plan seem, politically, like an IT marketing job to get projects going. Action items go far beyond projects. Here are some general actions we have developed and implemented recently.

- Change facilities and workspace.
- Implement the gathering and use of lessons learned in business departments.
- Discard some old, obsolete tools.
- Implement a knowledge base in IT to deal more efficiently with problems and new opportunities.
- Implement guidelines for small IT projects.
- Work with selective departments to improve effectiveness through eliminating exception work.

In fact, a rule of thumb from over 35 years of doing strategic planning is that 40–50% or more of the action items should not be project-based. You might think that the non-project items should be carried out individually and not be included in the strategic plan. Including them in the plan has several benefits, including:

- Management becomes more aware of what other changes are necessary.

- Implementation of systems often requires non-project work related to facilities, procedures, policies, and work assignments.
- Inclusion emphasizes to management that the value of IT is more than the components of IT.

Thus, they are included for both practical and political reasons.

In our example of the weight loss and travel objectives, potential action items include:

- Sign up for a weight loss program that includes food.
- Start exercising more.
- Work on a new attitude toward eating.
- Plan the first trip.

Of these only the last is a project plan. The others are non-project actions. Not that there is many-to-many relationship between the factors. They are interdependent. If you don't plan a trip, for example, then you might lose motivation to lose weight. If you don't lose weight, you may not have the savings to take the trip.

This chapter deals with the implementation of the IT objectives through strategies and specific action items. Why have three levels? Why not just have objectives and action items? Consider this example. Let's suppose you have an objective to improve business process performance. And that you have an action item to implement a network management software package. For an IT person it is clear that if you improve the network performance, the processes that depend on the network will see improved response time. For everyone else, it is a big leap to get from general, vague objectives to detailed work in one step. That is the reason for the strategies. They accomplish the following:

- Strategies provide umbrellas for action items.
- Strategies are a means of demonstrating what is needed to carry out and fulfill an objective.

The relationships between objectives, strategies, and action items are all many-to-many.

This structure has proven its worth time and again politically. Let's say that a business manager states that he or she supports an objective and that really makes sense. Sounds good, right? It means nothing until you present the action items. Actions items require managers to spend money or make decisions — some of which may be unpleasant. When you present the action items, you are surprised to see that the manager pans some of the action items and voices opposition. What do you do? With the linkage of the planning factors you can show that:

- If some action items fail to be implemented, the strategy fails.
- If the strategy fails, the objective is not achieved.
- If the action items fail, then some of the issues and opportunities are not dealt with.
- If the issues and opportunities are not addressed, the affected business processes suffer.

That is one of the major reasons to use the list and table approach presented in this book.

Structure of Strategies and Action Items

Let's consider the wording of strategies and action items. Recall that objectives were worded in two parts. The first was the IT objective and the second was the benefit or impact on the business and its processes. Here are some proven guidelines.

- Strategies should also be divided into two parts as with objectives so that they relate to the business. This is particularly with IT strategies that relate to infrastructure and architecture. Doing this helps in both understanding and justification.

- Both strategies and action items should be defined based on categories. This will ensure completeness.

From experience it is useful to organize IT strategies into categories. In this way, you will not miss any area. Here, we consider the following areas.

- General IT strategies
- IT staffing strategies
- General business process strategies
- IT staffing and organization action items
- Application systems and information strategies
- Architecture and infrastructure strategies
- Project strategies
- Methods and tools strategies

The categories for action items are:

- Technical and technology action items
- Application system and information action items — these are not discussed in detail since they are business specific
- Business process-related action items
- Methods and tools action items
- Policies and procedures action items
- Project action items

As with objectives, constraints, and issues and opportunities the use of categories provides structure so that your planning lists will be comprehensive and integrated.

Discussion of IT Strategies

Having given the areas of IT strategies earlier, let's consider how these should be written up for review and analysis. Here are some of the elements to consider (see Figure 10.1).

The importance of the strategy relates to the positive benefits to the processes. On the other hand, the impact if the strategy is not done defines the negative effect of either not carrying out the strategy, or only partially implementing it.

How the strategy arose is important since some may wonder why it did not appear in the last plan. In fact, since strategies do not change that much in one year, you will still want to update the wording and analysis. You can also point to deteriorating factors that contributed to the strategy.

For ease of review it is best if you develop bullets under each of these items. Since some are subjective, you can refine them during reviews. What does the review of these write-ups accomplish?

- The wording of the strategy can be clarified and understood to business managers.
- Support for the implementation of the strategy will be gained, paving the way for the related action items.
- Managers will understand both the importance and urgency of the strategy to the business.

- Title of the strategy
- Description of the strategy
- Importance of the strategy to the business and IT (alignment)
- Impact if the strategy is not achieved (urgency and negative alignment)
- Related strategies (so as to give mutual support)
- General resources required to achieve the strategy (scope of implementation)
- Definition of success if the strategy is implemented (vision of the strategy)
- Factors and background that gave rise to the strategy (how the strategy arose)

Figure 10.1 Elements of a Strategy.

- Opportunities for process and workflow improvement within and across business units; greater integration of processes.
- Interfaces to business partners.
- Customer interfaces.
- New capabilities to improve business unit performance and productivity (e.g., decision support and expert systems).
- How new systems and technologies can benefit the business and IT over a 1–2 year time horizon.
- Upgrades to current infrastructure to maintain high service levels and control support costs.
- New application systems and replacement for legacy systems.
- New or improved software for increasing collaboration in the business.
- General policy and procedure changes that improve IT value and business performance.
- Improvements in the data architecture and structure to provide greater value of information to the business.
- Measurements of IT and processes to identify potential opportunities and raise the awareness of the need for change.
- Improved vendor management to increase vendor performance as well as to facilitate the transfer of knowledge to internal staff.
- Improvements in methods and tools and their use by IT staff through training, sharing of knowledge, and gathering/using lessons learned.
- Enhancements to project management and project oversight to effect cumulative improvement in the planning and execution of work.

Figure 10.2 Factors to Consider in Defining Strategies.

Some of the things to consider when defining strategies for IT are given in Figure 10.2.

General IT Strategies

In this section we consider a number of IT strategies that apply to IT in general. As with the objectives in Chapter 9, we analyze some of these to see how they could be improved (Figure 10.3). This shows our thought process which you should consider when you develop your strategies. Due to the politics of change, always consider wording to be important.

- Streamline processes to improve efficiencies.

  Sounds good, but it implies that IT has a lot of power that they may not have. So you might say instead, "Facilitate and assist business units in improving their work performance effectiveness and efficiency."
- Maintain flexibility to respond to new service needs.

  Flexibility is almost always desirable. However, the technology, systems, demands of operations and other factor greatly limit the flexibility available. Consider using instead, "Address business needs through a combination of proven technologies and system and through process improvement techniques."
- Drive economies of scale through shared best practice.

  This one has been seen several times. It is too filled with jargon with "economies of scale," "shared," and "best practices." Replace it with "Strive to implement common methods and solutions to IT work so as to effect cumulative improvement."
- Make IT funding decisions based on value to the business.
  This should be happening already. Drop it.
- Drive constant year-to-year operational productivity improvements through monitoring best-in-class IT benchmarks.

  The use of benchmarks sounds nice, but it is difficult to do since firms in even the same industries have unique IT conditions. In addition, the improvements relate to actions not to monitoring others. Monitoring is too passive.
- Integrate IT planning with the development of business objectives to ensure alignment of IT and business goals.

  This looks good. However, it is dangerous because it can be interpreted to mean that IT will participate in business planning. Drop it.
- IT planning and business planning must be integrated to ensure that limited IT resources are used effectively.

  Similar comments to the above. This one would apply to firms in which their activities are heavily involved in E-business.
- Link the IT budgeting process to the business objectives.

  Difficult to do given the generality of business objectives. IT budgeting is linked to IT operations and the strategic plan. The strategic plan links to the business objectives.
- IT resources will be allocated based on the priority of business objectives.

  Not true. IT resources are allocated-based operations, business initiatives, business strategies, and business issues.

Figure 10.3 Examples of General IT Strategies.

IT Staffing Strategies

Figure 10.4 gives examples of strategies related to the IT staff. Strategies here should address:

- Hiring and integration of new staff members
- Collaboration to improve teamwork

- Maintain a high level of professional and technical expertise.
  Achieving this may not be affordable. This needs an addition. To what end?
- Attract and retain high-caliber staff committed to the business and IT vision.
  People can be committed to a business vision, but how can you tell? I might be incompetent, but I am enthusiastic about the vision!
- Identify and facilitate the sharing and movement of talented people.
  It is better to say, "Allocate resources for maximum business benefit through collaboration and teamwork."
- Create an environment that maximizes intellectual productivity.
  This is too vague. What is the environment?
- Develop training programs and clear career paths for all IT staff, encouraging education on emerging technologies.
  You also want to focus on improving skills with current technologies. Thus, you want to add something on achieving cumulative improvement.
- Foster technology proficiency in all staff.
  How about business knowledge too? See the next one.
- Find opportunities for IT staff to get more familiar and more knowledgeable with the business as well as increasing their technical skills and abilities.
  This is a good one since it facilities the alignment of IT to the business.

Figure 10.4 Examples of IT Staffing Strategies.

- Advancement of skills through work, training, and knowledge sharing in both business and IT
- Career advancement of IT staff

General Business Process Strategies

Some examples of business process strategies are given in Figure 10.5. Note that these strategies improve on process performance while not interfering with the actual management of the work.

Application Systems and Information Strategies

Listed in Figure 10.6 are several candidate strategies pertaining to systems and information. That a number are given reflects the focus of the strategies in many strategic IT plans.

- Ensure that business processes are compliant with security and privacy requirements.
     This is probably too narrow. You might want to add something on productivity.
- Incorporate IT knowledge sharing and transfer among departments.
     This is not clear. Moreover, why do business units need IT knowledge?
- Encourage cross training of individuals.
     This should be expanded to include other ways of increasing skills.
- Implement and support the use of lessons learned and experience among business employees to improve process performance.
     This speaks to the business processes directly and defines the IT role.
- Work closely with each major business unit to understand and document the business requirements.
     This could be endless. The word "requirements" is IT related. The phrase "understand and document" is too passive. There is no benefit or action stated. Instead, use "Work with business units to improve work by addressing key business needs."
- Analyze business requirements collectively and develop a proposed technical model that correlates to the business model.
     This is probably a nice dream, at best. It would take too much time and effort to do it. By the time you are really into this, the requirements have changed and you have to redo what you have done.
- Use the enterprise architecture to guide the deployment of systems that automate key processes.
     Drop it. It has too much jargon. Many processes cannot be totally automated. You need more than the architecture to do this.

Figure 10.5 Examples of Business Process Strategies.

Architecture and Infrastructure Strategies

Along with the previous set of strategies, this often consumes substantial space in the strategic plan. Examples are given in Figure 10.7. Caution! You want to keep these to a reasonable level so that the plan will not appear too technical.

Project Strategies

Projects are the major avenue by which IT improves business processes. Thus, this is very important and should be drafted carefully. The focal points are:

- Process selection
- Project management and oversight

- Expand data integration to enable collaboration between business units and to create synergies that can be leveraged.

  Too much jargon. How about "Expand data integration and access so that the value to multiple business units is increased?"
- Increase application development capacity.

  This is unclear in a business sense. What is "capacity?" Does this mean spending more money? If so, what does the business get in return?
- Implement large projects on time, within budget, and with a high level of customer satisfaction.

  Satisfaction comes not only from IT does for you, but from what you did for yourself. The implication is that a more passive business is implied. Another problem exists with the use of the word "large." Drop or change this one.
- Improve the effectiveness and efficiency of systems by increasing functionality, simplifying business processes, and reducing system modifications.

  Well, any system will go through modifications to meet changing requirements. So reducing them may not be good. One time we found that several applications with no modifications over several years were not used at all! Another problem with this one is "improve." Must be that the situation today is not very good. Probably drop it.
- Use IT to support business requirements and to achieve cost reduction through more effective and efficient use of IT resources.

  This is probably acceptable since it is sufficiently general and includes business factors.
- Drive rapid development of new services.

  Why aren't we doing this now? You might change this to use the word "timely" and eliminate the word "new." Then you would to add at the end the business benefit.
- Exploit intranet technologies that enable employees to communicate, access data, follow up on open issues, order goods or services, and perform other functions.

  This is probably too detailed to be a strategy. Move it into action items.
- Purchase application packages if they provide best-of-class, cost-beneficial and required services instead of using custom development.

  The problem here is that the focus is on the solution, not the requirement. It is better to say, "Select and implement the application system that best suits the business need and has the most effective life cycle cost."
- Implement an application architecture that enables IT to quickly deliver and upgrade strategic computer applications.

  This is too fuzzy. More than the architecture is needed for applications.
- Maintain an applications and technology infrastructure that exploits an architecture that enables 24 × 7 technical and business operations.

  Not bad. This relates clearly the architecture to the business.
- Demand near-term, business-focused results from development efforts.

  What about efforts that are longer term? If you only focus on short-term work, you advance neither IT nor the business in a strategic sense. Major change requires substantial time so that this would imply only tactical benefits.
- Reduce time and cost of implementation by building modular systems that leverage existing technology and infrastructure.

  Ah, modularity. A wonderful word used since the 1970s. Overused and abused, it is not clear here what the benefits to the business are. In addition, building modules, documenting, and testing them for reuse is very time consuming. Many projects could not afford this.

Figure 10.6 Examples of Application Systems and Information Strategies.

- Select IT products and services that support performance, cost-effectiveness, and sustainability.

  What happened to delivering business value? Maybe, this should read as "Select and integrate products and services that cost-effectiveness address current and emerging business needs."
- Orderly sunset and support of legacy products/technologies.

  What if some business unit totally depends on a legacy product? Why is IT using legacy stuff? Too many issues arise with this one. This should be changed to emphasize the new as well as the old. You might consider instead, "Maintain a stable, value added set of products and technologies that serve the needs of the business work."
- Optimally exploit existing products/technologies.

  See the above strategy.
- Implement a data architecture that will provide a uniform and secure mechanism for data acquisition, storage, retrieval, and update.

  OK, but it should go beyond the data architecture and include software. It should contain some business benefit related to effective use of information.
- Maintain sufficient backup and disaster recovery expertise to minimize the effect of catastrophic events on the information technology infrastructure.

  Add business resumption and indicate that the benefit is reliable operations of the processes. Also, add cost-effectiveness relative to risk since you could spend a lot of money here.
- Support and work towards implementing a shared or common IT infrastructure where there is no strategic reason to justify differentiation.

  This sounds too much like imposed standardization. Drop the last part of this one and substitute something on the business benefits.
- Plan for new capacity and configuration requirements for the integration of video and voice into the network infrastructure.

  Not bad. How about adding something on what capabilities the business gets as well as the benefits of these capabilities?

Figure 10.7 Examples of Architecture/Infrastructure Strategies.

- Project implementation
- End user participation and ownership

Figure 10.8 gives some examples.

Policy Strategies

In many strategic plans there will be a need to refer to improving policies related to technology infrastructure, business roles, work, and resource allocation. Three examples are provided in Figure 10.9.

- Improve the success rate of IT projects.

  No one would seem to argue with this at first glance. Also, it appears regularly in strategic IT plans. However, it implies that you don't have much success now. A better approach is to use "Achieve cumulative improvement in project performance through issues management, lessons learned, and effective business participation."
- Apply "best practices" in managing technology projects.

  This is fuzzy. What are best practices? Reading this a manager might think that they are not applying them now. Everyone has a slightly different idea. Moreover, to business management it implies that you are not following best practices now. Drop it.
- Implement a standardized approach for managing projects of all sizes.

  This is a good point. However, the wording applies a lack of standardization now. So, replace it with "Expand consistent and proven project management techniques to all projects regardless of type or size to ensure business value."
- Establish templates, lessons learned, and issues databases to support cumulative improvement in project performance.

  These, together with collaboration are critical success factors for projects.
- Ensure that there is adequate business involvement in projects to achieve the benefits.

  There should be one strategy that addresses business involvement. Too often, the business units want IT to assume project ownership so that they can be less accountable.
- Select projects that contribute to business objectives, improve business performance, or address business issues.

Figure 10.8 Examples of Project Strategies.

- Define and implement policies that result in priority being given to work with the greatest business value.

  This is an excellent policy since it leads to the enforcement of alignment to the business at all three levels.
- Implement an architecture and necessary standards to encourage resource sharing, reusability, and portability.

  This sounds good, but its real benefit to the business is not clear. Moreover, how this could be accomplished is still fuzzy. This strategy has appeared in strategic plans we have seen going back to the 1960s. How the architecture improvements will improve the cost-effectiveness of IT should be spelled out.
- Define the roles and responsibilities of IT and the business units in implementing new systems solutions.

  While you might not want to phrase this strategy in these terms, nevertheless, you want a strategy that emphasizes the importance of the role and associated responsibilities of the business units to ensure benefits and success.

Figure 10.9 Examples of Policy Strategies.

Discussion of Action Items

In the sections that follow we examine specific action items and make comments that either validate, negate, or improve on them. You will want to write up each action item. Here are the critical elements to address:

- Description of the action item
- The type or category of the action item
- The urgency of the action item relative to the business and IT
- The impact if the action item is not carried out
- Summary of steps needed for implementation
- Benefits of the action item
- Related action items
- Resources, decisions, etc. required for implementation
- How success in implementation will be judged

As you scan this list, you will see that some of these are subjective, based on knowledge and experience. No problem. You will circulate these for review so that they can be updated. Make sure that the language used is relatively dry and not political. The passion should be in the strategies and objectives.

Technical and Technology Potential Action Items

Along with project ideas, this is probably the most frequently cited category in the strategic plan. Examples appear in Figure 10.10. We list these without comment since action items are so specific. A general comment is that each should give some business benefits.

IT Staffing and Organization Action Items

Action items in this category apply to:

- Work assignments
- Hiring and integration of new staff

- Implement systems to provide a foundation upon which web-based services can be added without major modifications.
- Create easily navigable/user friendly web sites that are compliant with accessibility regulations.
- Implement consistent and transparent technologies to ensure easy constituent entry points and access to data.
- Maintain a messaging/e-mail infrastructure that facilitates communication and collaboration.
- Assess sufficiency of present Internet firewall capabilities.
- Implement desktop video conferencing.
- Create a single sign-on for users.
- Implement VOIP telephony.
- Implement electronic forms.

Figure 10.10 Examples of Technical/Technology Action Items.

- Hire staff members educated in both information technology and areas of business.

  This is useful since it carries out the goal of alignment.
- Train our staff through a mixture of alternative methods of learning that include academic courses and short courses in the classroom and online.

  This is OK. However, you might include shared knowledge and experience since people learn as much or more that way than through formal training.
- Provide staff members with assignments that reinforce and extend their training.

  This one makes the assignments too dependent upon the training. What about their experience and knowledge?
- Encourage rotational assignments within IT for staff.

  This should already be in process and should not require an action item.
- Perform peer reviews in connection with the design of processes and other technical work.

  How about "Perform reviews of IT work that result in gathering and using experience?" And, "Perform reviews of work that is sensitive to the importance and risk associated with the work."
- Provide opportunities for research into new technologies.

  The company is not a university. The research should be based on business needs and opportunities. Drop this one.

Figure 10.11 Examples of IT Staffing and Organization Action Items.

- Skill and knowledge improvement
- Work measurement and management
- Collaboration and joint work

Some examples are discussed in Figure 10.11.

Business Process-Related Action Items

Some of these action items are proposed as Quick Wins in later chapters. No problem. You still want them as action items. Why? Because by the end of the planning work, you can demonstrate the value of the plan by showing the implementation results of some of the action items through Quick Wins. Figure 10.12 gives examples of Quick Wins.

Policies and Procedures Action Items

Listed in Figure 10.13 are some examples of action items that pertain to policies and procedures. There are useful to include in the strategic plan since they offset the project focus of other action items and also reveal that you have thought through the requirements of implementation of the IT strategies.

- Eliminate exceptions in a process.
    Exceptions can kill the efficiency of a process. It is useful to consider going into a friendly business unit and eliminating, replacing, or modifying the exceptions. Think of it as clean-up.
- Combine two processes.
    This can formally be accomplished through integrated software. However, you can also work on the processes directly by analyzing and improving process interfaces.
- Implement a lessons-learned process in business units.
    This is one action item that we have employed repeatedly. The business knows what to do, but the knowledge of how best to do it is unevenly spread among regular employees and King and Queen Bees. The lessons learned can directly improve process performance by getting into how the work is performed.
- Retrain business staff in both the process and system.
    Individuals often enter business departments one at a time. As such, they do not receive much formal training. Over time, the process deteriorates as people get into bad habits. Retraining in both the system and process can address. You can make it even more effective by including the lessons learned in how to do the work.

Figure 10.12 Areas of Potential Business Process Action Items.

- Develop and update IT security plans.
- Support the development of business resumption plans for all departments.
- Prepare risk assessments for all critical IT systems.
- Develop a structure/template for manuals and training materials related to information and systems.
- Define enterprise architecture standards.
- Implement an improved user request process and procedures.

Figure 10.13 Examples of Policies and Procedures Potential Action Items.

Project Action Items

Project action items pertain to specific projects as well as to the project management process. Listed in Figure 10.14 are potential actions for the project management process.

Examples

In applying the method we have found that you want to identify potential strategies and action items at the same time you are working on issues and opportunities, and objectives. If you try to do this sequentially, by moving from objectives to strategies, and then from strategies to action items, it will take too long.

There are useful tips regarding the review of the strategies and action items. For issues and opportunities as well as objectives you first circulate lists.

- In addition to the IT strategy list, add a table that relates the IT objectives to the IT strategies. This will give managers a context for review. Also, if they question a strategy, you can point to the corresponding objective.
- Action items are detailed. As such, they are easier to grasp — as long as the technical action items are worded in business-friendly terms. However, the list by itself lacks meaning. It is almost impossible to know if these are really needed and if they are consistent

---

- Implement new decision criteria for evaluating IT projects that result in greater alignment to the business and its needs.

    Instead of being in a reactive mode, the strategy is to proactively define new project opportunities with the involvement of the business units. Proactively generated projects often give better results, in part due to increased business commitment.
- Collect and share information on issues across projects.

    The same issues in projects recur again and again — only the details change. Thus, experience in dealing with issues can be a starting point for resolving the issue — thereby avoiding reinventing the wheel.
- Assign a lead and backup project leader to each major project.

    This has many benefits while still ensuring accountability, including: (1) backup if one leader departs; (2) support for junior project leaders; (3) improved analysis and decision making (two heads are better than one) and (4) the capacity to show both negative and positive factors to users (good cop, bad cop).
- Gather and use lessons learned from projects during project work.

    Lessons learned are often gathered at the end of the project when people have left and everyone is tired. No surprise that there is no improvement. Gather lessons learned as you go and relate them to tasks in project templates or work breakdown structures.
- Devote more project meetings to discussing issues and lessons learned rather than status.

    Status meetings are often worthless. No one wants to admit that they screwed up. Instead, gather status ahead of the meeting. In the meeting summarize it and devote the time to sharing experience and discussing issues.
- Implement multiple project analysis for tracking and issues management.

    Projects are often tracked individually. Yet, resources, issues, and methods and tools are shared across projects. So, it makes sense to implement high-level project standardization so that you can perform multiple project analysis.

Figure 10.14 Examples of Project Potential Action Items.

with other parts of the plan. To show the need give the table of action items versus issues and opportunities. For linkage to the strategic plan, include the table of strategies versus action items.

Lessons Learned

With the strategies and action items defined, there are a number of IT tables that can be created. These include:

- *IT strategies versus action items.* You could either place an "X" if an action item supports a strategy or a number on scale of 1–3 or

1–5 indicating the importance of the action item to the attainment of the strategy.

- ***IT objectives versus IT strategies.*** The entry is an "X" if a strategy supports an objective.

- ***IT objectives versus action items.*** This table is derived by combining the first two tables. Given the difference in scale, this one is not that frequently used.

- ***IT strategies versus issues and opportunities.*** This shows that you have the issues and opportunities covered by the strategies. You can place an "X" if the issue or opportunity is addressed by the strategy.

- ***Action items versus issues and opportunities.*** This is a good table since it shows how the issues and opportunities are addressed. The "X" approach can be used. Don't think that all issues and opportunities are addressed. Some will be uncovered due to resources, priorities, etc.

- ***Architecture and infrastructure versus IT strategies.*** The entry is an "X" if the implementation of the strategy applies to the element of the architecture. This can help justify the action items related to technology since the IT strategy can be linked to issues and business processes.

- ***Architecture and infrastructure versus action items.*** The "X" approach is used. You want at least a few action items here to show that the infrastructure needs upgrading to respond to business needs and control support resources.

Note that there are no tables involving constraints. Constraints were politically useful in showing that you cannot achieve objectives in a short time horizon.

Next, you can relate strategies and action items to the business processes in the following two tables. Both of these tables are used in the strategic planning work since they are the key links to the business factors as discussed in Chapter 12.

- ***IT strategies versus business processes.*** The entry should indicate the benefit of achieving the strategy in terms of business process performance.

- *Action items versus business processes.* The entry is the impact of the action item on the process — helping to justify the action item. Here, infrastructure improvements will map to many processes.

With the tables defined earlier relating business factors to processes, you can combine tables to develop the following:

- *Business mission/vision/objectives versus IT strategies.* This may not be that useful since the IT strategies are on a different scale.
- *Business mission/vision/objectives versus action items.* Same comments as the previous one.
- *Business strategies versus IT strategies.* This is not bad. By showing how the IT strategies support business strategies, you can gain support for them.
- *Business initiatives versus IT strategies.* While business strategies are general, the business initiatives are business projects and programs that management is placing resources on. Thus, this is an important table.
- *Business initiatives versus action items.* This is another good table. Experience has shown that this can result in very rapid approval of the corresponding action items due to management attention and importance.
- *Business units or departments versus IT strategies.* The entry can be the benefit to the business unit if the strategy is implemented.
- *Business units or departments versus action items.* This is a marketing table to gain business unit management support. The entry is the benefit from the action item to the specific department.
- *Business issues versus IT strategies.* This is a table of negative intermediate alignment of IT to the business.
- *Business issues versus action items.* This, along with tables pertaining to IT current activities, demonstrates the benefits of the action items. As such, it is immediate or operational negative alignment of IT to the business.

Politics

The IT strategies are not likely to generate that much management interest. However, it is a different story with action items. They are political at their core since their implementation may potentially:

- Take resources from current and other planned work.
- Provide more or less benefits to some business units versus others.
- Reveal the extent to which IT is IT focused versus business aligned.

That is why in the previous section, we stressed bland wording — no need to arouse latent problems.

The center of political marketing of the IT and business process strategy lies in three areas:

- The action items and their approval
- The assignment of resources to action items
- Successful implementation of the action items

Taking a hard line, if you fail in any one of these to any substantial degree, the value of the entire planning effort is in question. Plans are nice, but results and change are better.

What to do Next

Take the current IT strategy plan and extract both the strategies and action items. With this you can answer the following questions:

- Are the strategies covered by the action items?
- Which action items were not approved? Why?
- Since the plan was approved, what changed with the urgency of the action items that were not approved?

- What was the impact on the business processes and issues due to the lack of approval?
- What happened to the strategies given that not all action items were implemented?
- What was the mix of approved action in terms of:
  - Technology versus application and other action items?
  - Project versus non-project action items?
- Are the strategies related to business factors?
- Are the strategies clearly related to the IT objectives, or are they treated as separate lists?

Summary

This is the last of the three chapters in developing the planning elements of the strategic IT and process plan. We emphasize again that these be defined in parallel. Here are some final guidelines from the discussion in this chapter.

- The strategies need to relate to the business — even those involving architecture and infrastructure.
- Many, if not most, of the action items should not be project ideas.
- Resist the temptation to roll over the unapproved action items into this plan. At least the wording and description should be updated. Moreover, in the description of the action item you want to indicate the deterioration that occurred due to the lack of implementation.

Chapter 11

Create Strategic IT and Process Plans for Business Units

Introduction

Here is a chapter that you won't find in many other strategic planning books. In this chapter we show how you can develop strategic IT and process plans for selected business units. We do this for several cases. First, there is the situation where there is no overall strategic IT plan. But shouldn't this be a requirement beforehand? Not necessarily. As you will see in the example at the end of the chapter, there are political and practical reasons why you have to develop the plan for a critical business unit without the strategic IT plan.

The second case is that where there is an accepted and endorsed strategic IT plan. Then, it is important politically to show how the business unit plans are compatible and draw upon the overall plan.

The Value of Strategic Business Unit Plans

This looks like a great deal of effort with limited payoff. Wrong. The effort is limited for several reasons:

- Only a few business units will be selected due to limited resources.
- Within a business unit, only a few critical processes will be considered.

This limits the scope.

What is the benefit and payoff? Past experience has shown that the following benefits are often realized.

- The strategic IT and process plan overall is validated.
- Business units more clearly understand the plan and the benefits of the planning since it applies to them.
- The strategic business unit plan can result in tangible, rapid benefits.
- This strategic business unit plan can help structure future business requests for IT services — supporting a more proactive IT approach.
- Business units will assume a greater degree of ownership. Their participation and contribution will be greater. Why? Because they see this in their own self-interest.

If there is no strategic IT plan or it is flawed or ignored, the strategic plan for the business unit can serve as a model for the overall planning. This is the case in the example at the end of this chapter.

There is also a political competitive advantage *vis-a-vis* other business units. If your department is the only one with a strategic plan, you will appear more organized. This means that both upper management and IT will listen more carefully to what you have to say. We have also seen that people in other departments may seek to transfer into your department because it appears that you are more structured and organized.

There are additional benefits to both IT and the business units. For IT, the strategic business unit plan provides a focus for future requirements. Moreover, any and all change requests can be validated against the plan. This can either eliminate, change, or support the request or change of requirements. Most important, the business unit now has a vision of how the work could be performed better.

For IT there are benefits as well. First, IT staff can better under-stand what they need to do to support the business unit. They can, for example, search for new systems and technology that could meet the business unit needs. Second, having the strategic business unit plan makes the department's needs more visible and understood. Third, the IT staff can better understand how the business operates and the problems that they face.

Why these Strategic Plans are Often Ignored

So if it is so valuable, logical, and useful, why isn't it done? Research reveals the following reasons:

- There is no formal mechanism for mapping the overall plan into the business unit. The action items in the overall plan are **assumed** to address the business units. However, the actions items only address part of the requirements and issues of the business unit.
- IT lacks resources to do the planning for a business unit. The issue here is the role of IT in doing the plans. It makes no sense for IT to do these plans, since then IT would own them and the business unit might ignore the plan for their own unit. The approach is to coordinate having the business unit staff perform the planning for themselves out of self-interest.
- There is a concern if you do a strategic plan for one unit, then others will want one too. So? This is not bad. Later on, when there are available resources, more business units can be addressed.
- "We didn't do this level of planning before and things are still working." Perhaps, this is true. However, without process plans many opportunities for improvement will go undone and not pursued. Process change will be treated ad hoc.

- "If we do the plan and there are no IT resources, the effort will have been wasted." Not true. There can still be work done within the departments.

Identify Key Business Units

The first step is to identify the business units for which strategic IT and process plans will be developed. A good starting point is the table of business units versus processes. Developed in an earlier chapter, this provides a rating of importance and involvement of the business unit in the process work.

Previously, during the creation of the plan, several key planning tables were defined. These were:

- Business issues versus processes. This table indicated which processes contributed the most to the major business issues.
- Mission, vision, or business goals versus processes. Here, the extent to which the performance of a process affected the element of the mission or vision, or specific business goal was given as the table entry.

Now, we can combine each of these with the table of business units versus processes to obtain:

- *Business issues versus business units*. This table indicates the contribution of the work of the specific business unit to the individual business issue (called *Negative Importance*).
- *Business mission, vision, or goals versus business units*. Here, the entry is the importance and role of the activities of the business unit to achieving a specific objective (called *Positive Importance*).

This gives us two of four ways to select which business units to work with.

There are two other ways to rank business units. The first is political. Here, you would rate those business units highest that were most amenable to change and improvement. This a good place to start to show how the planning works. It also allows you to show results fast. Not bad.

The other approach is to rate the business units on the basis of the extent of automation. Here, the departments with the least automation and systems might offer some of the best opportunities. The problem is that these departments may not be strategically important. After all, their automation needs have been ignored or bypassed for years.

From experience, a mixed approach is often the best. Start with the political ranking to show results. This will not only yield benefits, but also provide you with a reference sell to help market the planning to business identified through positive and negative alignment. Of these two, the most common method is to select the business units with the most significant business issues.

Develop Strategic Plans for Business Units without an Overall Strategic IT Plan

Recall that in Chapter 1 reasons were given for firms not producing a strategic IT plan. If this is the case in your organization, then what is the justification for doing your own strategic IT and process plan? We gave some of the reasons earlier in this chapter. Here are some more:

- If we do this planning, the results will go nowhere because there is no overall plan.
- There is no overall guidance or help in developing a plan for a business unit.

These are more excuses. Again, the reason to do it is self-interest. To improve your processes and those linked to other related business units.

If you develop the strategic plan, how do you explain it to others? Here are some justifiable reasons.

- We need to set a direction for our work.
- Employees need to understand the importance of the work and how it will change over time. This will improve motivation and also get them more supportive of change.
- We need to make work improvements in a more systematic manner.

The approach to developing the strategic plan for a business unit follows from the approach in this book as defined in earlier chapters. However, due to the more limited scope of the business unit versus the overall organization, there are some modifications necessary.

Here are the initial steps with these changes.

- Identify the processes in the business unit. Rather than name only a few key processes, you want to come up with a more comprehensive, complete list. This will include smaller processes that relate to the key ones in terms of interfaces with information, shared staffing between resources and shared facilities.
- Map the business vision, mission, or objectives of the organization to the department. You can proceed as before and link these to the processes you just identified.
- Determine the issues, opportunities, and problems in the business unit. Opportunities here include potential uses of automation as well as organization, staffing, policy, and procedure change.
- Link business issues to the processes. Here you will not only consider the overall business issues, but also those in the business unit. Start with the lists provided in Chapter 8.

So far you have connected the work to both the negative (issues) and positive (objectives, mission, and vision). We assume that the business unit does not have its own objectives or strategies. In this case, the next step is to define the business objectives for the business unit.

How do you go about defining these with limited time, money, and even interest in the business unit? Given the press of daily work, inertia, and resistance to change, this would seem formidable. Not really. Start with the most important processes. Define objectives for each of these processes. To get these answer the following question.

> If the process worked as intended without problems, how would the business unit and organization benefit?

The answers here point to the future vision of the work. Knowing the benefits, you can define the objectives.

Let's take an example of bank branches. A bank branch can be thought of in terms of the following activities: teller and ATM operations, lending, new accounts and sales, and note and other activities. After you make a list of the processes, you can define key objectives in terms of:

- Retail customer relations
- Business customer relations
- Common transaction performance
- Exception transaction performance

You have the issues and opportunities in hand. Next, you can determine the barriers or constraints that prevent you from achieving the goals in the near term. Here is a list to get you

- Financial limitations.
- Time limitations — the amount of elapsed time tolerable for a change.
- Space restrictions.
- Work restrictions. Given the volume of work, you may only be able to squeeze in a limited amount of change.
- Management perception of the importance of the business unit. This would govern visibility and how much attention you can expect to receive.
- Outside regulations and rules imposed by governments, unions, and others.
- Employee restrictions. This includes the limitations imposed by the geography of the area, the resource pool, and related factors.
- Cultural and social limits. These impose boundaries on what is possible. For example, some cultures may have slow days due to weather, and so forth.

Figure 11.1 Examples of Constraints.

started (Figure 11.1). It is similar to those in Chapter 9, but made specific to a business unit.

In our bank example, constraints include:

- Company policies and government regulations
- Union rules, if these apply
- Business rules governing the work
- Financial limitations
- Facility limitations
- Staff capability limitations

The next part is to define the strategies to achieve the objectives without violating the constraints. The easiest approach is to work with the list below and flesh out detailed strategies under each bullet.

- Workspace allocation. How much space is allocated to specific activities.
- Workspace layout. The layout of the area where an activity is performed.
- Policy interpretation. There is usually some flexibility in how some policies are interpreted.

- Procedures for doing the work. This includes documentation as well as guidelines for performing the work.
- Staff assignments. Who does what work? This includes items such as assignment to shifts, assignment to exception work as well as regular work.
- Methods and tools used to perform the work.
- Staff skills and training.

In our bank branch example, some strategies are:

- Work assignments to busy, normal, and slow periods
- Space layout in each of the four branch areas
- Guidelines for handling regular work
- Guidelines for handling exception work
- Staff training in systems and processes

For the potential action items, use the same list as for strategies. As you define these, sort them into the categories in Figure 11.2.

You now have the elements of the strategic IT and process plan. As you are doing this, you can be assembling the related tables as defined in Chapters 8–10. Some of the key tables are:

- Issues and opportunities versus processes
- Issues and opportunities versus action items
- Objectives versus processes
- Strategies versus action items
- Action items versus issues and opportunities

Of course, there are many more. But there are limited time and resources available. These are key ones because (1) they validate the interconnection of the planning elements and (2) they can be employed to sell the changes to others.

How should you communicate with people during this work? For business employees in the department, get them involved. You want

- Actions that can be done quickly in the business unit without management approval. These could include:

  o Additional guidelines for doing work
  o Sharing experiences in customer relations and work
  o Staff retraining in the work
  o Retraining of staff in computer systems
  o A review of shadow systems
  o A review of workarounds used in the business unit
  o Sprucing up the facilities — painting, furniture, signage, and so forth

- Actions that can still be handled in the department, but that require more time and resources. If a peak period of work is coming up, some of the changes in the first group would appear here.

  o More substantial facilities work
  o Improving the documentation of processes and work
  o Major retraining of staff

- Actions that require upper management approval, but no IT involvement. Examples are:

  o Changes in the interpretation of policies
  o Handling some specific types of exceptions
  o Handling specific types of customers
  o Major staffing reassignments

- Actions that require IT work and resources, but not upper management approval. Some of these might be:

  o Minor systems changes
  o System maintenance changes to fix problems
  o Incorporating a shadow system into a supported system

- Actions requiring both upper management and IT involvement. These are typically major projects that require substantial resources.

Figure 11.2 Categories of Action Items.

them to own the work. If you do it by yourself, you own it. Not good. Use the methods of communicating as defined earlier for the overall strategic planning effort.

For IT, you can indicate that you are trying to understand better the issues involved in the work and determine improvements that could help IT in responding to work requests. You want to indicate that after the plan is produced, the user requests will be aligned to the strategic plan. This should make any IT manager happy in that it will reduce the effort required to deal with the requests. Moreover, it will be harder for them to put off your requests since they are better justified.

How should you present the plan to upper management and IT? After all, they may see this as a threat. They may see this as an attempt to usurp their power. Here are some key points.

- For upper management present some of the lists as you do the work.
- To get them excited point out some of Quick Wins that are possible.
- Try to implement some of the Quick Wins during the planning work so that you can demonstrate results to upper management. This shows that you are serious about improvement.

For IT, you want to present the plan in terms of the tables. Give special attention to action items. Include all action items to show IT that the action items are not just of things IT should do. From experience, if the action items are 85% non-IT, then that would be valuable in showing how business focused the plan is.

Project the Overall Strategic Plan Down to a Business Unit

Now, suppose that there is an overall strategic business plan. The plan may speak in general terms about issues, goals, and so forth. Another input to the planning effort at the business unit level is the mission and/or vision. How does this change if there is a strategic IT plan? Not too much. You will add the strategic IT plan to the business plan for inputs into the business unit planning process.

These are the inputs externally to the planning process. Work with these first. Figure 11.3 provides a list of actions that can be taken.

- Extract the business objectives and mission/vision into lists related to the following: employees, departments, customers, processes, and systems and technology.
- Try to identify business issues. You may need to use your own knowledge here to supplement what is the business plan. Sometimes, you can find these in the plan when the plan identifies challenges or opportunities. Often, they do not want to call it a problem or issue unless the situation is dire.
- Get the IT objectives and relate them to business processes.
- Do the same for IT strategies and action items.
- Pull out the business strategies related to the business objectives.
- Relate the following to the business processes:

  o Business objectives
  o IT objectives
  o Business issues
  o Business strategies
  o IT strategies

Figure 11.3 Actions in Mapping the Strategic Plan to a Business Unit.

Next, move to the business unit itself. You can measure a business process from the corresponding figure in Chapter 16. Make the elements of the list local to the business unit. How do you address processes that cross departments? Seek out their cooperative and participation. Do this based upon their own self-interest. If they show no interest, use the employees who interface with the other departments as the source.

Collect information as indicated in Chapter 5. Next, start to prepare lists of issues and opportunities, objectives, strategies, and action items as was done in earlier chapters. We refer you to these to avoid repeating what was said earlier.

There is an additional wrinkle here. You want to map these to the corresponding ones to the business and strategic IT plans. Here are some of the tables to develop.

- Issues and opportunities versus general business issues
- Business unit objectives versus mission, vision, and business objectives
- Business unit strategies versus business strategies

In some instances, the strategic business plan objectives, and so forth may appear too vague. Then you should try to map them to the processes in the business unit. Since you have mapped the planning elements such as objectives, strategies, and so forth to the internal processes, you can now combine the work so that the strategic business plan elements relate to those of the business unit.

Potential Problems with Strategic Business Unit Planning

Let's consider potential problems by type. Keep in mind that we have experienced all of these in our previous planning efforts.

- There seems to be absolutely no interest in doing the plan — from both management and employee perspectives. Then you want to start with measuring the processes and identifying issues and their impacts to get people more motivated. You can also start the planning work very informally. You need participation, but you can do a lot to get the ball rolling.
- IT attempts to take over the planning. You might be surprised at our response. Don't discourage it. Ask them to participate in the detailed process analysis. They will probably back away since they don't have extra resources and because they don't want to be bogged down in the detail.
- Some upper-level manager questions the planning effort. They may think or say, "You have all of these extra resources available to do planning." That is why the planning effort must be work in addition to regular work. This does not necessarily mean that it will take longer. Individuals who are busy can usually fit this in since it is a limited effort.
- The plan has been completed, but there is no interest in implementing change. This should be expected even though it appears on the surface to be depressing. Remember that change is not

easy. Expect and anticipate inertia and resistance. Focus on some of the easy changes first. Try to implement some of these during planning to create momentum. If these do not work, keep measuring and reporting on the issues and problems. You should act "neutral" — even if you put in a great deal of effort. How do you do this? Just calmly mention the issues and do not press for action. You might indicate that you can live with things as they are, but that the department is missing out on some good opportunities for improvement.

Measure Your Planning Work and Plan

There are several areas of measurement that have proven useful. These include: (1) measuring the business unit before the planning work; (2) measuring the work and department effort during the work; (3) measuring communications with IT, other business units, and upper management; and (4) measuring results after the plan. Let's consider each of these in turn.

Figure 11.4 gives a list of potential items for measurement before the planning work.

- What changes and improvements have been carried out in the past two years? Were these measured? Were they lasting?
- What surprises have there been with respect to business processes? Significant surprises reveal that there is lack of measurement of the work.
- What is the extent to which information about the work (guidelines) is shared among employees? Lack of sharing indicates a lack of collaboration and cumulative improvement.
- To what extent does the work rely on shadow systems and workarounds? This would indicate problems with systems in handling all of the work as well as inefficiencies in the process.
- Are there any measurements relating to work quality, effectiveness, and efficiency? Related to this is whether there has been an effort to improve the work.

Figure 11.4 Measuring the Business Unit Before the Planning Effort.

- During the planning effort were there surprises that caused major revisions in the planning lists and tables? This may indicate problems in data collection.
- To what extent were employees involved in the planning effort? What is the percentage of employees that were involved?
- Was the interest of the employees increasing during the planning work?
- Were interim findings during the planning work presented for review and approval?
- Related to the previous one, were some Quick Wins found and implemented?
- What was the distribution of effort in doing the planning between developing tables and lists versus communications? Communications should be dominant.
- Did the planning lists and tables improve with reviews?

Figure 11.5 Measuring the Planning Work.

- What communications occurred with upper management? What was their reaction?
- What communications occurred with IT? What was this organization's reaction?
- How was the IT and strategic plan for the business unit revealed to management — gradually with informal communications first or formally? It is better to have extensive communications before the presentation. That will build momentum.
- What was the extent and nature of communications with other, related departments? Were they supportive in participating and providing information?
- What was the reaction of IT to the plan? What role did they play during planning?

Figure 11.6 Measurement of Communications Related to the Strategic Business Unit Plan.

For measuring the work and participation during the planning effort, consider the items in Figure 11.5.

Communications is a key to planning. It is valuable to keep the items in Figure 11.6 in mind as the plan is being developed.

Figure 11.7 provides things to consider in measuring the results of the planning work and implementation of the plan action items.

Update the Strategic Business Unit Plan

You only need to update the plan if there is significant change in the business unit. Otherwise, you can stick to measurement on a

---

- What were the aspirations and expectations of management of the business unit before the planning work? What changed over the horizon of planning and after the plan?
- Did management endorse further planning? Did they initiate the planning with other business units?
- Were there tangible, short-term results from the planning?
- Was there improvement in employee morale? Was there a drop in employee turnover?
- Do employees now share information among themselves after the planning effort?
- What issues and problems remain after the initial changes due to the planning?
- Are managers and employees more aware of how their work relates to the overall business?

Figure 11.7 Assessment of the Results of the Business Unit Strategic IT and Process Plan.

periodic basis. This keeps the effort minimal and lower profile. A review every six months would seem to be most suitable frequency.

When you update the plan, you can follow the guidance in Chapter 16. Things are easier than is the case with the overall strategic IT and process plan. Here are some steps.

- Review the updated strategic business plan to see what is new.
- Review the strategic IT plan to detect any shift in priorities.
- Look into the processes to see what new problems and opportunities have surfaced.

The goals and strategies of the business unit plan have not changed. So, the focus is on issues and opportunities. Then you can create action items in response.

Examples

In a transportation agency the IT group was mired in legacy technology. The business users wanted to move ahead and get progress.

The strategic IT plan did not exist. Why? Because if you are only in maintenance mode, the future is fixed. Just more of the same. Thus, there was no interest in strategic planning in IT.

Government agencies, in general, are very political. This situation was no exception. There was a great deal of infighting and mutual suspicion. IT had made promises of change, but had never delivered. The logical thing would be to change IT. Not possible. The IT manager had close personal ties with the head of the agency.

The problem was how to initiate change. The effort centered on the operations division. This is the largest business unit in a transportation agency. Some of its critical departments include:

- Bus operations
- Vehicle scheduling
- Driver assignments
- Vehicle maintenance

Overall, this division accounts for all of the revenue, the use of federal funds, and over 85% of the employees.

If the planning effort started as an strategic IT plan for the division, sparks would have flown. The effort never would have even started. The approach taken was to develop business process plans first. Some of the key processes were:

- Driver scheduling and assignments
- Interface between drivers who belong to the Teamsters Union and the agency
- Bus scheduling
- Bus maintenance
- Customer service
- Route planning
- Management information related to fare revenue, ridership, and so forth

The method described in Chapter 6 was employed for each of these. As the plans were developed, the new vision for each process was defined. At this point, the next step was to identify requirements to achieve the long-term vision. This included not only policies, facilities, and procedures, it also encompassed automation. The automation requirements included what new systems and technology were needed and how they would benefit and integrate into the processes.

At this time, IT realized what was going on and tried to take over the planning. However, the division management asserted ownership and approved the IT and strategic process plan for the division. They also approved action items which went to the board of the agency for approval. These were approved and work started — with limited IT involvement.

There is another chapter to this story. After some of the systems were implemented, the IT manager resigned. The new IT manager employed the same approach to develop an overall strategic IT and process plan that include marketing, accounting, payroll, finance, and other business units.

You might say that this is too unusual to include as an example. Not at all. First, people learn about the politics of planning from examples like this. Second, this is real life since planning points will change. Change threatens the status quo which in turn puts individual's power at risk.

Now let's consider an Asian example. An European manufacturing firm had a subsidiary in Indonesia. While there were both strategic plans for the overall business and IT, these did not seem relevant to the conditions with which the Asian division had to cope. The challenge was to develop a strategic IT and process plan for this business unit that would align with those of headquarters.

Management in Indonesia felt that they needed a direction and plan for both positive and negative reasons, including:

- The need to raise morale by showing employees how they were important to the overall firm (positive).

- They wanted to reduce the level of interference and microman-agement of corporate on their activities. By showing they were organized and supportive of the direction of the business, they could have more effective autonomy (negative).
- They wanted to see process improvement. Past efforts that focused on one individual process had not been lasting or really effective (positive).

The approach in this chapter was applied to six key processes and 11 supporting processes. Initially, little was relayed to corporation. As the strategic planning progressed, a number of Quick Wins were implemented. Measurements and data collection revealed more issues. Some of these related to the central systems provided by IT at the corporate level. Heretofore, Indonesian management had not been able to define the problems and their impacts in fitting the systems into this Asian cultural and political environment. The analysis revealed a number of shadow systems and workarounds that were essential in doing the work. This information was used to convince corporate IT to make changes so as to eliminate most, but not all of the shadow systems.

With this success and the plan completed, the plan was presented to corporate management. To say that they were surprised was an understatement. They later mandated that operations in all of the countries in the region develop their own strategic IT and process plans aligned to the overall plan. Since creation, the plan has gone through three iterations and updates, resulting in more improvements.

Lessons Learned

One thing from experience is that it is sometimes valuable to start the overall strategic IT and process planning work with one division or business unit. This gives you experience. It shows that the method works. Then you can scale up the plan to include more of the business.

Another lesson learned is that you should anticipate rising expectations as well as resistance. Resistance often comes from senior employees who like things as they are and who have informal power in the status quo of the work. The rising expectations can come from the junior employees. Often, it is here that you will receive the most support for change. To dampen expectations, you should indicate that some problems are not easy to solve. Also, point out that recognizing that a problem exists is the first step toward a lasting solution.

Politics

Many IT organizations are protective of their role. They may do it as their responsibility to develop these plans. Several trends have strengthened this feeling. First, key processes often span departments so that no one department owns the process. Second, many software packages such as Enterprise Resource Planning (ERP), Supply Chain Management (SCM), and Customer Relationship Management (CRM) also cover these multidepartment processes. However, IT lacks the knowledge to do it.

What to do Next

Figure 11.8 contains a checklist of questions you can employ to evaluate your strategic planning relative to departments and to assess the need for strategic business unit plans.

Summary

We consider this chapter to be important for several reasons. The justification for doing strategic planning is often to achieve longer

---

- What problems have surfaced that resulted from different understandings of the direction for the business unit?
- Have the changes made to systems resulted in very marginal benefits?
- Have the business processes remained unchanged for some time?
- Have the processes been subjected to real analysis and measurement?
- Is it difficult to interpret the strategic business plan in terms of the activities in the business unit?
- Do the employees know their processes and procedures and how they relate to the growth and performance of the business?
- Do the people in the business unit tend to operate as semi-independent groups? Is the whole greater than the sum of the parts?

Figure 11.8 Questions Related to Strategic Business Unit Plans.

term changes in the business. This can often be done most effectively by getting down to the business unit level and the detailed work.

One benefit is to justify the strategic planning through results and applicability. Another benefit is to trigger change in the business units. These changes in turn can affect and enhance the overall strategic IT and process plan.

There is even better justification to developing the strategic business unit plan.

- To be effective over the long term, the management and employees of the business unit should have a clear sense of direction.
- To carry out orderly change and improvement, you really do need to have a plan.
- Having a strategic business unit plan gives greater say and control over the business.
- The strategic business unit plan helps management and the organization by indicating how the business unit can help achieve both long- and short-term business goals.

Chapter 12

Build and Market the Plan and Planning Method

Introduction

This chapter focuses on two major related activities in the strategic planning. One is the creation of the strategic IT and process plan. Here, the attention goes beyond completing a document. It includes establishing a strategic planning database.

The other is concerned with the marketing of the planning process and the plan to management and employees. If management authorized the planning work, then why is marketing or sales necessary? For the following reasons.

- Past planning efforts have not resulted in any significant change.
- This is the first time that the strategic plan has been created.
- There does not appear to management that a strategic plan update or effort is needed now.

As you will see, marketing is needed almost from the beginning through implementation of the action items. Also, this part of the chapter expands on the comments and suggestions on marketing in previous chapters.

Why are these two activities united in this chapter? One reason is that you want to begin the marketing while you are still doing the planning. This will ensure a better reception for the strategic plan when it is finished. You also want to avoid springing any surprises. If management knows what is in the plan, then they can move beyond it to lending support for the resource allocation. That is the most critical point in the marketing effort since the plan fails if there is no implementation.

Define the Future Vision of Processes and IT

In Chapters 7–10 you create a number of lists and tables related to both business and IT. One of the first steps in developing the plan is to employ these to define a longer term vision of both the business processes and IT.

For the business processes you want to define a combined version of the processes. In that way, you can better define common future requirements for IT resources, architecture, systems, and infrastructure. This vision would provide a generalized view of how work would be performed. Two examples come to mind. The first was several years ago in which a common vision of how customers could use the web to interact with the company. More recently, we have developed visions for several organizations using web 2.0 technologies and capabilities.

Turning to IT the vision involves defining how the following would be accomplished:

- End user relations in terms of business unit requests, implementation, and other activities.
- Application systems capabilities and structure. This could include expanded use of integrated software packages or the expanded use of web-based software (e.g., Salesforce.com, google.com).
- Modern infrastructure and architecture.
- Staffing capabilities and resource allocation.

- IT project management, process improvement, and change management.

Consolidate the Planning Tables

Another step is to consolidate the lists and tables created earlier. During the development of these earlier, you conducted some preliminary reviews with employees and managers in both the business and IT. Here, you will work to make them final.

Since we have discussed the specific tables and lists in detail, we provide some guidelines here to help in putting things together.

- People often have difficulty seeing the impact of general items in the plan such as objectives and strategies. Therefore, a good way to review them lies in the corresponding tables that relate to issues and opportunities, and action items.
- Here is a good approach for sequencing the reviews of the plan consolidation:
  - o The planning lists
  - o The tables that relate action items and issues and opportunities to business processes
  - o The IT objectives and strategies mapped to the processes
  - o The IT factors mapped to each other
  - o The IT factors mapped to the general business factors such as business objectives, business issues, and so forth

The benefit of this method is that it is incremental. Once someone has performed a review at one level, it is easier to move to the next level. An additional benefit is that most of the questions and problems will surface early since the later presented tables are drawn from the earlier ones.

- Be willing to make updates to the tables. However, you really want to understand what is behind their concerns and comments.

This will give you insight into their perspectives and assist you in dealing with politics and potential future resistance to change.

Create Strategic Planning Databases

The strategic planning database is a repository of information on planning elements for both business processes and IT. The value of the database has been proven many times in the past. Here are some of its applications.

- The staff involved in strategic planning change. The database makes it easier for the new staff to get up to speed.
- After the completion of the plan, requests for information and clarification may come from both business and IT managers. Having the database makes responding to these requests easier.
- You really want to achieve cumulative improvement so that each time you update the strategic plan, you improve the quality, completeness, and effectiveness of the work in less time with less work. Having the database makes this much easier to achieve.
- Some issues seem to be handled. However, events cause the issue or some other item to reappear. Using the database will make it less likely that you will miss the recurrence.

But there is another benefit to having this in an organized structure — power. Having this information gives you substantial influence since management will likely call upon you for more analysis. This may seem too Machiavellian, but it is a reality.

Let's consider the elements in the strategic planning database. Figure 12.1 contains those pertaining to the business processes. Figure 12.2 applies to the business planning data. Figure 12.3 presents the data elements for IT projects while Figure 12.4 gives those for IT planning factors. No one is expected to use all or even most of these. You should start small and grow the databases over time. Note that process improvement methods such as Six Sigma and Total Quality

Business process

- Process ID
- Process name
- Key business department
- Degree of involvement and ownership by the key department
- Other business departments involved
- Date record was created
- Created by
- Date of last update
- Updated by
- Process description
- Overall current process condition
- Trends in the condition of the process
- Supporting systems
- Rating of the supporting systems

  - Quality
  - Completeness and coverage of work
  - Reliability

- Process goals
- Key transactions
- Interfacing processes
- Nature and condition of process interfaces
- Known shadow systems
- King and Queen Bees
- Supervisors to contact
- Key employees to contact
- Potential process issues
- Active process issues
- Impacts of active process issues
- Process opportunities
- Quick Wins planned
- Quick Wins executed
- Results of Quick Wins
- Process performance

  - Volume of work performed
  - Cost of process
  - Number of employees involved in work
  - Employee turnover
  - Peak periods of work
  - Condition of training
  - Condition of procedures
  - Existence of guidelines and lessons learned in how to do the work

Business department

- Department ID
- Name of department

Figure 12.1 Data Elements for Business Processes.

- Manager of department
- Number of employees
- Ownership role of the process

Process issues

- Issue ID
- Issue title
- Issue description
- Type of issue
- Potential severity and importance of the issue
- How to detect the issue
- Guidelines to prevent the issue
- Guidelines for dealing with the issue
- Likely issue impacts

Figure 12.1 (*Continued*)

Business vision

- Vision element ID
- Title of vision element
- Type of vision element
- Importance and emphasis
- Date created
- Status
- Last updated
- Description
- Applicable business units

Business mission — similar data elements as vision
Business objectives

- Objective element ID
- Title of objective
- Type of objective
- Related objectives
- Importance and emphasis
- Date created
- Status
- Last updated
- Date objective was dropped from the business plan
- Description
- Applicable business units
- Applicable business processes

Business issues

- Business issue ID
- Business issue title

Figure 12.2 Data Elements for Business Planning Factors.

- Type of the business issue
- Status of the business issue
- Importance of the business issues
- Urgency of the business issue
- Description
- Comments
- Business units impacted
- Business processes affected
- IT systems and activities involved
- Date that the issue surfaced
- Date that the issue was dropped from the business plan
- Actions taken on the issue

Business initiatives

- Initiative ID
- Title of the business initiative
- Type of the initiative
- Status
- Description
- Comments
- Business units impacted
- Business processes affected
- IT systems and activities involved
- Date of initiation
- Date of completion
- Benefits of the initiative
- Impacts after implementation
- Lessons learned

Business strategic plan

- Year or issue of the plan
- Who created the plan
- Level of detail in the plan
- Extent of change from the previous version
- Direct relevance to key processes
- IT inclusion in the plan

Figure 12.2 (*Continued*)

Management (TQM) follow the same lines in process analysis as do Business Process Management (BPM) and Business Activity Measurement (BAM). Specific comments on each group of databases are included at the start of the figures.

Figure 12.5 deals with the key strategic IT and process planning tables. There include process, IT, and business factors. They were

IT project

- Project ID
- Title of project
- Description
- Status of project
- Date started
- Date completed
- Description
- Project leader(s) ID
- Business units
- Project issues
- Estimated cost
- Actual cost
- Project lessons learned
- Estimated benefits
- Realized benefits
- Comments

Project leader

- Project leader ID
- Name of project leader
- Status of project leader (active, departed, and so forth)
- Areas of expertise
- Date first become project leader
- Last date of project management role
- Project experience
- Technical experience
- Business experience

IT project issues

- Issue ID
- Title of issue
- Status of the issue
- Date when issue was created
- Created by
- Date last updated
- Updated by
- Description
- Comments
- Impact if not done
- Guidelines for resolution

Lessons learned

- Lesson learned ID
- Title of lesson learned
- Status (active, inactive)

Figure 12.3 Data Elements for IT Projects.

- Type or category
- Date created
- Created by
- Date updated
- Updated by
- Description
- Situations to which it applies
- Estimated benefits from using the lesson learned
- Guidelines for using the lesson learned

Figure 12.3 (*Continued*)

IT objectives

- Objective ID
- Title of objective
- Type of objective
- Date created
- Created by
- Date of last update
- Updated by
- Description
- Related objectives
- Comments

IT strategies

- Strategy ID
- Title of strategy
- Type of strategy
- Date created
- Created by
- Date of last update
- Updated by
- Description
- Related strategies
- Comments

IT issues

- Issue ID
- Title of issue
- Type of issue
- Issue urgency
- Issue importance
- Issue impacts if not addressed
- Date created

Figure 12.4 Data Elements for IT Planning Factors.

- Created by
- Date of last update
- Updated by
- Description
- Related issue
- Comments
- Actions

IT opportunities

- Opportunity ID
- Title of opportunity
- Type of opportunity
- Urgency of opportunity
- Importance of opportunity
- Impacts if not addressed
- Date created
- Created by
- Date of last update
- Updated by
- Description
- Related issue
- Comments
- Actions

IT constraints

- Constraint ID
- Title of constraint
- Type of constraint
- Impact of constraint
- Date created
- Created by
- Date of last update
- Updated by
- Description
- Related constraints
- Comments

IT action items

- Action item ID
- Title of action item
- Type of action item
- Status
- Date created
- Created by
- Date of last update
- Updated by
- Date of approval

Figure 12.4 (*Continued*)

> - Date of completion of action item
> - Results of implementation
> - Comments on the action item
> - Lessons learned from implementation

Figure 12.4 (*Continued*)

Business-related tables

- Business process versus business process. This table explains the *interdependence* among processes.
- Business objectives/mission/vision versus business processes. This table shows which processes are *positively aligned* to business goals.
- Business strategies versus business processes. This table indicates the *relevance* of processes to the strategies.
- Business initiatives versus business processes. This table reveals the *focus* of the business on the work.
- Business issues versus business processes. This table shows the *impact* and contribution of business processes on the major business issues (*negative alignment*).

IT-related tables

- IT objectives versus issues and opportunities. This table shows how objectives *cover* the issues and opportunities.
- IT objectives versus IT constraints. This table shows how the constraints *restrict* the IT objectives.
- IT objectives versus IT strategies. This table indicates how the strategies *carry out* the objectives.
- IT objectives versus action items. This table shows how the action items *follow through* on the objectives.
- IT strategies versus action items. This table shows how the action items *fulfill* the strategies.
- Issues and opportunities versus action items. This table indicates how the issues and opportunities are *resolved* through action items.
- IT objectives versus IT projects. This table indicates how the IT projects, when completed, *implement* the objectives.
- IT objectives versus infrastructure/architecture. This table reveals the *level of importance* of elements of the infrastructure and architecture to the objectives.
- Issues and opportunities versus IT operations. How issues and opportunities *impact* IT operations is the subject of this table.
- IT strategies versus IT operations. This table deals with the *benefit* of achieving the strategies on the operations.
- Action items versus IT operations. How action items *improve* IT operations is the focus on this table.

Figure 12.5 Strategic Planning Tables.

IT- and process-related tables

- Issues and opportunities versus business processes. This table shows the *impact* of the issues and opportunities on the work.
- IT objectives versus business processes. Indicated here are the *long-term benefits* of the objective on the work.
- IT strategies versus business processes. This demonstrates the *intermediate term* benefit of the strategies, if achieved, on the processes.
- IT projects versus business processes. How IT projects will *change* the process is the subject of this table.
- Action items versus business processes. How the action items will have an *immediate impact* on the work is covered in this table.
- Infrastructure and architecture versus business processes. This table shows the *technical dependence* of the processes on the infrastructure.
- IT operations versus business processes. The focus here is on how the processes are *maintained* by IT operations.

Business- and IT-related tables

- IT objectives versus business objectives/mission/vision. This table shows *strategic positive alignment* of IT to the business.
- IT objectives versus business issues. Here is revealed the *strategic negative alignment* of IT to the business.
- IT strategies versus business strategies. This table demonstrates the *intermediate alignment* of IT to the business.
- IT strategies versus business initiatives. The contents of this table demonstrate the *fulfilment* of the initiatives.
- IT projects versus business initiatives. This table gives the *support* of IT to the implementation of the business initiatives.
- Issues and opportunities versus business issues. Here is shown the *contribution* of IT issues and opportunities to those of the business.
- Action items versus business issues. This table demonstrates how action items *alleviate* business issues.
- IT objectives versus business units. How business units benefit from the *achievement* of the IT objectives is the subject of this table.
- Issues and opportunities versus business units. This table shows how issues and opportunities *affect* the business units.
- Action items versus business units. Shown here are the *benefits* of action items to the business units after they are completed.

Figure 12.5 (*Continued*)

developed in Chapters 7 (alignment) and here in Chapter 12 (creation of the plan). Note that not all table combinations have been included.

Assume that you build these databases over time, what do you do about updating them? View the creation and maintenance of the tables as a continuous effort. You collect the information as you work with departments and business units. When you have some downtime, you can use this time to do updating and analysis.

Business Process Databases

The main database is that of the business process. The other databases are support and references for this database. Here are some specific comments pertaining to these databases.

- It might seem that maintaining this information would be a nightmare. Not really. If you look down the list of databases and their elements, the ones that change are mainly those dealing process performance and issues.
- These databases can support substantial management analysis. For example, you could develop a ranking of processes based on performance. You could also rank them based on issues and their impacts. Another use of the databases is to do cross process analysis of issues. It can be both enlightening and practical to see how the same issue applies to several processes.
- Elements of the process plan can be inserted into the business process database. This makes the process plan more available for analysis.
- The data element, overall current process condition, and several others are subjective. They are useful in helping to analyze groups of processes for future work. This also applies to the data element, trends in the condition of the process. This element describes deterioration or improvement over the past year.
- There are several elements related to interfacing processes. Since processes are becoming more integrated and highly related to each other, this can be useful in support multiprocess analysis. There is also a field to describe the nature and type of interface. This can, for example, indicate the degree of dependence of one process on another.

- There are several data elements related to supporting systems. These are the main systems supported by IT that are used by the process. In addition to naming them, there are fields to assess characteristics of system performance relative to the process.
- There is a field to identify shadow systems as well as one for King and Queen Bees. These are not stupid fields to include. The King and Queen Bees are good contact points. With regard to shadow systems, once you have found one you don't want to forget it.
- For process issues you can begin with those listed in Chapter 8. There are two data elements. The first is for those that are likely to occur (potential issues); the second is for active issues. There is a field for the impact of the active issues on the work.
- Quick Wins and their implementation are covered in Chapter 8 (identification) and Chapter 14 (implementation).
- In the business department database there is a field related to ownership role of the process. This field would indicate the extent to which the department exerts ownership of the process. As such, it is an indicator of involvement and direction of the work.
- In the process issue database, there are a number of fields that merit explanations. The type of issue is a lookup table. Examples of issue types include: staffing, procedures and training, policies, systems, shadow systems, exceptions, management, interfaces with other processes. Additionally, there are five data elements that are more subjective on how to deal with the issue: potential severity of the issue, impact of the issue, detection, prevention, and action. This database is very useful across multiple processes.

Databases for Business Planning Factors

The data for these business planning factors are the result of the work addressed in Chapters 5 and 6. There should be a lookup table for business units, business processes, and the types or categories of the vision, mission, objectives, and initiative. There is a field for status to indicate whether the element is active or not. This allows you to keep a history of vision, mission, and so forth to track evolution over time.

There is an element for importance and emphasis. Not all mission, vision, and objective items are created equal. This field allows you to assign a weight to the item that you feel management feels through their actions — not their words. Words are cheap — actions are expensive.

Consider now the data elements for the strategic business plan. You will note that they are mainly subjective. Why even have this stuff? Because it gives you more structure when you review the strategic business plan — building on what was presented in Chapter 5.

Databases for IT Projects

These databases should already be in place in IT so that you can perform both single and multiple project analysis. They are included because we have found that many IT groups do not have a structured database for retaining project information after the completion of projects.

With regard to benefits, these should come from a checklist. Benefits should all be tangible with the intangible or fuzzy benefits rolled into the tangible ones.

For the project leader you can use this database to capture expertise, project experience, and that applicable to both business processes and technical areas. Both the issues and lessons learned databases can serve as a repository to support projects and other IT work. After being associated and involved in IT for over 40 years, experience shows that the same issues and lessons learned apply to IT work again and again. The only difference lies in the details of the work. The "newness" of either a lesson learned or an issue lies in the detail. Both of these databases support a more standard, consistent, and structured approach for IT work. Both support cumulative improvement in IT.

Databases for IT Planning Factors

There are additional lookup tables that should be developed. Several of these relate to the type of the objective, strategy, and so forth. There is a distinct list of types for each planning factor — due to the level of detail involved in the planning factor.

For issues there are several subjective data elements. These are: urgency, importance, and impact if not done. Note too that issues and opportunities are in a separate database.

Tables Related to Strategic Planning

The data elements in these tables can include both ratings and comments. After a review, we have added a point of focus for each even though these have been discussed earlier. Note that in order to establish these tables, you would want to have reference lists of business and IT factors.

How do you create and maintain the databases? You can use either database management or spreadsheet software — whichever you are most comfortable with. The database management tool is best suited for larger and more complex planning efforts.

From experience it is not a good idea to wait until the strategic plan is either near completion or completed. Then it is too late. You may not remember all of the information. Moreover, if you are going to enter all of the information at one time, it can be both daunting and tedious. Thus, it is preferable to start creating the database when you begin the planning work. You can keep adding to the database and updating it as the planning work goes on. This is always possible since there will be downtimes when you are waiting for meetings or responses. As such, the planning effort is a foreground task, while the database work is a background task.

Develop and Document the Plan

There are several documents that need to be addressed. These include:

- Overall strategic IT and process plan.
- Business unit strategic IT and process plan (covered in Chapters 7 and 11).
- Presentation of the plan to upper management (covered in Chapter 3).
- Presentation of either the overall or business unit plan to divisions, business units, and IT (covered in Chapters 3 and 11).

For the strategic IT and process plan, let's consider the goal of the document. It is not just to get the plan approved. It is also to spur support and enthusiasm for implementation and change. These goals turn the document from being a dry, technical document to something that is business-oriented. So, the first guideline is to minimize the technical jargon, concepts, and terms in the plan. Make it all business. The business is the main audience for the plan.

A second guideline is to avoid being bogged down in detail. The detail can be addressed separately. Where there is a need for detail is in the impact of issues and opportunities and the benefits of the action items.

Figure 12.6 gives an outline with comments on each part of the document. Overall, you want to keep the length to, say, 20 pages. Of course, you have much more information. But you can use that later in reviews of implementation, resource allocation, and so forth. Note that there is no separate section for the business analysis as that would step on the toes of the business strategic plan.

- Executive summary. This should show the alignment of IT to the business, a summary of issues, objectives, and strategies. More detail can be given to action items and their benefits.
- Introduction. This section describes the approach for strategic planning, the organizations involved, and some of the lessons learned from the planning work.
- Business processes. This contains an overview of the condition, issues, and opportunities for the key processes. This is a down to earth assessment of the impact of problems and might also highlight process deterioration. Also, given is the future vision for the processes.
- IT and business processes. Here you want to define the IT planning factors in terms of their relation to the work and processes. This makes it easier to understand and can gain more support. This also shows the relevance and real-world nature of the IT planning items.
- IT planning tables. This is a short section that presents how the IT factors are interrelated. It shows consistency and shows the overall direction of IT. Included here is the vision of IT.
- IT and business factor planning tables. This is the section that reveals and covers the three levels of alignment of IT to the business.
- Action items. A separate section is devoted to action items. Here you can cover the following:
  o Benefits from the implementation of Quick Wins (see Chapter 14).
  o Action items and business processes — benefits.
  o Action items and issues and opportunities.
  o Project ideas mapped to processes, business initiatives, business issues, and strategies.

Figure 12.6 Outline of the Strategic IT and Process Plan.

When you review the above figure, you will find it similar to what you see in a 30 second television commercial. This starts with the problem and its impact. Then it moves to the benefits of the solution. The commercial closes with the desired actions.

Positive and Negative Marketing

Normally, people think only of positive aspects of strategic planning. Examples are:

- "With the strategic plan, we can fix a number of business problems."
- "The strategic plan will provide for direct business benefit and improvement."

These statements were not created out of thin air. They come from real experience. What is the problem with these statements? They are detached from reality! The strategic IT and process plan is a roadmap for change and improvement in both IT and the business. As such, a roadmap is just that — it tells you where you should go and how to get there. However, the strategic plan does NOT get you there. That follows from resource allocation and implementation.

In terms of positive marketing, we have found that you cannot do that much. Why? Because, as you saw in the examples above, you risk overpromising. The plan is completed, but the action items are not really implemented so there is disappointment and discouragement.

What approach should you take to marketing? Do what doctors, medical firms, and so many others do:

> The basic approach in marketing during strategic planning work should be negative.

This sounds terrible. It is not. What you will emphasize are the following:

- How situations will not improve and further deteriorate unless there is a plan.
- Without a plan, fixes, actions, etc. tend to be short term and detailed. They are neither systematic nor long lasting.
- Unless resources are allocated, the action items will die on the vine.
- If there is no change through implementation, there will be a continued decline in the performance of either or both of IT and the business.

This should not be considered as new. This is how a doctor sells you on an operation. This is how expensive medications are promoted. Negative marketing exploits the fear of not taking action. For over 20 years we have used the negative marketing methods to overcome resistance to change and surpass the inherent inertia.

Specific Marketing Activities

There are four major areas for marketing related to the strategic planning. We will examine each of this, keeping in mind the comments in the previous section. In each of these we focus on self-interest and assume that going into the phase of the work that there is substantial negative sentiment. If, of course, things are more positive, then you can adjust the marketing accordingly.

Marketing before and at the start of planning

To sell the planning effort, you want to focus on problems that have occurred because there was no plan in place. Do not overpromise with potential results. Focus on the continued deterioration and problems if there continues to be no strategic plan. Highlight these problems:

- The same problems will keep recurring.
- The projects are not all of great benefit to the business.
- Projects that were discarded were sometimes better than the ones selected.
- Processes will continue to deteriorate. More exceptions will surface. Both the efficiency and effectiveness of the work will suffer.
- Morale in both IT and business units suffers because there seems to be a lack of unified direction of IT. IT work seems like an odd collection of work.
- People get reassigned among projects and work frequently. Less is accomplished due to the lack of overall direction.

Marketing during the planning effort to management

During the planning effort you want to accomplish several things. By doing marketing as the planning is being performed, you are also marketing the end product strategic plan. First, you want to show that the planning effort is worthwhile. Uncovering potential Quick Wins and getting them implemented goes a long way to accomplishing this goal. Assume that management sees value in the planning in tangible results.

Another goal is to demonstrate progress. You have to show management interim deliverable items. This has always been difficult in an area that used to be treated as fuzzy. The method here provides with the ammunition to show progress. You have the lists and tables that you can roll out. The Quick Wins also help here.

The third goal relates to larger scale planning. It goes way beyond Quick Wins. You want to demonstrate the alignment of IT to the processes and the business. Again, the method helps since it works with the three levels of IT-business alignment. Start with the operations alignment and proceed upward to strategic alignment.

Market the action items for resource allocation

Prior to the completion of the plan you want to start the marketing to get resources and support for the action items. Don't wait until the completion of the plan. You will lose momentum and have to restart the marketing.

Point out that many, if not a majority, of the action items are not related to IT projects. Therefore, they do not require resources. This puts the managers at ease since these relate to policies, procedures, etc. For the projects, you want to emphasize the impacts on the business if the projects are not funded and provided with resources. Again, negative marketing. This is effective since it counters any feelings that IT overpromises with projects and then fails to totally deliver results. Stress the negative effects on business processes and operations — not on IT (that would be self-serving).

Market the implementation of action items

You would think that your marketing was successful that implementation would not require marketing. Not true. When you actually start implementing change, you will run into resistance. We refer here to the tips and guidelines in the implementation chapters — Chapters 14 and 15.

Examples

In one organization, we discovered a strategic IT plan that seemed very complete and addressed the major business and IT issues. However, nothing was done with it. The planning was totally decoupled from the strategic resource allocation. The allocation occurred three months after the plan had been completed so that any momentum from the plan was lost through the time gap.

Another problem with the plan was in the details and structure. The action items were buried in the middle of the plan. So it took effort to dig them out. Additionally, a number of items were treated in technical terms. Managers felt that they had to get a "technical interpreter" to explain what this part meant. Another problem was that there was little interconnection between the parts. Objectives were not clearly related to strategies, etc. This made the plan difficult to follow.

In many plans, the scope is restricted to IT. This misses a good opportunity to show the benefits of the action items, strategies, etc. in terms of the real work. In Chapter 1 a number of reasons were given for including the business processes with the IT planning. Here is another one — justification of the action items. Including the business processes forces the plan to be more business friendly and directly related to the work, as well.

Lessons Learned

We have some good planning methods fail because they lacked an easy way to create the plan. Often, there would be little communications with business managers until the plan was completed. The results were often marketing failures. Why? Because the managers' lack of involvement and participation translated into a lack of ownership.

Another reason that many methods fail is that they end with the approval of the plan. That is far from the end — just the beginning. The real resistance will occur first when you attempt to get resources for the action items. Some managers that said "Yes, yes" to the plan now say "No, no" because they do not want to relinquish their priorities and resources. Wait, it does not end there. When you get to implementation you will likely experience substantial resistance to change. That is why we have covered this in Chapters 14 and 15.

Don't brush aside the planning databases that have been presented. The effort to construct them can be spread across months. Remember your long-term personal and organizational goal is that strategic IT and process planning improve in quality, completeness, and take less effort. Only if you collect, organize, and retain the experience and knowledge will this be possible.

To demonstrate how useful the databases can be, let's consider the database on process issues. You can use the list of these issues as a checklist across multiple, different processes. This is valuable for both practical and political reasons. First, showing this to business departments reveals that you are organized and structured. It shows that you have learned from experience. Second, in seeing the list, departments will start to see that they have many issues in common with other departments and business units. From experience this can lead to greater collaboration among departments — something that is really needed. Most of the time inter-department contact is at the management or exception level. A greater degree of collaboration can lead to more process improvements.

Politics

When you are completing the draft of the plan, the tendency is to sit in your office and get it done. Not so fast. It is better to spread out the work. This gives you more time to review the lists and tables with managers and staff. It is best politically if there are absolutely no surprises in the strategic IT and process plan. Managers and most people are uncomfortable with surprise information. They may wonder why it took so long to uncover.

In doing marketing you probably should not refer to this as "marketing." This has too many negative political connotations. It is better to say that you are explaining the planning approach and results. Remember in political terms all communications are political. Thus, you must really think about what and how you convey information. You do not want to raise false expectations since resources are only allocated later. On the other hand, you do not want to overly downplay what is possible. The key is to indicate that you will require their continued support AFTER the completion of the plan for resource allocation and for implementation.

Remember what was said about the political value of the strategic planning databases. This is not simply work, it is also valuable knowledge that can be drawn upon again and again. That is why we suggest in the next section that you get going on these databases right away.

What to Do Next

Here is a list of potential actions that you can pursue now.

- Begin to create some of the planning databases in a spreadsheet. This has several benefits. First, it will force you to be organized in how you collect information. Second, you will be able to find gaps in the information. Third, there is almost immediate value of the information in developing the strategic IT and process plan.
- Evaluate the marketing effectiveness of the past IT strategic planning work. You can use the checklists in Chapter 16 to help you get started in terms of results. You can gauge the extent of participation as well as awareness of the strategic plan. Taken

together you can examine both communications and performance of the planning effort. You can follow a similar approach
for strategic resource allocation (see Chapter 13).

- This action was suggested before, but it deserves more attention
  here. Take the current IT strategic plan and create the lists and
  tables using the tips in Chapter 5.

Summary

If you follow some planning methods, the effort to finally create a
draft of the strategic plan is a monster task. Not so with the
approach in this book. You have been gathering information and
creating drafts of lists and tables related to the strategic plan all
along. This makes the assembly of the draft of the plan incremental
and much easier.

The time saved due to the incremental update of the planning
lists and tables gives you more time for communications, sales, and
marketing. Again, don't downplay the importance of marketing.
Not many things sell themselves. This is particular the case with
strategic plans. Marketing begins and continues throughout
the cycle of strategic planning — from initiation through plan completion, to resource allocation, and finally to action item
implementation. Don't stop the marketing effort with the completion of the plan. As has been shown and discussed, your marketing
is just starting.

While this chapter dealt with the creation of the plan and
marketing, a third key subject was that of the strategic planning
databases. These are important for technical, business, and political
reasons.

PART IV

IMPLEMENT THE PLAN

Chapter 13

Perform Strategic Resource Allocation

Introduction

For most books, completing the plan and getting it approved is the end of the book. After all, you have the action items approved and are ready to go. Not so fast. Approval is only the first step in getting them done. You need to get resources and then do the implementation. There are two kinds of action items — ones that don't require resources which you can do and those that require resources. For the latter there is another step — fighting for resources to do the work.

The first part of the battle is to flesh out the plans for the project ideas and other work that is in the list of action items. Why weren't detailed plans drawn up in the strategic IT planning process? Too many action items. Not enough time. Project leaders are often too busy to develop plans for the projects in the strategic plan. Recall that enough was done in terms of objectives, benefits, costs, issues, and general schedule before. But not at a detailed level.

The second part is then for these to compete to gain resources. We will examine each of these two activities in sequence.

What are the categories of work struggling to get or retain resources? A list appears in Figure 13.1.

In defining the slate of work to be done, experience shows that it is best to prioritize within each of the below categories first. Then, funding and resources can be allocated between the categories.

- Strategic IT and process plan action items. This consists mainly of projects identified in the plan
- Current work including operations and support
- Active projects
- Maintenance and enhancement
- Backlog of work
- Emergency fixes
- Targets of opportunity
- Other new project ideas, not from the plan

Figure 13.1 Types of Work Competing for Resources.

There are several major concerns in the resource allocation:

- The more you can allocate to projects, the greater the progress toward intermediate and long-term goals for IT and the business.
- The more you can allocate to support, maintenance, operations, and enhancement, the more you support short-term goals.

From this you can see that there is a basic measurement of any IT group:

How the resources are allocated is indicative of the focus of the business and IT — short term or longer term.

Or, actions speak louder than words.

If there is no Strategic Resource Allocation...

It may be the case that there is no formal resource allocation used in your organization. What do you do then? One option is to just propose each project idea from the plan for separate review and approval. This can hit or miss. The problem is that there is no consistent overall review. Resources are being allocated ad hoc, on a case-by-case basis. Even with approval, you are not done. You probably will then have to fight to get each resource on an individual basis. Since this might not be successful, you may either have to substitute resources or delay some work on the project. Alternatively, you may find that you cannot do the project at all. But it has been approved. One potential outcome is that you will be blamed for being a poor leader.

Here are two better approaches. The first is to push for a formal strategic resource allocation process. While pursuing this, you can apply a backwards approach. Before you push for project approval, line up the resources in advance. If you cannot get them, then you could modify or delay the proposal of the project to management. This does seem to be a backward approach, but it recognizes the political realities of the situation — given that resource allocation is not well organized.

Prepare the Detailed Project Plan for an Action Item

Normally, the project leader assembles the project team and creates the project plan. Work is assigned. The plan is created and reviewed. However, this will likely come later after the strategic resource allocation.

Let's review what we have so far. We have the idea for a plan. There is a business purpose, some benefits, a general estimate of cost, an estimate of the schedule. However, this is not sufficient for the project to go into battle with existing projects and other work that have strong backing. You need more.

There are some specific objectives that you seek to attain:

- There should be a clear sense of urgency as well as defined benefits. Benefits are not enough by themselves, since managers could say, "Well, if we don't do this project, there will not be any real impact since we have lived without the results of the project for a long time."

- The resources that are identified should minimize the demand on people that are in high demand. This will reduce the conflict and increase the chances of success in getting approval.
- The plan should give confidence that the project can be completed on time and within the budget. Risk must be under control.

A tall order — but doable. Start with the work. Using past experience and work, you should either have a *project template* or work breakdown structure for the project as a starting point. A template is a set of high-level tasks and milestones. Dependencies are defined as well as general resources.

There should also be a list of potential issues who apply to various projects. If this exists, go through the list and identify those that apply to this project. Also, you should map these potential issues to the tasks and milestones. Why do this? Because you want to demonstrate that you understand the potential risks and issues and have identified the work to which they pertain.

The third step is to make a list of the people who will be required for the project. If you do not know them all by name, then you can put down the job title of the person that is needed. Assign these resources to the tasks. For each critical person that is in demand, think about how you can minimize their involvement in the tasks, how to get them released from the project, and why you really need their unique skills and experience.

Next, break up the general tasks in the template or breakdown structure into smaller chunks of, say, two weeks in duration by defining detailed tasks. If this is too much work, then start with those tasks that have the most potential issues. Keep the level of detail to two weeks. This is credible. However, if it is too detailed, people may get lost in the detail. Also, you want flexibility to refine the plan after it is approved.

These steps prepare you for the next step of refining the budget estimate that was defined earlier during planning. Here are some tips. Isolate the equipment, facilities, and other non-labor expenses from those involving labor hours. For these examine how much of this expense would have to be incurred if the project was not done. This often shows that the project has incremental cost. For the labor hours try to relate these to the tasks in the plan.

Think of all of this stuff as the internal part of the project planning. The external part of the effort is to go to the departments or areas that will benefit from the project. There are several related things to do. The first is to estimate the impact if the project is not done. Here you must work with the department to assess the deterioration and effects if the project is not done. General statements do not count here. Focus on detailed work. Let's suppose that the project will fix problems in the current business process. What if these are not fixed? What will happen? After all, the process has remained broken for some time. Find example transactions that will highlight the impact of the problems in the work. Make sure that these are common and not rare or exception transactions.

Next, turn to the benefits. Assume that the project is completed successfully and that the process is changed. Take the example transactions and define new ones that demonstrate the benefits and that the problems in the process have been addressed. Many people stop here. Do not! You have to explain what the department will do to realize tangible benefits. Here are some examples.

- There are fewer errors and less rework resulting in labor savings.
- Employees can be reassigned to higher quality work.
- A higher volume of work can be completed, increasing productivity.
- Customer service levels can be improved because information can be obtained faster and easier and transactions can be completed faster.

- Employees can be shifted to other jobs or made redundant so that there are direct savings.

In Chapter 3 we discussed presenting the project ideas to management. It is worthwhile emphasizing some key points. First, the benefits and the overall project should be presented by the department managers and staff. After all, they will be accountable for the benefits. They also have more credibility than you do. The presentation focus should be on this. The lesser part of the presentation dealing with the project plan itself can be presented by the project leader. This part of the presentation can emphasize the template structure, the resources required, and the potential issues. Bringing up the issues seems negative, but it is not. First, it shows that you are realistic about the project. Second, you want to set the expectations of management at a realistic level.

Now let's consider in detail each of the areas that the new projects will be in competition with. In each category we will examine how to reduce resources in the area as well as how to set priorities for the area.

Current Work and Operations

This is sometimes a catch-all category that includes work such as the activities in Figure 13.2.

In terms of getting resources for the projects generated by the strategic IT and process plan, it would appear that only the item dealing with application software operations support would be relevant. However, many projects often require resources beyond that of application programing.

Given these areas, you seek to prioritize within each of these. The purpose is as much to understand where the resources are going as it is to make potential changes in resource allocation.

- Network support. This includes daily network operations, network management, tuning, performance measurement, network maintenance, upgrades, and similar activities.
- Hardware support. This encompasses hardware testing, upgrades, maintenance, and installation.
- Systems operations. Included here are operating systems upgrades, fixes, system backups, restores, diagnostics on the system.
- Security services. Maintenance of access codes, updating security software, firewalls, anti-virus, spyware and other security-related functions are in this category.
- Application software operations support — work needed to keep the application running on an on-going basis. This is often called production support.
- Administrative support.
- Help desk and end user support.
- Training and upgrading of IT staff capabilities.

Figure 13.2 Current Work and Operations.

Here are some measurements that have proven useful.

- Distribution of support by user area. Network support, for example, could be apportioned based on the number of users or devices in the business departments. This chart would serve to indicate whether support is disproportionate to the size or importance of the department. In one case, we found that an excessive set of resources were supporting only a few employees dealing with the general ledger. This led to a review and redistribution of resources to operational departments.
- Distribution of support by area of the architecture. This chart would be useful in organizations with complex IT architectures. The purpose of this analysis is find areas that require more support due to complexity, age, or size of that part of the architecture. An example was made comparing multiple data centers in a large organization. As a result of the analysis, several enhancements and changes to the architecture were made to streamline support and reduce requirements.
- Distribution of support by business process. Generating this sounds, at first, complicated, but it is similar to the first chart in

that you would focus on the business departments involved in the specific process. This chart could reveal that an individual business process was consuming a disproportionate share of resources. As an example, the processes around the general ledger were shown to consume an excess of resources — which led to later modernization.

These measurements are based on work. You can also consider measurements based upon personnel. Here, you could create a table in which the rows are the staff members and the columns are activities. You would place an "X" if a person could perform work in that activity. This table helps to reveal the extent of flexibility or lack thereof for the staff. As such, it reveals what is possible in terms of resources for the planning generated project ideas. It has long been an issue that specific application systems require highly technical skills and experience so that moving application programmers between areas is often not possible to any great extent. This is in part due to the in-depth knowledge needed of the business rules and processes.

Within categories first and then across the categories, one approach is to rank the work. Many times there are multiple ways of ranking. However, since support is difficult to pin down in terms of risk or benefit, experience shows that is best to rank on the basis of what happens if the work is not done. This negative ranking can really help to set priorities. After all, if you want to get resources, you have to first eliminate some of the things that people are now spending time on.

Active Projects

This looks like the best potential place to get resources. These employees could work on the new projects. However, there are some factors to overcome, including:

- There is momentum in any existing project.
- The users who participated in the project want the project results.

- Socially, team members may want to stay together.
- No one wants to admit that there is either no need for a project or that the needs have greatly changed.

So, before we discuss how to evaluate an existing project, let's discuss what is politically possible for change in an on-going project. Here are some options:

- Change the scope of the current project to include work that would be carried out by a project generated by the strategic plan.
- Taper the resource level so as to move incremental resources to the new project.
- Start a new project and then transition over staff from the current project.

Some observations here are useful. First, once a project is funded and gets going, the reviews of the project tend to be limited to that of determining progress. This gives the strategic review for resource allocation the chance to do a more in-depth review. Second, if you start a new project up, this acts to create competition for resources. Moreover, there will be pressure on the existing project to show results faster.

Figure 13.3 gives a checklist for evaluating a current project. Note that this is more comprehensive than you would use due to time constraints. However, it does provide a sense of what is possible in the review. A side note — you can also use this checklist to evaluate your own project.

Maintenance and Enhancement

Maintenance can be defined as work to improve system performance, fix problems in the system, and restore functions in the system according to the requirements. Maintenance might be considered just technical work. The effort is triggered by a problem detected by

- Need for the project.

  o Is the original need for the project still there?
  o What have business departments been doing in the meantime during the project work without the project results? You may see that they have coped rather well and the need for the project is not that urgent.
  o What if the project were to be stopped today? What would the impact be? Could users function without the project end result?

- Project status

  o Start with the traditional measurements of percent complete, budget versus actual costs, and schedule versus planned work. However, these are trailing indicators.
  o More modern indicators consider the management of issues that give to slippage and failure. Some of these measures include:

    ▪ Distribution of open issues by type. If more of the issues are external, that is not within the project, then the project may be in trouble because of the difficulty in resolving management and other outside issues.
    ▪ Age of the older outstanding issues. The longer that an issue remains unresolved, the more the project team must make assumptions.
    ▪ Percentage of remaining work with issues. This is easily calculated using project management software, such as Microsoft Project. Active issues are assigned to tasks — present and future. The percentage is based on the ratio of project hours with issues to total project hours remaining.
    ▪ Earned risk. This is the percentage of work with issues that have been resolved versus the total amount of work with issues. This reveals the progress made by the project.
    ▪ Average time to resolve an issue after it has been identified. You can also examine this by the type of the issue.

- Management of the project

  o Number of times that the project schedule and plan have been changed due to new requirements and other modifications. This shows the stability of the project.
  o Turnover of the project manager. What was the reason for changing the project manager?
  o Unplanned work. During most projects new, essential tasks have to be done that were not anticipated at the start of the project. The measure here could be expressed as the ratio of new, unplanned work to the total hours of the work in the project.
  o Use of standardized structures and templates to track issues, tasks, and work.
  o The role of the project manager. Does the manager do all of the project management planning himself or herself, or are team members involved in updating their own work and tasks?

- Project morale

  o Turnover of project team members and staffing changes and substitutions.
  o There are subjective measurements also. Examples are what team members discuss when together, how eager they are to work on the project, and so forth.

Figure 13.3: Checklist to Evaluate an Existing Project.

either IT or the business employees. A request is submitted and approved. The work is performed. The changes are tested and placed into production.

Some divide maintenance and enhancement based on the level of effort required. That is, if the number of hours of work required for the change is less than X hours or dollars, then it is maintenance. We have found that this is artificial. People may "low ball" the estimate to get it into maintenance.

Examples of maintenance are to fix an interface problem between systems, correct the navigation between screens, and repair business rules. Examples of enhancement include: new reports, additional data elements, more business rules to handle additional transactions; a new interface between systems.

At first blush, it would seem that this work has to be done since there is a problem. The reality may be quite different. People have learned from experience that maintenance requests and work are not given careful scrutiny. If something is labeled an enhancement or change to meet new requirements, then there may be a more in-depth review. These factors may lead people to try to slip enhancements in as maintenance. After all, when you are repairing "A," why not include change "B" at the same time. This is frequently done. If carried out to any substantial degree, there is a resource drain into work that had little or no justification. This robs resources from work on current projects and operations support as well as from the action items of the strategic plan.

Let's now turn to enhancements. *Enhancements* are changes to a system to meet new or additional requirements. User departments typically complete a form that includes the following items in Figure 13.4.

The process may then require a business unit manager to review the request and approve it before it goes to IT.

Then the form is reviewed by someone in IT. This person will contact the requestor for additional information to estimate the resources needed to make the change and to gather detailed

---

- Date of request
- Requesting person and organization
- Identification of the system
- Nature of the change
- Benefits from the change
- Urgency of the work

Figure 13.4 Typical Enhancement Request Items.

requirements. After approval, the changes are made, tested, and the system is updated and put into production. Thus, ends the cycle.

There are several problems with this approach. There is no verification of the benefits either estimated before the change or validated after the change. Many enhancement requests fly "under the radar" of senior IT management. A second problem is that there is often no review of the urgency. IT staff take the user statements of urgency at face value. Overall, the process is neither fair nor balanced. Projects and the action items from the strategic plan are under the microscope. These items are not. The result is often a drain of resources that prevents or delays new work that may have major or significant business benefit and impact.

For over 25 years, we have employed a different process. Let's return to the request form. This approach is applied to both maintenance and enhancement. The key items in the new form are given in Figure 13.5.

Let's now examine some of these items. Benefits validation means that the business unit must indicate what will change after the enhancement is placed into production. The benefits must be tangible. Examples are:

- Direct labor savings
- Increased productivity so that the same people can do more work
- Less time in doing rework
- Increased revenue

- Date of the request
- Requesting person and organization
- Identification of the system
- Nature of the request
- Benefits
- How the benefits will be validated and measured
- What the business would do if the change is not approved
- What the business would do if the change is deferred
- What other work is related to this request
- What the business department will do in support of the change

Figure 13.5 Items to be Included in a Maintenance or Enhancement Request.

Business departments have to explain how they will make changes after the enhancements have been completed.

The next two items on what the business unit will do if the change is not done or deferred speak to the urgency of the request. These are more specific than in the first form since they require the business manager to indicate how they will continue to do work. If the impact is substantial, that adds to the urgency.

Often, a simple request is just the tip of the iceberg. There may be many other changes lurking out there. The user may have identified a symptom of a problem and not the problem itself. If this is the case, then after the change is made, the problem may mutate, but does not go away.

The last item pertains to the work that the user department is willing to do. This includes testing, documentation, as well as changes in the business process, policies, facilities, and staffing.

When many requests come in, they are handled one at a time. This can lead to problems. If some IT staff are not busy, the user department may get lucky and the work performed right away. It is fairer and preferable to bundle requests. This can be done by having a specific schedule for submitting requests. If something is truly urgent, then it falls into the category of emergency fixes discussed later in this chapter.

The review should encompass not only this request, but also current work and other outstanding requests. This provides for a greater understanding of the overall work required for the business unit. Work can be better planned as the IT staff knows the internals of their systems.

After the work is completed, the business department should be required to give evidence as to the following:

- Effectiveness of the change
- The benefits actually achieved
- How the benefits were realized

This step has many benefits, including:

- The business unit sees that the benefits are taken seriously.
- IT morale is improved because of the tangible benefits.

This addresses the IT morale issue that IT staff sometimes wonder about the value of their work — especially in maintenance and enhancement.

In the last two IT organizations we managed, this approach reduced requests by over 60% from what went before with the reduced form cited earlier in this section. People don't want to fill out the additional information. They may not be held accountable. After all, if the earlier form is used, then they have little involvement or effort. Thus, submitting a request is relatively painless. This can generate more marginal requests.

We can now turn to analyzing the maintenance and enhancement work. Figure 13.6 gives a list of potential measurements of this work. Note that not all of these could be carried out due to limited resources. Measurements could be carried out prior to the strategic resource review as well as during the strategic IT and process planning effort.

In strategic resource allocation, it was previously indicated that it is useful to set priorities within categories and then between these to get the overall allocation. Here for maintenance and enhancement there are several practical ratings. From the work on alignment in

---

- Division of all maintenance and enhancement work by business unit or department. This is useful to reveal fairness. In the past, IT often reported to the manager of accounting. Then often, a disproportionate amount of work went into accounting systems. It also shows the extent to which the work is aligned to the business goals and business issues.
- Division of maintenance and enhancement work by system. This can indicate the health of the systems and reveal individual systems that require major work or even replacement.
- Percentage of requests that were approved and undertaken. This can reveal the rigor in the submission and review process.
- Percentage of requests approved by business unit. This can indicate the degree of fairness and balance.
- Estimated effort versus actual effort by groups of requests. This can help improve future estimation.
- Schedule performance — estimated duration versus action duration by groups of requests.

Figure 13.6 Potential Measurements of Maintenance and Enhancement Work.

the strategic planning work, you know which are the key processes and systems in terms of each of business goals (positive alignment) and business issues (negative alignment). The first step is to create a table wherein the rows are the requests and the columns are the business processes or systems. The entry can be either an "X" if the request applies to the individual process or system, or could be a subjective rating indicating the degree of benefit to that process or system on a scale of 1–5. Using this you can develop the following tables.

- Maintenance and enhancement table for positive alignment. In this table the rows are the requests and the columns are the business goals. The entry is the extent to which the change will help the achievement of the business goal.
- Maintenance and enhancement table for negative alignment. The rows are the changes and the columns are the business issues. The entry is the extent to which the change will alleviate the individual business issue.

If there are many changes, then these can be bundled into groups by department or type.

All of the above steps seem that extra work. To some they appear as "overkill." However, they support the clear goal of getting additional resources for the planning action items. This justifies the additional effort.

Backlog of Work

A piece of work in placed in the backlog if it has been reviewed and approved for work. However, either resources are not available or that the work does not have priority over existing work. It is not just new projects that are on hold. It can also be maintenance, enhancement, and operations work as well.

The concept of a backlog of orders is common in manufacturing and other industries. In IT a backlog can give confidence to staff that there is much more work to do. This is psychologically good. Another benefit of a backlog is that it can apply pressure to get the current work and projects completed.

But there is an underlying point.

> Nothing in the backlog is truly urgent. People have learned to do without the results of the work.

If some item in the backlog was urgent, it should have knocked out some of the existing other work.

Often, the backlog is not managed. It accumulates. Work is selected from the backlog when the specific, applicable resources are made available.

Some managers give a higher priority to the backlogged work than the strategic plan action items. The reasoning is that these backlogged items have already been approved — before the plan was approved. So they should take priority. A big mistake.

One of the applications of the strategic IT and process plan is to control the backlog. During the strategic resource allocation the items in the backlog should be reviewed. Does this mean that the things should be killed off? No. That would be politically dangerous. They were approved and some business groups may be very disappointed if they are killed outright.

Here are some actions that can be taken.

- See if an item in the backlog can be combined with an action item from the strategic plan.
- Determine if the need for backlogged item is still there. Maybe, there can be additional small changes that can be made to avoid doing the backlogged item.

In any event, the action items from the strategic plan should take priority over the items in the backlog.

Here are some lessons learned from managing backlog in 10 IT organizations. When something is approved, it raises expectations among business staff. They may think that finally they will get resources and results. If the work is then placed in the backlog, morale drops and the employees and managers affected may think they were misled. That is why during the project or work review for approval, consideration of available resources and funds should be a high priority. This avoids raising false expectation. The lesson learned may be to not approve the work since neither money nor people are available.

Another idea is to retain a fixed number of items in the backlog in each category of operations, maintenance, enhancement, and projects. This is politically important. Why? If the backlog keeps growing, management may think that IT is not very effective or efficient since the list keeps growing and never declines.

As to the psychological value of the backlog among IT staff, our approach has been to avoid highlighting the backlog and even downplaying its importance. This will get the staff to focus on the current work.

Emergency Fixes

Resources are drained in our daily lives by the need to handle emergencies — at work and home. While dealing with these, time is taken away from other work and fun. Then, after the emergency you have to recover and have some downtime. This is followed by getting up to speed and back to what you were doing or going to do before the emergency. You probably know some people who lives seem to move from one problem to another. They never seem to make headway. They are always reacting to events.

The lessons of time management are to take charge of our lives. Exert more control. Try to anticipate potential problems and issues. Make efforts to prevent these.

Examples of emergency fixes and work include the ones in Figure 13.7.

There are others, including critical employees who quit or suddenly become ill.

Organizations sometimes behave the same way as individuals. We worked with one IT group that was always reacting to problems — network problems, application problems, user "emergency requests" and so forth. The list goes on and on. When we examined the situation, we found that:

- Many of the problems were, in fact, preventable.
- Many others were predictable based on past experience.
- Some were not really emergencies.

- A software application experiences failure during batch processing.
- There is a network outage or overload.
- A virus is brought in by an employee and spreads.
- A manager wants to have a change made to an application — now.

Figure 13.7 Examples of Emergency Work.

We also discovered that some employees in IT and even some supervisors seemed to thrive on emergencies. Like a fire department, responding to and dealing with emergencies made them feel worthwhile. The IT manager often proudly discussed and presented how many emergencies were dealt with. However, no progress was made toward strategic goals. Eventually, the IT manager was replaced and work began to reduce the extent, range, and amount of emergency work.

During strategic resource allocation, a common approach is to allocate some percentage of resources to emergency work. This is based upon past experience. Often, nothing is done to take actions to reduce emergency fixes. That is why in earlier chapters we mentioned that some suitable action items are to reduce the extent of emergency work. This is similar to a fire department which carries out inspections of buildings and requires homeowners to clear the land around their houses to reduce the potential damage from brush fires.

There are several potential actions to take during the resource allocation. One is to give higher priority to fixing problems that have been recurring. Another is to implement a management review of emergency requests and work before work begins. Experience shows that this review can significantly improve productivity of IT staff and lead to higher morale and work quality.

Targets of Opportunity

What is a target of opportunity? Something that arises that is unexpected. These are the positive opportunities and surprises. The negative ones have been addressed as either IT or business issues.

Examples relating to IT and business processes are listed in Figure 13.8.

Since technology change is more predictable than business change, the IT targets have usually been incorporated into the plan.

- Information technology

  o A new product from a vendor;
  o New pricing of system services and/or technology products;
  o New vendor of services or products;
  o New release of a product that has substantial new features.

- Business processes

  o A change in organization that affects the process;
  o A change in management of the group that performs the process;
  o External factors such as a drop in sales or sales increase;
  o Staffing changes due to retirements and so forth. that create new
    opportunities for changing a process;
  o New government regulations that affect the process.

Figure 13.8 Examples of Targets of Opportunity.

Remembering that the strategic plan deals with both IT and business processes, it is most often the case that the surprises come from the business process side.

How can these affect the resource allocation? When they arise, they attract attention and notice. Managers may want to seize the moment and devote resources or make changes in resource allocation to include or take advantage of a target of opportunity. This can then divert resources from the actions of the strategic plan.

Given that targets of opportunity are a potential threat to realizing the benefits of the plan, you want to head this off by trying to incorporate these into the strategic IT and business process plan. This was addressed earlier in the book. However, there is a time gap between the approval of the strategic plan and the resource allocation. If this is only a few weeks or a month, there is not much risk of a new target appearing. The longer the gap between plan approval and resource allocation, the greater the likelihood of substantial targets of opportunity.

If a new target of opportunity arises after the plan approval, the approach is to incorporate it into the plan action items before the allocation occurs. In that way, you take advantage of the opportunity and employ it to strengthen the support for the action items.

This is best seen by example. Consider the list of business process examples earlier in the section. The last one is rare since organizations are given substantial time to respond to government regulations. External factors can affect a process in terms of scaling up or down the work. A substantial increase in work that was not anticipated and is expected to continue can make improvements to the process a high priority. The plan action items might be able to be modified to allocate more resources to process support.

The other examples pertain to changes in staffing and/or management. Why are these opportunities? Because they provide a chance to make changes in the business process that would not have been possible before with previous managers and staff. These changes should trigger a review of the action items before the allocation to see how best to take advantage of these.

Other New Project Ideas, Not from the Plan

Wait a minute. Didn't the plan include all of the potential projects? Yes and no. Yes — the strategic plan covered the known projects that were either proposed or identified. However, there could beÿnew ideas that some manager identified during or after the planning process. Also, there is a political situation. If a manager wanted a new project and it was not included in the strategic plan, he or she may decide to propose it directly during the strategic resource allocation.

Like targets of opportunity, these compete with the action items of the plan for resources. However, the other new project ideas are usually much better planned and marketed. After any new project idea has a constituency that gains something from the project — power, resources, efficiency, effectiveness, etc. If the idea was discarded or dropped during the planning work, it is politically difficult to attack it. The reason is that you appear to be defending the planning process at the expense of the idea.

A political approach to this problem is to organize the supporters of the project action items that are in the plan. Point out the threat that this project poses in terms of resources and funding to them and their projects.

Now let us suppose that the idea comes from upper management and cannot be dismissed or easily attached. What should you do? Try to unite this project idea with some of the action items in the plan. If you can successfully do this, then everyone wins. The manager gets his or her project. The business department gets the project that was in the plan.

A Proven Method of Resource Allocation

Having discussed the categories of areas that demand resources, we can turn to the allocation approach itself. We assume that the work has already been prioritized within each category. What is left is the overall allocation among categories. The method we have employed many times involves developing a number of rankings and ratings based on different criteria. Here are some criteria that have proven useful in the past.

- Short-term stability and benefits. Here, all of the pieces of work are sorted by whether they provide short-term benefits and stability. Obviously, for this one many of the action items of the plan appear at the bottom.
- Long-term contribution to the mission and vision. This favors both the on-going projects as well as the action items of the strategic plan. This can balance out the first ranking. In this one you would rate based on doing the least amount of work in maintenance, operations, and enhancements while still ensuring operational stability.
- Alleviation of the business issues. This rating favors enhancements, current projects, and some of the action items of the plan. This

particular rating is very powerful since it speaks to the business urgency.

- Intermediate-term benefits. This favors all but the major project ideas in the plan that require major resources.
- The risk in the work. This rating is based upon the potential or actual problems and barriers to the work across all categories. Many action item project ideas involve change, process improvement, and/or new systems and technology and so would fall toward the bottom of the rating.

There are a number of ways to carry out the rating process. You can have a small group of managers assign numerical values of 1–5 (1 is low; 5 is very high) or high, medium, and low. Then their scores can be averaged to get an overall rating.

When an allocation is developed through one of the rating methods above, it can be assessed in several ways. In each case a table is constructed wherein the rows are groups of the top ranked items from the lists generated above.

- Division of resources across business units. Here, the columns are the business units. The entry is percentage of resources devoted to this business unit in terms of total resources. This can show whether an individual ranking fits with the perceived importance of the business departments. This rating can help prevent a disproportionate share of resources going to one area.
- Division of resources by product or customer type. The columns are types of products or customer groupings. The entry is the percent of resources supported the individual product or group. For example, in banking you might consider the resources required to support consumer customers versus business customers; or, credit card products versus lending products.
- Division of resources versus mission or vision elements. Here, the columns are the elements of the mission or vision. Note

that both of these include elements for continued, successful operations so as to include maintenance and operations. The entry in the table is the percent of resources applicable to that mission or vision element. Note that an activity can apply to multiple objectives, vision or mission elements so that the percentages exceed 100% in total.

- Division of resources versus business issues. The columns are the business issues. The entry is the percent of resources that help resolve or mitigate the issue. Some categories may be unrelated to a specific business issue. This table is useful in showing how the business issues are covered.

So, we have several ways to rate the projects and work as well as different ways to evaluate or review the ratings. The ultimate mix of work that is approved depends on the situation and firm. However, there are some very useful observations possible. Regardless of all of the wonderful business plans, and mission and vision statements, what is really going on is often revealed by how the resources are allocated. This is where the "rubber meets the road."

Timing and Frequency of Strategic Resource Allocation

During times when technology and the business are very stable, the strategic allocation process is undertaken annually. This was the case in many organizations for years. However, with a more dynamic and fluctuating business environment, there is a need for more frequent allocations to better respond to business requirements.

If the allocation is not undertaken with enough frequency, then management can get frustrated because of the lack of available resources to pursue some new requirement. The result is often an ad hoc, unplanned reallocation of resources. This can be very disruptive to both IT and the business:

- The IT staff must drop what they are doing and turn to the "urgent" work newly identified.

- The business managers and employees hear about this change and find that their project has been stopped. They must now make contingency plans since they will not be getting the new or enhanced system on schedule. Morale can drop.
- The area affected by the "urgent" project suddenly receives a lot of attention. This can affect morale there as well when people thought they were doing the work OK.

There is the other extreme. The pain of too many reviews is the effort required to do the allocation as well as the disruption to projects and other generated by the new allocation results.

Deciding on the frequency of the resource allocation depends on the firm and its situation. Ideally, an organization would stick to its past resource allocation until there were enough new ideas and factors to have another allocation. However, this is too indefinite. Just doing the resource allocation can raise fear about the projects.

A common approach is to do two resource allocations per year. The most we have seen is four — that was a very fluid and dynamic setting. If you have two resource allocations, the work is limited. However, you are more responsive to management needs for specific new projects. The review also places positive pressure on current projects to show results.

Having covered frequency, let's turn to the timing. Assume that the annual business year starts on January 1. In our discussion earlier, we indicated that the strategic IT and process plan should be finished by mid-year. This allows time for the input of the action items into the business plans. Thus, the resource allocation should occur after the plan has been completed and at the early or middle stages of the business planning. If the strategic plan was completed in July, the resource allocation should occur by October — preferably earlier. The second resource allocation can occur in the period from February to April. This has the added benefit that the strategic planning effort can be sensitive to the latest allocation that occurred shortly before the start of the next strategic planning effort.

Examples

A major bank was trying to rapidly modernize their application systems. Resource allocation was being performed annually. Resources were found to be drained by other activities. It was recommended that both strategic and tactical resource allocation be implemented. Strategic resource allocation occurred quarterly. Resource allocation was then fine tuned weekly. This was successful and much progress was made.

In a local government agency there was a strategic plan. However, there was no overall resource allocation. As a result, while the plan was very good and approved, no progress was made on the action items. Management complained and decided to establish a committee to oversee IT and do the allocation.

A manufacturing firm in China had a substantial IT department with modern software. However, they were too busy to do the strategic plan for IT, much less processes. Resource allocation was performed ad hoc. The first problem occurred when the company grew and the IT applications and infrastructure could not keep pace. More resources were piled into IT, but there was little change. Eventually, the firm was taken over by another company which absorbed their IT group.

Lessons Learned

A key lesson learned is to assess the extent of change after the allocation. This not only tests the effectiveness of the allocation, but also can lead to other benefits. First, the staff realizes that what they work on matters. That is, there are more important things than doing routine maintenance and minor enhancements. Second, the resource allocation helps to align IT better with the strategic goals of the organization.

If there is strategic resource allocation, then it often follows that there should be a followup to ensure that the allocation that was mandated is being pursued. This is important in that it reinforces the importance of what is worked on with the employees and managers both in IT and the business.

Politics

Politics is often very active during resource allocation. All of the planning activities do not get the same attention as the actual assignment of people and money to projects and other work. That is why in many organizations, the allocation is not formal and structured as we have presented. Instead, it is more informal, not transparent, and sometimes not even announced. People are just told that their priorities have changed. Sometimes, no reason is given.

What to do Next

Examine the current method of allocating resources today in your organization. Figure 13.9 gives a list of things to consider along with comments.

If you want to make changes to a resource allocation method, you might be tempted to directly propose a new approach. Don't even bother to consider this as managers may not see any problem with the current approach. What you want to first do is to pin down the effects on work and projects of changes or the lack of change in the resource allocation. This will get support for something new.

Summary

This chapter has presented a structured method for resource allocation at a strategic level. This activity closely links to the

- How often is the allocation performed?
- Is the method known to the staff? It should be transparent to be enforceable.
- Were there any surprises from the allocation?
- What really changed in the work after the allocation?
- How are the plan action items considered during the allocation process?
- What surprises occurred between allocations? Hopefully, not very many.
- Who is involved in the allocation?
- Do the managers who are involved in the allocation get a disproportionate share of resources?
- Does the allocation ever result in a current project being killed? If so, this would indicate that the allocation is serious.
- What information is gathered prior to the allocation?
- Does the allocation result in reduced maintenance, operations, and enhancement work?

Figure 13.9 Evaluating your Current Resource Allocation Approach.

strategic planning effort since a structured, formal method gives credibility to both the allocation and the planning work.

If there is no formal strategic resource allocation, it is hard to see how projects from the plan can be started, except on a case-by-case basis. This requires more effort and can result in more disruption to the work. Overall, think of the strategic plan as the "What." Consider the strategic resource allocation as the "How."

Chapter 14

Implement the Plan — Short Term

Introduction

This chapter addresses methods for implementing the Quick Wins developed by the strategic IT and process plan. Since there are many potential changes that could impact the same employees and departments we need to define an organized approach. This is in the next section where the Quick Win implementation strategy is developed.

Following this, we cover specific areas of Quick Wins. These include:

- Business process Quick Wins;
- Department interface Quick Wins;
- Systems Quick Wins;
- Infrastructure and facility Quick Wins;
- Staffing and skills Quick Wins; and
- Project management Quick Wins.

This is followed by the initial and then successive waves of Quick Wins. We also consider resistance to change. After all, just because management approves of the Quick Wins, this does not mean that the employees will go along. Given inertia and politics, anticipate and expect that there will be resistance. In that way, you will not be surprised when it arises. The last part deals with measurement specific to Quick Wins. Since you will not be implementing these Quick Wins by yourself, we will assume that there is a project team that will coordinate the implementation.

Develop a Quick Win Implementation Strategy

Because of the number of Quick Wins you will want to implement these in groups. What happens if you rush into implementation?

- You encounter unanticipated problems. The solution of these diverts you from the Quick Wins and slows down the effort.
- You fail to overcome pockets of resistance. Queen and King bees may yet rise up to resist change.
- Management expectations are now raised to such a high level that it is impossible to satisfy them. Thus, management is let down and may not support the change effort to the extent necessary.

What is a Quick Win implementation strategy? The ***Quick Win implementation strategy*** is a roadmap for how the Quick Wins will be undertaken or sequenced in stages. Some of the activities are preparation for the long-term change (addressed in the next chapter). As such, they may have costs, but limited benefits. Other changes are procedural or policy related and so have benefits. You want to add up the benefits, costs, and risks of all of the activities in each phase of implementing Quick Wins. But there is more than one way to carry out the change sequencing based upon politics, technology, organization, and processes. That is why the Quick Win implementation strategy is so important.

The Quick Win implementation strategy forces people to think about how multiple things in different areas will be undertaken and successfully carried out. A benefit of the strategy is that with success, you increase the employees' morale and motivation for further Quick Wins.

Up to this point, the strategic planning process and plan have not resulted in any change. The rubber meets the road when you develop the Quick Win implementation strategy. Think of the change implementation strategy as a large table. The first column of the table consists of two groups of rows. The first group of rows consists of areas of Quick Wins. The second group of rows focuses on performance measures. The second, third, and other columns refer to phases of Quick Wins. In that way, you can manage a large number of Quick Wins. Keep in mind that many Quick Wins lead to long-term change so that they are compatible with the long-term action items. The last column indicates the final set of Quick Wins. Figure 14.1 gives an overall schematic of the change implementation strategy or roadmap. Figure 14.2 reveals how the table is completed.

How do you complete the table to generate a potential change implementation strategy? Here are the first two steps that are shown in Figure 14.2.

Areas of change	Current	Phase 1			Phase N
Performance measures					

Figure 14.1 General Structure of the Quick Win Implementation Strategy.

Areas of change	Current	Phase 1		Phase N change	Long term
1	2	3		4	
Performance measures					

Figure 14.2 Sequencing of the General Structure of the Quick Win Implementation Strategy.

- Identify the areas of Quick Wins (labeled 1 in the diagram). These can be processes, departments, policies, systems, IT infrastructure, customers, or suppliers. You want to be complete in terms of identifying what will change. Below the dark line you will need to list performance measures such as cost, schedule, risk, and benefits. You can also include perspectives. That is, what will employees, managers, customers, or suppliers get from the changes in the entries above the line.
- The columns are the row headings, the current situation, phases or waves of Quick Wins.
- In the second column you have the current state or situation (labeled 2 in the diagram). Here, you would indicate with some comments issues that have surfaced in each area of change. Then, below the line you indicate the overall impact of the current situation.

It is appropriate to make some observations now. First, you want to be complete in the row headings. Note that unlike IT projects or other work, implementation here has potentially a much broader scope. So it is difficult for people to understand the scope of the Quick Wins that will be taking place and their ramifications.

Second, you want to ensure that managers and employees are "on the same page" in that they have a common perspective of the current situation. That is the purpose of the second column. It shows the issues above the line and the impacts below the line.

Now let's move to the other steps.

- For each area of Quick Wins (each row above the line) enter the changes in the appropriate columns (labeled 3 in the diagram). This is now an alternative change implementation strategy.
- But what does it mean? Now you must "add up" all of the Quick Wins in each column and determine the impacts below the line (labeled 4 in the diagram). This helps you to see the effects of

Table 14.1 Quick Win Implementation Strategy Score Card.

Factor	Score	Comment
Elapsed time required to get the Quick Win implementation strategy		
Extent of participation by team		
Extent of participation by the team members		
Number of alternative Quick Win implementation strategies generated		
Extent of changes made to the implementation strategy as a result of collaboration		
Participation by management in the evaluation and trade-offs of alternative Quick Win implementation strategies		
Feasibility of the Quick Win implementation strategy given available resources		

the change. It will assist you in evaluating alternative Quick Win implementation strategies.

This approach can reveal the benefits of Quick Wins in spreading out the risks and in phasing in the many changes.

How do you evaluate your Quick Win implementation strategy? A potential score card appears in Table 14.1.

This score card is significant because you are attempting to judge the quality of the selected Quick Win implementation strategy as well as the range of alternatives considered and the extent of participation by the change management team, the strike force members, and management. The factors for the score card are listed below.

- Elapsed time required to develop the Quick Win implementation strategy. This is obviously important. However, it should not be short since that may mean little participation or collaboration.

- Extent of participation by the team. It is critical that the team understands the ramifications of carrying out multiple Quick Wins in different areas in the same phase. They must be heavily involved and committed so that when problems arise in implementation, they are comfortable with the setting of the agenda of change.
- Extent of participation by the team members. Team member participation is important since they can point out resource conflicts and other problems that the change management team might not be aware of.
- Number of alternative Quick Win implementation strategies generated. This shows the range of what was really considered.
- Extent of changes made to the Quick Win implementation strategy as a result of collaboration. This indicates the effectiveness of collaborative work.
- Participation by management in the evaluation and trade-offs of alternative Quick implementation strategies. This reveals the extent of management support.
- Feasibility of the Quick Win implementation strategy given available resources. This is very important since you can have a wonderful strategy that falls flat on its face because it is infeasible.

You are going to have to sell the Quick Win implementation strategy. You don't market the Quick implementation strategy by marching around with presentations. That will fail. Managers have to participate and understand the trade-offs that were made in the rejection of some alternatives. They have to understand the passion that people have in being able to do their own work as well as the change work. That is critical.

How do you involve management in the development of Quick Win management strategy? Here are some reasonable guidelines.

- Show them the process and the tables. This reveals the method.
- Now keep the managers informed by showing them some of the alternative Quick Win management strategies. Be sure that someone from the strike forces is helping and participating. Management must see that employees are involved since they will be dependent upon them for implementation success.
- Involve management in the final selection by going through trade-off and alternatives.

Now let's consider different types of Quick Wins for implementation.

Business Process Quick Wins

Here, we consider a wide range of Quick Wins involving policies, procedures, shadow systems, and workarounds. Policy Quick Wins result in complex change. When you change a policy, you have to consider how the policy will be interpreted in terms of the work. This is the same as in the law where legislation is enacted and then interpreted by the court system. Many people make the mistake that people assume how the policy is to be interpreted. However, most of the time, it is not automatic. Table 14.2 can help here.

In the first column (labeled A) you enter the areas that the new policy will address. In column B you place the current policy in terms of interpretation. In column C the new policy is placed for that area. Column D contains the interpretation of the new policy.

Table 14.2 Analysis of Policy Quick Wins.

Areas covered by policy	Existing policy	New policy	Interpretation of new policy	New procedures
A	B	C	D	E

The last column (E) is for the new procedures required to support the policy.

You cannot rely on what managers say about the use of current policies. You need to talk to different supervisors. After all, different supervisors may interpret the same policy differently. You also want to talk to employees without the supervisors around to see how they do their work. This might be a different result that what you heard from the supervisors.

On implementing new policies you define both the interpretation of how the policy is to be employed and used as well as the procedures. Here are some questions to answer with regard to new policies:

- Are there any new exceptions generated by the new policy?
- Are exceptions to the old policy covered by the new policy?
- Are there fuzzy or unclear areas of the policy in terms of what the policy applies to?
- Can people get around the policy? An example might be a policy to use a specific method or tool if the work is more than a certain cost. Some people might then state that the cost was lower, thereby avoiding the policy.
- Is the new policy consistent with the systems and automation in place? If not, then there must be systems changes before the policy is changed.

There may be opportunities in Quick Wins to eliminate one or more exceptions. This is carried out in the simplest cases by changes in procedures. However, in some cases there may need to a policy change. Some guidelines here are:

- Focus on the problems and extra work that the exception generates.
- Show how the new approach that eliminates the exception will work.

- Indicate how any questions or issues that remain with that exception will be handled.

Recall that a shadow system is a system created within a department. It can be automated through database management software or spreadsheets. There are several approaches to take with a shadow system.

- You can eliminate it. Here, it is treated as an exception so that the above guidelines apply.
- You can formalize it. This means that it will become part of the standard business practices until the long-term changes are put into place.

If you formalize it, then typically this means some systems work, development of procedures, and training. Then, you have to explain how it will be used in conjunction with the regular work.

A *workaround* is a set of procedures that are followed because the existing system does not handle or address a specific collection of transactions or work. People have gotten in the habit of using the workaround. It is ingrained by habit. What are alternatives here?

- You can eliminate the workaround by changing the system to handle the work. This is a good idea, but it may go beyond what is possible in a Quick Win.
- You can formalize and streamline the workaround so that the workaround is performed more consistently and efficiently.

It may be the case that you have to add some additional work steps to prepare for the long-term change. Examples of this are:

- Measurements of the work
- Additional editing or quality control work
- Improved customer service

Employees are often naturally resistant to new work. They feel that they are already working at full steam. Thus, it is important to stress the following points:

- The additional work is temporary and will disappear when the long-term change is implemented. This can help get the employees to support long-term change faster to get rid of the work.
- The additional work is necessary and should have been performed all along.
- Demonstrations of how people can do this additional work and their regular work must be done so that the people feel comfortable with the feasibility of the total workload.

Now that you have covered the employee part of planning, it is time to consider the supervisors and managers. Of course, the supervisors are going to be involved during the planning as are some of the middle-level managers. However, you also want to do planning with supervisors without the employees. There should be an initial meeting to go over the following items:

- Potential problems with employees in terms of resistance.
- Identification of individuals in the department or group who should be trained in the changes first, second, and so forth (sequencing of employees).
- Timing of the implementation in terms of peak or trough workload periods.

As the planning progresses, you want to have follow-up meetings with the supervisors to determine how things are going, what their reactions are, and also address these specific points.

- Can specific individuals be freed up from their regular work to participate in the change effort?

- How can the supervisor review work after changes to ensure that reversion or fallback does not occur?
- How will resistance be addressed — either covert or overt?

Managers need to be assured that the work will not be disrupted. Therefore, you should have some employees and supervisors in the meetings with managers when you provide updates. This will also show the managers that the employees and supervisors are committed to the changes.

Do you have to do all of this planning if you are just implementing Quick Wins? Yes, for several reasons. First, it shows that the change management team and management are sensitive to their concerns and feelings. Second, it gives the employees a greater sense of ownership in the change process. Third, you may uncover hidden issues that were not noticed before. Some issues may be more substantial or less important than previously thought.

Department Interface Quick Wins

This can be tricky. Here are some situations. You are implementing Quick Wins in one area that impacts another group. Alternatively, you are implementing Quick Wins in work that spans multiple groups. The approach is basically the same as that for a single group. However, you should employ these guidelines.

- Focus on the issues in the current interface and the problems generated for both groups.
- Even if the two groups are of unequal power or prestige, you should treat both groups as equals.
- When doing training, focus on the problems with the interfaces and their impacts.
- Train both groups at the same time so that the training and message are consistent.

- Involve employees and supervisors from both groups in the planning work and meetings.

Systems Quick Wins

For Quick Wins these changes must not take more than a few weeks. Any extensive change would fall into the major change and not Quick Wins. The scope of any systems change must be very limited. Testing must be included.

What types of changes could be made to systems in such a short time? Here are some examples.

- New or modified reports
- Modified screens in terms of data element placement or text on the screen
- Automation of simple exceptions
- Modifications of business rules to eliminate workarounds
- Changing of permissions and security levels
- Simple modifications to interfaces

Infrastructure and Facility Quick Wins

There are many potential infrastructure Quick Wins, such as:

- Network cabling upgrades
- Reorganization of network segments and subnetworks
- Implementation of simpler system software upgrades
- Security policy and procedure changes

Let's turn to facilities. Changing someone's workplace when it has been the same for many years is difficult. You have to think about where and how people will work during the changes. It is important that they see some benefit from the change. In one case, a facility layout change resulted in people being more cramped and poorer lighting. It then had to be redone. Employees should be involved in terms of selecting furnishings and colors. You can imagine the feeling of powerlessness when someone comes in and tears up and reorders the place.

Staffing and Skills Quick Wins

Let's first consider some examples that can be considered Quick Wins. Suppose that you had a customer service group in which everyone was allowed to answer any call. You found in the analysis that a number of employees could not handle the difficult or complex calls. As a Quick Win, it was decided to create a position of specialist so that other employees could refer the calls to these people. In order to implement this and similar shifts, the following steps are required:

- Define and get approval for new position.
- Develop procedures and standards for the new position.
- Screen current employees to determine those who qualify for the new position.
- Train the employees who will be specialists.
- Train other employees on call referrals.

As you can see, there are multiple steps. However, each is reasonable.

All of the changes require additional training. Rather than address it in each area, it is covered here. Training begins with defining the new procedures for the work. You want to have those for the current work on hand along with the issues that were identified earlier. The next step is to develop a short training outline in preparation for the training materials. Here is a successful outline:

- Overview of current work. This is familiar to people and it shows that you respect what they do.

- Issues involved in the current work. This gets the employees to acknowledge again the need for change and improvement.
- Change management approach. Here, the Quick Wins are described along with the long-term change.
- New policies and procedures. These are presented in a summary form.
- Detailed procedures and workflow.
- Benefits and measurement from the change. This shows that the implementation is to be taken seriously. It also helps to set expectations.

You can probably reuse the work on the new process and changes that was done earlier.

Project Management Quick Wins

There are a number of potential Quick Wins related to improving the management of projects in IT. Let's assume for the moment that projects are managed in a traditional manner wherein each project leader operates on their own to create and update plans. Then some or all of the following changes will yield rapid results (see Figure 14.3).

Rather than working with all project leaders, you might start a pilot effort with the junior project leaders. Why not the senior ones? Because the junior ones are more amenable to change.

Tips on Implementing the First Quick Wins

After all of this planning, the installation of the first Quick Wins should be easier. It will be. However, there can still be issues that arise.

- People get pulled off of the change effort due to pressing regular work. This is addressed in the next section.

- Set up meetings for project leaders to share experiences and lessons learned. This should aid the junior project leaders and provide a forum for the senior ones.
- Sit down and make a list of common project issues. This is the start of a standardized issues database.
- Have each project leader identify issues associated with their projects. They can use the list from the previous step as a starting point.
- Get some of the project leaders to have their team members update and define their own tasks. This will increase participation and yield more accurate schedules.
- Have the project leaders link the issues that they identified to tasks in the plan. This will support expanded issues management later.
- Collect the current project plans and extract the high-level tasks from these plans. Make these standardized in terms of format, words, etc. This is the start of building templates.
- Have project leaders retrofit their schedules into the templates. Now you are on the path to being able to easily do multiple project analysis.
- Change the nature of project meetings from status toward discussing issues and lessons learned. This will not only raise morale, but also improve productivity.

Figure 14.3 Examples of Project Management Quick Wins.

- Pockets of resistance still surface even if the supervisors, managers, and many employees support the change.

To kick off the change, an upper-level manager should introduce the Quick Wins. The manager should not only explain that change is needed, but give fairly detailed management expectations and a timetable for change.

You can now follow the training outline given in the planning section to implement the change. Wherever possible you should convert everything that you identified in your strategy for implementation at the same time so as to reduce disruption. You should create a quiet and calm atmosphere and then kick-off the training for the change.

In the training for the change, have the supervisors and employees perform the training. They know the language and their fellow workers. They can answer questions more quickly and easily than the change management team. However, several members of the team should be present.

After you have carried out the Quick Wins, monitor the work. Get opinions of employees. In this initial change this is crucial to build confidence for further change. Here are some guidelines.

- Encourage employees to pose questions as they do their work.
- Have a supervisor on hand to address any concerns.
- Ask employees after a few days what they think.
- Gather positive opinions and write these down.

What if you find that you have to make some modifications to the new procedures? Be careful here. What may be happening is that people are attempting to revert back to the old process. They may be testing you to see how far they can go. Think through any changes with the project team and supervisors outside of the ears of the employees. Do not improvise on the spot. There is no need. If you do, you may be sending a message that you are desperate to have the employees carry out the change.

A useful thing to do is to hold a group focus meeting. This can be done several times. The first one can be after 3–4 days of operation. Another can be held a week later. The supervisor and a member of the change management team can co-chair the meetings. Here are some things to cover in the meetings.

- How is the work going now?
- What are any problems that have arisen? Do not attempt to address these in the meeting. Write them down for later analysis with the supervisors and members of the team.
- What are some lessons learned and guidelines that they have identified in how to do the work? Answers here can be helpful for both further Quick Wins and long-term change.
- What are the benefits of the changes? Here you want people to identify the benefits along with how they impact the group. What do the benefits result in?

Dealing with Resistance to Change

Employees may continue to raise issues and potential problems from planning through initial operation after the implementation of the Quick Wins. This can occur in the middle of training, for example. Typically, an employee will ask "How will we do xxxx?" You should take this initially as a positive step in that they are trying to visualize how something will now be done. It starts to become resistance if the same individuals raise similar questions repeatedly. Here are some guidelines to handle this.

- Do not respond with a hair trigger idea.
- Gather more details using the supervisor and other employees to delve into the situation.
- For each question go into impacts, need for action now, and other related problems.

Additional Quick Win Implementation

Let's suppose that you have just carried out one round of Quick Wins. Maybe it went well. Typically, however, the road was bumpy at first. The project team and management have gone through a learning experience. This is a good time to gather more lessons learned. Here are some additional steps to prepare for more Quick Wins.

- Revisit the schedule and sequencing of Quick Wins to see if there have to be any changes.
- Involve employees who were successful in the effort in later waves of Quick Wins. This is very useful to generate more grass roots support for change.
- Gather and use comments from employees as testimonials.

In general, the successive waves of Quick Wins will carry out more and greater changes. However, you are better prepared with the experience.

Once the Quick Wins are implemented, it is tempting to think that marketing of the change effort can stop. It can't. Employees who resist change may start rumors that things are not going well. Managers who oppose change and see a power shift may lobby to slow down the pace of change. Trust us, these things happen frequently.

It is imperative that you keep key managers informed about status, issues, and progress. You should get them involved in some of the issues. As changes occur, invite managers to visit with employees after the changes have been made and the work has settled down. You want hands-on involvement in addition to formal presentations and informal meetings.

In terms of formal presentations on Quick Wins, here is an outline that we have used many times.

- Summary of the overall change implementation table — gives an overall perspective.
- Quick Wins that are active now — zoom in for detail.
- Results of the implementation planning for the Quick Wins.
- Summary of the issues and problems in the current work — reinforces the need for change.
- Example of a transaction — before and after change — proves the change.
- Benefits from the change — relate to the transaction.
- Surprises and lessons learned — this is often of great interest to the managers who get more insight into the work.

Using these steps management becomes more hands-on without getting in the way of change or micromanaging change.

Measure Quick Win Results

There are several ways to measure the implementation of Quick Wins — at both the planning and implementation levels for both employees and management.

The purpose of the employee planning score card is to assess how the employees performed in the implementation planning. It is used to help in future implementations of Quick Wins. It also helps to evaluate the change management team effectiveness. This score card is shown in Table 14.3.

Some comments on the factors in the score card are:

- Quality of participation in planning — this is subjective but important. The score can be arrived at through discussions in meetings.
- Number of meetings held with employees. You may want to add the total time here as well.
- Number of surprises encountered in implementation that should have surfaced during planning. You may also want to include the types and impacts of the surprises. This will help to improve your future efforts.
- Lessons learned gathered during planning. This is always important.
- Elapsed time for the planning. This should get shorter as you implement more Quick Wins.

Table 14.3 Quick Win Implementation Planning Score Card for Employees.

Factor	Score	Comments
Number of employees involved in planning		
Percent of total employees involved in planning		
Quality of participation in planning		
Number of meetings held		
Number of surprises encountered in implementation that should have surfaced during planning		
Lessons learned gathered during planning		
Elapsed time for the planning		
Performance of the project team		
Planned versus actual schedule		
Planned versus actual cost		

Table 14.4 Quick Win Implementation Planning Score Card for Management.

Factor	Score	Comments
Number of supervisors involved		
Percent of supervisors involved		
Number of meetings with supervisors		
Number of surprises encountered		
Extent and impact of surprises		
Extent and degree of participation		
Performance of the project team		
Support of supervisors with employees		
Performance of management involvement		
Resolution of issues by supervisors		
Resolution of issues by managers		

The intent of the planning score card for management is to evaluate the role of management and supervisors as well as the project team. Table 14.4 contains a potential score card.

Remarks on the specific factors are as follows:

- Number of supervisors involved. Almost all should be involved.
- Number of meetings with supervisors. There should be many formal and informal meetings or gatherings.
- Number of surprises encountered. Surprises are also a reflection of the supervisors and management.
- Extent and impact of surprises. You definitely want to include impacts here.
- Support of supervisors with employees. This is subjective and should be addressed.
- Performance of management involvement. This is subjective and can be estimated by the change management team and the supervisors first.
- Resolution of issues by supervisors. This includes outcomes as well as elapsed time to resolve issues.
- Resolution of issues by managers. Same comment as above.

Table 14.5 Quick Win Implementation Results Score Card for Employees.

Factor	Score	Comments
Number of employees trained		
Percent of employees trained		
Employee turnover during and after change		
Number of surprises in training		
Number of surprises in implementation		
Impact of surprises		
Extent of surprises		
Elapsed time to install		
Planned versus actual schedule		
Planned versus actual cost		
Cost and effort of surprises		
Performance of the project team		
Willingness of employees to embrace change		

The goal of the employee implementation score card is to assess how effectively the employees embraced, participated, and supported the changes. The score card is given in Table 14.5.

Remarks on the specific factors are as follows:

- Employee turnover during and after change. This indicates both positive and negative factors (e.g., you lose a Queen bee).
- Number of surprises in training. Surprises can surface during both implementation and training. You might include the types as well.
- Number of surprises in implementation- same as above.
- Impact of surprises. This can be financial, morale, structural, and so forth.
- Extent of surprises. This is the scope or range of surprises.
- Willingness of employees to embrace change. This is subjective and can be estimated by the change management team and supervisors.

The manager implementation score card addresses management and supervisory participation in the Quick Win implementation work. It is shown in Table 14.6.

Table 14.6 Quick Win Implementation Results Score Card for Managers.

Factor	Score	Comments
Extent of supervisor involvement		
Degree of support of supervisors for change		
Extent of management involvement		
Degree of support of managers for change		
Elapsed time for supervisors to resolve issues		
Elapsed time for managers to resolve issues		
Number of issues surfaced		
Number of issues resolved		
Extent of revisions needed		
Enthusiasm of supervisors		
Enthusiasm of managers		
Performance of project team		

Comments are:

- Extent of supervisor involvement. This is critical and should include quality of involvement.
- Degree of support of supervisors for change. This is an overall measure in terms of actions taken by supervisors that indicate support.
- Extent of management involvement. This is a balance between micromanaging and aloofness.
- Degree of support of managers for change. This is an overall measure in terms of actions taken by managers that indicate support.
- Elapsed time for supervisors to resolve issues. This can be an average.
- Elapsed time for managers to resolve issues. Same as above.
- Number of issues surfaced. This can also include the type of issues.
- Number of issues resolved. This is a measure of completion.
- Extent of revisions needed. Surprises may require revisions.
- Enthusiasm of supervisors. This is subjective and can be estimated by employees and managers.
- Enthusiasm of managers. This can be estimated by supervisors.
- Performance of change management team.

Examples

For a major insurance company, we were brought in to turn around a failing strategic planning effort. This effort involved three full-time employees and had gone on for four months. There was not much to show for their effort. While they went to a training class involving a somewhat exotic planning method, they lacked the experience to implement the method successfully.

We looked over what they had done and the business units that they had worked with. We revisited the business units to find issues and problems that could be resolved with Quick Wins. We successfully did this in two departments with the team. This raised morale and got the planning going again. At the same we wanted to begin to create the planning lists and tables identified in earlier chapters. Rather than start from scratch, we used sample lists of issues and opportunities, objectives, and strategies to get going. That worked. After about three weeks, two of the team members were released to return to their regular work. The third and remaining person finished the plan with a little coaching.

Lessons Learned

One lesson learned is that you should be open to all types of changes and improvements during the planning work. Here are some tips:

- When an issue or opportunity surfaces, see if it could be handled by a Quick Win. Even if it cannot, you have more justification for a bigger effort since you requested the quick change.
- Do not get overwhelmed by just concentrating on Quick Win opportunities. Remember that your key is the strategic plan. Instead, you should concentrate on those Quick Wins that are easiest, have the greatest benefit, and the least risk.

- Do not try to implement Quick Wins yourself. By involving more people, you gain more support. Also, doing it alone diverts you from the other parts of implementation of the plan action items.
- Give credit to the employees and supervisors for the Quick Wins. If you take the credit for yourself, then there could be resentment.

Politics

Here are things from experience relating to politics of change. One of the major areas of risk is that the resistance by the King and Queen bees. When you get to implementation, resistance that was once in the background may now surface. It may not surface openly as a challenge, but as repeated questions. Many change implementation methods stress the importance of getting these people on board. However, this may not always be possible. If you push too hard for their support, you may compromise the changes. Then, the successive waves of change may be in jeopardy. Moreover, word will spread that the change effort can be manipulated.

How do you address these people? First, you have them identified through the planning work. Second, you can involve lower-level employees in planning first. Then, you can bring in the King and Queen bees. Both supervisors and employees should be encouraged to support the change and answer any questions that the "bees" raise.

Another situation is that an individual may not openly resist during the planning and implementation. They may just continue to do the work as if there was no change. Supervisors need to oversee these people to detect this. Then, the supervisors can step in and take corrective action.

Another area of risk surfaced in the Legend Manufacturing situation. Once it is seen that the Quick Wins work and that there are real benefits, there is often a tendency to speed up the change. As has been pointed out, this can be very disruptive. What is the best way to deal with this? Assume that it will happen and address it in planning with the managers and supervisors. Point out the problems of change too quickly.

What to do Next

Why wait until the end of the planning effort to implement Quick Wins? Try to get some implemented during the planning process. First, this will show results. Second, it will indicate that the planning is serious. Third, you will gain more interest and participation in the remainder of the planning work. Fourth, you will gain experience that will be valuable later after the plan has been approved and the action items are ready to be implemented.

Summary

Implementation of Quick Wins is a proven approach to implement both near and long-term change as defined in the strategic IT and process plan. Many strategic planning efforts end up having no benefit because they only concentrated on the big changes. Too bad, they could have gathered ideas for Quick Wins which would have ensured the success of the planning work.

If you are successful with Quick Win planning and implementation, then the installation of longer term change will be easier and more predictable. A critical success factor is the gathering of lessons learned during this work.

Chapter 15

Implement the Plan — Long Term

Introduction

At first thought, this chapter should deal with guidelines for implementing systems. However, there is much more involved with a focus on processes. There have been many approaches to process improvement: re-engineering, Total Quality Management (TQM), Six Sigma, and IT systems by themselves. There have been many failures for each of these as well as successes.

- Re-engineering focuses on major rework of a process. It does not encompass IT. Moreover, large-scale change is often impossible given that the work and many transactions have to still follow the same business rules.
- TQM has been used successfully in manufacturing and some other areas. But it fails in service areas.
- Six Sigma has had some successes, but involves a substantial investment in training. Neither TQM nor Six Sigma link to IT.
- Downsizing or rightsizing by itself without process improvement often results in a deterioration of work and the process.
- Putting in a system is one thing. However, to get the benefits you have to change staffing, processes, and so forth.

The approach in this book is a combination one that includes IT, process improvement, change management, and organization change.

After the Quick Wins...

From the last chapter, we implemented a sequence of groups of Quick Wins. These not only provided benefits in themselves, but also accomplished the following:

- Narrowed the requirements since some were addressed through Quick Wins.
- Built up momentum and support for change among the business employees.
- Helped to identify people who might resist larger change later.
- Kept employees involved in the change effort so that they would come up with major new requirements.

These benefits have occurred from many of our projects. In fact, we would not now implement a major system without the Quick Wins.

So, after these Quick Wins have been completed and measured, do you just wait for the system to be ready? No. You want to maintain the participation of the employees. Here are some actions that have proven useful.

- Train staff in the new process with the system being simulated. This is valuable since it puts attention on the process. If you wait and combine process and system training, people will be drawn mainly to the system. Think of the process as the method and the system as the tool. You want to train in the method first; then train in the tool.
- Continue to gather lessons learned among employees. This will improve collaboration and sharing of information and result in further work improvement.
- Try to identify more Quick Wins. You never want to stop this.

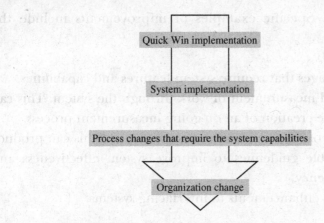

Figure 15.1 Sequencing of Implementation.

Sequencing of Change

Figure 15.1 presents an overall logical approach for implementation.

This diagram highlights the overall approach to change. Why go through all of this detail in a book that deals with strategic IT and process planning? The goal of the strategic planning is to get both short- and long-term change and improvement in the processes. To achieve this goal, you have to have a successful method for implementing the change. Otherwise, you could make some changes and implement some systems, but the benefits will fall short of both requirements and needs.

The first step, that of Quick Win implementation, was covered in the previous chapter. The key to success here was the use of the Quick Win implementation strategy or roadmap to sequence the Quick Win changes.

In the second part the system is implemented. The next section will address training in the new system using a more interactive approach. At the end of this phase of change, the system is being used as well as the Quick Wins.

The third part is concerned with major process improvement and change that is only possible after the system has been implemented. Specific examples of improvements include the following:

- Policy changes that require system features and capabilities.
- Automated measurement of work through the system. This can support the creation of an on-going measurement process.
- Gathering of experience in using the system. This can produce very valuable guidelines to improve system effectiveness and work efficiency.
- Additional enhancements to interfacing systems.

At this point in the implementation, the employees are tightly linked to both the system and the process. They may be doing different work or work differently. The old organization does not fit with what they are doing. So, the fourth part is to change the organization to better manage and perform the work. This is logical. Reorganizing first, without knowing how the work will change, makes less sense.

Modern Systems and Process Training

A good approach is to expand the training method of the Quick Wins in Chapter 15. For doing this, the steps would be as given in Figure 15.2.

Here are some additional tips from experience.

- Relate how the new transactions support the overall business goals.
- Give time for the employees who are doing the training to cover benefits, differences, and guidelines on how best to use the system.
- If you are going to train multiple groups, make sure that you use employees from the previous training group in the next one. This will be instrumental in achieving ownership and involvement.

- Review the original process as a starting point. By surfacing the issues and impact again, employees can realize how far they have come.
- Next, go over the current process after the Quick Wins. Highlight not only results and improvements, but also the remaining problems that can only be addressed by the system implementation and further process change.
- Rather than plunge into the training, take a little more time and use the same example transactions to present and review the vision of the work after the complete system and process improvement implementation. This shows where things are headed.
- Now, you have the past, present, and future. You are ready for introducing the change due to the system. Show how the work will be performed with the system by using the same transactions. The benefits and improvements can be highlighted.
- Give an overview of the system.
- Move away from the system and back to the process. Have employees do detailed training in the system in the context of the process. Thus, they would show how to do the real work using the system and new procedures.

Figure 15.2 Training Steps.

At first glance, you might think that the first four steps are extraneous and not needed. They are very useful in providing focus and direction. The method has been proven on television. Where? You can see on many stations late at night around the world. It is the informercial. People in the audience participate in demonstrations and discuss the benefits. Overviews of before and after are provided at the start. The role of IT is that of the moderator or host of the show. Again, the role of IT is to help and coordinate — not to do. If you do it, you own it. The employees don't.

The above method has the benefit of gaining much more participation. Another benefit is that employees see exactly how the system is to be used in the context of, not separate from the process. A third benefit is that employees will take ownership of the training through participation.

What about documentation for the system? Embed it in the process. The document should not be a system manual like that for a software package such as a spreadsheet. The document should fit the process. For documentation, we have long used playscript in which the procedures appear in columns. Column 1 is the step of the transaction. Column 2 is who or what (computer) does it. The third column consists of the procedures — what to do in the step. Here is another tip. Add a fourth column for guidelines on HOW to do the step better or best.

Process documentation should be distributed to staff either in paper or online. We think that they should have access to it for three weeks to a month. After that, they would go to their supervisors for access. Why not have it available all of the time? Because it can become too much of a crutch. Why memorize it if you can read about it frequently? This reading takes time from work and reduces productivity so we suggest that they have limited access.

Playscript dates over 2000 years old — to the Greek plays. It has the advantage of being easily understood and updated.

Each project is unique in type, the country, culture, business rules, and other factors. Nevertheless, we can make some observations relative to four types of projects:

- Projects related to application software packages. This is more common today. Installing a software package presents different challenges due to marketing and fast implementation expectations.
- Projects related to enhanced existing software. Here we are referring to situations where, for example, an existing online system is redesigned in terms of the user interface. More capabilities are added as well. So, to users it may represent something very new, but under the skin it is much the same.
- Projects related to custom software. This is software that is developed in-house.
- Projects related to infrastructure and architecture. Major network upgrades, changes in operating systems, and other systems changes are examples.

As you will see, each of these has its own pitfalls and opportunities. Often, the choice for an application system is based on the lesser of comparative evils. This indicates that process change, Quick Wins, and change management become more important due to the limitations of any application system solution. The purpose of these sections is to indicate how the strategic IT and process plan as well as the focus on process improvement and change impact the software and technology implementation.

Projects Related to Application Software Packages

A firm has conducted an internal analysis of their needs for a process(es) and determined that the existing application systems cannot be modified. Nor are there resources or time for system development. The lure of a package is undeniable:

- It is possible to install the software package quickly to achieve more rapid change.
- Some customization of the package is possible through control tables.
- There usually is substantial marketing hype about all of the benefits.
- Consultants are available to assist with the implementation.
- Existing customer tout the advantages of the software.

So, the organization proceeds to evaluate and select among different packages in terms of features and functions. Leading examples of types of software are Enterprise Resource Planning (ERP), Supply Chain Management (SCM), and Customer Relationship Management (CRM).

It all seems so structured. The package is proven and works. However, if you review various surveys, you find that:

- There is a substantial failure rate in which the package was never fully installed.

- Even when implemented, many firms cannot pin down firm, tangible benefits.

This can be quite discouraging — especially since the package may have been identified during the strategic planning process.

Here are some guidelines to ensure a higher likelihood of success.

- Focus on the functions rather than features. Features are nice to have. Functions are requirements. For example, if you were selecting a car, then heated seats are a nice feature, but not a needed function unless you live in a cold climate. However, excellent gas mileage is essential so that car performance is the key.
- Look at what you do not get with the package in addition to what you get. Consider Figure 15.3. The box represents the requirements. There are two packages A and B. Let's assume that A has many more features than B, so it is preferred in terms of features. Now, look at the drawings in the box. The coverage of the requirements is shown by the inside drawings. System B covers more requirements than A. We would select B because:

> In software package selection, it is as important to see what you did not get as what you get.

Now, look at the area between the outside rectangle and the shape for System B. This represents the requirements that are not addressed by the software package. What do you do about this? How do you address these requirements? You could customize the software package — not likely. You could keep some of the old system that handled these requirements. Alternatively, you may have to invent new, additional systems that provide these capabilities.

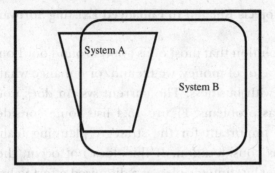

Figure 15.3 Comparison of Two Packages in Terms of Functional Coverage System Requirements.

- Often, people want to fit the package into the existing process. This has a number of problems. First, you are likely to get fewer benefits since there will be less change in the business process. Second, customizing the package to fit the internal process that includes many exceptions and shadow systems may neither be possible nor affordable. That is why most firms change their processes to fit with the system. This seems like a natural choice. However, a firm can lose some competitive advantage with other firms using the same systems and, hence, similar processes. That is one of the reasons why Wal-Mart has tended to develop their own software.

There are other problems as well. One is that the business unit staff and managers may have inflated expectations with regard to schedule and benefits after dealing with the vendor of the software and their consultants. Of course, they probably understated the extent of process change that would be required — knowing that this might scare them off.

Another problem is that the firm will have to rely on outside support for some time until the internal staff can get up to speed. This transition may never occur. The IT staff may question their role. Where will the staff go who worked on the old system?

Projects Related to Enhanced Existing Software

This is the solution that most of us apply around our homes. Instead of spending a lot of money, we fix and/or enhance what we have. It is the same with business. The current system does not work even though it has problems. Figure 15.4 lists some considerations for this option. Important for the strategic planning team is to give these serious consideration. If this does not occur, then management may see the strategic plan as a disguised effort to bring in some package or build new software. In these times, you want to clearly demonstrate that the current software cannot fulfill basic functions in a process that has changed over time.

Projects Related to Custom Software

System development has often been favored by IT groups. There are several reasons for this. Development is more creative work than maintenance and enhancement for one. Second, development represents more job security. Third, the IT organization can more closely meet the business unit requirements. The strategic IT and process plan should indicate the dynamic factors related to projects so that both the urgency and importance are known. Specific project analysis would indicate the degree of risk and issues that could argue

---

- Are the changes so extensive that they create risk in terms of software bugs and stability?
- How steady and reliable are the IT staff members who will be doing the changes?
- Are the software changes well understood and agreed upon?
- What is the approach for transition of the software changes into production?
- What requirements cannot be accommodated by the software changes? How will these requirements be addressed?
- Will the modified system support the potential growth and change in the business over time? The strategic IT and process plan should have identified what potential business changes will be arising.
- What software problems will remain after the changes are made?

Figure 15.4 Factors to Consider for Using Existing Software.

- What can be salvaged from existing systems?
- Can the design and development effort be streamlined given the identified Quick Wins?
- What is the role of the business unit staff?
- How can requirement changes be controlled?
- Can the current system be enhanced so that it can last until the new system is available?
- Are the business rules well known and agreed to by the business units and IT?
- Will the developed software be available in time and in synchronization with business needs (as covered in the strategic IT and process plan)?
- What is the resource impact on other projects and work?

Figure 15.5 Factors to Consider Related to Custom Software.

against development. In addition, the strategic resource allocation should provide information on resource availability and priorities. Some questions related to custom software are given in Figure 15.5.

Projects Related to Infrastructure and Architecture

It might seem unusual to include these here since they do not involve application software. But the strategic IT and process plan include actions related to the IT architecture and infrastructure. Infrastructure here refers to the components of the systems and technology. Architecture refers to the integration, interfaces, and structure of the systems and technology.

Examples of potential projects in this area include:

- Major system software upgrades and changes.
- Implementation of new technologies such as web 2.0 applications and cloud computing.
- Consolidation or expansion of computer centers.

There are a number of managerial considerations in the implementation of projects such as those listed above. These are given in Figure 15.6.

- Has the business benefit of the change been identified? More important, what will happen if the change is not made?
- Often of greater importance, have the risks and business impacts been determined if the change is not carried?
- What will be the impact on business operations during the implementation of the technology?
- What are the longer term staffing requirements to support the new technology?
- What are staffing requirements for implementation? How will these impact other work? The strategic resource allocation should have identified the other projects and work. Of particular interest in terms of business processes is the effect on the resources that support the current operational technology during this transition.
- Does the new technology offer potential benefit and additional capabilities for the business processes over the longer term?

Figure 15.6 Factors to Consider Relative to Infrastructure and Architecture.

Process Change after System Implementation

In the past, the work would end with the system being implemented. Benefits and costs would be tabulated. As a sidenote, the actual measurement of the benefits is sometimes not done. Resources may not be available. Management may want to move on to other things since you cannot undo the past if the benefits are sufficient. There is a problem here. If the business unit sees that the benefits will not be measured, then they may not push through the changes that could generate the benefits.

For political reasons, you have to keep the feet of the business unit on the fire. There are several mechanisms for doing this.

- Proactive measurement of the business process (discussed in the next chapter).
- Handling of residual issues. This keeps IT linked to the business process.
- Continued collection and use of lessons learned and implementation of further Quick Wins.
- Implementation of substantial process change made possible now by the availability of the new, operational system.

The last point is the focal point of this section. What are examples of substantial process change after implementation?

- Change in roles of supervisors and staff. In one collections department, work was previously manually assigned by supervisors. The new computer system took over this job and dealt out the accounts to the staff. The supervisors then could use the systems to analyze the performance of collections staff.
- Change in how the work is performed. Going back to our collections example the new system could analyze the characteristics of all delinquent accounts. This allowed for a new group to be established to handle customers who were chronically behind in their payments.
- Changes in policy made possible by the capabilities and flexibility of the new system. This occurs frequently after ERP systems have been installed.
- Shift of workload between and among business departments.

These and other changes are made in line with both the process plan for the individual process and the strategic IT and process plan. Taken together they provide the direction for the business process.

These changes can disrupt department operations and negatively impact productivity. Therefore, you want an organized approach for these changes. The sequence of the changes can have a major impact on the business unit. The approach we have employed is that followed in the previous chapter with Quick Wins (see Figure 14.2 and the discussion of the figure). You want to develop an implementation roadmap and strategy for change. The row entries are the major changes. The columns in the table are the phases of changes. The performance measures in the table can remain.

Organization and Staffing Changes

A two-pronged approach has proven useful here. One effort is to define work and tasks that should have been done, but were never performed during staffing limitations. Why is this necessary? To raise morale and improve overall productivity. A basic point is:

> There will be more support for change if the employees can identify their new roles after the changes have been implemented.

The second effort is to create the new, modified organization. If you proceed top-down, you will have problems with the fit of the people into the work and its supervision. Proceed bottom-up. What does this mean? Begin with developing work descriptions and measurements for the employees directly involved in the work. Having done this you can proceed to define the roles and responsibilities of the supervisors. You can continue to work up the organization.

How do you further motivate the people for change? During the initial data collection in Chapter 5, it was indicated that it was useful to identify clerical work and work that people did not really like to do. Now, you can capitalize on this information and demonstrate how the new process will result in less of this type of work.

What about downsizing and rightsizing? If the company is in a panic or there is a severe downturn, here is the appropriate place and time for doing it. To make the downsizing effort less painful, you can do have them discover during Quick Win implementation and training the changing nature of work and the roles of the staff. Some will see the "writing on the wall" and may bail out and leave. Through this preparation the downsizing will not come as a surprise.

What types of people tend to leave? From experience the following are some.

- Junior employees who lack seniority
- Senior employees who do not want to change and decide to retire or leave

When a senior person leaves, many think that this is very bad. You lose a lot of experience. The department is weakened in its abilities as a result. That would be true IF you keep the work the same.

When you do the organization change, you can start addressing exceptions. If a senior person departs, they take the knowledge of exception processing with them. This frees up the rest of the staff to redefine how to handle the exceptions. Often, you just can eliminate them or merge them into common work.

Examples

In one major bank we implemented new processes and systems across multiple departments. The areas of the bank were:

- Installment lending
- Credit card
- Leasing
- Real estate lending
- Commercial lending

The activities in each area included:

- Application processing
- Payment processing
- Customer service
- Collections
- Charge-off and recovery

Upper management was not interested in GANTT charts or other project management stuff. This was too much detail. They wanted an overall implementation strategy. This is big version of the roadmap or strategy for Quick Win implementation presented in Chapter 14.

The result was Table 15.1. In this table, the rows are the banking areas and the columns are the activities. For the table entry, the phase was given. For example, the first phase was labeled "A" and consisted of installment lending collections. This implementation gave experience and knowledge for both collections and installment lending. This led to the areas labeled "B." Other letters stand for later phases of implementation. Staffing limitations only allowed for three implementations to be undertaken at one time. After a project was completed, management wanted two numbers put in the square or entry — the cost of the work and the tangible benefits. What was the deciding factor in the selection of where to begin? The bank had suffered major losses in that area and wanted rapid results. As in many instances, the driving factor for change was urgency.

This multiple project implementation spanned over four years. With the management change and technology change, you would think it would fail. It never ran into problems. Why? Here were the critical success factors.

- Employees were involved all along the way. Employees from one group would train the next group.
- Lessons learned were gathered continuously. These lessons learned were incorporated into improvements in the systems as the implementation progressed.

Table 15.1 Phases of Implementation across the Bank Activities.

Areas	Collections	Charge-off	Servicing	Payment	Application processing
Installment lending	A	B	C	D	E
Credit card	B	C	D	E	F
Leasing	C	D	F	G	I
Real estate lending	D	E	G	H	I
Commercial lending	E	F	G	H	I

- There was a regular stream of milestones and tangible results. Management from the business units made the analysis and presentations of the results so that they owned the implementation.
- The strategic IT and process plan was embodied in the roadmap in Figure 16.2 so that all could see the direction of the work.
- The training approach presented above was used throughout and was very successful.

There is a sidenote to this example. One employee, whom we will call Ralph, was in the second group to be changed. Ralph resisted change. He fled or transferred to another group. We then changed that group. He fled again. Finally, he saw that either he would have to leave or begin working in the new process. He chose to stay and become part of the change. Later, he became a stronger supporter of the new systems and processes — after four job changes!

Lessons Learned

One lesson learned is to think in terms of integration. Change management, process improvement, and IT are all integrated together. If these are not treated together, then problems are likely to arise. In the implementation phase of work, the system has been customized, built, or purchased. It is ready to go. You do not want to touch this as it could result in delays. The process improvement has also been defined. So, the dominant part of implementation is change management. Change management deals with the people and organizational side of change. Change management addressed the politics of change. Thus, while integrated the attention, as far as methods, are concerned goes to change management.

What if some problem arises? An example might be a requirement that was not addressed in the system or the Quick Wins. Given all of the data collection, analysis, meetings, and collaboration, this might seem rare. However, it does happen. You would obviously first analyze it and ask the following:

- What is the new requirement?
- What gave rise to this requirement? Was it political in the sense of trying to delay the implementation?
- What other requirements did we miss in the analysis?
- What has changed in the work to give rise to the requirement?

What are potential actions? The first is to turn it down. Then, the process would deal with the requirement in the way it had done before. Another action is to defer the requirement until after implementation. While this will not delay the implementation, it will create problems in deciding how to deal with it until after the implementation. A third potential action is to handle it through process change without IT work. This is one of the best options. The fourth action is to halt the implementation and modify the system to handle this new requirement. This can delay the implementation for weeks or months. Code has to be designed, programed, and tested. Then, the modifications have to be integrated with the rest of the system — consuming more time. This should be avoided since morale can be affected as can work on other projects. Moreover, management confidence can be shaken. Remember too that many "new" requirements are politically based. Some people want to delay implementation by proposing changes. Some managers may want to put their stamp on the implementation. One tip here is to keep the implementation low profile. Another tip is that you should indicate a formal approach to any new requirements. Here, you would include the above questions.

Another lesson learned is to leave a few lingering issues and problems at the end of implementation of the new system. Why do this? Don't you want to address all of the issues? It is often not possible due to the schedule and demands on staff time. Addressing the issues could delay implementation with all of the effects mentioned in the preceding paragraph.

What are the benefits of having lingering issues? It keeps IT in touch with the process. Most of the time when implementation is finished, IT staff move on to other work. This can give the process an opportunity to regress back to older ways. By having the issues, IT and the people involved in the change can remain with the department and observe the work. We have found not only that this is useful, but also that some of the issues later take care of themselves through process and organization change.

Another lesson learned concerns the business users involved in implementation. If you rely on the same people all of the time, they can get burned out. Moreover, the other business unit staff will start seeing them as part of the change team and IT. Not good. It is preferable to involve more business users. During requirements gathering, you involved the more senior business employees. During implementation, you can get more junior people involved. Why them? Because they will be more supportive of change. Some may see the opportunity to advance their careers through involvement in implementation. Up to a point, the more users the merrier.

From experience, you want to keep gathering lessons learned during implementation. What can be gained from this effort? Here is a list from experience.

- Guidelines for using the system to handle exceptions.
- How a shadow system can either be eliminated or combined into the system.
- Elimination of some exceptions and workarounds.
- Guidelines on how better to perform the work.
- Information on individual staff performance to see who takes the greatest advantage of the system.

Politics

The politics really hits the fan here. People who held off resisting change now see that things are serious and that this is their last chance for resistance. What are their points that you should be prepared for? Here is a list.

- The new system does not handle the work in the way it should. You have almost analyzed the common work to death. Quick Wins validated the analysis through the changes. Thus, this comment most often applies to an exception. That is OK. You could address this during process change.
- There is no provision to handle certain exceptions. The same comments as the one above apply here.
- The system is too difficult and complex to use. This can because the new system has a much different user interface. It is not that it is complex — just different. To head this off from being raised, during training you want to have junior staff demonstrate their understanding of the new system.
- We cannot learn the system and do our regular work at the same time. Probably true. However, because changes were introduced in phases, the process is more gradual. Usually, after the Quick Wins the employees embrace the new system since it is a tool to make their working lives easier. One problem with sudden system implementation without Quick Wins is that there is too much change at one time.
- There is no real benefit from the new system. Well, you already have the benefits of the Quick Wins. The Quick Wins are consistent and supportive of the new system. Therefore, the benefits of the new system follow. This point is usually just one of resistance.
- The procedures associated with the new process are not how we do our work. This should have been prevented in the definition and refinement of the process and its procedures during the Quick Wins. Some people are not used to change and so may raise this point.
- The new system is too inflexible. No system ever is totally flexible. That is the nature of automating business rules. Flexibility exists

somewhat with the system, but mainly rests with the process in which the system is encapsulated.

- The new process does not address some of our serious issues. It should be the case that the system handles the common work. The Quick Wins and later process change handle other issues. However, none of this can address embedded organizational and staffing issues. These are addressed later.

From your own experience, you can probably add many more excuses. The thing to keep in mind is that if you have involved a substantial number of business employees in the implementation and analysis, have carried out Quick Wins, and designed the process improvement, then most of the reasons behind these points lie in fear of change, fear of loss of power, and general resistance. The problem is that many IT people accept these statements at face value and do not question them. You can use the above list at the early stages of implementation to point out that some people may like the status quo. As such, they may pose seemingly legitimate reasons for stopping. If you accept one of these points, then you risk showing or shutting down the implementation.

If you are getting some success in implementation, there can be efforts to expand the work and include other departments. Managers may try to jump on board the implementation. What should you do? Don't turn these people away. That will just make enemies for now and later. Instead, show interest in what they say. Indicate that additional changes will come with process improvement and the organization review. In addition, you can point to the original list of requirements and issues that the system and process improvement were designed to address.

There is the psychological shift when one moves into implementation. Let's examine this further. People who once supported change now express reservations. Why? Because change is happening. It is really going on. We call this *mid installation paralysis*. It is not infrequent. People buy books that they do not read. They buy music

- Did someone measure the benefits after implementation?
- Were lessons learned gathered during the implementation?
- If so, were they applied to later implementations?
- Was resistance to change anticipated?
- If so, what was done to deal with resistance?
- How were employees involved in the implementation?
- What did employees say about the new process after implementation?
- Who participated in training in the new process and system?
- Was there an effort to create guidelines on how to use the new system more effectively?

Figure 15.7 Assessment of Previous System Implementations.

and electronics that they do not use. Why don't they want to proceed given the time and money invested? Here are some reasons: (1) they really did not want to change; (2) when the time for change came, it appeared too challenging; and (3) other activities diverted their attention. Whatever the reason, you should expect this to occur to some extent. It is nature. Again, the words "inertia" and "resistance to change" come to mind. The way to deal with this is first to anticipate that this will happen. Focus on having more junior staff learn and perform the new process. This will show people that it can be done. Because of the waves of Quick Wins, this is less likely to occur since the employees are better prepared for change.

What to do Next

One step to take is to examine several past system implementations. Figure 15.7 gives a checklist of questions and areas to assess.

More guidelines are given in Chapter 16 on measurement and updating the plan.

Summary

This chapter has focused on the long-term change and improvement of work as directed by the strategic IT and process plan.

As such, the approach is different than that of implementing a system. The basic difference is that:

> The focus is on improving the work through changes in the systems and processes.

Rather than attention limited to the new system and its features. Using this approach you use the functions and features of the new system that are directly relevant to the work.

The overall approach to change is a mix of IT, process improvement, change management, and organization change. It draws upon some of the best features of the methods in these areas. Using this method there is less risk of failure, reversion, or deterioration since motivation of the employees for change is key to the method.

> The goal of the process improvement and systems change is cumulative improvement that is lasting.

Why does this approach lead to longer lasting change? Because the method focuses on ownership of the process and its systems by the employees who perform the real work.

Chapter 16

Measure Planning Results
and Update the Plan

Introduction

This chapter addresses two areas. The first is to provide measurements for many activities related to the strategic planning effort. The second is to describe how to update the strategic plan. In each of the measurements more items are provided than you would likely use. The purpose of this is to provide you with a choice.

Should you only measure after the approval of the plan and the implementation of the action items? No. You want to measure often — as often as resources permit. Why? Because you want to ensure that management is aware of the measurements. This is for business and political reasons. Often, during the planning effort, the visibility to management is limited. Measurements help to keep their interest and support. Moreover, if there is consistent flow of measurements, then management will feel more comfortable with the work. They will be less likely to intervene and impose their own measurements — ones that might not be favorable.

In physics, there is a law that applies here. It is the Heisenberg uncertainty principle. The essence of this is when you use light to observe something, the light particles disturb what you are trying to measure. This applies here in this chapter. Measurements can tend to change attitudes toward the work. People start to realize that something is a problem. Previously, before the measurement, they just accepted the problem as part of the work. Now they see it in daylight.

Business Process Measurement

For a number of reasons, it is valuable to measure a business process in the early stages of strategic planning. These include:

- Identifying problem areas in the process and their impacts to the business and employees. Measurement will not catch all of the problems, but the major ones should be relatively easy to identify.
- The act of measuring a process shows people that there is going to be a serious effort related to the work.
- Politically, the measurements reveal to management and employees of the need for change.
- If there is later process change and improvement, then you will need both before and after measurements to assess the benefits. People's memories are sometimes short and they may not recall the problem after it has been fixed.

The list of measurement items for the business process is given in Figure 16.1. Note that you will not have time to use all of these. You want to be selective. What measurements should you choose? Well, you definitely want to include those that point to issues and problems in the work. You also want to include overall measurements that assist in the before and after analysis.

How do you conduct the measurement of the process? You could carry out formal interviews. However, we have found that people often will not be open and give honest answers. Instead, they may give you the answers you want to hear — to be pleasant and sometimes to get back to work sooner.

One approach that has worked many times is to observe the work and talk with employees informally. To measure adequately, you should get down to the actual work. Once you have gained their confidence, you can talk to them informally in groups during breaks. When you review the list of items, there are numbers that are subjective. Your measurement will be based on these meetings.

- Number of people directly involved in process by department. This can reveal both involvement and ownership of the process.
- Related processes. A process typically does not stand alone. It is interdependent with other work in the department and across departments.
- Total labor cost of the process.
- Total cost of the process. This includes facilities, IT, overhead, labor, and other costs.
- Turnover of employees by department. This can reveal one of the effects of problems in the work if it is high. In a customer service unit in a transportation agency, the turnover at the start of the planning was in excess of 70% per year!
- Turnover of employees involved in the process. This is a more direct measurement of the process, but may difficult to get due to the effort to pin down who and who is not involved in the work.
- Systems provided by IT.
- Open change requests and systems work. This can be obtained from IT.
- Total IT cost attributed to the process. This may be only available by department.
- Volume of work performed. For online work, this can be measured by the number of transactions. This can be refined by measuring transactions by type. If customer contact is involved, then the telephone system can provide statistics.
- Frequency and distribution of work. This helps to identify the peaks and troughs of the work.
- Average time to perform a transaction or specific piece of work.
- Number of reported and known problems by type. A good source here is what was reported or discovered by IT. Another source consists of employees. You can sometimes get this information by asking them what has changed in the last year.
- Age distribution of the problems. This requires some idea of when a problem was first noticed.
- Last time that the employees involved in the work were formally trained as a group. If this is a long time ago, then it may reveal that people have gotten into some bad habits.
- The training approach that is used when a new employee is brought into the process to do work. Often, the new employee is assigned to a senior employee — a King or Queen Bee.
- Extent of dependence on the King and Queen Bees. This can reveal the number of exceptions. You can sometimes get this by asking such questions as:

  o "How often do you have to ask someone for help with work?"
  o "What happens to this work if no one is available to help?"
  o "Compared to a year ago, do you ask for help more or less often?"
  o "For what items do you have to ask for help?"

- Percentage of work in exceptions. This may have to be a rough estimate based on what the King and Queen Bees do.
- Number of shadow systems. Recall that a shadow system is one that can be manual or automated and is not supported by IT. Often, it is critical to performing the work. A substantial number of critical shadow system can indicate potential for additional systems work. This is good source for opportunities for the strategic plan.

Figure 16.1 Potential Measurement Items for a Business Process.

- Percentage of the work that requires one or more shadow systems. This can indicate the degree of dependence of the employees on the shadow systems.
- Extent of rework. It may be the case that specific employees are assigned to perform corrective work.
- Number and type of workarounds. A workaround occurs when employees have to work around a limitation in a process or system. Workarounds consume more effort and require more process knowledge.
- Age and condition of training materials and procedures for the process. Look at this documentation and determine when it was last used and updated.
- Knowledge of the staff about the policies governing the process. Here, there can be both formal and informal policies. Informal policies are often developed over time by the senior staff and supervisors for reasons of efficiency and effectiveness.
- Awareness of employees of the importance of the process to the organization. This can indicate motivation. This may be discovered informally in talks with the people.
- Extent of collaboration in the department in doing work. Teamwork in many cases is very helpful and helps to raise the levels of skills and knowledge. If, on the other hand, people work in isolation, then there can be problems wherein people repeat the same mistakes.
- Sharing of lessons learned among employees. Lessons learned here relate to the "how" of the work. You might be able to get this by asking "How do you do the work differently now as compared to a year ago?"
- There are some useful ratios such as those listed below. However, these do not pertain to all processes.

  o IT cost to total process cost. This can indicate the degree of automation of the work.
  o IT cost per employee. This can show the extent of IT investment in the work.
  o Cost per transaction. This may be useful as a trend if past historical data is available.
  o Ratio of King and Queen Bees to total employees. This can show the extent of exception work.
  o Volume of work per employee.
  o Revenue per employee.
  o Cost per employee.
  o Number of problems per volume of work.

Figure 16.1 (*Continued*)

Alternatively, you could hand out part of the list of measurements and solicit their opinions. Take notes since their comments are often more interesting and insightful than just the measurement.

If possible, you should also try to pick up trends. Some of these are:

- Volume of work
- Turnover of employees

- Number of employees involved in the work
- Changes in the mix of the types of work being done
- Changes in the extent and nature of IT support and activities
- Changes in problems and their impacts

IT Measurement

Of all of the departments in a firm, IT seems often to be the one focused on measurement of itself. This is, in part, historical. Many years ago, IT was little understood and viewed by some managers as a necessary activity, but supportive. This lead to IT having to justify itself to management. Of course, the situation has totally changed. IT is now critical to most firms. Thus, the objectives of IT have been transformed to include:

- Assessing the cost-effectiveness of IT. This measures the comparative costs of IT as well as work in IT.
- Determining the degree of alignment of IT to the business. This can be seen in terms of work supporting critical processes and effort toward achieving the business mission and vision.

Some organizations go beyond this to consider the extent to which IT provides a competitive advantage.

With these expanded measurement goals, it follows that more measurements are needed for IT; some of which go beyond IT itself and into the business. Suggestions for items to consider in IT measurement are given in Figure 16.2.

Of course, this list is not exhaustive. You should employ it as a starting point. Of particular interest are the measurements for surprises and performance measures related to projects.

If you are successful in carrying out the strategic IT and process plan, then you might see the following improvements:

- A decline in the number of surprises due to improved communications and a generally more proactive approach and style.

- No. of IT employees.
- Distribution of IT employees by category — operations, development and maintenance, and so forth. This can be revealing in that if the number of staff involved in software development and implementation is small, it can limit what IT can do to support the business goals, mission, and vision.
- Distribution of IT employees between projects and other activities. This pertains to the software-related staff members. This can serve as a measure for new work on the horizon. Of similar interest, is that of percentage of resources devoted to projects versus support.
- Percentage of projects that were generated proactively to improve processes and support the business and strategic IT plans. This can reveal the degree to which IT is reactive or proactive.
- Average duration of projects. This is important in that if there are projects that seem to be endless or time consuming, these are draining resources from other potentially more beneficial work. Experience shows that it may show a reluctance to terminate projects that are in trouble.
- Measures of standardization in IT.

    o Are there standardized templates or work breakdown structures for all project work?
    o Is there a formal method for identifying new projects?
    o Is there a method for measuring multiple projects at the same time?
    o Is there an organized approach for identifying, structuring, and applying lessons learned?
    o Is there a project office or someone who tracks projects, maintains issues and lessons learned, and provides support for project leaders?
    o Is there a structured approach for managing and tracking issues across all work, including projects?
    o Is there a issue on database that is used and updated?
    o Are milestones just recorded or are they reviewed? What is the depth of review of critical milestones?
    o Is there a formal change control process for architecture?
    o Is there a formal change control process for projects?
    o To what extent are change requests examined and justified?
    o Is there an organized approach for terminating a project?

- Communications measurements

    o What is the extent of contact with upper management?
    o What are the nature and extent of contacts between IT and business units?
    o What are the nature and extent of contacts between IT and its vendors and suppliers?
    o Are there standardized outlines for all IT presentations?
    o Are there standardized outlines for all major documents?
    o What is the process for generating, reviewing, and updating documents?
    o To what extent do meetings deal with issues and lessons learned versus status?

Figure 16.2 Potential Items for Measurement of IT.

- Vendor and supplier relations measurements

  o Is there a method for assessing vendor performance?
  o How are problems with vendors identified and tracked?
  o Are vendors required to share a common project plan and set of issues?
  o What is the process for evaluating new vendors?

- Technology-related measurements

  o How many legacy systems are there?
  o What resources are applied to maintaining old, legacy technology, and systems?
  o What is the approach for selecting new technology?
  o What is the method for implementing and testing new systems and technology?

- Maintenance and enhancement measurements

  o Is there a formal method for placing changes in application systems into production?
  o Is maintenance differentiated from enhancements?
  o What is the method for justifying and reviewing maintenance and enhancement work?

- Failure and success measurements

  o Is there an approach to gather lessons learned from failures and problems?
  o Do issues and problems tend to be repeated?
  o Is there a definition of success?
  o What is the definition of failure?
  o Are lessons learned gathered from successes?
  o Does the IT group celebrate successes?

- Project measurements

  o What is the percentage of labor hours and projects that yielded real, tangible benefits to the business?
  o Percentage of projects completed on time?
  o Percentage of projects completed within budget?
  o Is there a formal method for reviewing budget and schedule variances?
  o To what extent are there shared tasks in projects?
  o What is the extent of collaboration across project teams?
  o What is the percentage of project ideas that were not followed up on?
  o What is the distribution of project work across business units?
  o Are issues tracking across projects?
  o Are common issues in multiple projects identified and addressed in a standard manner?
  o What is the average time to resolve an issue?
  o Are potential and open issues related to the tasks and milestones in the plan?

Figure 16.2 (*Continued*)

- Surprises. This is an interesting and revealing category.

  o Number of surprise requests from upper management? This can be indicative of the communications with upper management.
  o Number of surprise requests from business units.
  o Number of surprise system failures.
  o Number of surprises related to project problems and overruns.
  o Number of surprises from vendors in their work.

- IT staff and skills

  o Number of hours allocated and used related to training of IT staff.
  o Is there an on-going approach for assessing staff skills and knowledge in IT?
  o What is the turnover of IT staff? How has it changed in the past few years?
  o Is IT overly dependent on a few critical employees?

Figure 16.2 (*Continued*)

- Greater standardization in the management of regular work and projects.
- A greater emphasis on issues and risk management.
- Increased scrutiny of maintenance and enhancement so that it is reduced to deploy more resources in projects.

Over time, there should be signs of cumulative improvement. There should be fewer new issues. Lessons learned should improve skills. The use of templates, lessons learned, and issues management should make project performance more consistent and easier to estimate and plan.

Project Measurement

The measurement of a project often relates to percentage of work completed, budget versus actual expenses, and schedule versus plan. However, this is just the tip of the iceberg. Much more is possible. Moreover, these measurements reflect the impact of problems when it is too late to do anything.

Figure 16.3 contains a more robust list of measurements — many dealing with issues management. Should you apply these to all

- Standard measurements

  - o Budget versus actual costs on a period and cumulative basis.
  - o Percentage of work completed in the project.
  - o Comparison of the baseline schedule and the actual schedule.

- Issues-related measurements

  - o Total number of issues — potential, open.
  - o Total number of open issues.
  - o Number of open issues by type. The types include work, methods and tools, user, management, vendor, process, technology, team members, and so forth.
  - o Percentage of open issues that are not under the control of the project team (called uncontrolled issues). If this is low, then the project is probably in greater danger.
  - o Average time to resolve an issue by type. This should indicate that it takes longer to resolve uncontrolled issues.
  - o What is the age of the oldest outstanding major issue? A long time can indicate that the project is in trouble since the project team may have to make assumptions on the outcome of the issue to continue work.
  - o What is the percentage of future tasks with open or potential issues?
  - o What is the percentage of remaining work with open or potential issues? This is one of the most valuable and revealing measurements.
  - o What is the distribution of work with potential and open issues overtime? If the end work in the project has a substantial percentage of work with issues, this could a flag of future disaster.

- Milestone-related measurements

  - o Is there a formal method for selecting which milestones are to be reviewed?
  - o How are milestones reviewed?
  - o Is there a regular schedule for milestones?
  - o What is the percentage of milestones in the future? A high number can indicate that the project has major work ahead regardless of progress made.
  - o What is the percentage of milestones in the future with risk? This is important because it can reveal the potential problems and risk ahead.

- Project setup, update, and tracking measurements

  - o Is there a baseline schedule?
  - o Are schedule changes made in a formal manner?
  - o Is there a standardized project file?
  - o After the project is ended, is the project file placed in a repository?
  - o Are all plans created from templates?
  - o Are detailed tasks defined by the project leader or team members? What is the extent of collaboration among the team in creating the plan?
  - o Do team members update their own tasks?
  - o Are lessons learned discussed in the planning of near term tasks?
  - o Are lessons learned gathered on a regular basis as work is performed?

Figure 16.3 Potential Items for Project Measurement.

projects? No, of course not. It is impossible due to the available time and resources. However, they can be applied to projects that meet some or all of the following criteria:

- The project involves work to support a major business process.
- The project results will ease or resolve a significant business issue.
- The project may be small, but involves major risks and issues (such as new technology or a new system).
- The project is highly visible to upper management and business units.
- The project is important to IT operations.
- The project duration is long.
- The resources involved in the project are very substantial.

Using this screening, we have found, from experience, that about half of the projects fit some of these criteria. It might seem impossible to do this without a great deal of effort. However, if you link the issues to the tasks and milestones, use a flag to indicate whether an issue is open, and standardize on the use of the project management software, it is reasonable.

Project Termination

This is not a pleasant subject. Some think that project termination equals project failure. In fact, there are good reasons to terminate a project. One is that the original need for the work is no longer needed. Another is that there is new work that is more pressing. These and other reasons are valid. Consider the questions in Figure 16.4.

Architecture Measurement

There are many potential measurements of systems and technology. Listed in Figure 16.5 are some potential measurements.

- Is there a formal review process to determine whether to terminate a project?
- What is the percentage of projects that were terminated? If this is very low, it may indicate that there is limited project review.
- What is the percentage of projects that should have been terminated? This can reflect a lack of will on the part of upper management or IT management.
- Were lessons learned gathered from a terminated project? Often, people just want to move on and forget.
- Were terminated projects slowed down and shut down in an orderly manner?
- How were resources reassigned from a terminated project? It is best if the resources are moved as soon as possible.
- Were reasons given to the staff about the terminations? Were these credible?
- What was communicated to the business units affected by the termination?
- How are lessons learned from terminated projects applied to current and future work?
- What is the distribution of reasons for terminating projects? These can include the following:

  o Lack of need for the project
  o Lack of support and involvement from the business unit
  o Running overbudget or behind schedule
  o Lack of resources to continue work
  o Inability to resolve significant issues in the project
  o More urgent needs for resources in other projects and work
  o Problems with the methods and tools used in the project
  o Problems with the systems and technology

Figure 16.4 Potential Items for Measuring Project Termination.

Planning Process Measurement

Figure 16.6 gives a list of measurements for the strategic planning process. You would employ this before you embark on an effort to create a new strategic IT and process plan. You can also use it during and after the strategic planning process.

Planning Measurement

Separate, but related to planning process, is the strategic plan itself. A list is given in Figure 16.7.

- What is the division of costs between network — hardware and software support?
- What is overall network and system performance? How has it changed recently?
- What is the number of online users? How has it changed over the past year?
- What is the division of resources across the application systems?
- What are the number of open issues related to:

  o Network operations?
  o Hardware operations?
  o Systems software?
  o Security software?
  o Internet connectivity?
  o Application systems?

- What are the number of recurring issues and problems in the above areas?
- What is the age of the components of the architecture?
- Interface-related measurements. This is usually a drain on resources.

  o Interfaces between networks
  o Interfaces between application systems
  o External interfaces with outside networks

- Is there a problem reporting and tracking process?
- Is fixing a significant recurring problem treated as a project?
- Can the architecture accommodate growth? What problems have occurred during growth spurts?

Figure 16.5 Potential Items for Measuring Architecture.

Work and Support Measurement

Given that the strategic IT and process plan should result in a shift in work and support, it is useful to measure these areas. These are covered in Figure 16.8.

How Often Should a Plan be Updated?

Traditional wisdom and practice indicates an annual update cycle. However, given business change as well as internal factors relating to technology, it may be useful to consider more frequent update. But isn't this a lot more work? Not really as you will see from the next section.

How do you determine if you should update more often? Here are some signs.

- What is the number of IT managers and staff involved in plan development? The more people you involve, the greater their understanding and support.
- Who was involved in writing the plan? What happened to them after the plan was completed?
- What was the duration of the planning effort?
- Was the planning effort synchronized with the schedule for the business plan?
- What was the effort required to generate the plan?
- Are lessons learned gathered in preparation for the planning work?
- Is there an organized process to update the plan?
- What is the frequency of the plan update?
- Are there events between planning cycles that significantly change the plan results? If this is substantial, it may indicate that more frequent updates are necessary.
- To what extent are business units involved in the planning work?
- What is the extent of communications during and after the planning work with:

  o Business units
  o IT staff
  o Upper management
  o Selected, critical vendors

- Were significant new project opportunities identified during the planning work?
- Was it easy to gain access to managers and employees during the planning work?

Figure 16.6 Potential Items for Measuring the Strategic Planning Process.

- Business priorities changes, causing action items in the plan to be pushed back.
- Projects that were approved, funded, and started are suddenly stopped or given a lower priority.
- There appears to be substantial business changes that the plan never addressed. That is not the fault of planning, but of new events.

What should you do? Consider doing the plan update twice a year. There are a number of benefits of this decision, including:

- It will be easier to do the update given the shorter elapsed time.
- Politically, it will indicate to management that IT is responsive to business needs.
- Doing the update will make the plan more visible and relevant.

So, if the plan was last updated in July of one year, it would be updated again in January of the following year.

- Does a formal strategic IT plan exist?
- Is there frequent reference made to the plan by the IT staff, upper management, and business units? Or, does it seem to just sit on a shelf?
- Is there a formal link between the strategic IT plan and the strategic business plan?
- Is there an effort to demonstrate alignment of IT to the business on three levels: tactical, intermediate term, and long term?
- To what extent are business processes part of the plan?
- What is the percentage of action items that were approved?
- What is the percentage of action items that were implemented?
- What is the percentage of action items that are not projects?
- What changes in maintenance, operations, and enhancement after the plan was approved?
- Was the strategic plan formally reviewed and approved?
- Was there a strategic resource allocation process to deal with the action items?
- What was the number and type of projects terminated due to the plan? There should be some since the project action items will require resources.
- What were the number and type of technologies considered and rejected by the plan? This can show that the planning effort was selective.
- Does the plan relate issues to objectives and issues to action items?
- Are strategies differentiated from objectives?
- Is there a formal section that relates the business factors to the planning factors?

Figure 16.7 Potential Items for Measuring the Strategic IT and Process Plan.

Update the Plan

Let's first determine what is involved. In essence, you will update the lists and tables of the plan. Wow! This looks like a lot of work. Not really. The objectives haven't changed. Nor have the business processes or organizations. There is not likely to be major new technology since new technology and systems are introduced incrementally, most of the time being backward compatible. Nor have the systems and staffing in IT changed much. So, where is the change? In issues, opportunities, and action items. Maybe, there is some need to update strategies.

Nevertheless, the update gives you the change to consider new projects. You would start with the ones that were rejected during the earlier planning. To this you could do a quick canvassing of departments to search for new opportunities. There are typically some new business needs. You have to take a two-pronged approach. First, you

Project and support work

- What is the percentage of tasks that are assigned to one person? This would indicate the extent of teamwork.
- What percentage of tasks take longer than two weeks? Longer tasks are more difficult to track.
- What is the percentage of tasks that exceed their estimated duration?
- What is the percentage of work that involved vendors that is joint with vendor staff? This can indicate the extent to which knowledge is shared.
- What is the number of methods without tools?
- What are the gaps in either or both of methods or tools? What efforts have been made to eliminate these?
- What is the number of methods and tools for which there is no internal "expert?"
- Are new methods and tools systematically evaluated?
- Are there measures for method and tool effectiveness?
- How is support managed? As small projects, we would hope so as to provide for greater management.
- What is the distribution between planned and unplanned support?

Results of work

Listed below are some potential measurements for the benefits from the work.
- What is the volume of work being performed?
- What is the average time to perform a transaction before and after?
- What is the condition of business process before and after work?
- To what extent was there reduced staffing in the business units?
- Was there a reduction in clerical work?
- Was there reduced training time in the department to learn the new process?
- Was there reduced rework?
- Was there a change in the condition of the business procedures?
- Are the procedures followed to a greater extent?
- What are the nature and extent of exceptions?
- Are there guidelines that support the procedures?
- Have the power and influence of King and Queen Bees changed?
- Are lessons learned shared among business employees?
- What is the extent of collaboration among departments?
- Is there an improved ability to handle new work without making them exceptions?
- Can the new process handle a greater volume of work?
- Is there a change for new employees in the business units to become productive?
- Is there improved teamwork among business employees?
- What is the number of shadow systems in the business unit — before versus after the change?
- What is the business employee turnover before and after?

Figure 16.8 Potential Items for Measuring Work and Support.

look to upper management for signs of what is needed directionally. Second, you look to the departments and the business processes for requirements.

There may be some specific new challenges. Here are some examples.

- Challenge 1: New technology

    The first step is to determine if there is a true business or IT benefit. Most of the time it is better to pass on these. The next step is to determine the fit with the existing architecture. What would the technology replace in the architecture? What can you get rid of? What other changes would have to be included? For example, if you made a major network change, you might have to change the electronic mail system. Concurrently, you would want to ascertain the maturity of the new technology. For example, are there supporting products, guidelines, and available support from vendors?

- Challenge 2: New business needs

    Often, new business needs can be addressed by enhancements to current systems. However, if it is radically new, there you have several issues. You first have to determine the details of the need and how it arose. Why is it new? Why wasn't it there before? One action to take is to link these needs to existing projects and the business processes. If you can do some bundling of the work, there might be economies of scale.

- Challenge 3: New management

    We previously stated in communications that you should seek out new managers and let them know about the key IT initiatives. You can also use this opportunity to suggest areas where they can make their "mark." If you wait for them to contact you, then you are in a reactive mode and on the defensive — not good. You should have some idea of what to tell any new manager at any time — good preparation. You also need to have information on changes in management early. This requires something of a small intelligence network to learn about changes early.

Now, we proceed to the actual updating. Here are the steps. Note that these can be performed in parallel even though they are listed in sequence.

- Step 1: Review the objectives and constraints first. There should be few, if any changes. The same applies to the business processes.
- Step 2: Review the business goals, mission, and issues. Again, there should be little change since these are directional and long term.
- Step 3: Examine the action items. Which ones were completed? Which ones were terminated before completed? Which were not approved?
- Step 4: Having looked at both ends of the plan you can review the strategies.

These steps can be construed as your internal update of the plan. Note that business issues are absent from the steps. However, there are also external factors. Before the update work begins alert the IT and business supervisors to find out what has changed since the last update. Ask them if there have been significant changes in:

- The actual work in the process
- How work is being measured
- The staffing related to the business process
- Policies and procedures

This work can elicit changes due to competitive pressures.

Now comes one of the bigger tasks. That is the review of the business issues. How do you do this since many of the issues are implicit and not stated outright? Go to the processes and see what issues have surfaced. This will give you a tactical view. Then, turn to upper management and try to elicit what has changed. Your position is:

- IT is here to support the business.
- It is important that IT gets a "heads up" on issues to have time to respond.

Having gathered this information, you can first proceed to update the lists. Given the stability of some of the items, you want to concentrate on:

- IT strategies
- IT issues and opportunities
- Business issues

You can then update the tables related to:

- IT
  - o Objectives
  - o Constraints
  - o Strategies
- Business
  - o Business objectives, mission, and vision
  - o Business processes
  - o Business issues

That leaves potential action items. From experience, you want to make a list. Start with the ones left over from the last planning effort. Next, consider potential project ideas. These would stem from the challenges mentioned earlier as well as the business issues. Assume that the projects that are generated by the plan are completed, what else is there to do? Next, try to think of other non-project ideas such as changes in policies, procedures, facilities, work assignments, and other areas mentioned earlier in the development of the plan.

You can now add the action items to the lists and create the related tables. Critical tables include the following:

- Issues and opportunities versus IT strategies
- IT objectives versus IT strategies
- IT strategies versus action items
- Action items versus issues and opportunities

For business and IT joint relationships, you have:

- Issues and opportunities versus business processes
- Action items versus business processes
- IT strategies versus business processes

For alignment, you have:

- Business issues versus business processes
- IT strategies versus business mission or vision
- IT strategies versus business issues
- Issues and opportunities versus business mission or vision
- Issues and opportunities versus business issues
- Action items versus business mission or vision
- Action items versus business issues

This will indicate both positive and negative alignment.

The process of communicating the update of the plan follows the same guidelines as with the plan itself.

As an aside, the update to the plan can lead to more effective strategic resource allocation. That is, while the first planning effort focused on the plan, the update was brief so that more attention could be given to the resource allocation method.

Examples

In a manufacturing firm, the planning process was implemented in several autonomous business units successfully. During the plan updates, the planning process was adapted to the individual culture and schedule of the business units. The planning process withstood five changes of management in two years. This was a tribute to middle management who supported the planning effort.

The planning process was implemented first in the major operational division of a transportation agency. The overall management did not see the need for an strategic IT and process plan. The test of the method came with an emergency shortage of finds and layoff of personnel. This made the plan important and of high priority. After the plan was updated for the agency, resource allocation kicked in and resulted in a major shift of IT resources — to the better.

Lessons Learned

With respect to measurement, consider carrying out the first measurement informally. This will have less visibility and lead to lower expectations of change. Then with experience, you can formalize the measurement methods. This approach minimizes risk and potential problems while giving you an opportunity to reveal results from measurements.

There are a number of lessons learned from past updates of plans in different organizations. The first guideline is:

> Think of the strategic planning effort as a continuous process.

Doing this makes you look for new issues and challenges as work is performed. Remember if you "drop the ball," you may miss something significant.

Keep an eye on project ideas that were again rejected. Try to communicate with departments about how priorities were set. Politically, you want to stress the relative importance of project ideas.

If the plan update is carried out twice a year, consider only proposing new project ideas on an annual basis. This can lead to more focus on results using non-project ideas.

Politics

Measurements can be very political. Many people suspect, from past experience that you have a hidden agenda. You want to indicate that through the process of measurement problems can be surfaced to management. With formal measurements there is greater credibility.

Politics can surface during the updates. Some managers may not see the need to do it. Alternatively, they may not recognize any benefits from the past effort. How do you market the update? Don't even consider preaching the benefits of planning. Go instead to what problems the plan mitigated or dealt with. Also, indicate that the planning effort is not that substantial.

What to do Next

Look over the past two years in your organization to find instances of management change. What was their impact on the IT activities and the plan? Could the results of the management change have been predicted?

What new technologies were implemented in the past two years? Did they measure up to the hype that originally caused people to be interested in them? What were the lessons learned from both successes and failures?

Looking back did the plan reflect business needs in terms of business issues and objectives? To what extent did the action items mitigate the business issues?

Summary

This chapter has focused on two different, but related areas. One is that of measurement. The second is that of the plan update. These are related because the measurements can provide valuable input into the update of the strategic IT and process plan.

There were many specific potential measurements provided. Which ones you start with is not as important as starting a measurement effort. People are often too busy to measure. Then, they later fail to understand what they accomplished.

Chapter 17

Conclusions and Actions
to Take

Introduction

We have covered the major areas of strategic IT and process planning: These are listed in Figure 17.1. These are listed in a sequential order, but, again, you want to do many of these in parallel so as to reduce the elapsed time and cost.

Given that so many planning efforts either fail outright or fail to deliver the intended results, the first part of this chapter focuses on failure — the method, the implementation, and more specific problems during planning. Moving from this negative stuff, critical success factors for the planning method, the planning effort, and the plan implementation are presented. This covers both the good and the bad. There is no ugly! (joke).

The bottom line is the business requirements force the need for an effective strategic IT and process planning effort. Guidelines are given for success. These focus on major themes of structure and organization, collaboration, issues management, and lessons learned. Finally, to get you started, a number of specific actions are suggested along with tips for doing these.

- Internal assessment related to planning

  o The existing planning method
  o The strategic plan
  o Existing systems and technology
  o Existing infrastructure and architecture
  o Current projects and work in IT
  o The business mission, vision, objectives, and issues
  o Business processes

- External assessment

  o Strategic planning methods
  o Business trends
  o Trends in business processes
  o Trends in systems and technology

- Development of the strategic IT and process plan

  o Issues and opportunities
  o Objectives
  o Constraints
  o Strategies
  o Action items
  o Creation of tables

- Determination of a business unit strategic IT and process plan

  o From the overall strategic IT and process plan
  o To the overall IT and process plan

- Strategic resource allocation

  o Competing activities for resources
  o Resource assessment
  o Resource allocation

- Implementation Quick Wins from the plan

  o Quick Win strategic implementation roadmap
  o Quick Win installation and measurement

- Implementation of longer term change

  o Policy changes
  o Staffing and organization changes
  o Projects
  o Process change

- Measurement

  o Business processes
  o Current systems and technology

Figure 17.1 Areas and Topics in Strategic IT and Process Planning.

---

o   Current projects and work
o   The planning method
o   The planning process
o   Resource allocation
o   Quick Win results
o   Projects and longer term results

Figure 17.1 (*Continued*)

Why Planning Methods often Fail — 16 Reasons

Reason 1: The method does not fit the culture of the firm

Culture is a major underlying factor in the operation of any organization. There are layers of culture, including:

- Culture of the country of operation
- Culture of the organization overall (as developed at headquarters)
- Culture of the organization in the country of operation
- Culture of the division, department, or business unit

To see that culture can play a major role, let's consider an example. A firm is focused almost totally on short-term results. Planning is very difficult in this culture. A standard strategic IT planning method would likely fail. What could you do to deal with this culture since you cannot change it through planning easily? Start with a focus on finding issues and problems. Then you can start defining Quick Wins. The implementation of these Quick Wins can generate momentum to expand the time horizon of the planning effort.

How do you understand the culture? When you start the planning effort get down to where the work is performed. Cultural factors are dominated by work. By starting here you can understand the culture. You can:

- Ask why some problems were not addressed.
- Suggest possible changes and improvements and gauge the reaction of the employees and their supervisors.

From this you can see that a planning method must be adaptive to any and all cultures. One thing this implies is flexibility to deal with both short- and long-term horizons. Another thing is that by dealing with both processes and IT, you have additional flexibility. You can start with either one.

Reason 2: *The method is too exotic or arcane*

To have a reasonable chance of success, a planning method must be easily understood without a lot of training. This means it must be common sense and reflect how people would plan their own lives. Also, it means that there must be a minimum of jargon and fuzzy words. Nothing gets in the way of planning more than if you have spend a lot of time explaining what some planning words means. People get turned off.

The cost of using an exotic method can be high. Cost elements include:

- Training costs in learning the method
- Elapsed time and effort to get proficient in the method
- Use of consultants in employing the method
- Recurring training costs involved with the method
- On-going consulting costs

So, why do firms sometimes rush to adopt some new method? Here are some of the reasons we have seen from experience:

- Management was approached directly by the consulting firm pitching the method. They jump at this so-called opportunity without a thorough review.
- Past planning efforts had failed. However, there was no examination of the reasons for failure — which rested with the firm, not the methods. Thus, they are set to try another method.
- If a method uses esoteric words and ideas, it seems to be attractive to people. It is out of the ordinary.

- The firm wants to develop a plan and is drawn to the method that has the most marketing support.
- The firm learns of the method from another company. That company is using the method and is enthusiastic about it. However, there are no results. But based on the recommendation, the firm picks it anyhow.

How do you head off the adoption of such methods? Ask some common sense questions, such as:

- If the method is so good, why aren't more firms using it?
- Why did this method surface so recently?
- When you strip out the jargon, what is the essence of the method in common sense words? Maybe, you can use this as part of the method to use.
- How long would it take to learn and use the method?

If a manager wants to use one of these methods, experience shows that you should not resist directly. You will be viewed as being too negative. Instead, concentrate on issues in the implementation of the method.

Reason 3: Too much outside help is needed

While this can be linked to the previous reason, there are instances in which a firm becomes over reliant on a consultant to do the planning and produce the plan. If the firm surrenders much of the planning work to outside help, there can be substantial problems in addition to the cost.

- There is a lack of knowledge transfer from the consultant to the firm's employees.
- The consulting firm owns the information in the sense that they both gathered it and organized it.

- It is probably less likely that the action items will be implemented since there is a lack of internal ownership.

What is the minimal level of internal involvement in the work? First, the employees should develop and document the planning elements (issues and opportunities, objectives, and so forth). Next, they should do all of the presentations of the plan to management. Third, they should take over the updating of the plan. These three tasks ensure that the employees will own the plan. Probably, the best role for consulting assistance is in the coordination of the internal planning work and the providing of guidance from their experience. That will ensure a more effective transfer of knowledge. However, many consultants do not want to do this since it means less initial revenue and either reduced or non-existent future revenue.

Reason 4: The method is too expensive to implement

Expenses do not multiply just from exotic methods or over-reliance on consultants. They can get expensive for some or all of the following:

- The planning required the involvement of too many people — distracting them from the work.
- The planning work concentrated on big projects and ideas — leading to much greater expenses later on.
- The planning effort required the heavy involvement of a few key people. The result is that their other work suffered which led to systems problems.

Some managers think that if you pay more, you get more. This is sometimes true for housing. If a house does not sell, rather than lowering the price, you raise it to appeal to a different audience. Moreover, a big expense seems impressive in terms of what was spent in planning.

Experience shows that the major expense should be employee time — not that of consultants or the purchase of a method. If you adopt a method that delivers short-term results, the planning effort will be more limited in duration. This leads to lower costs. In addition, the Quick Wins financial results can mitigate the planning cost as well as justify it.

Reason 5: *The method takes too long to implement*

In projects, if a project takes too long to complete, it has a much higher likelihood of failure. One reason is that people lose hope and turn to other solutions. The original need disappears. Another reason is the requirements can change — further lengthening the project duration.

These points apply to planning. If the planning takes too long, expectations tend to melt. People start taking actions in contravention of the plan. After all, they have to keep the business going. The information can become stale and less relevant. Value of the plan information can rapidly decay due to business and IT operations as well as outside factors.

A guideline we have employed is two and three months maximum elapsed time. This puts pressure on to get the thing finished. The only reason to extend this is to implement Quick Wins. Since these deliver tangible benefits, they can justify a longer effort.

Some think that if you take longer, you get better results. Not true. Many of the issues and opportunities should surface in a short time. The business factors usually are known. Moreover, it is possible that expectations for the plan are raised if you take longer. They associate duration and effort with value.

Reason 6: *The method does not address resource allocation after completion of the plan*

This is a common failure of many planning methods. They just cover the development of the plan. To be complete and to better ensure results, a planning method should address how to get the resources to undertake the implementation of the action items. Otherwise, the action items are not done. The excellent planning work could have been largely wasted. Strategic planning loses credibility and gets a "black eye."

Reason 7: Using the method, you are not likely to get Quick Wins

Many planning methods focus on identifying major work and project opportunities. This is all good, but it does not go far enough. During the strategic planning, this is a golden opportunity to find Quick Win opportunities that otherwise would not have been either discovered or implemented. The Quick Win benefits can sometimes exceed the cost of the strategic planning work.

However, you have to guard against the other extreme — settling for just short-term wins. While these can result in more immediate results, the longer term actions provide support for the mission and vision. Additionally, some of the Quick Wins might become undone later without the longer term action items.

Reason 8: The method is not tested in our industry

Each industry has unique characteristics in terms of processes, customers, organization, and so forth. For example, it has proven difficult to take process improvement methods employed successfully in manufacturing and apply these to service industry firms. One reason for this lies in the difficulty of measuring the service firm activities. There can be more subjective factors.

So, it is useful if you are not a pioneer in your industry for a method. Remember the saying, "Pioneers are ones who get arrows in their backs." The pioneering firms endure the learning curve in applying the method to their industry. This can make the planning very expensive and probably more prone to failure.

Reason 9: The method only deals with IT and not processes

Most strategic IT planning methods focus on IT. This has some benefits. First, the scope of the planning is reduced. Second, the staff involved in the planning need a lesser understanding of the business.

These advantages are more than compensated for by the problems.

- The relevance of the plan to IT may be just fine, but that to the business may be questionable.
- An IT plan that does not focus on processes puts the IT management team at risk. They may be seen as out of touch with the company's needs.
- If implemented, the plan action items may produce marginal benefits.

Reason 10: The method ignores the real-world politics

Some methods are quite formal and academic. This is fine in a book and might get by in a classroom. However, as we have seen, strategic IT and process planning can result in change. Change threatens the political status quo.

Why don't these planning methods spend more time and focus on politics? One reason is that they may only been employed in politically friendly environments. These do exist and in substantial numbers. However, in many firms the atmosphere oozes with politics. Another reason is that they have been created by academics or theoreticians who sometimes do not want to give importance to politics. That might make the world too dirty.

On the other hand, we are not saying that the planning work should just be political. You just be aware of and take advantage of the politics. Why? To get the plan done. To gain support for the plan. To get resources for implementation. To get results!

Reason 11: There is a lack of measurement in the method

If you use anything new, you want to be successful. Therefore, when you buy a tool to do something around the house, you have a good idea of the use of the tool. You also have expectations of the benefits. It is the same with planning methods.

Measurement is not something you do at the end with the plan. As the chapter on measurement indicated you have to measure processes, systems, the planning, resource use, implementation — a wide range of factors. Yes, this takes some time. However, it gives you a better idea of where things stand and pushes you to fix problems.

Reason 12: Using the method, the plan is not easy to update

Every planning approach has some specific techniques for collecting and organizing information. This is the same with tax preparation software. Some packages require you to enter all of the data each year. The better methods roll over the information which you then update. This will catch more errors and the software can suggest some opportunities for deductions.

An important criterion for selecting a planning method is to see what is involved in updating the plan. The plan update should be incremental, based on what you have from last time. This can result in more effective work and cumulative improvement. It also gives you the time to expand the scope of the business units and their processes to be considered. Moreover, you can develop IT and process plans for business units. Thus, the value of the planning to the business increases over time.

Reason 13: The method does not fit firms of our size

A number of methods are quite expensive, labor intensive, and time consuming to implement. In process improvement, Six Sigma and Total Quality Measurement (TQM) are two examples of this. To be viable over the long haul a strategic planning method should be scalable. This is important for even large firms. Why? Because a scalable method can be projected down to individual business units.

Reason 14: The method requires a lot of management involvement,
but this is not possible

The method in this book points to heavy management involvement at two major milestones. One is to initiate the planning effort. The second is to get resources for the actions of the strategic plan. Why only these two? Because acceptance of the plan is implicit in the approval and support for resources for the action items.

A basic point is that while the strategic plan is important, there are so many other activities of equal or greater importance to managers. Everyday business situations and issues tend to dominate management time. So, it is unrealistic to expect a great deal of management involvement.

There are several reasons to have limited management involvement, even if it were possible. First, if managers get more involved, they may color the planning results for individual reasons (politics again). Second, they may start micromanaging the planning work. This can drive you crazy. Third, even well-intended involvement may suppress the surfacing of issues and opportunities. Remember the sayings about bearers of bad news.

Reason 15: The method does not involve business unit managers
and staff to any degree in developing the plan

Some planning methods limit the involvement of the business unit managers to reviews of the final draft of the plan. One reason for this is the focus on IT. Another reason is that they may see substantial business involvement as either impossible, undesirable, or impractical.

However, substantial business involvement is essential to effective implementation of the action items of the plan. Their involvement and participation gives them more of a sense of ownership. In addition, their participation ensures that the plan will be more realistic and relevant to the business.

Reason 16: The method relies too much on technology solutions

Some planning methods rely on getting software solutions at the expense of Quick Wins and other areas of change. IBM, many years ago, did this with their planning approach. Their method devoted attention to areas of the business that needed new software applications. This is probably the case with airplane manufacturers who supply planning models to airlines to project the number of plans required. Technological solutions are just one piece of the planning puzzle.

Why Implementing a Planning Method Fails — 25 Reasons

Failure can only occur from the selection of the wrong method. You could have the "perfect" technique, but it still has a substantial likelihood of failure in implementation. Some of the reasons given below are within the scope of the planning work. Others are more dangerous since they are external to strategic planning. As in the earlier chapter dealing with objectives and constraints, you have to work to get around these. You cannot change them since they are not under your control.

Reason 1: The company lacks direction

This sounds impossible. What we mean is that the company is totally focused on short-term results. To management long term is this year. Many of these organizations are driven by events and the processes. They are reactive.

We have encountered this situation several times. Instead of walking away or giving up, search for an entry point involving the business processes. You can start by evaluating the processes to look for issues and their impacts. This gets attention. Then, you can point to the need to have some direction for the process. This leads to process planning. After this, turn to alignment of the processes to the business. Then move to IT. See how they are aligned to the direction of the processes as well as their current condition. Step-by-step you create the strategic IT and process plan.

Reason 2: There is a lack of stability in IT

One situation is where there is turnover among IT managers and supervisors. Another is staff turnover. It is difficult if the faces keep changing. However, the focus of the plan is not on the individuals. It is lower down where the work is performed. There has to be greater stability here. In one case, we helped in the strategic planning over a three-month period. During this time the IT manager changed three (yes, three) times — a revolving door.

In this situation, you want to concentrate on the details of the planning. Seek limited involvement of IT managers, but keep them involved. When do you really need their help? One time is in the presentation of the plan. A hint here — let them take credit for the plan. Then, you need some involvement during resource allocation.

However, even here this is limited since many of the action items pertain to processes and should be supported by the business managers. For the technical action items you can point to the problems that will arise for the business if the underlying problems are not addressed.

Reason 3: IT has a short-term focus

The IT management and staff may be totally devoted to fixing problems, keeping operations going, doing some enhancements and, maybe, several smaller projects. There is not much tolerance for long-range planning.

What can be done in this situation? As before, focus on the problems and their impacts. Show that there is a need and direct benefit to IT from considering the long-term view. These benefits include:

- Systematic problems can be addressed.
- IT can sit back and view their alignment to the business.

- The staff morale can improve since they can move away from just solving today's problems.

Reason 4: The company has no one with planning experience

Most companies don't have the luxury of full-time planners. Actually, our experience shows that this is an advantage. If the individual doing the planning has other, regular work, then there is less dependence on the planning as a job. There are many advantages of having the staff such as project managers and systems analysts.

- They learn more about the business processes.
- They get more contacts with staff and managers in business units.
- Their regular work will improve with the experience.
- They get a change of pace.

All of that said, if the method used is too exotic, then the application of the planning method may fail due to their lack of experience.

There is another point. If a company hires a person who has done planning in the past, they will come with baggage from past experience, including the planning method used in their past position. This may or may not be good.

If the planning is performed as work in addition to regular work, there will be a push to get it done to work on their regular work. If it is full-time, then the planning may be stretched out. Using the method presented in the book, it has been proven that the IT staff members are more than capable of doing the planning with some guidance.

Reason 5: Quick Wins are identified, but not implemented

This often results from not preparing management for Quick Wins. Another reason is that people take the position that "Nothing can be implemented without a thorough review." Here are some suggestions for Quick Wins:

- Seek the lowest level of approval to implement the Quick Wins. Management is often interested in what is done and results. The "how" is often left to department supervisors as long as they follow company guidelines.
- If the staff can test the Quick Wins in the business units, implementation can follow.
- If you have to go to management, then (1) it appears that you have no authority (why should they deal with you?) and (2) management may feel that they are doing your job.

The strategy is to test implementing Quick Wins to test resistance to change as well as to show results.

Reason 6: There is a lack of measurement as the planning is being done

People get involved in the planning and so feel that they have no time to measure. The previous chapter highlighted many measurement areas. If you measure, several things to keep in mind are:

- You become more aware of what is going on.
- You want to do the work so that the measurements will be successful.
- Overall, you become more careful and your work is more planned and measured.

One reason that people do not measure is that it seems to them to slow down the work. It does not. Time management methods teach you to measure constantly. So, do weight reduction programs.

Another reason is that they do not see the benefits. Traditional project management methods preach the post-implementation review. But this is too late. You want to measure as the work in the project is done. In that way, you can correct problems before the end of the project.

Reason 7: Only one or two people are doing the planning

If the planning is done by one or two people, they own the plan. Not good. You can have one or two people overseeing the planning work. But the people doing this should not do the plan. They should *coordinate* the planning work — not do it. Remember that participation leads to commitment. Commitment leads to ownership. The people coordinating the planning should not own it.

Another point to keep in mind is that you want only one or two people to coordinate the planning. Any more than this affects accountability.

Reason 8: There is an over focus on the IT part of the plan

This has been discussed before. Disregarding or short changing the business process part can lead to actions items that have no business benefit — even though they help IT. Here are some tests for an IT action item:

- It should directly help the business processes to be more effectively and efficient (direct benefit).
- If, on the other hand, it helps IT staff only, then it should release IT staff to do other work that assists the business (indirect benefit).

Why does this problem occur? There is a comfort level in doing what you are familiar with. IT may not have had substantial contact with business units.

The best approach is to start with the business processes. In that way, you will not become bogged down in the IT planning materials.

Reason 9: There is a lack of creativity in finding solutions

In the chapters on defining issues and opportunities, objectives, strategies, and action items (Chapters 8–10), we suggested a number of techniques to find solutions. There is no need to repeat this. Basically, here are some options to consider:

- Do nothing. This shows the effects of deterioration as well as importance.
- Throw money at it. This shows the limits of financial solutions such as new systems.
- Only short-term solutions. This can show why a long-term approach is needed. It also reveals the systemic problems in the work.
- Long- and short-term improvements without major systems work. This can demonstrate the need for systems projects.
- A mix of process improvement and systems work. Usually, this is the desired approach.

You should never assume that people will instantly be creative. Many people have been conditioned to accept things as they are. Considering the above list will trigger new ideas.

Reason 10: There is too little or too much outside information

Everyone can see the problem with too little information. It hurts the extent of analysis. Moreover, it impacts the political credibility of what you have done. In addition, if you have only performed a cursory outside analysis, then someone may come along with some other outside trend, product, and so forth and affect the trust in the planning. That is why we devoted Chapters 5 and 6 to data collection and outside information, respectively.

It would seem that you can't have too much information. But it is true. You can become overloaded with outside data. What are some of the potential impacts we have seen?

- Too much time was spent on outside information so that it detracts from the internally focused work that is so politically important.

- If someone has a great deal of external information, there is a tendency to want to use it in the plan. Then, the danger is that the strategic IT and process plan looks a lot like a business and technology assessment — too passive.

A key test of external information is relevance. Once we encountered a fellow who was involved in planning and almost totally centered on external information. He knew a tremendous amount of data — like a walking, talking encyclopedia. However, little was relevant to the company. He had to be removed from the team. Later, he surfaced at another firm doing the same time — with the same problems. The test of relevance is whether what you see affects either or both of business processes or systems and technology.

Reason 11: The consultants are over controlling the planning effort

Let's ask and answer some questions. Why does the consultant want control? First, it ensures that they are essential to the work — more money. Second, through control they ensure that their method will be used.

Why does a company cede control to consultants for strategic IT and process planning? First, they feel that they lack expertise. Second, they think that if the consultant has their name on the work, it is more credible. Third, the employees have a lot of other things. Having the consultant assume a greater role eases their work.

The major downside is that the consultant owns the plan — not the company. When questions, additional work, and updates to the plan appear, there is a tendency to rely on the consultant. Should this continue, it puts the strategic plan on the side of, not inside, the work.

In addition to defining the consultant's role at the start, you must reinforce this during the planning. Ensure that the consultant works with employees from the start. There should be a joint project plan for the work. There should also be periodic reviews with the internal staff (consultant not present) to verify the roles and responsibilities. All presentations should be given in large part by employees.

Reason 12: There is a lack of follow-up after the plan is approved

That is the problem with many planning books. The plan is approved and the story is at an end. But you know from the chapter on strategic resource allocation that the fight is just beginning. Many people accept the plan because they see it as just paper and a presentation. It gets real when the implementation of the action items in the plan threaten their resources and work — and their power.

Start planning for the struggle for resources during the planning. Try to determine what the sources of available resources. In military terms, try to identify the "soft" targets from which you can obtain resources. Sounds negative, but it is very real. If you get started after the plan, you have to do a lot of research and data collection. During this time you lose the momentum generated by management approval. You want to maintain a continuous flow.

Reason 13: One or several managers attempt to dictate the plan contents

A strategic IT and process plans points to new actions and projects. These represent CHANGE. Some managers and staff in both the business and IT may feel threatened by this. Their work will be affected. As will their power and control. Things will be different. The reaction of some managers is to try to take over some or all of the direction of the plan.

The best approach from experience is to anticipate that this will happen and plan for it during the planning work. This will make you want to try to detect potential resistance and also spur you on to line up support for the plan.

Another guideline is to develop the lists and tables in sufficient detail that it will be difficult for a manager to institute changes. You can help yourself here by distributing drafts of planning elements to a number of managers at one time. If a manager knows that the information is in circulation, he or she will be more reluctant to make changes.

Reason 14: There is a lack of informal management and business unit contact during planning

A frequently used process in strategic planning is to go out and collect information after the planning work has been kicked off. Data is collected over several weeks. There is a regular, almost daily contact with business managers. Following this the planners return to their desks and start performing analysis. Several months can elapse before the first draft of the plan rolls out.

There are a number of problems with this situation, including:

- *Expectations.* During data collection, business managers may get the feeling that some of their problems will be fixed with the plan. This was not corrected. So, there is bound to be a letdown and even hostility when they see the plan.
- *Feedback.* There was no feedback from the information collected. Furthermore, the plan analysis may be in contraposition to the data they provided.
- *Missed opportunities.* If you try to collect all of the information from a manager at one time, you may miss important information. You also lose the opportunity to correct information from later analysis.
- *Lack of ownership.* The managers do not feel they are a part of the planning effort. They clearly do not feel that they own the plan.

Here are some guidelines. First, never indicate that all of the information has been collected. Just like Freddy in the *Friday the 13th* movies, you want to indicate that you will be back. Second, the return visits can include:

- Gathering additional information
- Getting feedback on lists and tables of the plan draft
- Soliciting details and support for the plan action items and for strategic resource allocation

Through these contacts you can keep the interest and involvement in the planning not only alive, but increasing. You can also use these meetings to gain support for the action item implementation.

Reason 15: Interim results are not presented for feedback and involvement

Look at this from the perspective of a manager. You gave information to the planners. Weeks and months pass. Suddenly, you are given a complete draft of the plan. For a busy manager this is too much to swallow. So, what do you do? You first put it on the shelf of the pile to be done. Then, the planner contacts you for feedback. You give it a cursory read and maybe make a few suggestions. That is it. The planners seem happy to get the feedback and publish the plan. You go back to work. When the time comes for getting resources, ah too bad. Everyone is committed.

This somewhat extreme example reveals why recurring feedback and involvement are key to success. Start with reviews of the planning lists. Then move to the tables.

Reason 16: Too few business units and processes are considered in the plan

In several strategic planning failures we turned around, this was the case. The planners thought that if they contacted a few departments, that would be sufficient. It was not. The other departments felt left out. The plan failed to gain support.

It is not realistic to expect that you can contact all departments in a large corporation. However, here are some guidelines that were used in the turnarounds.

- *Positive importance.* Identify the departments that are critical to revenues for the firm.
- *Negative importance.* Determine which departments and business units contribute to the business issues.
- *Geographical spread.* You want to include business units in key markets and operations of the organization.
- *Mix of support and operations groups.* You want to include some support groups to show relevance and to gain support.
- *IT involved and IT neglected.* Here, you reach out to both those units that have heavy dependence on IT and those that have received limited IT support.

This strategy helps you to gain political support for the plan and its implementation.

Reason 17: *It is not clear how the plan aligns to the business*

In many strategic IT plans there are good ideas for application systems, hardware, networks, and infrastructure. It is sometimes difficult for a business manager to read this and make the leap to determine how it applies to them. This can lead to lack of support for the plan. Moreover, it can lead some managers to question the direction of IT.

By including the business process planning into the strategic planning, all parts of the strategic plan have to relate to the key business processes. This will gain more management and business unit support.

Reason 18: *There is a lack of schedule synchronization with the business*

In several cases we have observed, an excellent plan was produced. The plan was then reviewed and approved. Then nothing happened because the business plan had yet to be released. This lack of coordination and synchronization means that momentum for the plan is lost. You later have to start again to generate interest. You also may have to update the plan. Credibility declines. The steps to synchronize the plan with the business have been discussed in previous chapters and should be followed to prevent this problem.

Reason 19: No one is doing measurements

Planning takes time. There are also very limited resources. With these factors in mind it is not surprising that measurements of processes, the planning work, and so forth are not undertaken. Some also take it for granted that everyone agrees on the state of what could be measured.

Measurements are critical because there is need to gain a consensus understanding of the processes and planning. Measurements also provide the opportunity to generate more support for change. Measurements also provide you with the basis of the before and after comparison.

Reason 20: There is no gathering of lessons learned

Often, the objective is to produce the strategic plan within the time and resource constraints. However, it is so much more. You want to gain resources for implementation. Then, you have to implement the action items and measure results.

You also want to reduce and improve future planning efforts. All of these are supported by gathering lessons learned, organizing them, and applying them. In addition, lessons learned are powerful and inexpensive action items related to both IT and business processes.

Reason 21: Issues that are identified are not tracked and managed

In doing the planning, you encounter issues and problems. Sometimes, if these do not directly bear on the plan, they are dropped and later ignored. Don't let this happen.

Use these in the plan as opportunities for improvement. You will also gain political traction since managers will see that you listened to them regarding issues.

Reason 22: *There is a bad mix of action items*

One of the most frequent problems with plans is that the action items are entirely devoted to potential projects. To many managers this seems self-serving on the part of IT. They (IT) are just using the plan to push some projects.

For credibility and value, you want to include many non-project action items. That is why we spend so much time and space on these in Chapter 8.

Reason 23: *Planning is being done without sensitivity to politics*

Politics has been a major emphasis in this book. Since the strategic IT and process plan may result in significant changes to processes, systems, and technology, the planning effort is political. The plan is a political document. Recognizing this from the inception of planning can prove rewarding and lead to more extensive implementation of change.

The key political goals are:

- Recognition of the need for improvement and change
- Support for resources to implement action items
- Implementation involvement and support of action items

Reason 24: *There is no follow-up for action items*

Many strategic planning books end with the completion of the plan. As we have seen, this is just a starting point for change. During the planning effort you want to concentrate on implementation of the action items — not just defining them. The benefits of implementing some action items before completion of the plan have been discussed in depth.

Reason 25: The plan does not address past problems

Sometimes, the individuals involved in planning want to center their attention on new opportunities. This is somewhat natural since new is more exciting and interesting than old.

The strategic IT and process plan should really be directed toward existing issues and opportunities. You can have more traction and support if you can show that the contents of the plan address a range of existing problems — even some that people have just accepted and given up on. That is not to say that you ignore new opportunities. However, you want to relate these to the current issues and problems.

Critical Success Factors in Selecting a Planning Method — 20 Factors

We looked at failure before in this chapter. Now and in the next sections, we go positive and look at factors for success. The factors in this section can provide guidance in evaluating both your current planning approach and new ones that arise. Remember that while a new planning method may arise out of need or discovery, it can also stem from the creators' desire to make money.

Factor 1: The method must be common sense

If it takes several times to read and understand a planning method, then other people will likely have the same problem. When you use a method with exotic terms, instead of gathering information for the plan, you end up spending a lot of time explaining the planning method. Additionally, you probably will have to justify why such a method was adopted. It is better to use a jargon-free approach so you can focus on the plan and not on the education of the method.

*Factor 2: The method should be able to be carried
out with little or no outside help*

Why do people rely on outside help? There are many reasons. They feel that they don't have the time. This means that the strategic planning is not viewed as critical. Another reason is that people feel that they lack the experience in doing planning. However, as you have seen in this book, with checklists and tables, it is not that intimidating. A third reason is that the organization has selected some exotic method that requires outside help. An example is Six Sigma for process improvement. The discussion in the previous factor on jargon methods applies here.

The more that you rely on outside help, the less ownership you have of the plan and its contents. Also, you become dependent on the consultants when you have to get resources. You also may require assistance during implementation. This does not look good in the eyes of upper management.

*Factor 3: The method should present a detailed approach
for addressing the alignment of IT to the business*

Many IT planning methods begin centered on IT. Alignment is considered later. This is a big mistake. You want to start with the business processes to ensure that the plan contents are aligned to the business. Then during the planning, you produce tables that relate specific IT factors to those involving the business processes and business. Alignment should be considered and analyzed throughout the planning work.

Factor 4: The method should fit the culture and country of the firm

Most methods are marketed and promoted as being culture and country independent. They do not contain specific rules or guidelines to address these issues. Yet, cultural and country background influence the IT and business activities and thereby planning. Some of these factors include:

- The maturity of IT in the organization
- The impact of competition in the country
- How management and employees view the concept of time and urgency

The approach we have taken has been applied in many different countries and cultures. It works for several reasons. First, it relies on self-interest. Second, it is common sense.

Factor 5: *The method should not require exotic methods or tools*

Some planning methods require the use of specialized methods and software tools. This not only requires a substantial investment, but also slows down the planning effort. You should be able to get by with standard database management software, e-mail, spreadsheets, and presentation software.

Factor 6: *The method should lead to updating later with limited effort*

If the plan is a document of text, then it is more challenging to read and review. Also, it will take more time to review. If, on the other hand, the approach is based on lists and tables, updating is easier. You just start with the lists and move to the tables. Reviews are faster since you can show the before and after versions and highlight the changes and additions.

Factor 7: *You should be able to determine progress of the planning during the work*

Some planning efforts resemble a black box. You may not see anything until the completion of a draft strategic plan. Here, you can determine status and progress by reviewing the state of the planning lists and tables.

Factor 8: *The method should be scalable up or down*

Many methods for process improvement involve many people and are expensive to implement. As such, they are out of reach for mid-size and smaller organizations and business units. The method here can be undertaken with a small department or the entire organization as seen in Chapter 11.

Factor 9: *The method should support parallel tasks to reduce elapsed time*

In the use of any planning method, there is the potential for doing parallel work. In our approach, there is no reason why you cannot work on the process and the IT areas concurrently. The same applies to the development of the planning lists and tables. You are limited by the time available. There is an additional benefits of multitasking and parallel work. There is a greater possibility of synergy between elements of the plan — leading to greater consistency and value.

Factor 10: *It should be relatively easy to deal with staff changes in the planning*

In some cases, we found that the strategic planning effort was placed on a substantial hold while someone new was brought in. Then, the new person had to get up to speed on the planning methods that were used. Momentum was lost. This is dangerous if the method mandates that the planners do most of the plan creation.

Here, since the method is both jargon-free and collaborative, it is possible to involve more people in the planning. The role of the planner is coordination — not doing all of the work. In addition, since the method relies on lists and tables, it is easier to get someone new involved in the planning.

Factor 11: The method should require limited upper
management involvement

This has been addressed before in the failure section. The critical management points of involvement are:

- Kick off the planning work
- Review and endorsement of Quick Wins during the planning work
- Review of the planning drafts
- Review and approval of the strategic IT and process plan
- Support for getting resources for the action items
- Review of the implementation of the action items

Some methods require major involvement of management. But they do not have the time. It is not urgent. More management involvement can color the plan contents and lead to micromanagement.

Factor 12: The method should have a focus on business
processes, not just IT

By including business processes, you ensure that the IT parts of the plan are applicable to the business. Additionally, the IT parts of the plan will have a more narrow scope — being driven by the processes.

Factor 13: The method should have been applied before
in the same or similar industries

One industry is very different from another. Take, for example, manufacturing and service firms. It is easier to apply some process improvements such as TQM and Six Sigma in manufacturing than in service firms. It is the same with planning methods that center on statistical measurements.

If the method has been applied to other firms in the same industry, then you have proof that it works in similar firms. Also, you have some of the same issues, objectives, and so forth.

Factor 14: The method should be accompanied by
guidelines on how best to use the method

Let's say that you want to fix an outdoor sprinkler system. You go to a home improvement store and get the pipes and tools. Then you start work. You first try to remove the sprinkler heads. They break off due to rust, dirt, and corrosion. Now, you have to replace much of the pipe — major scope creep. That is what happened to us. The lesson learned is that it takes expertise and experience to do many substantial tasks around a house. In this case, we needed a gardener with a hand-made tool to remove the sprinkler head without breaking the pipe.

It is the same with planning methods. They all tell you what to do. But success lies in what they tell you about "how" to do the planning effectively and efficiently.

Factor 15: The method should support getting Quick Wins

Quick Wins are important for several reasons. One is that sometimes a policy, procedure, staffing, or facility change can fix a problem. Not all problems require an IT solution — rather, they require a systematic solution.

Another reason is that Quick Wins help to produce momentum and results to aid in the acceptance of the strategic plan. As such, Quick Wins are politically useful.

Quick Wins are also politically important because these show that IT is not just focused on IT work. Instead, they are focused on providing and suggesting solutions. This gives both added value to IT and improves the tactical and mid-term alignment of IT to the business.

Factor 16: The method should deal with strategic resource
allocation after completion of the plan

If strategic resource allocation is performed without being linked to strategic planning, then there is a greater likelihood that the planning action items may not be given the proper amount of emphasis and importance. That is what is behind Chapter 13.

*Factor 17: The method should require extensive collaboration
during the planning work*

Collaboration has many benefits. The planners can do more coordination. The people involved in the planning accept ownership through involvement and participation. Collaboration also will produce less disagreement later on.

Of course, you cannot get everyone involved. That is not possible. Instead, you want to involve a reasonable representation of the managers. Since business processes are part of the strategic planning, it is valuable to include some employees who are doing the actual work.

*Factor 18: The method should address gathering information
from the current plan*

This is one of the starting points in the planning work. However, it is not restricted to the planning document. It also includes lessons learned from planning, resource allocation, and the implementation of the action items of the plan.

*Factor 19: The method should address the future
of the business processes*

Fixing problems in a process is good. However, these changes or fixes can be undone later. To ensure that the process improvements are relevant longer term, you should define the future direction of the business work. You cannot do this for all of the work. Our approach was to direct attention to specific, common, and frequent transactions. Then the level of work is reasonable.

*Factor 20: The method should support drafts of the plan to be easily
updated after feedback*

By relying on lists and tables the plan is more easily understood and updated. When the plan is actually written, then the text is for introducing and explaining the items in the planning lists and tables (Chapter 12). Experience shows that this reduces the time between the last review of the tables and lists and the completion of the plan draft and final plan.

Critical Success Factors in Strategic Systems and Process Planning — 20 Factors

This is a good place to gather together some of the ideas that are critical to the success of the planning work and the plan itself. Given what you have already read, none of this is new. Rather, it is a summary that you can employ as a checklist to keep yourself on track.

Factor 1: Maintain steady informal communications with management

You certainly don't want to run into manager's offices everyday. However, you want to communicate informally to a number of managers — not just one. This will get them more interested in the planning. In these meetings, you can start with status. Then, give them some of the planning lists and tables. It is also valuable to liven this up with stories or examples of what you have learned. You can also communicate regarding the Quick Wins.

Factor 2: Have regular reviews of lists and tables

When you have a "strawman" of a list or table, get it out for review. When you received feedback from some of the people, issue an update. This will be useful in reaching the managers who did not respond to do so. This technique gives more momentum to the planning. You don't want to wait for everyone to respond. Issuing updates puts more informal pressure on people to respond. Later, you can indicate, truthfully, that people had multiple chances to participate — providing political coverage.

Factor 3: Give the credit for the work to others

It is natural for people to take credit for what they do. However, experience shows that if you give the credit to the people who provided information, did reviews, implemented Quick Wins, and so forth, then the credit will reflect back on you. Taking credit for something takes credit away from others. This approach has proven itself again and again in our planning work.

Factor 4: Try to develop the plan using parallel tasks

Data can be collected in parallel in both the business and IT. Once you have gathered sufficient information, you can create the lists — at the same time that you are gathering data. Same with the tables. In several planning jobs, we have data gathering, preparation of lists, development of tables going on simultaneously. Not only will you get done faster, but you will generate more momentum.

Factor 5: Work to identify and implement Quick Wins as you do the plan

Many Quick Win opportunities do not require upper management approval. Examples are procedures and how to do the work. So, there is no need to wait until the plan is completed. Implement them as soon as possible. It is not bad to have a substantial number of the action items in the strategic plan implemented upon the completion of the plan. This shows the value of the strategic planning work and supports the endorsement and implementation of the remaining action items.

Factor 6: As you are doing the plan, make an effort to restructure the strategic resource allocation approach

The success of the strategic IT and process plan rests on whether you get the resources to carry out the action items. If the resource allocation method is not sensitive to the strategic plan, the actions may end on the "cutting room floor." So, to prevent this you want to raise the resource decision process early in the planning effort. In that way, when the plan is completed, there will be a more friendly process for resource allocation.

Factor 7: Demonstrate the alignment of IT to the business during the planning work

Through the measurements given in Chapter 16, you can start showing characteristics of alignment in the early stages of the planning work. Then as the plan progresses, the Quick Wins and lists and tables can show improvement in alignment on all three levels.

Factor 8: Develop "strawman" materials for review

Never wait until things are finished. Get things out there for people to respond it. Also, responding to something is much easier than trying to find things from scratch. In the later case, it is difficult for people to become instantly creative in thinking up issues, and so forth. It is much easier to circulate a checklist of items. You can indicate that these were drawn from past experience and readings. That is why Chapters 8–10 give you a lot of material to start with. As the people respond, the items on the checklist take on a life relevant to their work.

Factor 9: Work with a number of different business units during the planning

During the planning work, you want to spread yourself among different business units. Do this on a daily basis. If you spend too much time dedicated to one area, you risk getting bogged down in the detail. You might also raise expectations of what can be accomplished. Another benefit is that you gain a wider perspective. One tip is to follow a transaction as it flows between departments.

Factor 10: Anticipate resistance as well as a lack of interest in the planning effort

The strategic planning effort points the way to change. This can give rise to resistance. That is why we have so much time on this. If you anticipate resistance and are prepared for the excuses and reasons people give, you are better prepared to respond. If you do not respond, they may think that resistance won the day.

At the other extreme is a lack of interest. Why does this arise? Don't people realize that it could mean change in their work? They should be interested. However, they may have past planning and change efforts come and go — with no visible benefit. Use this to your advantage by playing down expectations. Show that this time the work is different since it is process focused and includes Quick Wins.

Factor 11: Demonstrate how feedback was incorporated into later drafts of the plan

Using the method of lists and tables, it is easy to demonstrate the changes. Another thing that you want to do is to describe how their input affected the write-up of the individual planning items. Keep a list of the people who contributed to the plan. Add this to both the presentation of the plan and the planning document. Give them the credit that they deserve by acknowledging that they have a lot of other things to do at the same time.

Factor 12: Create a "strawman" mission or vision to relate the plan to if these do not exist

In some organizations there is no overall mission or vision. In other instances where it does exist, it has shortcomings. Use the techniques in Chapters 5 and 6 to analyze the mission or vision, or to develop a "strawman" version. Important! Do not indicate that this is the mission or vision. That would likely be resented and seen as intrusive. Instead, label these as objectives. When you get these reviewed, you can do it at the same time as lists are reviewed. In that way, they will not stand out. Your goal is to get these nailed down so that you can relate them to processes and to the IT planning factors.

Factor 13: Focus management attention on resource allocation

Not only should you try to anticipate the resource allocation after the plan is finished, you should also raise the resource issue once you have reached some of the planning milestones. These include:

- The first time there is a complete set of planning tables
- When Quick Hits have been implemented

Since the planning effort is demonstrating results, raising the resource question will gain more support. When we have done this, some managers started actively to prepare resources. Several marginal projects were cancelled. Pressure was applied to control support, maintenance, and enhancements.

Factor 14: Try to avoid asking management for help
during the planning effort

Why would you think of asking for support? Some line managers may question the planning effort. Others may refuse to cooperate or participate. These might be managers who have a large degree of autonomy as long as they show results. If upper management has to step in for you, the line managers may become resentful. The senior managers may start wondering if the planning effort is worth it.

To deal with these difficult managers, go work with other departments. Get the attention of the difficult managers through reviews — which take less time.

Factor 15: Do not overpromise results from the plan

People participate with you in the plan development. They are feeling optimistic. It is natural to encourage them. Avoid this. Point out that the real tests are resource allocation and implementation. Indicate that these are the areas in which you will really need their support and involvement.

Factor 16: Be on the constant lookout for new opportunities and Quick Wins

In many strategic planning efforts, the work is approached in phases. For example, once you have a reviewed set of issues and opportunities, you move on to other parts of the plan. Not a good idea. Once people have participated, their minds start to stir. New ideas are likely to be defined. It is this way with system requirements. The traditional approach is to have the requirements defined and approved and then move on to design, development, or system acquisition. However, it is highly probable that new requirements will arise as they think about the project. You should assume this to be the case. In one successful company, Quick Wins were defined. Then we went to another area of the firm. When we came back, some of the Quick Wins had been implemented. New ones surfaced.

This example reveals several lessons learned.

- Keep in steady, regular contact with departments during the entire planning process.
- Do not be afraid of having new ideas surface. This is a positive and reveals a greater willingness for change.
- View additional ideas as positive. It reveals an attitude that will support implementation.

Here are some questions to ask when something new arises.

- Why did this arise now?
- Why was it missed before?
- What has changed since we first gathered information?
- How are the existing issues and opportunities affected? Should they be updated?

Factor 17: For each issue or opportunity consider the non-systems and financial solutions first

Often, systems staff members jump to systems solutions for problems, requests, and so forth. Encourage the consideration of non-systems alternatives through Quick Wins, organization change, process change, and so forth. These do not require money and do not require IT resources to any great extent. A rule we have always used with IT groups we have managed is to consider systems work as a last, not a first, resort.

Factor 18: Avoid hiding of information to avoid miscommunications

Why do people not share information? They may be afraid of what the information means. However, they also feel a sense of power with the information in their possession. Avoid this. Be open in providing information. We don't mean posting it on a web site. Instead, we mean that you should circulate the information. Another aspect of your attitude is to be neutral. You are dispassionately coordinating the planning work. Don't get too excited about some of the information. Some may think you have a hidden agenda.

Factor 19: Consider doing a business unit strategic plan in parallel to the overall plan

This seems like double the amount of work. However, it is not since many of the planning items apply to both the enterprise and business unit plans. There are a number of benefits to this approach.

- You can validate the enterprise analysis and findings through the department plan.
- The department can start with what you have gotten together at the enterprise level.
- You will gain important political support from a key business unit.

Factor 20: Incorporate pet ideas of managers into the plan

Sometimes, a manager will have a pet project idea or some other change. He relates this to you. What should you do? Try to incorporate it into the plan. In addition, you should try to link it to issues and opportunities, objectives, and strategies. That will justify the inclusion into the plan. It will also ensure that you will get a higher level of support from that manager.

Critical Success Factors in Plan Implementation — 20 Factors

In addition to the ideas for planning, we also gave you many tips for implementation. Success in your planning effort depends on getting real, tangible results. As in the previous section, you can use this as guidance to measure the implementation.

Factor 1: Implement Quick Wins before the plan is completed

This has been discussed before. In several cases, we were able to implement all of the Quick Wins prior to the completion of the strategic IT and process plan. Beyond generating support for the plan, another benefit related to savings. The Quick Wins actually more than paid for the planning work. When someone said that, "These changes would have been made without the plan." The response is that they were not done and most had laid there dormant for months or years. It took the planning work as a trigger to get these changes more visibility.

Factor 2: Maintain the measurement work

As you implement the Quick Wins and long-term change, there is sometimes a tendency to think that measurements are no longer needed. This is not true. You have to keep marketing the value of the planning by showing results. Otherwise, people's memories may fade and you will encounter more problems when you later update the plan.

Factor 3: *Work politically to gain support for change during and after the planning effort*

The politics do not end when the implementation is proceeding. There will likely be resistance even after implementation. There may, for example, be attempts to revert the process back to the old ways. The lesson learned here is that you cannot let down your guard. Assume that it is political from the start to the finish.

Factor 4: *Make the plan a living document so that it is frequently informally updated*

If the strategic plan is sold and assumed to be fixed — only to be updated each year, then there can be problems. First, new opportunities and business changes may either change or render part of the plan irrelevant. IT, systems, and processes maybe stable, but business conditions can change with the wind. Thus, it is unwise to dismantle the planning work at the end of the resource allocation. You want to keep it alive at a maintenance level to support implementation and changes after implementation. In that way, you assure that the plan will remain relevant. Since it is based on lists and tables, it is relatively easy to make changes.

Factor 5: *Extend the planning method and plan to several business units*

Let's assume that you are successful in both planning and implementation. How can you capitalize on this success? One logical step is to create business unit IT and process plans for several business units. This will maintain the momentum you have. It will also demonstrate the value of planning down to individual business units. A third benefit is that you will gain more support for later updates.

Factor 6: Update the plan two times per year

In business today, there is substantial change. In the past, a standard method was to update the strategic IT plan with the same frequency as the business strategic plan — annually. However, many organizations are finding that they must change their business plans with greater frequency. This carries over to the strategic IT and process plan. We suggest twice a year. A greater frequency may require too much effort. People may think that the additional planning is excessive. Also, there may not have been sufficient change to justify an update.

Factor 7: Market the plan action items with a focus on processes

For the action items related to processes and application systems, the link to the business is obvious. Not so with infrastructure and network changes. The suggestion here is to focus on negative impacts — what happens to the process if the improvement in the systems and technology is not undertaken. People have heard so much of positive benefits and you can give them, but they are sometimes difficult to verify.

Factor 8: Market the plan action items in terms of the impact if not done as well as benefits

The argument in Factor 7 applies here as well. Management has heard so much of benefits. But they have lived without these changes for a long time. Why not live without for another year? By stressing the negative impact if not done, you instill a sense of urgency. This is the same approach doctors have used for thousands of years to get patients to agree to surgical procedures — fear if not done.

Factor 9: If the planning staff members are changed, ensure that there is overlap

At the start of the planning work, assume that there will be turnover. That is why you want to use a common sense planning method that is easy to understand and simple to transfer to someone. Our experience shows that two people working part-time on the plan is more effective than one person doing it full-time. One of the two is in charge so that accountability is ensured. Through shared work and experience, the organization is better prepared if one person departs or is no longer available.

Factor 10: Measure the projects from the strategic plan
as they are being carried out

Some of the action items of the strategic plan are project ideas. These get fleshed out with project plans. Resources are applied. A project leader is assigned. Work begins. Potential problems arise. The leader and team may not be aware of what business situation motivated the project idea in the first place. They may take the project on a path different from that envisioned in the plan. That is why it is important that the knowledge related to the project idea is related to the project leader and the team. It is also important to follow up with the project to guarantee that the project is not going off track.

Factor 11: Insert the strategic plan into work planning and reviews

Many times once the plan is finished and action items completed, the plan moves to gather dust on shelves. Not only is the strategic IT and process plan a living document, it is also an excellent tool to assist IT and the business grapple with everyday work. Here are some potential applications for the strategic plan on an on-going basis.

- Use the strategic plan to review projects to see if they are aligned to the plan.
- Employ the strategic plan to review requests for IT work from business units.
- Revisit the action items that were not implemented in the first round.

Factor 12: Use the plan to address new project ideas

Another application of the strategic IT and process plan is to apply to evaluate new project ideas that appear after the completion or update of the plan. Any new project idea should meet the following tests:

- The idea should support the key business processes.
- The idea should fit within the IT objectives and strategies.
- The idea should help to address issues and opportunities identified in the plan.
- The project idea should be aligned to business mission, vision, and/or issues.

Factor 13: Do an informal plan update four times a year

If the plan is updated twice a year, do not wait until one month before the update to start. Revisit the lists and tables of the plan more frequently. That will make the update easier and will also ensure that it is relevant. A lot can change in a few months. Moreover, the informal update keeps the plan as a living document.

Factor 14: Follow-up on the resource allocation to see
if it is done as directed

It is one thing to have management determine who works on what. It is another to check that this is followed through by actions. People can make a ton of excuses for not changing their work in their everyday lives. It is the same in business. You want to indicate the resource allocation will be tracked and then to do it.

Factor 15: Remeasure key processes on a regular basis

While processes do not change overnight, it is useful to measure key processes on a routine basic, say twice a year. If the employees involved in the work are aware of measurement, there might be improved performance. In addition, such measurements can provide early detection to problems with processes.

Factor 16: Use the web to examine trends in technology and processes ·

In the "old" days people received paper copies of magazines and journals that covered technology and business processes. Now, much of this is available online at no or low cost. As a background task you should keep apprised of the trends and products. In one class we asked students to find 50 such magazines and to determine how to get their information. In no time the class found over 150 periodicals — 120 were available at no cost.

Factor 17: Expand and maintain the issues and opportunities

In the strategic IT and process plan the objectives, constraints, and strategies do not experience much change between updates. These are directional factors. What changes are the issues and opportunities, and action items. So, it is a good idea to review the issues and opportunities by having regular contacts with managers and employees in business units.

*Factor 18: Keep contacts with business units to
support later planning work*

In keeping with Factor 17 you want to keep in contact with business units. You cannot only work with updating the issues and opportunities, but also continue with measurement efforts. This will make the update work easier later on. If you lose contact, then when the update comes rolling around, you may find that you have to start over — consuming time and energy when it was avoidable.

*Factor 19: Consider additional deliverables beyond the plan
in terms of results and technology assessments*

We have already indicated that department and business unit IT and process strategies are useful. In addition, you can create presentations based on reviews of the results of action item implementation. Another step is to initiate an assessment of new technology and systems that are related to your business.

Factor 20: Revisit action items that were not approved during resource allocation

In almost all cases not all action items are approved for implementation. Some, in addition, could not be done due to resource limitations. Do not give up on these. The action items were developed through detailed, valid work. They were then subjected to extensive view. The first step is to validate that there unimplemented action items remain needed. The next step is to review the implementation steps and resources required for them. At this point you can start marketing some of these to be considered for implementation.

Guidelines for Success

If you sit back and think of what has been covered you come up with five overriding points of focus. Each of these is covered in the following sections. Why are these valuable? On the positive side they yield benefits in terms of greater involvement and ownership of the plan and work. Second, they shorten the elapsed time for planning. Third, they can lead to cumulative improvement in your strategic IT and process planning. This cannot improve the quality of future planning, but also reduce the cost and time. Also, risk of failure and problems are reduced.

Focus: Structure and organization

A major component of the strategic planning approach is to provide structure and organization through checklist, lists, and tables. To this end checklists were provided for all elements of the plan. More checklists were given for communications, measurement, and the structure of the plan document and presentation. Structure may seem too confining, but it is a lot of value. First, the method is flexible in the details. That is where the work really shows up. Second, the structure increases the credibility of the planning effort. In addition, structure acts to prevent becoming sidetracking during the planning work. The structure provides the framework for effective strategic planning. The organization supports the development, marketing, and implementation of an effective strategic plan.

Focus: Collaboration and politics

These two themes, collaboration and politics, are not only linked, but also critical to the implementation of a realistic strategic IT and process plan. In collaboration you work with other people. Your role changes to one of coordination, instead of doing all of the work. This first results in participation. Next comes involvement. Then commitment. And, finally, a sense of ownership.

Politics has been addressed in every chapter. It is natural that IT staff and others would view the role of politics as getting in the way of the real planning work. This is not a good outlook, since it places the planners at a disadvantage. If you recognize and acknowledge that politics are alive and well, then your planning can be more effective. Dealing with politics means that you are very sensitive to people's self-interests — a good idea. Once you become sensitive to it, you can start taking advantage of the politics to advance the strategic plan and its implementation.

Focus: Communications

Another major thrust of the method and book is that of both formal and informal communications. Effective strategic planning requires implementation and results. To get these you have to have effective communications. Many books center only on the formal presentations. The informal communications are even of greater importance. These informal meetings, calls, and so forth pave the way for greater political support for the plan and ownership of the plan to assist in successful implementation of the action items.

Focus: Issues management

We saw issues in the issues and opportunities. But, we also saw issues arise as potential problems that could be encountered with the planning method, the development of the plan, the allocation of resources, and the implementation of the action items of the strategic plan. It is insufficient to provide you with a method supported by guidelines. Also, required are tips and suggestions to deal with some of the most commonly encountered problems related to planning.

Focus: Lessons learned

The last point of focus is lessons learned. As the old saying goes, "If we do not learn from the past and present, we are doomed to repeat the same mistakes in the future." To ensure that your planning efforts are increasingly effective, you should continue to improve your organization and structure. Keep tracking potential issues. Maintain communications. Still, these are not enough. You have to gather experience as you go — not wait until the end. In any project, gathering experience at the end is often too late. People have departed the work. Memories fade. So, you should sit down each week and document what lessons learned you have gained from the work. These lessons learned can be organized through the tasks in the project plan for the planning work.

25 Specific Actions to Take

Without actually doing the plan, there are a number of actions that you can take to get started. These become the basis of your planning work. These involve your time, but not spending additional money. Some of the best ideas fall into this category. We suggest that you can pursue these using a low-profile approach. This reduces political risks. It also does not raise expectations. In addition, the reactions and information you uncover can greater contribute to a successful planning effort.

Measure the effectiveness of the last planning effort

Some guidelines were given in Chapter 5 for reviewing the past planning effort. Of course, you want to consider the results of the plan in terms of what was implemented. However, you also want to measure what happened during the effort. Here are some questions to answer.

- Was resistance to strategic planning addressed?
- Why did some of the action items get dropped? Was politics involved?
- Is the plan referred to in daily work at all?
- What new ideas surfaced after the plan was developed that should have been uncovered earlier? This speaks to the issue of surprises.

Review the business mission and vision

You should have the business mission or vision at hand. Use the approach in Chapters 5 and 6 to analyze these in terms of specific perspectives. This can tell you something of the quality of the mission or vision as well as being useful to the planning effort.

Determine how the mission and vision are used

Related to the above you can assess the extent to which the organization is striving to achieve the elements of the mission and vision. How have things changed in the past year? Has there been noticeable progress?

Identify the key processes

This seems simple, but it is more complex. What does the word "key" mean? There are the business processes that are positive because they are major components of business operations. There are negative ones that contribute to business problems and issues. Some processes rank high in both lists. Doing this can help IT in determining alignment of both projects and current operations to the business.

Catalog the current IT architecture components and structure

Many firms have configuration management systems in place. This action items goes beyond this. Here you want identify the components in terms of age, issues, and other characteristics as discussed in Chapter 6. Look specifically at the interfaces between elements of the systems and technology.

Determine how resources are allocated in IT

This seems simple enough. You just sit down and write each employee's name opposite their major activity. Not so. You want to see how resources are allocated across business processes following the guidelines of Chapter 7. This is not the same as determining the allocation across departments. Since processes increasingly span departments, you want to be process focused.

Determine how resources are allocated among projects
and with non-project work

Within the allocation is that of project and non-project work. What you are after is to determine both the split of work as well as the trend in the division between these two areas. Movement away from projects shows the increase in demands just to keep things going. This shows a move toward reaction rather than proactive work (projects).

Study how projects were identified and selected

This can be very revealing. Where did the projects originate? Here is a list of sources.

- From upper management
- From business units and departments
- From the strategic IT plan
- From seeing a need in a business process
- From responding to problems in IT
- From new opportunities recognized in IT

You want to sort which are reactive and proactive. The more that are proactive the better. Of course, the more they are reactive, the greater the opportunity for the strategic IT and process planning process.

Determine how project results are measured

Having good projects generated proactively is one thing. Whether these resulted in measureable and tangible benefits is another. Strategic planning involves implementing changes that is definable and measurable. If nothing is measured now, then this does not bode well for those generated by the strategic plan. A good action item for the plan is to begin a measurement process for on-going and recently completed projects. Some will be reluctant to do this since the work is over. Measurement can erase lingering doubts as to whether the projects were worthwhile.

Communicate on the impact if the planning is not undertaken

If management or others are reluctant to take on the planning work, then instead of preaching the benefits, concentrate on the problems brought about by lack of planning. If someone has lived without something for a long time, it is natural for them to question why they need it now. You have to draw attention to lost opportunities, recurring problems, and issues that could be identified and acted upon based on the strategic plan.

Establish more informal communications

We are all busy in our daily lives. The reason why many marriages fail is poor communications. It is the same in business. You have to make the effort to communicate more. In addition, you have to measure how you are doing. One measure of success is the number of surprises. If there are few surprises, then you can feel that you are in touch with people.

Develop a process plan for a business unit

Separate, but related to, the strategic planning work is to develop a process plan for a major business process. Until you do this, many people will not see the benefit (again, inertia). Having an example is powerful ammunition for demonstrating the benefits.

Map the existing strategic IT plan into the lists and tables given in this book

If you already have a strategic IT plan, you can analyze it by making it into the issues and opportunities, objectives, constraints, strategies, and action items. Next, you can use the plan to create some of the planning tables. This is useful for several reasons. First, you can start the new planning effort faster. Second, you can determine what holes and gaps there are in the plan.

Develop sample planning tables

Discussing a method and planning seems very vague. By creating sample lists and some planning tables you solicit more interest. Moreover, it assists in giving you experience in doing future planning.

Identify potential issues, opportunities, and constraints

This is probably the easiest part of the planning elements to create. Why? Because they are more detailed than the general objectives and strategies. Take the ones from the plan and add to these some of these included in Chapters 8, 9, and 10. This is a starting point and gives you a headstart.

Create a database of issues and opportunities

As you gather the issues and opportunities, you will find that you need to find these a home for future use. The logical thing is to create an issues and opportunities database that can use either spreadsheet or database management software. This can be a useful political tool since it shows that you are effectively keeping the information alive.

Establish a database of lessons learned

We have discussed lessons learned a great deal. To make this useful, you should start to create a database of lessons learned. This is similar to that of issues and opportunities. They can be related to projects, IT activities, processes, and departments for future use. Doing this will make you more aware of lessons learned.

Study how resources are allocated in IT to new projects

The reasons to examine how resources are allocated are both proactive and reactive. It is proactive because you want to understand the process of allocation. It is reactive because you want to find problems in the resource allocation method. In the worst case there is no allocation method in use. Resources are assigned on an ad hoc basis. This does not bode well for the project action items in the strategic plan.

Determine what constitutes the accepted definition of overall IT and project success

Why is this needed? For one thing if there is no clear definition, then when you implement action items from the plan, the results may be seem as murky, at best. Another reason is defining success and failure gives the IT staff a better understanding of what is expected of them.

Examine how projects are managed and measured

One of the things that benefit the implementation of the strategic IT and process plan is that of clear and consistent project management and measurement. If there is no consistent method for these, then the credibility of your measurements from the plan can be questioned. It is better to have a clearly defined, general method for project management and measurement.

Attempt to develop a strategic IT and process plan for a business unit

If you are reading this, have an overall strategic plan, and want to try the method out, there are two steps. The first has already been covered — that of mapping the existing plan into the lists and tables. The second is to find a suitable and friendly business unit and create a strategic plan for them. This will build your planning skills and knowledge and will make the application of the method at the enterprise level easier.

*Assess the alignment of IT planning, projects, and operations
to the business*

The technique here follows that presented in Chapter 7. Performing the alignment analysis can reveal the need and benefit for doing the strategic plan. This can also be a useful tool in demonstrating why processes should be in the strategic plan.

Examine past project ideas that were not done

In looking at the past planning work, you can identify what action items including project ideas were not pursued. Here are some questions to answer.

- Why was the idea not followed up on?
- What happened since then in the business units affected by the project idea?
- Has, for example, the business process and work deteriorated further?
- Is there still a business need for the project idea?
- What did business units do after the idea was dropped?

Answers here can reveal a great deal about how the project ideas were generated as well as the quality of the analysis.

*Assess the impact of not including the business processes
in the strategic plan*

Suppose that your organization has an accepted IT strategic plan and that it does not contain the processes. Here is a list of questions to answer to determine the effect of not including the processes in the planning.

- What was the mix of Quick Wins versus project ideas in the plan? Quick Wins often pertain to processes.
- What was the level of support and involvement by business unit managers and employees? If there was little or none, then they might question the relevance of the plan to their activities.
- Were the project ideas aligned to business processes or just presented by themselves? If presented without the business processes, then questions may have arisen regarding importance and alignment to the business.
- What is the mix of application system work versus infrastructure and architecture work? Too much infrastructure and architecture work can indicate (a) major problems in IT systems and technology or (b) a lack of attention to the business processes.
- How much of the plan is concerned with the performance of business processes? If the plan focused on IT, then it is internally centered. This can be resented by the business.
- Are business unit managers even aware of the strategic IT plan and its contents? If not, then this may be a sign that they do not consider it relevant to their operations.

Determine how Quick Wins are discovered and followed up on

Have there been any Quick Wins? If so, how were they handled? What approval process was used? How was measurement performed? Did the Quick Wins get buried in the bureaucracy? Answering these questions will reveal a lot about how your Quick Wins will be treated.

Politics

In a case involving a European manufacturing firm, an outside consultant was hired to do the planning. The plan was made and delivered. No actions were taken since there was neither sufficient involvement nor ownership. When we were brought in to salvage from the plan, we asked for an electronic copy of the plan from the consultant. When we searched the history of the document, we discovered that the same report had been produced for at least three other clients. It had been reused and just modified several times. When confronted by the client, the consulting firm rebated their entire fee. Lesson learned — get an electronic copy of any planning document from a consultant!

In this book, we devoted a substantial amount of attention to politics and political factors. This is important because of the following logic:

- Companies depend on process performance for their livelihood and success (or failure).
- Processes have become more dependent upon the supporting systems and technology.
- The plan action items, if carried out, result in change. Change can affect the political balance in departments and between business units.

Don't view this as a sad, regrettable situation. It is a natural one arising from the growth and penetration of IT into the business. Remember that 30 years ago, IT sat on the sidelines and many did their work and then put data into a computer as an additional task. Systems existed beside, not integrated into processes. Rather than rejecting or ignoring the politics, take advantage of it. You will have more fun!

Conclusions

We have traveled a long road — from looking at planning, to developing the plan, to getting resources, to implementation of the action items, to measurement and updating. The scope has been much greater than just doing the planning.

Another dimension of scope is what was considered. Much space and effort has been devoted to including business processes and alignment of IT to the business. This is natural due to the increasing importance of IT to business performance.

Chapter 18

Planning Example —
Irish Farming Organization

Introduction

In this example, work was performed on a variety of projects over a six-year period. One of the first efforts was to develop a strategic IT and process plan. Much of the later work was spent on implementing the results of the plan. Results included an over 30% increase in annual revenue, 20% reduction in business costs, improved business and IT staff morale, and increased customer loyalty and support.

This example was selected for the following reasons:

- The plan was complex in scope.
- The organization and its managers were and are very traditional; change is not readily embraced.
- The organization is of substantial size and diversity.
- The scope of the example included not only developing, but also implementing and measuring the plan results.
- There was a substantial degree of politics, culture, and ambition — sometimes resembling a soap opera.
- There was management turnover necessitating on-going marketing of the effort.

461

In this chapter some of the key ingredients were:

- There was no business mission or vision and only a brief long-term business plan.
- The overall strategic plan was accompanied by the development of process plans and automation plans for key business units.
- The plan and its action items had to be sold to not only the business managers and employees, but also the IT staff.
- Being a cooperative the audience of the plan included the farmers who own the cooperative — you could sell management, but if the farmers did not understand and support it, your work counted for nothing.
- The critical business processes had not been measured or improved in some time — there was the normal feeling that if it was not obviously broken, why fix it?
- There were problems of morale, accountability, and the capability of central management to manage remote operations.

So, you can see that we have here the makings of a good drama. You can also see the need for a planning method, effort, and implementation that can be accomplished with limited resources.

Background of the Organization and Key Processes

We will call the cooperative Irish Farm (IF). IF was founded in the middle of the 19th century in Ireland by farmers. Over time, the cooperative grew and merged with other cooperatives. A cooperative is owned by the farmers. IF's goal is to provide services and goods to the farmers while at the same time operating at a modest profit.

Cooperatives exist around the world and provide economies of scale for the farmers who could not individually perform the functions.

Here are some of the business units of the cooperative along with a discussion of some of the processes and history.

- Headquarters. This is a single building located in the central of the region served by the cooperative. There are about 80 managers and staff. The standard headquarters functions are here: accounting, finance, marketing, human resources, and IT. Overall, there are over 1500 employees spread over five Irish counties in 20 business units.
- Retail stores. There are 29 retail stores. Each serves a local area. Some stores date back to the 1800s. Store locations have not changed and the stores have been remodeled several times. The customers include the general population as well as the farmers. The goods offered included those for the farmers as well as clothes, limited foods (meats, dairy products, and so forth), animal feeds, hardware, and dry goods. Stores vary in size and sales greatly. Do-it-yourself stores are starting to make inroads into their sales. Store managers operate on their own with limited direction from headquarters. There is a separate, old point-of-sale system in each store. Headquarters accesses the information through dial-up communications each day. Price updates are downloaded as are price labels. Key processes are inventory control, sales, store layout and planning, ordering, delivery, and related retail operations.
- Dairy operations. A fleet of trucks owned and operated by the cooperative pick up the raw milk from the farms and take it to the dairies for processes. There are four dairies. Samples of the milk are tested for water content and disease by the milk testing unit. Farmers are paid on the basis of quality and quantity of milk — to ensure not only health, but also track excess water being put into the milk, called "watering down." Key processes include: truck operations, milk testing, dairy operations, delivery of finished products.
- Mill operations. A mill produces feed for the cows. The main building is a five-story building in which raw materials are put in at the top and blended and processed. At the bottom molasses is injected and the result is animal pellets — similar to what you

would feed your cat, dog, or rabbit. Critical processes include: raw materials, inventory, processing, and finished goods.

- Marts. There are 11 marts in which farmers bring their cows to be sold and buy cows from others in auctions. Auctions are held several times a month. The marts, when created, were outside of towns in the late 1800s. Towns grew around them and far outside them — making this land prime real estate. Key processes include: auctions, payments to farmers, inventory of the stock, cash control, and related supporting processes.

There are other operations included mushroom farming, logging, and so on, but the above are the key areas of focus.

When the idea of developing the strategic IT and process plan was proposed, there was a great deal of skepticism from managers and employees. After all, they had worked without such a plan for decades. So, why do it now?

The marketing of the plan was composed of several ingredients. First, people had to be convinced of the need for the planning effort. Second, they had to be comfortable with the approach. For the need, trying to sell the planning work on the basis of benefits was rough. Rather, it was better to concentrate on the impacts and problems generated by not having a plan. This was accomplished by drawing attention to past problems and failures. These included wrongly acquired software packages, problems with current systems, and the excessive number of marginally valuable system enhancements.

To get people comfortable with the approach, several points were emphasized. First, being collaborative, they could get involved. However, requirements for involvement were shown to be limited to reviews so it would not consume too much time and effort. Second, a project plan was developed. The ingredients of the plan included those in Figure 18.1.

A number of people could see the need for an IT plan, but they questioned the reason for including business processes in the plan.

- Identification of four objectives

  o Technical — getting project ideas and concepts for improvement, both short and long term
  o Business — getting business focus and direction so that IT efforts were not only aligned to the business, but also would produce bottom line results
  o Political — make people aware of the potential for IT in the processes
  o Social — get individuals in different departments to work together where they had never done this in the past

- Scope

  o IT was included
  o Key business processes were included
  o Business objectives, vision, and issues had to be included since there was no strategic business plan

- Benefits

  o Specific IT project ideas
  o Changes in policies and procedures that would control marginal IT work so as to concentrate on higher value work
  o Improvements to business processes
  o Avoidance and control of marginal project ideas

- Plan and schedule — this followed the structure of the earlier chapters
- Issues

  o Participation by employees and management
  o Resistance to change and improvement
  o Limited resources to do the plan

- Costs

  o Some IT management and staff time
  o Consultant costs (minimized since this work was in addition to other work)
  o Limited involvement by business employees and managers

Figure 18.1 Elements of the Project Plan for IT and Process Strategic Planning.

The response was to indicate that if they were excluded, it was possible, even likely, that the results of the IT work would result in marginal tangible benefits to the business without process change.

Issues, Challenges, and Opportunities

As was stated above, there was no mission or vision of the organization. What do you do? If you ignore this and just go to the systems and processes, you are not likely to get much management involvement in the effort. This is due to the detail of that work along with the likely feeling of management that they never saw the need or benefit in a mission or vision statement.

Having decided to develop the business vision or mission, the next question is "How?" If you make a big deal of this, you take too much attention away from the strategic planning effort. Also, you don't have much time for this. Our approach was to develop a "strawman" mission or vision and run it by the managers one at a time. This required the least amount of effort. Moreover, if you know the business, there are only a limited set of options available.

To develop the strawman, you first make a list of perspectives or interested parties. Here we go again, like the rest of the book — lists and tables. Much easier to sell, update, implement, and update. It also ensures completeness and clarity. Here is the list:

- Management
- Shareholders — the farmers
- Employees
- Customers
- Business units and processes
- Suppliers

Look at the list and you can see that the first four are standard. Why add the last two? There are practical and political reasons. One is to give these importance and raise awareness. For processes we wanted the managers to know why change was needed and how important the processes were. Many managers held the often quaint view that if you get the organization right, the processes will sort themselves out. However, in every business unit in which there was more than one location, there were major inconsistencies.

Suppliers are important, because many of the potential changes and benefits would involve supplier relations and streamlining of the supply chain. This includes: planning, ordering, order confirmation, delivery notification, shipping, delivery, invoicing, payments, backorders, returns, and refunds.

For each one of these a list of potential elements for the mission and vision was created. These were then reviewed by each manager. Each manager rated the lists on high, medium, and low. This took little time and effort and did not represent a threat or major effort on their part.

Here is the final version:

- Management — accountability, performance orientation, up-to-date financial information.
- Shareholders — profitability, affordable prices.
- Employees — performance incentives, energizing work environment.
- Business units — availability of financial and performance information; efficient operations.
- Customers — access to wide range of goods at competitive prices; improved customer service.
- Suppliers — efficient logistics and ordering/supply chain; increased merchandise volume.

You could then create a nicely worded paragraph blending these in. We did not — on purpose, We wanted to be low key and profile. Later, the CEO asked us to develop this, but it was after the planning effort. Here, we wanted to show that this was just one small step in the planning process.

Why go through all of this effort? It helped create a swelling tide of support for the plan as it was developed, after it was completed, and during implementation. Moreover, it aided in overcoming resistance to change.

To gather information on issues and opportunities, we first made a long list of known problems and opportunities. This was reviewed, added to, and amended by an informal committee of business managers. The results were organized into three lists — process related, business related, and IT related.

Now let's consider some of the issues and opportunities related to a number of the key processes. These appear in Figure 18.2.

As can be seen, the issues involve both automation and basic processes. You might wonder as to why many of the issues were not addressed before. The answer is the same as that in many homes and

- Ordering

  o Implement electronic ordering and confirmations — almost all of the ordering required substantial manual processing.
  o Automate ordering-related transactions.

- Pricing

  o Pricing is set centrally and price shelf labels are printed in the stores; however, audit revealed that price labels are not accurate and incomplete.
  o Ensure up-to-date pricing and labeling.
  o Implement store auditing processes to verify price labels.

- Inventory management

  o Too many items are logged in the point-of-sale system as miscellaneous, throwing off inventory.
  o Improve inventory tracking.
  o There is a lack of information sharing among stores to support customer requests; information sharing of inventory among stores is needed for improved service and sales.

- Sales

  o Increase sales per customer.
  o Sell higher margin goods.
  o Improve sales tracking by types of goods.

- Receiving of goods at the stores

  o Goods often are left in the receiving area after being received.
  o Reduce handling of goods in receiving.

- Customer deliveries

  o The Cooperative maintains trucks to make customer deliveries.
  o Improve routing of trucks could reduce costs.
  o The mix of size and vehicle type has not been reviewed in years.

Figure 18.2 Issues and Opportunities.

- Invoicing to customers

  o This is often a manual process and prone to error.
  o Invoicing needs to be performed on a more timely basis.
  o Invoicing needs to be more automated.

- Accounting

  o There are substantial delays in accounting reporting.
  o More rapid and automated accounting is needed.

- Management analysis and reporting

  o Reports are standardized, but are very inflexible.
  o There are data discrepancies among reports.

- Credit control and review

  o The farmers own the Cooperative and can borrow and get credit lines from the organization. Controls here have been traditionally lax.
  o Consistent controls are needed.
  o A reporting and collection process should be implemented.

- Payments to suppliers

  o This process relates to ordering. Many payments require manual effort.
  o A modified process is needed wherein exceptions are separated out from the standard invoices.

- Mill operations

  o There are multiple processes here including feed production, ordering raw materials, receiving, bagging of feeds, laboratory operations.
  o The Mill management currently gets information from a variety of systems and processes.
  o There is a need for more integrated information.

- Mart operations

  o As was stated earlier, the Marts operate in a world of the 1870s.
  o There are substantial operational and financial benefits to consolidation.

Figure 18.2 (*Continued*)

businesses — people are caught up in daily operations and are not trained and are too busy to address these. There is also inertia and resistance to change.

Wait! There are more specific business issues (Figure 18.3).

As well as more detailed IT issues (Figure 18.4).

- It takes too long to get accounting done at end of period. This results in a delay of management information.
- Business processes lack long-term plans and strategies. Process work is addressed on an ad hoc or emergency basis. Such was the case in the conversion to the euro.
- It has been a long time since goods in stores have been reviewed. The result is often high inventories as well as a mismatch with customer demand.
- Store managers have substantial autonomy. This has lead to unacceptable variability in stock accuracy; sales; customer service.
- Many business units operate semi-autonomously. From a business view this leads to problems in tracking performance. Systems tend to be localized and not strategic — diminishing opportunities for economies of scale.
- Do It Yourself stores (DIY) are expanding — increasing competitive pressure.
- There is a need to get more control over store inventories and ordering. Ordering should be centralized in terms of initiation. This problem has contributed to higher costs and excess levels of stocks.
- There is no visibility of store inventories to the mill and to other business units through a wide area network. This makes it difficult to forecast production and to meet customer demand.
- There are insufficient rewards for better management in business units. There is no performance tracking system. Thus, there are limited incentives to excel.
- Many diverse activities in cooperative with varying financial results. However, IT gives the same priorities to all business units. IT efforts need to focus on activities that have strategic impact.

Figure 18.3 Specific Business Issues.

- Stores are not adequately networked with other businesses and head office. The impact is that there is limited visibility into operations, inventory, and stock levels.
- There is resistance to change in the business. This is in part due to country and company cultures. The impact is that the benefits of the investment in systems are not fully realized.
- Departments resist sharing of information and systems. Thus, many systems only support a local department's needs reducing the potential benefits of economies of scale.
- Some ledger-related systems are old. Excessive manual efforts are needed in processing.
- There is a lack of knowledge of vendor systems and work. The effect is increased difficulty in providing support.
- There are a number of software packages in use in single, small departments. This is not cost-effective and prevents systems integration.
- Minor software work consumes excessive IT resources. The result is a drain on available labor for strategic work.
- Systems efforts often focus on tactical not strategic goals with limited benefits.

Figure 18.4 Detailed IT Issues and Opportunities.

Objectives and Constraints

Aside from a mission statement and annual reports, the Cooperative did not have a strategic business plan. Knowing this, we created a strawman list of potential objectives and constraints. As with the issues, we then circulated the list to get reaction and to see which should be on the voting list. Then, that list was circulated more widely among business managers. Feedback was obtained, when feasible, in face-to-face meetings. We wanted to not just stop with business-oriented objectives, but also include systems impacts. Each objective is given along with a sentence on its IT implications (Figure 18.5).

Now let's turn to IT objectives (Figure 18.6). These were derived from the issues as well as the business issues. The approach was to develop a list within IT and then to review with selected managers. However, for them to fully understand it, a mapping had to be

---

- Increase head office control over operations. This will address the autonomy-related issues listed above. To support this, management requires more timely and complete information through systems and the network.
- Management capabilities need to be improved. Even with better hiring and training there needs to be more structured management information for support of operations and planning.
- Some areas are not efficient and require cost reductions through consolidation. This means more integrated information systems.
- Sales can be increased through improved store operations. For IT this includes better inventory information and merchandise control.
- Employee productivity needs to be increased. This includes both process change and automating clerical work.
- Improved management information is needed in terms of quality, timeliness, and completeness. This means that systems need to be more up-to-date and integrated.
- There should be a better system of rewards for performance. To support this will require automated performance measurement tools as well as score cards.
- Improved knowledge of inventory, products, and operations is needed. A process and integrated system is necessary to support this objective.
- There is a requirement to improve the accountability of managers and business units. This requires increased management information on a more timely basis.

Figure 18.5 Business Objectives.

- IT must be aligned to the business. Sounds good in any plan, but what does this mean? Here, it is that IT must support critical business processes and management requirements on three levels — everyday operations (today), projects (short term), and the strategic IT plan (long term). Type — general.
- Improved network integration among business units is necessary. This will provide for greater availability of information as well as more software integration. Type — infrastructure.
- Business processes must be integrated. Even with integrated systems, if there are separate business processes, the benefits of the system integration are wasted. Type — business processes.
- Management information needs to be improved to provide greater flexibility and availability. Type — information management.
- Business unit performance requires better and more complete measurement through software to collect, analyze, and report on the work. Type — measurement.
- More effective use of IT staff time and resources is necessary to address more strategic work. This means more stringent controls on minor work and support as well as more effective resource allocation. Type — IT resource allocation.
- Software selection needs to be better organized with a view toward integrating and interfacing with other systems. Type — software.
- More sharing of information on products, sales, lessons learned, and so forth will provide substantial business benefits in sales and cost savings. Type — information management.
- Vendor transactions for ordering, confirmation, and so forth. should be automated to improve traceability, sales, and reduce costs. Type — vendor management.

Figure 18.6 IT Objectives.

carried out between the IT objectives and the business issues and objectives. The objectives are also classified by type. By mapping with business objectives and issues and by examining the type, you ensure coverage of the objectives.

In any organization, there are many planning constraints. As was stated in an earlier chapter, these go beyond money and resources although these are often the major impacting constraints. Politically, it would seem that constraints would be depressing to people. It depends on how they are collected, organized, and presented. Here, the goal of the constraints was to ensure that the plan was realistic. As can be seen by the comments, the constraints also provide support for specific objectives (Figure 18.7).

- The IT staff resources are very limited and spread thin. There is little possibility of increasing headcount. There are two possibilities to respond to this constraint. One is to review priorities for work. The second is to employ more contractors, consultants, and students.
- Some existing systems are old and were designed for single departments. However, there are no resources to rewrite them; nor are there software packages available.
- With limited IT staffing, the Cooperative has had to rely on software packages. While these meet local needs in one department, they provide limited flexibility or capacity for integration with other systems.
- The Cooperative, by its nature, is geographically dispersed across four counties. This makes enhancing the network a high priority.
- Funding for IT work is very limited — even when departments place IT expenses in their internal budgets. IT projects should be linked more closely to business processes to gain support.
- The Cooperative is involved in a widely diverse set of business activities. The impact of this is to limit the scope of integration and economies of scale.
- The business units are not held accountable for benefits and changes to processes. This affects the extent of benefits of automation.

Figure 18.7 Constraints.

Strategies and Action Items

Strategies define major thrusts that support objectives. As was mentioned earlier, there is a many-to-many mapping between objectives and strategies. Strategies typically require several action items. Remember, too, that action items need not be project ideas. Instead, they can be policy, procedure, facility, and other changes. The same iterative process was employed for strategies and action items. The most attention and time in data collection went into issues and action items. Why? These are the most detailed and are of interest directly to employees since it affects their jobs.

During the initial collection of issues, we also asked about what specific actions managers and staff wanted. A number of these had nothing to do with IT. Why didn't we restrict it to IT? For several reasons. First, people often need to vent. The planning effort is one of the times they have a chance to do it anonymously. Second, process and organization issues are often intertwined with IT issues.

- There must be a focus on supporting key, critical processes. The implications of this on both the business and IT are substantial. First, more resources from IT should work to improve business performance through the processes. Second, routine support will have to be controlled — at political cost. Third, marginal value requests from departments will not be able to be addressed — also political. To mitigate these problems, it might be possible to outsource some of the requests for new work (category — policy related).
- More wide area network applications are needed to provide for wider information access and improved data collection along with an upgraded network. Without these, the benefits of some of the newer systems will not be realized since some business units cannot effectively access the network (category — systems, infrastructure, and processes).
- A process of measurement for business processes as well as IT and systems is needed to support key management and business goals. Measurements on a regular basis will also improve accountability (category — policy and process).
- To ensure accountability and participation, the roles and responsibilities in IT implementation work must be defined and supported by upper management. This is also necessary to achieve benefits from the IT work (category — policy).
- Information system and network links with suppliers and other trading partners should be implemented to support efficiency and improve profitability (category — systems).
- A greater level of interoperability must be achieved among the disparate systems. This will reduce data input, speed the availability of information, and improve data quality (category — systems).

Figure 18.8 IT and Process Strategies.

Third and most important, soliciting these ideas and then being able to do something about some of them gives support to the planning effort. Once again, the IT planning effort is often political.

Here are the strategies that were developed (Figure 18.8).
This list of strategies originally started with more detailed items. When you have developed your list of strategies, the first step is to ensure that these strategies, collectively, cover the system objectives as well as handle the issues and opportunities. The second step is to aggregate them to be more general so that you have only one strategy in a particular area.

As action items are identified, an analysis was performed to determine if there could be rapid actions (Quick Wins) to carry them out. Academically, this is not correct since you should present the entire plan first, get approval, and then implement the action

- Implement a VPN (virtual private network) for the stores. This will pave the way for greater integration (category — systems and infrastructure).
- Develop plans for key business processes. This is an essential step to provide direction to the business as well as IT. There are two additional benefits. The first is that any business requests can be evaluated in terms of the process plan. Secondly, the process plan will facilitate measurement (category — planning).
- Implementation of a system to give visibility of store inventory to other stores, the Mill, and headquarters will reduce overall inventory, improve customer service, and provide for better planning for the Mill in terms of feed production (category — systems).
- Implement a new purchasing and invoicing system. This will improve productivity and ordering speed (category — systems and processes).
- Provide more integration among the various accounting-related systems. This will yield faster and more accurate availability of information (category — mostly process with some systems work).
- Design and install a score card and measurement process for business processes across and within the departments. This improve accountability and productivity and support greater middle-level management involvement (category — process).
- Install a more comprehensive set of guidelines for the acquisition of software packages. This will reduce departments going out on their own, increase standardization, and support the measurement of benefits (category — procedures).
- Exercise greater controls over minor IT maintenance, support, and enhancement work so as to free up IT resources for strategic work. (category — policy).
- Design and put in place new procedures for business and user requests. This action item goes with the preceding item (category — procedure).
- Work to improve interoperability among existing systems. This will reduce manual work and effort. (category — systems).

Figure 18.9 Action Items.

items. But it is important to get political momentum and to gain support for the adoption of the plan. Here are the action items (Figure 18.9).

Planing Tables

These planning tables are presented after the lists of the IT planning items. However, in their development they were defined as the lists were finalized. Why? So that there would not be a substantial time gap between when the lists were reviewed and completed and the tables were presented. Moreover, it was decided not to present for formal review the lists without the tables since that would require employees and managers to construct the linkages on their own. A major time gap would have reduced momentum for the plan.

Space does not permit including all of the tables that were generated. This section includes some of the more interesting ones that received more attention. Note that presentation as a true table can be overwhelming; so we resort to lists. Instead of giving the information in a table format, we show it here in an outline form to make it easier to follow.

- Business vision versus business objectives

If there was a thorough, well-defined, and accepted business plan, this table would not be needed. However, we have found that many times even when there is a strategic business plan, the relationship between vision and objectives is not well defined. Note that we selected vision as there was no mission.

The approach for developing this and the following two tables is as follows. Rather than have business managers try to spend the time to define these from scratch, it is faster and more convenient to develop initial versions of the three tables and then get them reviewed by managers individually. Here is another lesson learned. Have them reviewed in two stages. In the first stage you would have managers with whom you have close association and involved. Then you would revise it and submit it to other managers individually. This method has several benefits. First, you can catch potential errors and political problems early. Second, the results will be more accurate since you will probably not be able to have managers review a draft more than once. After the second round of reviews, you would do a final update and send it to them. You should expect no response. If you get changes after the final version is sent out, then there could be a problem with the information. Alternatively, some managers may want to make political changes.

o Management: Increased accountability; performance oriented organization; up-to-date financial information

Increase head office control over operations; increase management capabilities; reduce costs; improve management information; improve accountability
Comment: This is a two-pronged approach involving systems and processes, and performance measurement

o Shareholder: Accurate and timely financial information; profitability

Increase head office control over operations; reduce costs; increase sales
Comment: Need to automate ordering, invoice processing, receiving to improve stock control

o Customer: Access to wide range of goods at competitive prices; improved customer service

Increase employee productivity; reward good performance; increase sales; increase knowledge of feeds; goods
Comment: Need to assess merchandise fit with customer needs

o Employees: Performance incentives; energizing work environment

Increase head office control over operations; increase employee productivity; improve knowledge of products; improve accountability
Comment: Implement measurements and incentive programs based on sales and operations performance

o Business units: Availability of financial and performance information

Increase head office control over operations; reduce costs; increase sales; reward good performance; improve accountability

Comment: Financial information is not readily available and pulling together much of the financial information requires substantial manual effort

o Suppliers: Efficient logistics; ordering chain; improved volumes of merchandise

Increase head office control over operations; reduce costs; increase sales

Comment: Need to automate ordering; invoice processing; receiving to improve stock control

- Business objectives versus processes

This table is essential to be able to map the business factors through the processes to the IT factors. You would think that most strategic business plans would include this table, but it is usually not formally included. This is the positive part of getting the relationship between business and IT. The negative part is that of business issues which we take up in the next table.

o Increase head office control over operations

There is a need for head office visibility into stores information and for improved stock control.

o Increase management capabilities

This is reflected in the need for improved measurements, performance reviews, incentive programs, knowledge sharing.

o Reduce costs

Cost reductions can come through more automation and improved productivity as well as through consolidation.

o Increase employee productivity; spend less time on clerical work.

More clerical work in ordering, receiving, and so forth needs to be automated; too many orders, deliveries, and so forth require excessive manual effort and recording.

o Improve management information in quality, timeliness, and completeness.

The new network with the stores needs to be used along with system enhancements and process changes in the stores.

o Reward good performance.

In stores, performance needs to be assessed in terms of sales and operations performance using score cards and checklists.

o Increase sales per store.

There is a need to have fewer outages; need to review store inventories and types of goods sold; expand knowledge of goods of store staff, consider implementing a two-tiered staffing in the stores — sales clerks and department specialists.

o Increase knowledge, product, inventory information across the stores, Mill, and so forth.

There should be a greater sharing of knowledge about customer needs as well as merchandise.

o Improve accountability of managers and business units.

This includes score cards; access to store information; performance reviews.

• Business issues versus processes

As was stated before, this is more political of the tables. This is because managers know their own relationship to the processes. When they see that a business issue relates to a process in which they are involved, they can become defensive. It is important to be ready for this by keeping the wording very dry and neutral. You can also assess potential reaction through the two-step review process.

o Improve end of period accounting. The processes are ordering, sales, receiving, accounting, management information.

o   Lack of process plans — all major processes.

o   Review of store merchandise — inventory, sales, management information.

o   Store managers have substantial autonomy — ordering, sales, management information.

o   Business units are semi-independent — management information; Mill operations, store management.

o   DIY (Do it Yourself) competitive pressure — pricing, ordering, sales, management information.

o   Future role of stores — sales, store management, management information, ordering.

o   Control over inventories and ordering — ordering, receiving, invoicing, sales, management information.

o   Mill needs to have visibility of store stocks — ordering, sales, Mill operations, inventory, store management.

o   Insufficient rewards for good performance — almost all processes.

There are several themes that are evident from this table. First, management information appears frequently. This shows the need for systems on a large scale that provide management as well as operational information. Second, it is evident that responding to business issues requires that multiple processes should be addressed.

Next, we turn to IT-related tables. There are many of these and there is never enough time to prepare all possibilities. Here, we concentrate on the major ones. The focus here to get from the IT objectives down to the issues and action items. Development of the IT-related tables could be done within IT, but politically this is unwise. You should have some business managers who are close to IT review these as a group. The managers might suggest rewording that makes the information easier to understand by non-IT literate managers.

- IT objectives versus IT strategies

  o Network integration of business units. Focus on critical processes; improve measurement.

  o Integrated business processes. Implement an improved and enhanced WAN, improve links with trading partners; define roles of business units in IT.

  o Cross department applications. This is a major focus of IT efforts.

  o Align IT to the business. IT can only be aligned to the business through effective performance of business processes.

  The theme here is to move to more heavily support critical processes and increase measurement.

- IT strategies versus IT issues and opportunities

  Space does not permit a complete association of all issues so this is summarized.

  o Support key processes. This fits most issues.

  o More WAN applications. This fits process-related issues across departments.

  o Process measurement. This fits all issues that are related to performance.

  o Roles and responsibilities of business units in IT implementation. This applies to all non-technical issues.

  o Links to trading partners. This maps to issues related to store operations and accounting.

  o Interoperability of separate systems. This relates to store-related issues.

- IT strategies versus action items

  o Support key processes. VPN for stores, process plans, new purchasing and invoicing system, control over IT support work, new procedures for business requests.

o   More WAN applications. VPN for stores, new purchasing and invoicing system, store inventory visibility.
o   Process measurement. Process plans, score cards, and measurement.
o   Roles and responsibilities of business units in IT implementation. New procedures for business requests, all systems projects.
o   Links to trading partners. Interoperability, new purchasing and invoicing system, VPN for stores.
o   Interoperability of separate systems. New purchasing and invoicing system; more accounting system integration; interoperability of store-related systems.

The next set of tables is to relate the IT factors to the business processes. There are four principal IT factors since we exclude the IT constraints. Note that the second table below, that of IT strategies versus processes, is a derived table since you would have IT objectives versus processes and IT objectives versus IT strategies. Therefore, you could map the IT strategies through the IT objectives via the business processes.

•   IT objectives versus processes

o   Alignment of IT to the business. All processes.
o   Integration of business unit activities. Store-related processes; headquarters processes.
o   Process integration. Same as the preceding.
o   Management information. All processes but the Mill.
o   Measurements of work and processes. Store- and vendor-related processes.
o   Better use of IT resources. All resources.
o   Software selection. Mill, Marts, and headquarters.
o   Information sharing. Mill, store processes.
o   Automate vendor transactions. Ordering, deliveries, receiving, invoicing, payments.

- IT strategies versus processes

  o Support key processes. All processes.
  o More WAN applications. Ordering, sales, inventory management, invoicing, payments, Mill operations, Mart payments to farmers.
  o Process measurement. All store-related processes.
  o Roles and responsibilities of business in IT implementation. All store-related processes.
  o Links to trading partners. Ordering, receiving, invoicing, payments.
  o Interoperability of separate applications. Mill inventory and store inventories; ordering, receiving, invoicing, payments; sales and inventory management.

- IT issues and opportunities versus processes

  o Stores are not networked with other business units; network applications are lacking — different to gain economies of scale and to obtain management and financial information.
  o Resistance to change from tradition. Process change must accompany system change.
  o Some ledger-related systems are old. More manual work is needed.
  o Software packages selected for single department needs in past. It is difficult to perform integration.
  o Much IT time goes into maintenance and small changes. Resources for key processes are limited.

- Action items versus processes

  o Implement a VPN for the stores. All store-related processes.
  o Process plans. All but the Mill which has limited plans in place.
  o Store inventory visibility. Ordering, inventory management, Mill, receiving.
  o New purchasing and inventory system. Ordering, inventory management.

o   More accounting system integration. Accounting processes.

o   Score cards and measurements — ordering, inventory, sales, receiving, delivery, Mill operations.

o   Software package acquisition — all semi-autonomous operations (e.g., Mill, Marts).

o   Control over IT routine support work — all processes.

o   New procedures for business request handling — all store and Mill processes.

o   Interoperability of applications — store-related processes; accounting-related processes.

Now that we have mapped both the business and IT factors to the processes, we can develop tables that link business and IT factors through the processes. Space does not permit the display of all possible tables. Thus, we include the one that links the strategic IT plan to the business vision. Other tables of interest include that of action items to business issues and action items to business objectives or business vision. These are where "the rubber meets the road" since they represent the bottom line of the plan.

• Business vision versus IT objectives

o   Management. Align IT to the business, increase accountability, performance-oriented organization, up-to-date financial information network integration of business units; integrated business processes, cross department applications, analysis of business unit performance.

   Benefits — provide visibility of information to headquarters units; improve management of processes; reduce manual labor.

o   Shareholder. Accurate and complete financial information, profitability — improved management information, cross department processes.

   Benefits — Improved business processes.

- o Customer. Access to wide range of goods at competitive prices, improved customer service, support for incentive programs.

  Benefits — higher morale, better management feedback.

- o Employees. Performance incentives, better work environment — network integration, cross dept. applications.

  Benefits — reduced manual work with information; support for performance.

- o Business units. Financial and performance information, improved processes — networks and integrated systems.

  Benefits — increased accountability; better tracking of performance.

- o Suppliers. Efficient logistics, ordering chain, improved merchandise volumes — improve analysis of business performance, more effective use of IT staff time, implement supplier links.

  Benefits — improve mix of goods through analysis of sales and merchandise; improve supplier relations.

- o IT. Effective support for systems, support of mgmt. Initiatives align IT to the business, integrated business processes, improve management information.

  Benefits — better support of key processes; improved information; better IT staff allocation.

During the planning process some key themes surfaced. Politically, it is often useful to list these separately as a form of summary since they show the learning curve of the planning process and further help to gain support for the planning process and the plan itself. These recommendations include:

- Develop process plans are needed for key processes
  Benefits
  - o Ensure consistent processes across the cooperative

- o   Provide direction for IT
- o   Reduce ad hoc work and costs

- IT needs to focus on cross department and integrated applications with suppliers and among business units.

  Benefits

  - o   Improved efficiency
  - o   More complete and timely management information
  - o   Reduced clerical and manual work
  - o   Process plans are needed for key processes

- Key store-related opportunities are: (1) improved stock control; (2) integrated purchasing and invoice processing; and (3) e-business with suppliers.

  Benefits

  - o   Improved controls and financial information
  - o   Improved ordering, receiving, and invoice processing
  - o   Reduced costs

- Management needs to implement structured measurements of stores and business units.

  Benefits

  - o   Provide more complete and consistent information on performance
  - o   Supports incentive programs
  - o   Improve productivity

- Implement more controlled approach for new project ideas and software package acquisition.

  Benefits

  - o   Ensure that benefits of software packages are attained
  - o   Ensure that software packages are integrated with other software
  - o   Reduce costs

What Happened after the Plan

Many planning books that give examples end the example with the plan completed. However, it is both interesting and revealing to see what changed during and after the implementation of the plan. Many of the things discussed in this section were not included in the plan. Academically, they should have been part of the plan. Why were they kept out? Politics.

If they had been included, the move could have been viewed as an effort to justify the plan. By not being included, they gave more credibility to the planning effort.

Let's turn first to the Marts. During the planning we questioned the need for so many Marts so close together. This led to a project to streamline them and reduce the number to eventually two. The key to this project was to encourage the farmers not to attend the local mart. One part of the project was to pay the farmers for the cows from headquarters and not at the marts. However, the main thrust was for IT to support getting information to the farmers so that they could decide, bid, and not attend the auctions. The first step was to establish a web site that included pictures of cows along with medical testing results. We felt that this would be great — more information than with Internet dating. But it had little impact. The second step was to implement auctions online through the Internet — eBay for cows. This was successful, but the attendance was still too high. Finally, we asked the farmers what else they needed. They all responded that they wanted to see the cows move. Apparently, medical tests are not enough. You want to see the cow walk around. So, we hired two students who drove around (others drive around today) and take video clips of cows. These were posted with the medical tests and pictures. That did it. Attendance dropped. The number of marts was halved. Not only were there savings, but there were very, very substantial profits by developing the land for housing, offices, and commercial stores.

Let's turn to the stores. It was clear in the development of the plan that two store managers were not handling their stores at all well. As it was obvious, they were replaced and sales increased. So you say, "Management was not doing their job." True, but the information and situation were not that evident. You could give credit to the plan. But don't even go there. Give the credit to management. They will be even more behind the planning effort.

Another area was the Mill. In reviewing the Mill operations, the systems for feed production were reviewed. At the last stage of this process, molasses is injected into the feed to produce pellets (the same as for cats, dogs, and rabbits). This cubing system was truly ancient, not just old. When we asked who programmed it, no one knew. However, both the users and IT expressed no interest. After all, it worked. However, it was a single point of failure. We found the name of the programmer and then, on a hunch, searched Irish death records and found he had been deceased for two years. We made a management presentation to replace the system. If it failed, then the Mill could not operate. With IT glaring at us from one side and Mill management from the other, we started the presentation. There were only three slides. The first was a title slide. The second described the project in terms of schedule and cost. The third was a copy of the death certificate of the programmer. The project idea was approved in five minutes!

After the planning effort, the laboratories that analyze the milk for disease, water content, and so forth sought a new software package on their own that could further automate the milk testing. This was justified to save time since the laboratory staff were harassed by the farmers for test results. This is natural since what the farmers are paid is dependent upon what the test results are. The system would have cost US$400,000 plus. When we looked at this, we came up with a simple solution in two weeks that negated the need for the software. By using Internet telephony a text message could be sent to each farmer on the test results. This effort surfaced due to the policy regarding software packages from the plan. Without the plan the software would probably have been acquired — a great, needless expense.

This strategic IT and process plan has been updated several times. Updating proved easy since the plan was based upon tables and lists. The lists were first updated and then reviewed. Then the revised tables were reviewed. Overall, a painless process so that managers who once thought an IT plan was a waste of time now became supporters. During the revisions a number of new project ideas surfaced. Many of these related not to systems and technology, but to the business processes. By the third update most of the plan focused on processes.

Lessons Learned

The first lesson learned was that over half the information collected pertained to either organization or process — not to systems and technology. If we had restricted the plan to IT, the effort would have failed since there was so much work needed for the processes. This has been a recurring theme in our planning efforts in over 25 countries. Regardless of the country or the culture, the process factors and issues tend to rule. Yet, if you were to go in and do a strategic process plan, you would probably be met with many yawns. By centering on IT strategic planning first and then moving into processes, you gain traction.

Another lesson learned related to collection of information. When employees or managers voiced a problem or reviewed something, we asked for an example. This approach was extremely helpful since it surfaced the details of the benefits and the impact if the problem was not fixed. Key to the planning effort is to develop a sense of urgency. Without that many managers would agree, but say that actions could wait.

A third lesson learned was to have some meetings to discuss areas of issues and processes in a group mode where employees across several departments participated. This surfaced many new results since these people often have little interaction with each other. This indicates that a major benefit of the planning effort, if carried out in a collaborative mode, is that of interdepartment sharing of knowledge. As a result of the planning effort, several ad hoc committees were established across departments. One was with the stores and the Mill. A second was among the stores.

Politics and Issues Encountered

There were a number of political factors encountered. We addressed these points in earlier chapters. The main issues are handled here as lessons learned.

- Some people saw no need for a plan. We addressed this by indicating what problems had occurred without a plan — much better than preaching the benefits of planning.
- There was an aversion to get involved because the initial focus was on IT. We handled this by focusing on processes and work. The IT factors then could be drawn out later.
- Limited management involvement through reviews helped in several ways. First, the limited time reduced visibility of the planning effort and so contained expectations for what would occur.
- The overlap of planning and implementing action items was excellent since it provided momentum.
- The incremental approach of tables and lists proved very effective in faster reviews and accelerated completion of the plan.
- The collaborative approach worked in that what one person saw as a problem could be refined by the thoughts of others.

Summary

This example is typical of what we encountered in planning efforts. There are several common themes.

- Processes are interrelated.
- There is more attention to processes than to systems and technology.
- Politics plays a substantial role as the managers and employees realize the potential impact of the plan and its action items.
- The planning effort tends to surface a number of opportunities for work — many of these can be addressed in the short term.
- A major benefit of the planning effort is that people across different departments begin to communicate. This is one of the more long-lasting benefits of the planning effort.

The critical success factors in the planning process and the themes in this book are:

- *Integration.* The success of IT planning depends on being integrated with process planning. The overriding theme is change management. After all, why do all of this work if there is no resulting change?
- *Collaboration.* The benefit and need of a collaborative effort are evident in gathering support.
- *Politics.* Never lose sight that the planning process is often very political — several wrong steps and it is dead.
- *List and Table Templates.* The approach of using lists and tables has proven itself again and again in terms of getting support for the plan, implementing the plan, and updating the plan.
- *Project Management.* Finally, treating the strategic IT and process planning as a project gives cohesion and structure to the work and allows you more easily to deal with the politics.

We wish you much success in your planning efforts.

Appendix A: Useful Web Sites

- www.cio.com — CIO magazine — a leading IT magazine with regular articles on IT planning
- www.forrester.com — long time IT research and consulting firm
- www.gartner.com — web site of the Garner Group, a large consulting group involved in IT planning and management
- www.managementhelp.org — basic help in strategic planning
- www.colorado.edu/ITplan — sample IT plan
- www.acf.hhs.gov/nhsitrc/it_planning/strategic_planning — government article with guidelines
- www.bitpipe.com — web site with planning articles
- www.techrepublic.com — web site that you can join free with many IT articles
- www.pmi.org — web site of the Project Management Institute
- www.strategyplus.org — Association for Strategic Planning
- bpmenterprise.com — gives resources for business process management
- bpminstitute.org — a non-profit organization supporting business process management
- bpm.com — another business process management web site
- isixsigma.com — an excellent site with articles and implementation tips for Six Sigma

- prosci.com — a company sponsored web site that has information on change management, re-engineering, benchmarking, and related topics
- change-management-toolbook.com — a web site for change management information
- change-management.com

Appendix B: References

Journals that contain articles on IT and process planning:

- *ACM Transactions on Information Systems*
- *Communications of the ACM*
- *International Journal of Project Management*
- *IBM Systems Journal*
- *Information Systems Management*
- *International Journal of Information Technology and Management*
- *Information Management Journal*
- *Journal of Global Information Technology Management*
- *Journal of Strategic Information Systems*
- *Journal of Systems and Information Technology*
- *Strategic Management Journal*
- *Strategic Planning*

Books related to strategic IT planning and process planning:

- Benson, R., B. Tom and W. Bill (2004). *From Business Strategy to IT Action: Right Decisions for a Better Bottom Line.* John Wiley and Sons.
- Burlton, R. (2002). *Business Process Management.* SAMS Publishing.
- Cassidy, A. (2005). *A Practical Guide to Information Systems Strategic Planning,* 2nd Ed. Auerbach Publications.
- Harmon, P. (2003). *Business Process Change.* Elsevier Publishing.

- Jeston, J. and N. Johan (2008). *Business Process Management*, 2nd Ed. Butterworth-Heinemann.
- Kaplan, J. (2005). *Strategic IT Portfolio Management*. PRTM, Inc.
- Lientz, B.P. and K.P. Rea, (2004). *Breakthrough IT Change Management*, Elsevier Publishing.
- Ward, J. and P. Joe, (2002). *Strategic Planning for Information Systems*, 3rd Ed. J. Wiley and Sons.
- Weill, P. (2004). *IT Governance: How Top Performers Manage IT Decision Rights for Superior Results*. Harvard Business School Press.

Appendix C: Checklists and Tables

This appendix gives a summary and comments for key lists and tables developed in the book. Space does not permit the listing of all possible combinations of tables. Instead we focus on those that have proven to be the most useful.

Business Related Lists:

- Business processes — usually limited to the top 10–15 processes.
- Business departments — major business units.
- Business vision — the state or status that the organization formally aspires to achieve.
- Business mission — the general approach for achieving the vision.
- Business objectives — goals that flesh out the mission.
- Business strategies — strategies and major initiatives of the organization.
- Business issues — identify problems and opportunities facing the business.

IT Related Lists:

- Issues and opportunities — these are both positive (opportunities) and negative (issues) affecting IT and processes.
- IT objectives — these provide an overall umbrella for the plan.
- IT constraints — these are basically issues that cannot be changed that affect the plan.

- IT strategies — there are directional intermediate-term goals that support the objectives.
- Action items — these can be project ideas, policy and procedure changes, facility changes, staffing changes for both processes and IT.
- IT projects — these are the currently approved projects (the project slate).
- Systems — these include all major application systems (e.g., payroll accounting, sales).
- IT architecture — the architecture includes server hardware, client hardware and software, system software, networks, application systems, and support systems.
- Current work — this is a list of types of work by IT. Examples are: maintenance, operations support, enhancements, development, network operations, projects, and miscellaneous. This category is useful to show the alignment of current actual work with the business.

Business Factor Tables:

- Business departments versus processes — this table indicates the involvement of the departments in the processes; you can indicate degree of involvement, ownership, and so forth.
- Business vision versus processes — achieving the business vision requires results from processes that generate revenue and costs; the entry here can be the degree to which the vision element depends on the performance of the specific process. This and the next table can be difficult to derive due to the generality of the vision and mission. You can develop this and the next as derived tables by combining business vision (mission) versus business objectives and business objectives versus processes.
- Business mission versus processes — the business mission supports the vision and so this table is analogous to the previous one.

- Business objectives versus processes — the entry here is the degree of importance of a process to achieve an individual business objective. The table and the next reveal the processes that positively support the business (positive importance).
- Business strategies versus processes — similar to the above. Note that you can use this table to construct the business objectives, mission, and vision versus process tables.
- Business issues versus processes — most business issues arise, result from, and worsen due to problems in the processes. The entry here is the extent to which a specific process contributes to the issue. Thus, if you select a key business issue, you can see what processes have to be repaired. This table reveals which processes are critical from a negative view (negative importance).
- Business vision or mission versus business objectives — this is really validation that the mission and/or vision elements are covered by the objectives. This is a many-to-many relationship.
- Business objectives versus business departments — this can be most easily obtained by using the business objectives versus processes and the business departments versus processes. By going through the processes, you validate the table and help to explain the table to others.
- Business issues versus business departments — this is also a derived table in that it can be generated by combining the business issues versus processes table and that of business departments versus processes table.

IT Factor Tables:

- Issues and opportunities versus IT architecture — for the IT-related issues and opportunities and some involving processes, this table reveals which parts of the architecture contribute to the issue or opportunity.
- Issues and opportunities versus systems — similar to previous.

- Issues and opportunities versus IT projects — this table show which issues and opportunities are addressed by the IT projects. The ones not addressed can be part of the strategic plan.
- Issues and opportunities versus current work — this table reveals the impact of issues and potential for opportunities for specific areas of work. This is useful in demonstrating the impact of issues on the current situation.
- IT objectives versus IT architecture — the entry here is the extent to which a specific IT objective depends on a part of the architecture.
- IT objectives versus systems — similar to the above.
- IT objectives versus IT projects — this shows the extent to which the current IT projects support each objective. This can be very useful in indicating which objectives require new projects and action items.
- IT objectives versus issues and opportunities — this is an important table in the plan and shows that the objectives cover the issues and opportunities. An entry is the extent to which the issue or opportunity relates to each objective.
- IT objectives versus IT constraints — this table shows that the IT objectives cannot be achieved in the short term. The entry is that the extent to which the constraint blocks the objective.
- IT objectives versus IT strategies — this is a many-to-many table in the IT strategies that are shown to cover the IT objectives.
- IT objectives versus action items — the entry is whether or not an action item supports a specific objective. This table could be called fulfillment in that it reveals that the objectives are supported.
- IT objectives versus current work — the entry is whether an IT objective is related to a specific area of current work. This table can show which areas are most important as well as highlighting which objectives are key relative to IT itself.

- IT strategies versus issues and opportunities — similar to that for IT objectives. However, we most often use the IT objectives table here to show the greater scale.
- IT strategies versus action items — this is useful table in that it reveals a grouping of many disparate action items.
- IT strategies versus IT architecture — this table is valuable for indicating the impact of the IT strategies on the architecture components. The table entry could be either whether the individual strategy supports an architecture component, or, alternatively, the benefit of achieving the strategy on the architecture.
- IT strategies versus systems — similar to that of IT objectives.
- IT strategies versus IT projects — this table reveals how a current IT project deals with an IT strategy. This can used in several ways. First, you can see which projects are marginal in that they do not support key strategies. Second, you can find the gaps in the projects that require new projects.
- IT strategies versus current work — similar to that for IT objectives versus current work.
- Action items versus issues and opportunities — this table is important in that it "closes the loop" by linking the start of the plan (issues and opportunities) to the finish (action items). This helps to justify the action items.
- Action items versus IT architecture — this table shows the more detailed impact of the action items on improvements in the architecture.
- Action items versus systems — similar to the above.
- Action items versus IT projects — this table shows the effect of the action items on the current IT projects.
- Action items versus current work — This shows what improvements the plan implementation will make on work in the relatively short term.

Business Process and IT Factor Tables:

These tables are important to build the derived tables in the next section. They also are important in their own right to show alignment to the processes.

- Issues and opportunities versus processes — the entry is the impact of an issue or opportunity on a process. This shows which processes are hurt by issues and could be helped through opportunities.
- IT objectives versus processes — this reveals coverage of the processes by the objectives — important in marketing the plan and getting people to understand it through the benefit on the work. The entry is the relevance of an objective to a process.
- IT strategies versus processes — similar to the preceding, this shows how groups of actions could benefit the processes.
- IT projects versus processes — this table indicates which projects are of benefit to individual processes. Network and other infrastructure projects benefit most processes.
- Action items versus processes — this shows the short-term benefit of the plan and completion of the action items on the processes. The entry is the benefit that the process will experience if the action items are completed successfully.
- IT architecture versus processes — this table is of interest in helping to justify investment in infrastructure by showing the relevance. The entry is whether or not a process depends on the element of the architecture.
- IT systems versus processes — this is more useful to business managers in that it reveals the dependence of the processes on individual application systems.
- Current work versus processes — the entry here is whether or not an area of work affects a specific process. Alternatively, the entry can be the percentage of effort allocated to that process. This table can show the overall allocation of work to the processes.

Business and IT Factor Tables:

All of the following tables are derived from the preceding tables through combination. For example, if objective A relates to process C and process C relates to business objective S, then objective A relates to business objective S. Note that some tables related to business strategies are not included since they would be similar to that of business objectives.

In a number of cases, we discuss positive and negative alignment of IT factors to business factors. Positive alignment occurs when an objective, and so forth helps to achieve a positive business objective or strategy. Negative alignment is when the IT factor mitigates the problems generated by a business issue.

- Issues and opportunities versus business objectives — the entry is, in words, the effect of an issue or opportunity on achieving a business objective. This helps to prioritize the issues and opportunities from a positive view.
- Issues and opportunities versus business issues — The entry is the degree to which the issue or opportunities contribute to an individual business issue. This table shows the negative importance of issues and opportunities.
- Issues and opportunities versus business departments — the entry is whether or not an issue or opportunity affects a department. This and the other tables involving business departments and IT factors help to show how a "genera" strategic IT and process plan can affect the department.
- IT objectives versus business mission or vision — this is, obviously, the most important table on long-term positive alignment of IT to the business.
- IT objectives versus business objectives — similar to the above. It is useful to do both of these tables since business objectives are more concrete than the mission or vision.

- IT objectives versus business issues — this table shows negative alignment. The entry is potential impact and benefit of achieving the IT objective on the business issue.
- IT objectives versus business departments — this table reveals how IT would help departments over the long term and serves to highlight long-term alignment to the department. The entry is the benefit of the objective to the department through the processes.
- IT strategies versus business objectives — the entry is the expected benefit of the strategy on achieving the business objective. This helps to show positive alignment.
- IT strategies versus business issues — like the table involving IT objectives, this table shows the negative alignment of the IT and process plan to the business plan. The entry is the effect of completing the strategy on the issue.
- IT strategies versus business departments — this table is useful in showing how a grouping of action items will benefit a department. The entry is the benefit of achieving the strategy on the department.
- Action items versus business objectives — this one is difficult to do because of different levels of detail. We prefer the following one.
- Action items versus business strategies — the entry is the expected impact of the action as a contribution to achieving the business strategy. This is part of the positive alignment.
- Action items versus business issues — this is part of negative alignment. The entry is the effect of an action item in mitigating a specific business issue.
- Action items versus business departments — the entry is whether or not a specific action item would affect a department. This almost always has to be done as a derived table using processes. It is useful in showing to department the immediate impacts of the plan on them and their work.
- IT projects versus business mission or vision — this table is useful in showing the contribution of IT projects to the mission or

vision. The entry is the estimated impact of the completion of the project on the mission or vision item.

- IT projects versus business objectives — similar to the above. This table and the one above help to show intermediate-term alignment of IT to the business.
- IT projects versus business issues — the entry is the contribution of the completion of an IT project to easing or eliminating a business — intermediate negative alignment.
- IT projects versus business departments — this shows the impact and benefit of current projects for departments. This is useful in getting more support.
- Systems versus business objectives — this reveals which systems support the individual business objectives (part of positive current alignment).
- Systems versus business issues — this is part of negative current alignment in that the entry is whether or not an application system is related to a business issue.
- Current work versus business objectives — this is part of positive current alignment in which an entry can be blank or "X" depending on whether the current work area supports the business objective.
- Current work versus business issues — this is part of negative current alignment and reveals the relationship of the work areas to business issues.
- Current work versus business departments — this can show departments how the current resources support their department. It can be shown with the table, action items versus business departments as well.

Index